CENTURY 21®

Computer Keyboarding 9E

ESSENTIALS, Lessons 1-80

JACK P. HOGGATT, ED.D.

Professor of Business Communication
University of Wisconsin
Eau Claire (WI)

JON A. SHANK, ED.D.

Professor of Education
Robert Morris University
Moon Township (PA)

SOUTH-WESTERN
CENGAGE Learning·

Australia • Brazil • Canada • Mexico • Singapore • Spain • United Kingdom • United States

Century 21® Computer Keyboarding,
Essentials, Lessons 1-80, Ninth Edition
Jack Hoggatt, Jon Shank

Vice President of Editorial, Business: Jack W. Calhoun

Vice President/Editor-in-Chief: Karen Schmohe

Acquisitions Editor: Jane Congdon

Sr. Developmental Editor: Dave Lafferty

Consulting Editor: Jean Findley, Custom Editorial Productions, Inc.

Marketing Manager: Valerie Lauer

Sr. Content Project Manager: Martha Conway

Manager of Technology, Editorial: Liz Wilkes

Media Editor: Sally Nieman

Technical Reviewers: Gayle Statman, Amy Cole

Sr. Manufacturing Buyer: Charlene Taylor

Production Service: GGS Book Services

Copyeditor: Gary Morris

Sr. Art Director: Tippy McIntosh

Cover and Internal Designer: Grannan Graphic Design Ltd.

Cover Image: Grannan Graphic Design Ltd.

Photography Manager: Deanna Ettinger

Photo Researcher: Darren Wright

For product information and technology assistance, contact us at
Cengage Learning Customer & Sales Support, 1-800-354-9706

For permission to use material from this text or product, submit all requests online at **www.cengage.com/permissions**
Further permissions questions can be emailed to
permissionrequest@cengage.com

Microsoft and Windows are registered trademarks of Microsoft Corporation in the U.S. and/or other countries.

The names of all products mentioned herein are used for identification purposes only and may be trademarks or registered trademarks of their respective owners. South-Western disclaims any affiliation, association, connection with, sponsorship, or endorsement by such owners.

ISBN-13: 978-0-538-44910-6
ISBN-10: 0-538-44910-1

South-Western Cengage Learning
5191 Natorp Boulevard
Mason, OH 45040
USA

Cengage Learning products are represented in Canada by Nelson Education, Ltd.

For your course and learning solutions, visit school.cengage.com

Printed in the United States of America
1 2 3 4 5 6 7 13 12 11 10 09

A Century of Innovation

Century 21® Computer Applications and Keyboarding, 9E Hoggatt and Shank

A Century of Innovation

Provide students with the best in keyboarding education from the proven leader in Business Education. The latest edition of *Century 21® Computer Keyboarding* prepares students for a lifetime of keyboarding success with innovative technology solutions that reflects today's business needs. Students tap into the latest keyboarding technology, learn to master computer applications, and increase their math and communication skills with this best-selling text.

Unparalleled Enhancements

- **NEW! Five additional lessons** provide a more complete integration of computer applications throughout the text.
- **NEW for Office 2007!** Integrates new document formats that support the defaults in Microsoft Office 2007 and still covers traditional document formats.
- *Century 21* works with the new *MicroType 5 with CheckPro™*—the all-in-one software solution for new-key learning and review, skill building, and document checking.

Proven Cycle Approach *— Learn. Improve. Enhance. Build.*

No other text does a better job of ensuring that your students understand and effectively use what they've learned. *Century 21's* **unique cross-curricular cycle approach** reflects a strong instructional design based on decades of learning success. Instruction is broken into two cycles. Students begin with a foundation in the **basics**, and then revisit content to **improve** skills.

Interactive Innovation

Integrated computer applications effectively prepare students for the business world by bringing technology into each instructional cycle. **Current technologies** including the Internet, e-mail, electronic presentations, and advanced word processing are addressed to prepare students for tomorrow's business environment.

Accurate Assessment with Triple Controls

Only *Century 21* uses **Triple Control** guidelines for timed writings and skill building. Three factors—syllabic intensity, average word length, percentage of high-frequency words—are combined for the most accurate evaluation of students' keying skills.

Exceptional Resources

The online companion site at www.cengage.com/school/keyboarding/c21 offers a stimulating, interactive learning environment. Students can find links for Internet research, online simulations, Career Cluster information, and more. Instructors will have immediate access to all necessary course materials including lesson plans, tests, and software ancillaries.

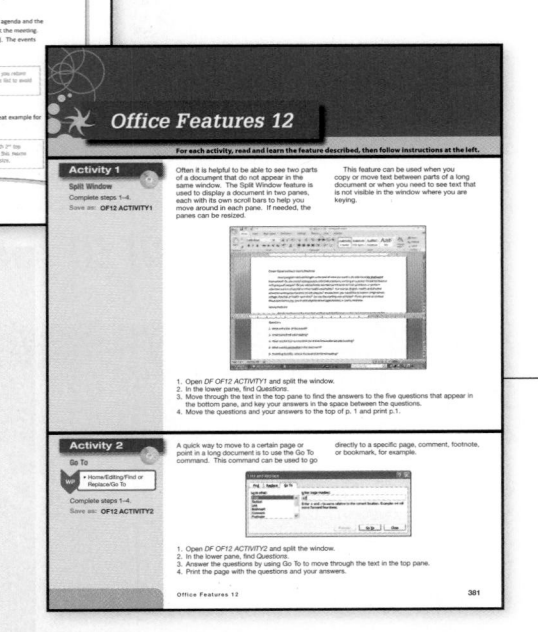

Established Cycle Approach

Cycle approach with cross-curricular themes reinforces skills and enhances learning in other disciplines. The cycle emphasizes a unique subject throughout—from source document to Internet activities.

- **Cycle 1:** Arts & Literature
- **Cycle 2:** Social Studies

Unit Opener

- **Format Guides** give overviews of document formats.

Lesson Opener

- **Warm-up drills** prepare students to key lesson material.
- **Lesson Objectives** identify key areas of learning throughout.
- **Scales** identify gross words a minute (*gwam*) to measure keying productivity.
- **Full-page model documents** show correct formatting and illustrate cross-curricular themes.

New for Office 2007

- **Office Features** offer specific instruction on Microsoft Office 2007 applications—Word and PowerPoint.

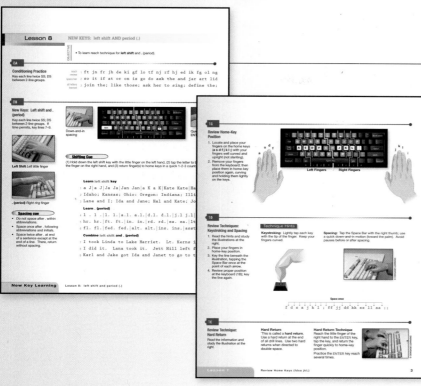

- **New-key learning** provides the basic skills for success.

- **New-key review** lessons provide an alternative for experienced students.

- **Correct keyboarding techniques** are emphasized visually. Keyboards help students with correct hand and finger positions.

- **Instructions** appear at left of page with **source copy** at right.

- **Balanced-hand drills** ensure equal use of right and left hand for maximum proficiency.

Timed Writings

- **Triple Controls** provide the most accurate evaluation of students' skills.

- **Lesson activities** are clearly labeled.

- **Icons** identify timings checked in *MicroPace* and indicate the difficulty of each timing.

Proofreading Practice

- **Script and rough-draft copy** provide real-world keying experience.

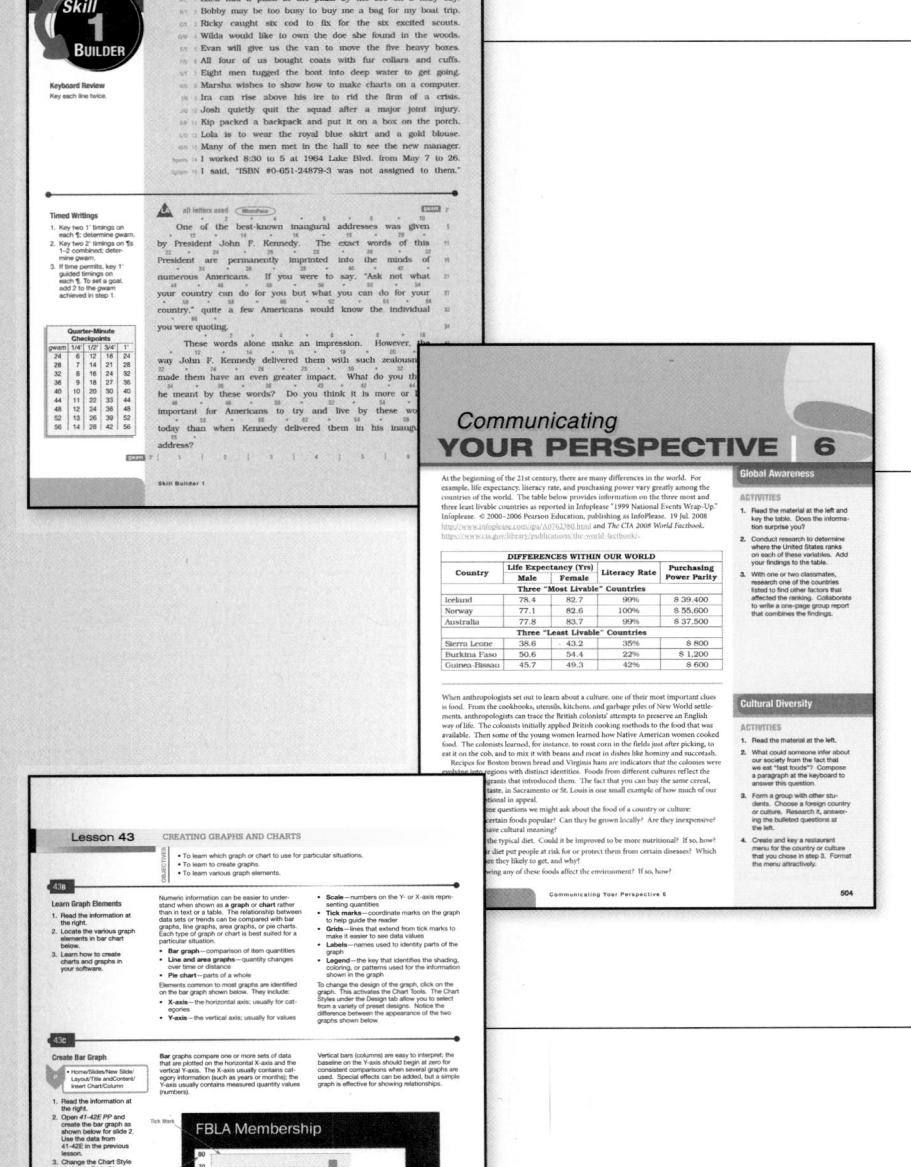

Strengthen Skills

- **Skill Builders** reinforce speed and accuracy for keyboarding success. The activities help students improve keying techniques and productivity.

Exciting Features

- **Communicating Your Perspective** activities focus on timely topics such as global awareness, cultural diversity, and ethics.
- **Special pages** invite individual and group participation.
- **Activities** combine keying practice with research and critical thinking.

Software Success

- **Computer applications** are integrated throughout the text to better prepare students for using these important skills.
- **Influential technology** such as PDAs, Internet, e-mail, database, electronic presentations, and spreadsheets are emphasized.

Innovative Instruction

- **Application Icons and Paths**—tab/group/command—provide clear directions on the ribbon to guide students to the commands within each application.

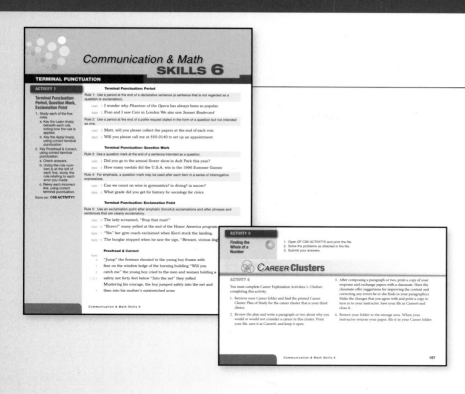

Cross-Curricular Reinforcement

- **Communication Skills,** such as grammar and punctuation, strengthen students' knowledge. Students complete exercises to apply rules given in the activity.

- **NEW! Math skills activities** reinforce the cross-curricular approach.

- **Career Clusters** reinforce the core standards and help students make a real-world connection.

Additional Features

- **Language skills** are incorporated into lessons.

- **Internet activities** enhance lessons and follow cross-curricular themes.

- Optional **word processing activities** introduce commands and provide additional practice.

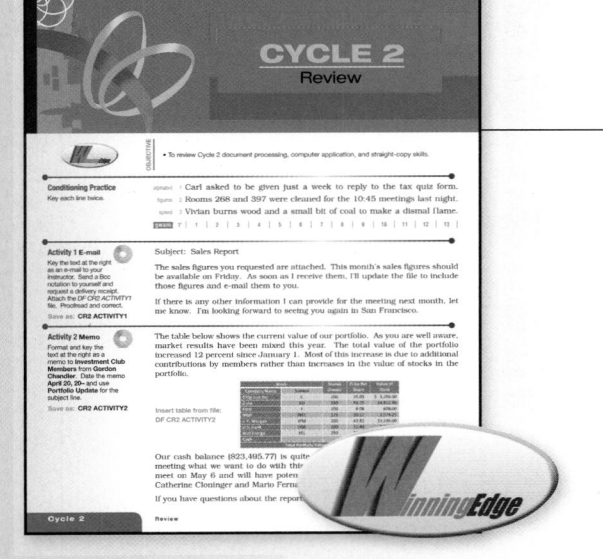

- Updated **Integrated Workplace Simulations** reflect new business topics, current technology, and actual job situations.
- **CD Icons** throughout the text identify data files.

Winning Edge activities and performance indicators throughout the Cycle Reviews and Assessments prepare students for competitive BPA and FBLA events.

Everything You and Your Students Need for Success

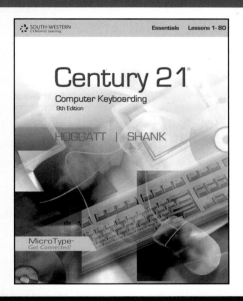

The Century 21 Family

Century 21 Computer Keyboarding 9E

Item	ISBN
Text, Century 21 Computer Keyboarding Essentials, Lessons 1–80	978-0-538-44910-6
Essentials Text, Lessons 1–80/eBook Bundle	978-0-324-67237-4
Workplace Enrichment Activities	978-0-538-44921-2
Spanish Language Supplement	978-0-538-44915-1
Style Manual	978-0-538-44916-8
Placement/Performance Tests	978-0-538-44922-9
Wraparound Instructor's Edition, Essentials, Lessons 1–80	978-0-538-44918-2
Instructor's Manual and Solutions Key	978-0-538-44919-9
PC Keyboard Wall Poster	978-0-538-44923-6
Instructor's Resource CD	978-0-538-44913-7
ExamView	978-0-538-44920-5
Instructor's Resource Kit	978-0-538-44944-1
MicroType 5 Network/Site License Package	978-0-538-44977-9
MicroType 5 with CheckPro Network/Site License Package	978-0-538-44983-0
MicroType 5 with CheckPro Demo CD	978-0-538-44986-1
Century 21 9E Sampler	978-0-538-44953-3

Preface

The ninth edition of *Century 21 Computer Applications & Keyboarding* provides a high degree of flexibility for moving between traditional and new content areas. This flexibility permits the structuring of courses to meet the needs of students, school districts, and the community. Instructors can determine where students will begin—with refresher lessons for those who have had prior touch keyboarding instruction, or with new-key lessons designed for true beginners. A placement test is available.

The 9th Edition presents choices in word processing, database, spreadsheet, and electronic presentation software features. It offers units on "Using Help," "Personal Information Management," and "Creating Web Pages," as well as workplace simulations that can be incorporated in your course as needed.

For this edition, South-Western/Cengage Learning surveyed business teachers, employed content reviewers, and met with focus groups to determine the needs of today's keyboarding students and instructors. The features of *Century 21 Computer Applications & Keyboarding, 9th Edition,* address those needs.

The *Century 21* family includes a full range of high-quality supplementary items to enhance your courses, including a Web site at www.cengage.com/school/keyboarding/c21. Thank you for choosing *Century 21.* Whether you are a new instructor, new to *Century 21,* or simply updating your *C21* materials, we know that you will find this edition an exciting solution for your classes.

ABOUT THE AUTHORS

Dr. Jon A. Shank is a Professor of Education at Robert Morris University in Moon Township, Pennsylvania. For more than 20 years, he served as Dean of the School of Applied Sciences and Education at Robert Morris. Dr. Shank retired as Dean in 1998 to return to full-time teaching. He currently teaches methods courses to students who are studying to become business education teachers. Dr. Shank holds memberships in regional, state, and national business education organizations. He has received many honors during his career, including Outstanding Post-Secondary Business Educator in Pennsylvania.

Dr. Jack P. Hoggatt is Department Chair for the Department of Business Communications at the University of Wisconsin-Eau Claire. He has taught courses in Business Writing, Advanced Business Communications, and the communication component of the university's Masters in Business Administration (MBA) program. Dr. Hoggatt has held offices in several professional organizations, including the Wisconsin Business Education Association. He has served as an advisor to local and state business organizations.

Dr. Jon Shank (left) and Dr. Jack Hoggatt

REVIEWERS

Karl Gussow
Fairfax High School
Fairfax, VA

Penny Guthrie
High Plains Technology Center
Woodward OK

Linda Inman
Pasco Middle School
Dade City, FL

Bonnie Lillibridge
Wickliffe High School
Wickliffe, OH

Karen Bean May
Blinn College
Brenham, TX

Billie Miller, Ph.D.
Cosumnes River College
Sacramento, CA

Kitty Olson
Blue Ridge High School
Greer, SC

Tracy Sanders
South Carolina Virtual School
Program
Columbia, SC

Mary Williamson
Peabody Magnet High School
Alexandria, LA

Robin M. Albrecht
Osbourn High School
Manassas, VA

Brenda Albright-Barnhart
Bolton High School
Alexandria, LA

Maureen Anderson
City Charter School
Pittsburgh, PA

Jeff Aronsky
La Mesa Junior High School
Santa Clarita, CA

Barbara Beasley
Taylor High School
Pierson, FL

Carla Bradley
Burlington High School
Burlington, WI

Ruby Calhoun
Cosumnes River College
Sacramento, CA

Marie N. Coleman
Sam Houston High School
Lake Charles, LA

Kathy Dunaway
Lloyd High School
Erlanger, KY

Peggy Eaton
Columbia Central High School
Brooklyn, MI

CONTENTS

Contents

CYCLE 2 Social Studies

NEW KEY LEARNING

RESOURCES

COMPUTER CONCEPTS

A **computer** is a machine that processes data and performs tasks according to a set of instructions. To do anything, computers must be given specific directions to follow. They get these directions from software. **Software**, such as that used for word processing, is a set of step-by-step instructions for the computer, written by computer programmers in a programming language like C++.

Computers also get instructions from you, the user. When you use the mouse (more in a moment about this tool) or the keyboard, you are giving instructions, or *input*, to your computer. That is why the mouse and keyboard are sometimes referred to as **input devices**.

Hardware is computer equipment. It carries out the software instructions. Hardware includes the central processing unit (CPU) as well as the monitor, keyboard, mouse, printer, and other *peripherals*. **Peripheral** is the name used for a piece of hardware that works with the CPU.

USING YOUR COMPUTER SAFELY
Follow these guidelines to use your computer safely:

1. Keep air vents unobstructed to prevent the computer from overheating.
2. Keep food and liquids away from your computer. If something does spill, unplug the computer and notify your instructor immediately.
3. Do not expose disks to excessive heat, cold, or moisture or to magnets, x-ray devices, or direct sunlight.
4. Use a felt-tip marker, not a ballpoint pen or a pencil, to write on disk labels.
5. Do not remove a disk from the drive when the in-use light is on.

STARTING YOUR COMPUTER
Follow these steps to start your computer:

1. Remove any disks from the disk drives.
2. Turn on the power. You may need to flip a switch or press a button on the CPU or press a button or key on the keyboard. You may also have to turn on the monitor separately.

Your computer may take a few moments to power up. The computer will execute a series of automatic steps that will load the **operating system**. The operating system—Windows® Vista, for example—is the program that manages other programs on the computer.[1] It will prepare the computer to receive your instructions and run software.

GETTING AROUND THE DESKTOP
The screen on your monitor is your **desktop.** Like the desk where you are sitting, your computer desktop is your main work area. It likely contains **icons** (picture symbols) for programs and documents, some resembling file folders that contain programs and documents. You probably have a taskbar or menu bar at the top or bottom of the screen (more about these in a moment). From here, you can start programs, find files, get information about your computer, and shut down the computer when you are finished.

A **mouse** is a tool for getting around the desktop. The same mouse actions are used in any software, though the results may vary depending on the software and version. Here are the basic ways to use a mouse:

- **Point**. Move the mouse (roll it on the work surface) so that the **pointer** (the arrow that represents the mouse's position on the screen) points to an item.
- **Click**. Press the left mouse button once and let go.
- **Double-click**. Press the left mouse button twice quickly and let go.
- **Drag**. Press and hold down the left mouse button and move the pointer to another location.

WHAT IS APPLICATION SOFTWARE?
You have probably heard the terms *application, application software*, and *application program*. They all mean the same thing. **Application software** is a computer program designed to perform a specific task directly for the user or for another application. Some common types of application software are word processing, spreadsheet, database, presentation, and Internet software.

---

[1] Windows® is a registered trademark of Microsoft Corporation in the United States and/or other countries.

STARTING SOFTWARE

Your computer gives you several different ways of starting programs, depending on the operating system and version. Here are two ways:

- If you have the Microsoft® Windows® operating system, click the **Start** button on the taskbar, point to *All Programs*, and click the name of the program you want to open. Your program may be inside a folder. If so, open the folder (by pointing to it) to get to the program.

- With Microsoft® Windows® operating system and Macintosh® computers, double-click the program icon on the desktop. Your program may be inside a folder. If so, open the folder (by double-clicking it) to get to the program.

Application software is displayed in a **window** on the monitor. The features of all windows are the same. At the top is the **title bar**. The title bar displays the name of the file you are working on and, for some programs, the name of the software (such as *Microsoft® Word*). If you haven't yet saved the document with a filename, the title bar will say something like *Document* or *unmodified*, along with the name of the software. Under the title bar, you may see a menu bar and one or more toolbars or button bars. These bars allow you to choose commands in your software. We'll talk more about them in the next section.

The title bar contains boxes that allow you to resize and close the window. At the bottom and right sides of the window are **scroll bars**. You can click or drag these bars with the mouse to navigate (move around in) your document. To learn more about resizing and navigating a window, go to the Windows® Tutorial on pages R5–R7.

CHOOSING COMMANDS

Most software gives you several different ways to choose commands. As you work with a program, you will find the ways that are easiest for you.

The Ribbon. If you are using the applications in the 2007 Microsoft Office System (such as *Word*, *Excel*, or *PowerPoint*), you will see a Ribbon at the top of your application window. The ribbon is comprised of tabs, groups, and commands.

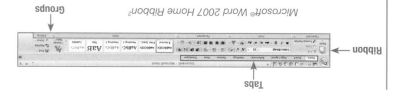

Microsoft® Word 2007 Home Ribbon²

Tabs · Ribbon · Groups

The tabs are located at the top of the Ribbon. When you click on a tab, the commands available in that tab are shown beneath the tab. The commands are grouped by purpose. The groups are shown below the commands. For example, the Microsoft Word ribbon shown above illustrates what happens when the Home tab is clicked. The Home tab contains five groups:

- Clipboard
- Font
- Paragraph
- Styles
- Editing

The first group, Clipboard, has four commands that are related: Cut, Copy, Paste, and Format Painter. To use a command, click it's icon. Notice the next group is Font. All of the actions you can perform related to fonts are contained in this group. The tabs of the Ribbon are **context-sensitive**, which means that they vary depending on what you are working on in your program. For example, the Picture Tools tab will only appear when you have selected a picture in your document, and the Table Tools tab only appears when you have selected a table.

Menus. A **menu bar** may appear at the top of your application window, just under the title bar. Like a menu in a restaurant, a menu bar offers you choices. From the menu bar, you can open a document, spell-check it, and so on. To open a menu and see its options, click the menu name in the menu bar. For example, to open the File menu, click *File*. For some software, you have to hold the mouse button down to keep the menu displayed. To choose a command, click it (Windows®) or drag down to it (Macintosh®). In some software, you can also open menus by tapping ALT plus the underlined letter in the menu name. For example, ALT + F opens the File menu. Menu names vary a little but are much the same across application software.

²Microsoft® is a registered trademark of Microsoft Corporation.

Toolbars. **Toolbars** let you choose commands quickly and easily. Most applications have toolbars. They have different names, such as *button bars*, in different software; but all toolbars are similar. They consist of icons or buttons that represent commands; some of the same commands found on menus. The standard toolbar contains icons for basic, often-used commands, such as saving and printing. Toolbars also exist for certain tasks, like formatting text or creating tables. In most software, pointing to a toolbar icon displays the name of the command. Clicking the icon executes the command.

Microsoft® Word 2003 Standard Toolbar

Keyboard shortcuts. Each application has its own set of **keyboard shortcuts** for opening menus and executing commands. Keyboard shortcuts usually consist of tapping a function key (e.g., F1, F2, F3) or tapping the ALT, CTRL, or COMMAND key plus some other key. For example, to open a file in *Microsoft® Word* for PCs, you would key CTRL + O. These shortcuts are often displayed on the menus and can also be found in the software's Help feature.

STARTING A NEW DOCUMENT

For many applications, starting the program starts a new document automatically. You can simply begin working on the blank screen that is displayed when the program has been loaded. If your software doesn't display a blank screen on starting up, if you want to start a new document later in your working session, or if you want to start a new document with another document already on the screen, do *one* of the following:

• Select the *New* command on the File menu or from the Office Button.
• Click the *New* icon, usually the first icon to the left on the standard toolbar.
• Use the keyboard shortcut for the *New* command.

A new document window will display. In some software, you may first see a **dialog box** that gives you setup options for your document. Tapping ENTER or RETURN or clicking *New* or *OK* will take you from the dialog box to a blank document window.

KEYING TEXT

Keying text in a new word processing document is easy. Simply begin keying. Text is entered to the left of the **insertion point** (the flashing line). You will use many features of your word processing software in the special Word Processing pages of this book.

SAVING A DOCUMENT

Saving a document places a copy of it on a disk in one of the computer's disk drives. This may be the hard (internal) disk of the computer or some kind of removable **medium,** such as a CD-ROM or thumb drive. This copy will not be erased when your computer is shut down. It is permanent until you delete or modify it.

Save any documents that you think you will need later. You can save a document anytime the document is on the screen—just after starting it, while you are working on it, or when you are done. Save often as you work on a document so that you will not lose your changes in case of a power failure or other problem. Follow these steps to save a document:

1. Select the *Save* command from the File menu, click the *Save* icon on the standard toolbar or Quick Access toolbar, or use the keyboard shortcut for the *Save* command.
2. If you did not save the document before, the software will display the Save As dialog box. In this dialog box, look at the *Save in, ___ Folder* box, or something similar. If the drive and/or folder where you want to save the file does not show, click the down arrow and double-click drives and folders until the box shows the correct location. The computer's hard drive is most often (C:); the drive that takes removable disks, (D:).
3. If you are saving the file to any kind of removable medium, insert that disk into the disk drive.
4. Key a name for the document in the box that says *File name, Name,* or something similar. Click *Save* or *OK* or tap ENTER or RETURN.

If you modify a document after saving it, resave the document by selecting the Save command (Step 1). The Save As dialog box will not appear this time because you already named the file.

window. The Close button in applications based on the Microsoft® Windows® operating system is the button containing an *x* at the far right of the title or menu bar. Each document window has a Close button, as does the software window.

- Use the keyboard shortcut for the Close command.

OPENING A DOCUMENT

Opening a document means retrieving it from wherever it is stored and displaying it on the screen. Follow these steps to open a document:

1. Select *Open* from the File menu or Office Button, click the *Open* icon on the standard toolbar, or use the keyboard shortcut for the Open command.
2. Choose or key the filename of the document. If you don't see the filename displayed in the Open dialog box, navigate with the mouse to where the file is stored by choosing the appropriate disk drive (and folder, if any), just as you do when saving a document. If you are retrieving a file from a CD-ROM or other external media, you will need to insert that disk into the disk drive to get the file.

CLOSING THE SOFTWARE

Choose one of these options for closing the application software:

- Select the *Exit* or *Quit* command from the File menu or Office Button.
- Click the Close button or *Close* box.

If you still have a file open and have not saved it, or if you have made changes to the file since your last save, you will be *prompted* to save the file. The computer is programmed to remind you of certain steps. These reminders are called **prompts**.

TURNING OFF THE COMPUTER

Follow these steps to turn off your computer:

1. Close all application software.
2. Remove any media from the disk drives.
3. Select *Shut Down* from the Start menu (Microsoft® Windows® operating system), Apple menu (Macintosh® computers), or Special menu (Macintosh® computers). On some Macintosh® computers, you can press the ON/OFF key instead.

CLOSING A DOCUMENT

Closing a document removes it from the window. If you have not yet saved the document, or if you have made changes to it that you haven't saved, you will be asked when you choose the **Close** command whether you first want to save the document. Choosing *No* will erase a document that has not yet been saved. For a document that has been saved, choosing *No* will erase any changes you have made to the document since last saving it. You can close a document in any of these ways:

- Select the *Close* command from the File menu or Office Button.
- Click the *Close* icon on the standard toolbar.
- Click the *Close* box or *Close* button. In Macintosh® applications, the Close box is at the top left of the

³Microsoft® is a registered trademark of Microsoft Corporation.

PRINTING A DOCUMENT

Follow these steps to print a document:

1. Turn on the printer. Make sure it is loaded with paper.
2. Display the document on the screen.
3. Select the *Print* command from the File menu or Office Button, click the *Print* icon on the standard toolbar, or use the keyboard shortcut for the *Print* command.
4. In the Print dialog box, select the print settings you want or use the settings that are already there (the **default settings**). In most software, the default settings print one copy of the document. When you are ready to print, click OK or *Print* or tap ENTER or RETURN.

The Microsoft® Word 2007 Save As Dialog Box³

CYCLE 1

Computers are not just for business anymore—they are for *every*one, *every*where!

In our world of fast-paced communication, almost everything we see on TV and the Internet, hear at rap concerts and Broadway musicals, or read in books and newspapers began as keystrokes entered into a computer by a keyboard operator.

To get the most value from high-speed computers, users must be competent at the input end—the keyboard. A computer processes data and text at the same speed for everyone. But a person who keys 50 words a minute produces twice as much work as a person who keys 25 words a minute for the same amount of time.

Lessons in Cycle 1 *reinforce* your keying skills. E-mail, reports, letters, and tables are some of the ways you then apply those skills, using the features of your word processing software. The Internet activities in these lessons represent an increasingly important use of keyboarding. A series of Communication and Math Skills activities can help you do error-free work. Activities focusing on Office Features aid in refining your software skills. You'll begin looking at career options in Career Clusters activities.

Here you have an opportunity to develop skills for traveling the Information Superhighway. Take it—straightaway!

Arts & Literature

Lesson 5

DIVISION & MATH CALCULATIONS

OBJECTIVES
- To learn division on numeric keypad.
- To learn to complete math calculations on numeric keypad.

5A

Keypad Review

Calculate the totals for the problems at the right.

A	B	C	D	E	F
20	92	872	613		
65	−43	−115	+716	438	704.9
39	+20	+178	−690	× 4.8	× 5.03
124	69	935	639	2,102.4	3,545.65

5B

Division

Learn Reach to / (Division Key)

1. Locate / (division key) on the numeric keypad.
2. Practice tapping the / key a few times as you watch the middle finger move up to the / and back to the 5 key.
3. With eyes on copy, key the data in Drills 1–3.
4. Verify your answer with those shown.

Drill 1

A	B	C	D	E
51.17	42	179	106	91
6/307	10/420	5/895	7/742	9/819

Drill 2

A	B	C	D	E
32.25	75.52	229.13	96.42	159.04
12/387	66/4,984	32/7,332	52/5,014	56/8,906

Drill 3

A	B	C	D	E
44.20	7.94	98.27	173.37	90.74
6.9/305	47.6/378	12.7/1,248	31.2/5,409	95/8,620

5C

Math Calculations

Use the numeric keypad to solve the math problems at the right.

1. Ken opened a checking account with $100. He wrote checks for $12.88, $15.67, $8.37, and $5.25. He made one deposit of $26.80 and had a service charge of $1.75. What is his current balance?

2. Jan purchased six tickets for the Utah Jazz basketball game. Four of the tickets cost $29.50; the other two cost $35.00. The service charge for each ticket was $1.50. What was the total cost of the six tickets?

3. Four friends went out for dinner. The cost of the dinner came to $47.88. They left a 15 percent tip and split the cost of the dinner equally among them. How much did each person have to pay?

4. Jay filled his car up with gas. The odometer reading was 45,688 miles. Jay drove to New York to see a Yankees game. When he got there he filled the car up again. It took 15.7 gallons. The odometer now read 45,933. How many miles per gallon did Jay get on the trip?

5. Mary bowled six games this week. Her scores were 138, 151, 198, 147, 156, and 173. What was her average for those six games?

6. There are 800 points available in the history class. Roberto wants an A in the class. To get an A, he needs to achieve 95 percent or better. What is the minimum number of points he will need to earn the A?

UNIT 1
Lessons 1-8
Review Letter Keys

Lesson 1   REVIEW HOME KEYS (fdsa jkl;)

This unit is an 8-lesson review of the letter keys. For 16 traditional new key lessons, see New Key Learning, pages 505–545.

OBJECTIVE

• To review control of home keys (**fdsa jkl;**), **Space Bar**, and **Enter**.

1A

Review Work Area Arrangement

Arrange work area as shown.

- keyboard directly in front of chair
- front edge of keyboard even with edge of desk
- monitor placed for easy viewing
- book at right of keyboard

© CENGAGE LEARNING

Properly arranged work area

1B

Review Keying Position

Proper keying position includes:

- fingers curved and up-right over home keys
- wrists low but not touch-ing keyboard
- forearms parallel to slant of keyboard
- body erect, sitting back in chair
- feet on floor for balance
- eyes on copy

© franksiteman.com 2007

Proper position at computer

Lesson 4 — SUBTRACTION & MULTIPLICATION

- To learn subtraction on numeric keypad.
- To learn multiplication on numeric keypad.

4A

Keypad Review

Calculate the totals for the problems at the right.

A	B	C	D	E	F
17	49	672	513	371	109
+83	+60	+415	+724	+564	+357
+52	+93	+808	+690	+289	+620
152	202	1,895	1,927	1,224	1,086

4B

Subtraction

Learn Reach to – (Minus Key)

1. Locate – (minus key) on the numeric keypad above the + (plus key).
2. Practice tapping the – key a few times as you watch the little finger move up to the – and back to the +.
3. With eyes on copy, key the data in Drills 1–3.
4. Verify your answers with those shown below the column.
5. Tap ESC on the main keyboard to clear the calculator; then key numbers in the next column.

Drill 1

A	B	C	D	E	F
27	50	893	798	523	401
–14	–26	–406	–235	–178	–300
13	24	487	563	345	101

Drill 2

A	B	C	D	E	F
84	56	996	829	759	83.6
–17	–38	–476	–514	–420	–41.5
67	18	520	315	339	42.1

Drill 3

A	B	C	D	E	F
99	89	505	807	978	63.4
–16	–10	–264	–234	–220	+37.5
–23	– 8	– 45	– 65	+461	– 8.9
–33	–17	– 87	–104	+309	–46.5
– 9	–24	–156	– 57	–218	+70.1
18	30	–47	347	1,310	115.6

4C

Multiplication

Learn Reach to * (Multiplication Key)

1. Locate the * (multiplication key) on the numeric keypad above the 9.
2. Practice tapping the * key a few times as you watch your ring finger move up to the * key and back to the 6 key.
3. With eyes on copy, key the data in Drills 1–3.
4. Verify your answers with those shown.

Drill 1

A	B	C	D	E
28	54	43	145	68.8
×13	×60	×89	×271	×19.3
364	3,240	3,827	39,295	1,327.84

Drill 2

A	B	C	D	E
603	109	837	468	219
× 24	× 72	× 55	× 90	× 34
14,472	7,848	46,035	42,120	7,446

Drill 3

A	$3 \times 5 \times 6 = 90$	D	$4 \times 10 \times 3 = 120$
B	$8 \times 7 \times 2 = 112$	E	$67 \times 13 + 89 = 960$
C	$2 \times 9 \times 4 = 72$	F	$7 \times 70 - 34 = 456$

Review Home-Key Position

1. Locate and place your fingers on the home keys (**a s d f j k l ;**) with your fingers well curved and upright (not slanting).
2. Remove your fingers from the keyboard; then place them in home-key position again, curving and holding them lightly on the keys.

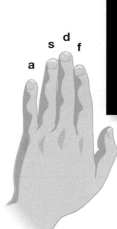

Left Fingers   **Right Fingers**

Review Techniques: Keystroking and Spacing

1. Read the hints and study the illustrations at the right.
2. Place your fingers in home-key position.
3. Key the line beneath the illustration, tapping the Space Bar once at the point of each arrow.
4. Review proper position at the keyboard (1B); key the line again.

Technique Hints

Keystroking: Lightly tap each key with the tip of the finger. Keep your fingers curved.

Spacing: Tap the Space Bar with the right thumb; use a quick down-and-in motion (toward the palm). Avoid pauses before or after spacing.

© CENGAGE LEARNING

Space once

f d s a j k l ; ff jj dd kk ss ll aa ;;

Review Technique: Hard Return

Read the information and study the illustration at the right.

Hard Return
`This is called a **hard return**. Use a hard return at the end of all drill lines. Use two hard returns when directed to double-space.

Hard Return Technique
Reach the little finger of the right hand to the **ENTER** key, tap the key, and return the finger quickly to home-key position.

Practice the **ENTER** key reach several times.

© CENGAGE LEARNING

OBJECTIVE

• To learn reachstrokes for **1**, **2**, and **3**.

3A

Keypad Review

Calculate the totals for the problems at the right.

A	B	C	D	E	F	G
45	74	740	996	704	990	477
56	85	850	885	805	880	588
67	96	960	774	906	770	699
168	255	2,550	2,655	2,415	2,640	1,764

2B

New Keys: 1, 2, and 3

Learn Reach to 1

1. Locate 1 (below 4) on the numeric keypad.
2. Watch your index finger move down to 1 and back to 4 a few times.
3. Key 14 a few times as you watch the finger.
4. With eyes on copy, key the data in Drills 1A and 1B.

Learn Reach to 2

1. Learn the middle-finger reach to 2 (below 5) as directed in steps 1–3 above.
2. With eyes on copy, key the data in Drills 1C and 1D.

Learn Reach to 3

1. Learn the ring-finger reach to 3 (below 6) as directed above.
2. With eyes on copy, key the data in Drills 1E–1G.

Drills 2–4

1. Calculate the totals for each problem and check your answers.

Learn Reach to . (Decimal)

1. Learn the ring-finger reach to the decimal point (.) located below the 3.
2. Calculate the totals for each problem in Drill 5.
3. Repeat Drills 2–5 to increase your speed.

Drill 1

A	B	C	D	E	F	G
144	114	525	252	353	636	120
141	414	252	552	363	366	285
414	141	225	525	336	636	396
699	669	1,002	1,329	1,052	1,638	801

Drill 2

A	B	C	D	E	F	G
411	552	663	571	514	481	963
144	255	366	482	425	672	852
414	525	636	539	563	953	471
969	1,332	1,665	1,592	1,502	2,106	2,286

Drill 3

A	B	C	D	E	F	G
471	582	693	303	939	396	417
41	802	963	220	822	285	508
14	825	936	101	717	174	639
526	2,209	2,592	624	2,478	855	1,564

Drill 4

A	B	C	D	E	F	G
75	128	167	102	853	549	180
189	34	258	368	264	367	475
3	591	349	549	971	102	396
267	753	774	1,019	2,088	1,018	1,051

Drill 5

A	B	C	D	E	F	G
1.30	2.58	23.87	90.37	16.89	47.01	59.28
4.17	6.90	14.65	4.25	3.25	28.36	1.76
5.47	9.48	38.52	94.62	20.14	75.37	61.04

For additional practice:

MicroType 5
Numeric Keypad
Lesson 3

Home-Key and Space Bar Review

Key each line twice single-spaced (SS); double-space (DS) between 2-line groups. Do not key numbers.

Spacing Cue

Tap the **ENTER** key twice to insert a DS between 2-line groups.

```
1 a  aa  j  jj  s  ss  k  kk  d  dd  l  ll  f  ff  ;  ;;  asdf  jkl;
2 a  aa  j  jj  s  ss  k  kk  d  dd  l  ll  f  ff  ;  ;;  asdf  jkl;
```
Tap the ENTER key twice to double-space (DS).
```
3 k  kk  a  aa  l  ll  f  ff  ;  ;;  d  dd  j  jj  s  ss  jkl;  asdf
4 k  kk  a  aa  l  ll  f  ff  ;  ;;  d  dd  j  jj  s  ss  jkl;  asdf
```
DS
```
5 la  la  jf  jf  ks  ks  ;d  ;d  ls  ls  aj  aj  kf  kf  d;  d;  k
6 la  la  jf  jf  ks  ks  ;d  ;d  ls  ls  aj  aj  kf  kf  d;  d;  k
```
Tap the ENTER key 3 times to triple-space (TS).

1G

Review Technique: ENTER (Return) Key

Key each line twice SS; DS between 2-line groups.

```
1 js  fk  ld  a;  kj  f;
2 ds  af  lk  ;j  aj  sl  jd  f;
3 fa  sd  j;  kl  f;  dj  ka  ls  al  fk
4 js  ;d  fj  d;  sk  al  sj  d;  jf  ;d  ks  la
5 dd  ;;  jj  ss  ff  kk  aa  ll  as  df  jk  l;  la  df
```

> Reach out with little finger; tap the ENTER key quickly; return finger to home key.

1H

Keyboard Reinforcement

Key each line twice SS; DS between 2-line groups.

```
1 as;  as;|lad  lad|jak  jak|adds  adds|ask  ask|sad  sad;
2 dad  dad|fall  fall|fad;  fad;|salad  salad|lass  lass;

3 as  a  fall  fad;  add  a  jak  salad;  as  a  sad  lad  falls
4 ask  a  lad;  ask  a  lad;  all  jaks  fall;  all  jaks  fall

5 as  a  fad;  as  a  dad;  ask  a  lad;  as  a  lass;  all  lads
6 add  a  jak;  a  fall  ad;  all  fall  ads;  ask  a  sad  lass

7 a  sad  lad;  ask  a  dad;  all  jaks;  ask  a  jak;  sad  dad
8 ask  dad;  as  a  lass  falls;  a  fall  ad;  ask  a  sad  lad
```

For additional practice:
MicroType 5
New Key Review, Alphabetic
Lesson 1

Lesson 2

OBJECTIVE

• To learn reachstrokes for **7**, **8**, and **9**.

2A

Home-Key Review

Calculate the totals for the problems at the right.

A	B	C	D	E	F
4	44	400	404	440	450
5	55	500	505	550	560
6	66	600	606	660	456
15	165	1,500	1,515	1,650	1,466

2B

New Keys: 7, 8, and 9

Learn Reach to 7

1. Locate 7 (above 4) on the numeric keypad.
2. Watch your index finger move up to 7 and back to 4 a few times without tapping keys.
3. Practice tapping 74 a few times as you watch the finger.
4. With eyes on copy, key the data in Drills 1A and 1B.

Drill 1

A	B	C	D	E	F
474	747	585	858	696	969
747	477	858	588	969	966
777	474	888	585	999	696
1,998	1,698	2,331	2,031	2,664	2,631

Learn Reach to 8

1. Learn the middle-finger reach to 8 (above 5) as directed in steps 1–3 above.
2. With eyes on copy, key the data in Drills 1C and 1D.

Drill 2

A	B	C	D	E	F
774	885	996	745	475	754
474	585	696	854	584	846
747	858	969	965	695	956
1,995	2,328	2,661	2,564	1,754	2,556

Learn Reach to 9

1. Learn the ring-finger reach to 9 (above 6) as directed above.
2. With eyes on copy, key the data in Drills 1E and 1F.

Drill 3

A	B	C	D	E	F
470	580	690	770	707	407
740	850	960	880	808	508
705	805	906	990	909	609
1,915	2,235	2,556	2,640	2,424	1,524

Drills 2–5

1. Calculate the totals for each problem in Drills 2–5. Check your answers.
2. Repeat Drills 2–5 to increase your speed.

Drill 4

A	B	C	D	E	F
456	407	508	609	804	905
789	408	509	704	805	906
654	409	607	705	806	907
987	410	608	706	904	908
2,886	1,634	2,232	2,724	3,319	3,626

For additional practice:

MicroType 5
Numeric Keypad
Lesson 2

Drill 5

A	B	C	D	E	F
8	786	4	804	76	86
795	69	705	45	556	564
78	575	59	6	5	78
60	4	446	556	666	504
941	1,434	1,214	1,411	1,303	1,232

Lesson 2   REVIEW LETTER KEYS (h, e, i, AND r)

• To review reach technique for **h**, **e**, **i**, and **r**.

2A

H and E Review

Key each line twice (SS); DS between 2-line groups.

Review h

1 j jh j jh|ha ha|had had|has has|ash ash|hash hash;
2 had had|hall hall|half half|dash dash|flash flash;
3 ha ha; had had; has has; a hall; a hall; sash sash

Review e

4 d de d de|seed seed|deal deal|feed feed|sale sale;
5 fade fade|keel keel|sake sake|lead lead|lake lake;
6 feel safe; a lake; a leak; a jade; a desk; a deed;

2B   Skill Building

Keyboard Reinforcement

Key each line twice SS; DS between 2-line groups.

home row
1 sad sad|jak jak|salad salad|lass lass|flask flask;
2 a sad lad; a sad lad; a dad; a dad; a fall a fall;

h/e
3 heed heed|shed shed|lead lead|held held|jell jell;
4 he has a shed; half ash; he feeds; a shelf; he has

all keys learned
5 jak jak|lake lake|held held|desks desks|half half;
6 a lake sale; she has half; he held a flask; a jade

all keys learned
7 held a; he has; a jak ad; a jade seal; a sled fell
8 he fell; ask a lad; he has a jak; all fall; a shed

all keys learned
9 a jade; she fell; a lake; see dad; she fed a seal;
10 he fell|has had|he had a jade desk|she held a sash

Lesson 2   Review Letter Keys (h, e, i, and r)   5

New Keys: 4, 5, 6, and 0 (Home Keys)

Use the calculator accessory to complete the drills.

1. Enter each number: Key the number and enter by tapping the + key with the little finger of the right hand.

2. After entering each number in the column, verify your answer with the answer shown below the column.

3. Tap ESC on the main keyboard to clear the calculator; then key numbers in the next column.

4. Repeat steps 1–3 for Drills 1–6.

Technique Cue

Tap each key with a quick, sharp stroke with the *tip* of the finger; release the key quickly. Keep the fingers curved and upright.

Tap the 0 with the side of the right thumb, similar to the way you tap the Space Bar.

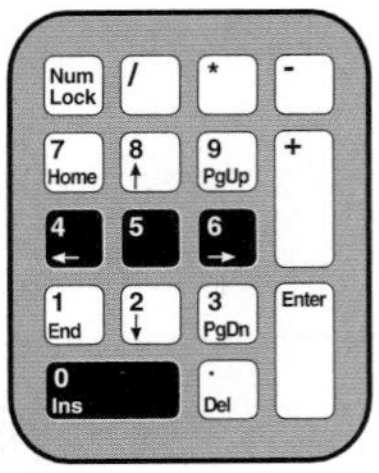

Drill 1

A	B	C	D	E	F
4	5	6	4	5	6
4	5	6	4	5	6
8	10	12	8	10	12

Drill 2

A	B	C	D	E	F
44	55	66	44	55	66
44	55	66	44	55	66
88	110	132	88	110	132

Drill 3

A	B	C	D	E	F
44	45	54	44	55	66
55	56	46	45	54	65
66	64	65	46	56	64
165	165	165	135	165	195

Drill 4

A	B	C	D	E	F
40	50	60	400	500	600
50	60	40	506	604	405
60	40	50	650	460	504
150	150	150	1,556	1,564	1,509

Drill 5

A	B	C	D	E	F
45	404	404	406	450	650
55	405	505	506	540	560
65	406	606	606	405	605
165	1,215	1,515	1,518	1,395	1,815

Drill 6

A	B	C	D	E	F
40	606	444	554	646	456
50	505	445	555	656	654
60	404	446	556	666	504
150	1,515	1,335	1,665	1,968	1,614

For additional practice:

MicroType 5
Numeric Keypad
Lesson 1

I and R Review

Key each line twice SS; DS between 2-line groups.

Review i

1 k i ki ki|did did|dial dial|side side|likes likes;

2 is is|if if|his his|file file|hail hail|hide hide;

3 filed his lease; a field; if she did; she did like

Review r

4 f r fr fr|free free|ride ride|rake rake|fear fear;

5 rare rare|hear hear|read read|real real|dark dark;

6 hear her read; red jars; hear her; dark red dress;

2D Skill Building

Keyboard Reinforcement

Key each line twice SS; DS between 2-line groups.

Technique Cue

- fingers deeply curved
- wrists low but not resting on keyboard
- eyes on copy

reach review

1 jh de ki fr hj ed ik rf jh de ki fr hj ed ik rf jh

2 his his|are are|jar jar|risk risk|if if;|shed shed

h/e

3 hear hear|she she|held held|heir heir|share share;

4 he held; had jak; hear her; had a shed; he has her

i/r

5 hair hair|risk risk|hire hire|iris iris|ride rides

6 a fair; hire a ride; a raid; a fire risk; her hair

all keys learned

7 is is|her her|jak jak|did did|fire fire|lake lake;

8 a lake; her jar; she did fall; hear a lark; see if

2E

Technique: ENTER

Key each line twice SS; DS between 2-line groups.

1 hear her;

2 ask if she is;

3 she had a real jar;

4 if she has a fair share;

5 ask if she likes red dresses;

6 ask dad if he has had a real sale;

7 he has real dark hair; she held a sale;

8 has a red shed; he hired her; he feels safe;

At the end of the line, tap ENTER quickly and begin the next line without pausing.

For additional practice:
MicroType 5
New Key Review, Alphabetic
Lesson 2

Lessons 1–5

Learn Numeric Keypad Operation

Lesson 1   NUMERIC KEYPAD KEYS: 4/5/6/0

OBJECTIVE

• To learn reachstrokes for **4**, **5**, **6**, and **0**

1A

Numeric Keypad Operating Position

Follow the instructions given at the right for positioning yourself to effectively use the numeric keypad.

© franksiteman.com 2007

Sit in front of the keyboard with the book at the right—body erect, both feet on floor.

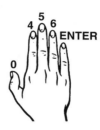

Curve the fingers of the right hand and place them on the keypad:

- index finger on 4
- middle finger on 5
- ring finger on 6
- thumb on 0

1B

Access the Calculator

Follow the instructions given at the right to access the calculator on your computer.

1. Click on Start.
2. Click on All Programs.
3. Click on Accessories.
4. Click on Calculator.
5. Activate the Num (number) Lock located above the 7 on the numeric keypad.

Lesson 3   REVIEW LETTER KEYS (o, t, n, AND g)

OBJECTIVE

• To review reach technique for **o**, **t**, **n**, and **g**.

3A

Conditioning Practice

Key each line twice SS; DS between 2-line groups.

h/e 1 held a sale; he has a shed; he has a desk; she has

i/re 2 fire risk; hire a; her side; like air; a fire; sir

all keys learned 3 as he fell; he sells fir desks; she had half a jar

3B

O and T Review

Key each line twice SS; DS between 2-line groups.

Review o

1 l o|lo lo|fold fold|doll doll|joke joke|load load;

2 also also|sold sold|road road|look look|hold hold;

3 a hoe; a joke; old oak door; load of sod; old oil;

Review t

4 f t|ft ft|fast fast|tied tied|heat heat|tilt tilt;

5 took took|feet feet|tear tear|date date|take take;

6 a tree; three kites; a fast jet; tree forts; a hit

3C   Skill Building

Keyboard Reinforcement

Key each line twice SS; DS between 2-line groups.

Technique Goals
• curved, upright fingers
• wrists low but not resting on keyboard

reach review 1 ki fr jh ft lo de ik rf hj tf ol ed took ride deer

2 if led for hit old fit let kit rod kid dot jak sit

h/e 3 hero hero|held held|heir heir|here here|hike hike;

4 he led|ask her|she held|has fled|had jade|he leads

i/t 5 its its|fits fits|kite kite|site site|first first;

6 a kit|a fit|a tie|lit it|it fits|it sits|it is fit

o/r 7 road road|fort fort|sort sort|rode rode|soar soar;

8 a rod|a door|a rose|or for|her or|he rode|or a rod

space bar 9 of he or it is to if do el odd off too for she the

10 it is|if it|do so|if he|to do|or the|she is|of all

Speed Check: Sentences

Key two 30" timings on each line.   Your rate in *gwam* is shown word-for-word below the lines.

`gwam` 30"

1 When do you think you will go? 12

2 Tara just finished taking her exam. 14

3 Nancy told the man to fix the car brake. 16

4 Val could see that he was angry with the boy. 18

5 Karen may not be able to afford college next year. 20

6 Jay took three hours to complete the chemistry project. 22

30"   2 4 6 8 10 12 14 16 18 20 22

If you finish a line before time is called and start over, your *gwam* is the figure at the end of the line PLUS the figure above or below the point at which you stopped.

Speed Building

1. Key each line twice SS; DS between 2-line groups.
2. Key a 1' writing on each line; determine *gwam* on each timing.

Key the words at a brisk, steady pace.

1 Pamela may make a profit off the land by the lake.

2 Eight of the firms may handle the work for Rodney.

3 Vivian may make a map of the city for the six men.

4 Helen held a formal social for eight of the girls.

5 He may work with the men on the city turn signals.

6 The dog and the girl slept in a chair in the hall.

7 Dianna may cycle to the city dock by the big lake.

8 Half of them may be kept busy with the sick girls.

`gwam` 1' 1 2 3 4 5 6 7 8 9 10

Speed Check: Paragraphs

Key two 1' timings on each ¶; determine *gwam* on each writing.

 all letters used   MicroPace   `gwam` 2'

•   2   •   4   •   6   •   8   •

Are you one of the people who often look from 5

10   •   12   •   14   •   16   •   18   •

the copy to the screen and down at your hands? If 10

20   •   22   •   24   •   26   •   28   •

you are, you can be sure that you will not build a 15

30   •   32   •   34   •   36   •   38   •

speed to prize. Make eyes on copy your next goal. 20

•   2   •   4   •   6   •   8   •

When you move the eyes from the copy to check 24

10   •   12   •   14   •   16   •   18   •

the screen, you may lose your place and waste time 30

20   •   22   •   24   •   26   •   28   •

trying to find it. Lost time can lower your speed 35

30   •   32   •   34   •   36   •   38   •

quickly and in a major way, so do not look away. 39

New Key Learning   Lesson 21: apostrophe (') and hyphen (-)

N and G Review

Key each line twice SS; DS
between 2-line groups.

Review n

1 j n jn jn|nine nine|torn torn|hand hand|noon noon;

2 neat neat|none none|land land|into into|dent dent;

3 no end; an ant; near land; nine nails; one to ten;

Review g

4 f g fg fg|go go|gone gone|ring ring|garage garage;

5 gift gift|golf golf|glad glad|goat goat|dogs dogs;

6 to go; he got; to jog; to jig; the fog; is to golf

3E   Skill Building

Keyboard Reinforcement

Key each line twice SS; DS
between 2-line groups.

Technique Goals
• down-and-in spacing
• eyes on copy

reach review

1 feet feet|kind kind|roof roof|high high|toil toil;

2 his jet; an old fort; do a long skit; she left the

n/g

3 song song|sink sink|long long|sing sing|fang fang;

4 log on; sign it; and golf; fine song; right angle;

space bar

5 do do|go go|of of|or or|he he|it it|is is|and and;

6 if it is|is to go|he or she|to do this|of the sign

all keys learned

7 she had a fine old oak desk; a jet is right there;

8 he told a joke; need for; she goes there at eight;

all keys learned

9 he took the jar along; she said he did it for her;

10 the list on the desk; go right after the jet goes;

3F

Technique: ENTER

Key each line twice SS; DS
between 2-line groups.

1 she is fine;

2 take a jet to go;

3 he is going to tattle;

4 she is the old song leader;

5 he took the song off of her desk;

6 he took the green dress to the store;

> Return quickly at the end of the line and begin the next line without pausing.

For additional practice:
MicroType 5
New Key Review, Alphabetic
Lesson 3

Lesson 21 — NEW KEYS: APOSTROPHE (') AND HYPHEN (-)

OBJECTIVES
- To learn reach technique for ' (apostrophe) and - (hyphen).
- To improve and check keying speed.

21A

Conditioning Practice

Key each line twice SS; then take a 1' timing on line 3; determine *gwam*.

alphabet	1	Glenn saw a quick red fox jump over the lazy cubs.
CAPS LOCK	2	STACY works for HPJ, Inc.; SAMANTHA, for JPH Corp.
easy	3	Kamela may work with the city auditor on the form.

gwam 1' | 1 | 2 | 3 | 4 | 5 | 6 | 7 | 8 | 9 | 10 |

21B

New Keys: ' (Apostrophe) and - (Hyphen)

Key each line twice SS; DS between 2-line groups.

Note: On your screen, apostrophes may look different from those shown in these lines.

Apostrophe *Right little* finger

Hyphen Reach *up* to hyphen with *right little* finger

Learn ' (apostrophe)

1 ;' ;' ;' '; '; I've told you it's hers, haven't I.
2 I'm sure it's Ray's. I'll return it if he's home.
3 I've been told it isn't up to us; it's up to them.

Learn - (hyphen)

4 ;- ;- ;- -; -; -;- -;- Did she say 2-ply or 3-ply?
5 We have 1-, 2-, and 3-bedroom condos for purchase.
6 He rated each as a 1-star, 2-star, or 3-star film.

Combine ' and -

7 ;' ;' ;- ;- ;-' ;-' -'; -'; up-to-date list; x-ray
8 Didn't he say it couldn't be done? I don't agree.
9 I told him the off-the-cuff comment wasn't needed.

10 That isn't a cause-and-effect relationship, is it?
11 The well-known guest is a hard-hitting outfielder.
12 Put an apostrophe in let's, it's, isn't, and don't.

OBJECTIVE

• To review reach technique for **Left Shift**, **.** (period), **u**, and **c**.

4A

Conditioning Practice

Key each line twice SS; DS between 2-line group.

o/t   1   told lost sort took toad toll fort foot tore forth

n/g   2   long gone sang gang rang grand signs grain negate;

all keys learned   3   front door; the lake; so little; large jet; had to

---

4B

Left Shift and . (Period) Review

Key each line twice SS (slowly, then faster); DS between 2-line groups.

Spacing Cue

- Do not space after . (period) within abbreviations.
- Space once after . (period) following abbreviations and initials.
- Space twice after . (period) at end of a sentence.

Review Left Shift key

1   j a Jan Jan|Kent Kent|Lane Lane|Nate Nate|Ida Ida;

2   Jake left; Kate said; Hans has a jet; Jane is here

3   I see that Jan; Jett and Hank Kent; Oak Lake Lane;

Review . (period)

4   1 .|1. 1.|fl. fl.|ed. ed.|ft. ft.|rd. rd.|hr. hrs.

5   .1 .1|fl. fl.|hr. hr.|e.g. e.g.|i.e. i.e.|in. ins.

6   fl. ft. hr. ed. rd. rt. off. fed. ord. alt. asstd.

4C   **Skill Building**

Keyboard Reinforcement

Key each line twice SS; DS between 2-line groups.

Technique Goals
- quick keystrokes
- eyes on copy

h/e   1   heir here then held shoe shed hide heat hear death

2   Heidi had a good lead at the end of the first set.

i/r   3   iris iron ring rifle right ridge rinse irate first

4   Kier is taking a high risk if he rides that horse.

o/t   5   took told lots oath notes those other joist hotel;

6   Olga has lost the list she took to the food store.

n/g   7   song sing gone long gang night signs grand ringing

8   Lang and she are going to sing nine songs at noon.

left shift/.   9   Lake Iris; Lila Lane; Lt. Jan Heredia; Lara Logan;

10   Ken Ladd is going to Illinois to see Irene Lanier.

New Key: TAB Key

The TAB key is used to indent the first line of ¶s. Word processing software has preset tabs called *default* tabs. Usually, the first default tab is set 0.5" to the right of the left margin and is used to indent ¶s (see copy at right).

1. Locate the TAB key on your keyboard (usually to the left of the letter *q*).
2. Reach up to the TAB key with the left little finger; tap the key firmly and release it quickly. The insertion point will move 0.5" to the right.

3. Key each ¶ once SS. DS between ¶s. As you key, tap the TAB key to indent the first line of each ¶. Use the backspace key to correct errors as you key.
4. If time permits, key the ¶s again to master TAB key technique.

Tab key *Left little* finger

 Tab ——▶ The tab key is used to indent blocks of copy such as these.

Tab ——▶ It should also be used for tables to arrange data quickly and neatly into columns.

Tab ——▶ Learn now to use the tab key by touch; doing so will add to your keying skill.

Tab ——▶ Tap the tab key firmly and release it very quickly. Begin the line without a pause.

Tab ——▶ If you hold the tab key down, the insertion point will move from tab to tab across the line.

Speed Check: Paragraphs

Key two 1' timings on each ¶; determine *gwam* on each timing.

E all letters used ⬭MicroPace⬭

```
         •    2    •    4    •    6    •    8    •
    Keep in home position all of the fingers not
   10   •   12   •   14   •   16   •   18   •
being used to tap a key.  Do not let them move out
   20   •   22   •   24   •   26   •   28
of position for the next letters in your copy.
         •    2    •    4    •    6    •    8    •
    Prize the control you have over the fingers.
   10   •   12   •   14   •   16   •   18   •
See how quickly speed goes up when you learn that
   20   •   22   •   24   •   26   •   28   •
you can make them do just what you expect of them.
```

For additional practice:

MicroType 5
Alphabetic Keyboarding
Lesson 20

U and C Review

Key each line twice SS; DS between 2-line groups.

Review u

1 j u|ju ju|just just|undo undo|rust rust|dust dust;
2 use use|hunt hunt|turn turn|hush hush|usual usual;
3 full sun; four fuses; a fungus; our used furniture

Review c

4 d c|dc dc|clock clock|cocoa cocoa|classic classic;
5 cute cute|dock dock|care care|luck luck|cost cost;
6 school dress code; ice chest; coat racks; a clock;

4E Skill Building

Keyboard Reinforcement

Key each line twice SS; DS between 2-line groups.

Technique Goals

- Reach up without moving hands away from your body.
- Reach down without moving hands toward your body.

3rd/1st
1 ice curt none north current notice council conceit
2 Nan is cute; he is curt; turn a cog; he can use it

left shift/.
3 Jan had taken a lead. Kate then cut ahead of her.
4 I said to use Kan. for Kansas and Ore. for Oregon.

key words
5 and cue for jut end kit led old fit just golf coed
6 an due cut such fuss rich lack turn dock turf curl

key phrases
7 left turn|could go|to the|can use|such as|for free
8 just in|code it|turn on|cure it|as such|is in luck

all keys learned
9 Joe can use the truck to get the desk for Lucille.
10 Jason hired Luke; Jeff and Jack did not get hired.

4F

Technique: ENTER

Key each line twice SS; DS between 2-line groups.

Practice Cue

At the end of each line, quickly tap the **ENTER** key and begin the next line without pausing.

· · · · · · · · · · · · · · ·

For additional practice:

MicroType 5

New Key Review, Alphabetic Lesson 4

1 Jake took the fruit.
2 Hank has her old journal.
3 He found the file on the desk.
4 I think Lane took her to the ocean.
5 Janet said she can take us to the dance.
6 Jane and Nick can take the car to the garage.

> **Keep eyes on copy before and after tapping the ENTER key.**

New Key: Quotation Marks

Key each line twice SS; DS between 2-line groups.

Note: On your screen, quotation marks may look different from those shown in these lines.

Quotation Mark: Press left shift and tap " (shift of ') with the *right little* finger.

1 ;; "; "; ";" ";" "I believe," she said, "you won."

2 "John Adams," he said, "was the second President."

3 "James Monroe," I said, "was the fifth President,"

4 Alison said "attitude" determines your "altitude."

Speed Check: Sentences

1. Key a 30" timing on each line.
2. Key another 30" timing on each line. Try to increase your keying speed.

1 Karl did not make the ski team.

2 Jay shared his poem with all of us.

3 Doris played several video games online.

4 Their next game will be played in four weeks.

5 She will register today for next semester classes.

6 She quit the team so she would have more time to study.

Keyboard Reinforcement

1. Key each line twice SS; DS between 2-line groups.
2. Key a 1' timing on lines 4–6.

Technique cue

- fingers curved and upright
- forearms parallel to slant of keyboard
- body erect, sitting back in chair

SHIFT key emphasis (Reach *up* and reach *down* without moving the hands.)

1 Jan and I are to see Ms. Han. May Lana come, too?

2 Bob Epps lives in Rome; Vic Copa is in Rome, also.

3 Oates and Co. has a branch office in Boise, Idaho.

Easy sentences (*Think*, *say*, and *key* the words at a steady pace.)

4 Eight of the girls may go to the social with them.

5 Corla is to work with us to fix the big dock sign.

6 Keith is to pay the six men for the work they did.

gwam	1'	1	2	3	4	5	6	7	8	9	10

Lesson 5   REVIEW LETTER KEYS (w, Right Shift, b, AND y)

OBJECTIVE

• To review reach technique for **w**, **Right Shift**, **b**, and **y**.

5A

Conditioning Practice

Key each line twice SS; DS between 2-line groups.

left shift/.   1 Lt. Jakes or Lt. Haas can take us to Jackson Hole.

u/c   2 just rice clue cone used curl duck luck such uncle

all letters learned   3 Hugh has just taken a lead in a race for a record.

5B

W and Right Shift Review

Key each line twice SS; DS between 2-line groups.

Review w

1 s w|ws ws|who who|show show|wait wait|whole whole;

2 saw saw|two two|wear wear|aware aware|sweat sweat;

3 where will; we wish; wear a sweater; I walked down

Review Right Shift key

4 A; A;|R; R;|C; C;|Al Al|Dan Dan|Sue Sue|Rick Rick;

5 Frank Ford called Carlos Garcia and Rosa Callahan.

6 Stan left for Chicago; Sue left for San Francisco.

5C

Keyboard Reinforcement

Key each line twice SS; DS between 2-line groups.

Practice Cue

Key at a steady pace; space quickly after each word; keep insertion point moving.

w/right shift   1 Dr. Woodward is in Austin; Dr. Choi will see Dawn.

2 Will and Wes left with Wanda Wilson two hours ago.

n/g   3 Gail sang|turn right|long ago|cotton gin|ten signs

4 Eugene sang a long song; Angela sang a short song.

key words   5 dig hair held soak risk shelf sick then wish world

6 oak land half down dial coal disk rock forks aisle

key phrases   7 we did|work with|send her the|take it to|and those

8 we should|to own the|she is to go|when he has gone

all letters learned   9 Jack and Sarah will go to the fair without Glenda.

10 Jake Wilson could not take it; Heather Fong could.

Lesson 20 | NEW KEYS: BACKSPACE, QUOTATION MARK ("), AND TAB

OBJECTIVES

- To learn reach technique for the **BACKSPACE key** and **TAB key**.
- To improve and check keying speed.

20A

Conditioning Practice

Key each line twice SS; then key a 1' timing on line 3; determine *gwam*.

alphabet	1	Jacky can now give six big tips from the old quiz.
CAPS LOCK	2	Find the ZIP Codes for the cities in IOWA and OHIO.
easy	3	It may be a problem if both girls go to the docks.

gwam 1' | 1 | 2 | 3 | 4 | 5 | 6 | 7 | 8 | 9 | 10 |

20B

New Key: BACKSPACE Key

The BACKSPACE key is used to delete text to the left of the insertion point.

1. Locate the BACKSPACE key on your keyboard.
2. Reach up to the BACK-SPACE key with the right little finger (keep the index finger anchored to the *j* finger); tap the BACKSPACE key once for each letter you want deleted; return the finger to the ; key.

Note: When you hold down the BACKSPACE key, letters to the left of the insertion point will be deleted continuously until the BACKSPACE key is released.

Backspace Key
Right little finger; keep right index finger anchored to *j* key.

This symbol means to delete.

Learn Backspace

1. Key the following.

   The delete

2. Use the BACKSPACE key to make the changes shown below.

   The ~~delete~~ backspace

3. Continue keying the sentence as shown below.

   The backspace key can be

4. Use the BACKSPACE key to make the change shown below.

   The backspace key ~~can be~~ is

5. Continue keying the sentence as shown below.

   The backspace key is used to fix

6. Use the BACKSPACE key to make the change shown below.

   The backspace key is used to ~~fix~~ make

7. Continue keying the sentence shown below.

   The backspace key is used to make changes.

5D

B and Y Review

Key each line twice SS; DS between 2-line groups.

Review b

1 f b|fb fb|bead bead|cabs cabs|bush bush|bath bath;
2 blue blue|debt debt|jobs jobs|both both|book book;
3 big brown rabbits; before he bats; big rubber bats

Review y

4 j y|jy jy|eye eye|oily oily|cyst cyst|daily daily;
5 dry dry|cry cry|tiny tiny|daisy daisy|enjoy enjoy;
6 early day; baby boy; really dirty; forty or fifty;

5E

Keyboard Reinforcement

Key each line twice SS; DS between 2-line groups.

Technique Goals

- Reach up without moving hands away from your body.
- Reach down without moving hands toward your body.

reach review

1 jn tf ki jh bf ol ed yj ws ik rf hj cd nj tf .l uj
2 swish den free kick look cedar fifth golf injured;

3rd/1st rows

3 no in bow any tub yen cut sub coy ran bin cow deck
4 Cody wants to buy this baby cub for the young boy.

key words

5 by and for the got all did but cut now say jut ask
6 work just such hand this goal boys held furl eight

key phrases

7 to do|can go|to bow|for all|did jet|ask her|to buy
8 if she|to work|and such|the goal|for this|held the

all letters learned

9 Corky has auburn hair and wide eyes of light jade.
10 Darby left Juan at the dog show near our ice rink.

`gwam` 1' | 1 | 2 | 3 | 4 | 5 | 6 | 7 | 8 | 9 | 10 |

5F

Technique: ENTER

Key each line twice SS; DS between 2-line groups.

For additional practice:

MicroType 5
New Key Review, Alphabetic
Lesson 5

Jo can take a train.
He has three large tents.
Orlando is at San Diego State.
I wish Sheila would take the class.
Juan has to work on Friday and Saturday.
Dr. Chen scheduled our test for the last day.

> At the end of each line, quickly tap the ENTER key and begin the next line without pausing.

`gwam` 30" | 2 | 4 | 6 | 8 | 10 | 12 | 14 | 16 | 18 |

New-Key Mastery

1. Key each line twice SS; DS between 2-line groups.
2. Key a 1' writing on line 11 and then on line 12.

To find 1' *gwam*:
Add 10 for each line you completed to the scale figure beneath the point at which you stopped in a partial line.

Goal: finger-action keystrokes; quiet hands and arms

CAPS LOCK/?
1 UTAH is the BEEHIVE state. What is HAWAII called?
2 Who did Mark select to play CASSIE in CHORUS LINE?

z/v
3 Vince Perez and Zarko Vujacic wore velvet jackets.
4 Zurich, Zeist, Venice, and Pskov were on the quiz.

q/p
5 Paula, Pepe, and Peja took the quiz quite quickly.
6 Quincy Pappas and Enrique Quin were both preppies.

key words
7 very exam calf none disk quip wash give just zebra
8 lazy give busy stop fish down junk mark quit exact

key phrases
9 if you can|see the|when will you|it may be|when he
10 where will|and the|as a rule|who is the|to be able

alphabet 11 A complex theory was rejected by Frank G. Vizquel.

easy 12 Lock may join the squad if we have six big prizes.

gwam 1' | 1 | 2 | 3 | 4 | 5 | 6 | 7 | 8 | 9 | 10 |

Block Paragraphs

1. Key each ¶ once.
2. If time permits, key a 1' timing on each ¶.

Paragraph 1   **gwam** 1'

Dance can be a form of art or it can be thought of   10
as a form of recreation. Dance can be utilized to   20
express ideas and emotions as well as moods.   29

Paragraph 2

One form of dance that is quite common is known as   10
ballet. The earliest forms of ballet are believed   20
to have taken place in Western Europe.   30

Paragraph 3

To excel at ballet, you must take lessons when you   10
are very young. It is not uncommon to see a three   20
year old in a dance studio taking ballet lessons.   30

Paragraph 4

In addition to starting at a very young age, hours   10
and hours of practice are also required to develop   20
into a skilled performer of ballet.   30

gwam 1' | 1 | 2 | 3 | 4 | 5 | 6 | 7 | 8 | 9 | 10 |

For additional practice:
MicroType 5
Alphabetic Keyboarding
Lesson 19

Lesson 6

REVIEW LETTER KEYS (m, x, p, AND v)

OBJECTIVE

• To review reach technique for **m**, **x**, **p**, and **v**.

6A

Conditioning Practice

Key each line twice SS;
DS between 2-line groups.

w/right shift 1 Wendy went with Wade to Walla Walla in Washington.

b/y 2 boy jury cynic tabby hybrid bylaw eyebrow syllable

all letters learned 3 Roberto Cain always fought with Jed on key issues.

6B

M and X Review

Key each line twice SS;
DS between 2-line groups.

Review m

1 j m│jm jm│man man│name name│game game│comic comic;

2 form form│came came│maid maid│harm harm│memo memo;

3 mimic the man; minimum amount; money market rates;

Review x

4 s x│six six│fix fix│box box│next next│exact exact;

5 axle axle│exit exit│axle axle│next next│oxen oxen;

6 next six exits; six extra boxes; the extra exhibit

6C

Keyboard Reinforcement

Key each line twice SS;
DS between 2-line groups.

Technique Goals

• Reach up without moving hands away from your body.
• Reach down without moving hands toward your body.

3rd/1st rows 1 buy amend fix men box hem but six now cut gem ribs

2 mint oxen buoy dent cube rant form went club fined

space bar 3 we it no of me do am if us or is by go ma so in ox

4 go to jet buy fan jam can any tan may rob ham lake

key words 5 if us me do an job the cut big jam was oak lax boy

6 also work cash born kind flex just done many right

key phrases 7 just a minute│if she could│is too big│make it work

8 to fix it│what if she│for our work│next day│to the

all letters learned 9 Jacki is now at the gym; Lex is due there by four.

10 Juan saw that he could fix my old bike for Glenda.

OBJECTIVE

• To learn reach technique for **caps lock** and **?** (question mark).

19A

Conditioning Practice

Key each line twice SS; then key a 1' timing on line 3; determine *gwam*.

alphabet	1	Zosha was quick to dive into my big pool for Jinx.
z/:	2	To: Ms. Lizza Guzzo From: Dr. Beatriz K. Vasquez
easy	3	The firms paid for both of the signs by city hall.

gwam 1' | 1 | 2 | 3 | 4 | 5 | 6 | 7 | 8 | 9 | 10 |

19B

New Keys: CAPS LOCK and ? (Question Mark)

Key each line twice SS; DS between 2-line groups.

Tap the CAPS LOCK to key a series of capital letters. To release the CAPS LOCK to key lowercase letters, tap it again.

Caps Lock
Left little finger

? (question mark)
Left Shift; then *right little* finger

Learn Caps Lock

1 The CARDINALS will play the PHILLIES on Wednesday.
2 Use SLC for SALT LAKE CITY and BTV for BURLINGTON.
3 THE GRAPES OF WRATH was written by JOHN STEINBECK.

Learn ? (question mark)

Space twice.

4 :? :? ;? ;? ?; ?; Who? What? When? Where? Why?
5 When will they arrive? Will you go? Where is he?
6 What time is it? Who called? · Where is the dance?

Combine Caps Lock and ?

7 Is CSCO the ticker symbol for CISCO? What is MMM?
8 MEMORIAL DAY is in MAY; LABOR DAY is in SEPTEMBER.
9 When do the CUBS play the TWINS? Is it on SUNDAY?

10 Did Julie fly to Kansas City, MISSOURI, or KANSAS?
11 Did Dr. Rodriguez pay her DPE, PBL, and NBEA dues?
12 Did you say go TWO blocks EAST or TWO blocks WEST?

P and V Review

Key each line twice SS;
DS between 2-line groups.

Review p

```
1 ; p ;p p;p|paed paid|open open|page page|cope cope
2 peak peak|plan plan|poem poem|plus plus|apex apex;
3 a pen; a cap; apt to pay; pick it up; plan to keep
```

Review v

```
4 f v|fv fv|five five|vote vote|have have|view view;
5 vast vast|even even|move move|cove cove|vase vase;
6 five jovial elves; vote for seven; view every move
```

Keyboard Reinforcement

Key each line twice SS;
DS between 2-line groups.

Practice Cue

- Use quick keystrokes.
- Eyes on copy as you key.

reach review

```
1 sw jn xs ;p fv jm de yj fr ki ft ol cd hj gf ju fb
2 jet jet club kick owned maybe sixth vacant shelter
```

3rd/1st rows

```
3 six view north maybe pencil number western mention
4 byway button known cute sent enjoy gems five gripe
```

key words

```
5 like each work kept turn made duty check just have
6 begin where jury down vote exist came eight except
```

key phrases

```
7 if they go|they kept it|without them|on their farm
8 to leave it|please expect|to review it|so much fun
```

all letters learned

```
9 Kevin does a top job on your flax farm with Craig.
10 Dixon flew blue jets eight times over a city park.
```

Technique: Spacing with Punctuation

Key each line twice SS;
DS between 2-line groups.

Spacing Cue

Do not space after an internal period in an abbreviation, such as Ed.D.

```
1 Dr. Cabrera has a Ph.D.; Dr. Wesenber has an Ed.D.
2 Lynn may send a box c.o.d. to Ms. Fox in St. Paul.
3 J. R. and Tim will go by boat to St. Louis in May.
4 Lexi keyed ect. for etc. and lost the match to me.
5 Mr. and Mrs. D. J. Vargas set sail for the island.
6 Ms. Franco may take her Ed.D. exam early in March.
```

For additional practice:

MicroType 5

New Key Review, Alphabetic
Lesson 6

New-Key Mastery

Key each line twice SS; DS between 2-line groups.

┌───┐

Technique cue

- Keep fingers curved and upright.
- Key at a steady pace.

q/z
1 zoom hazy quit prize dozen freeze quizzed equalize
2 Zoe was quite amazed by the quaint city of La Paz.

p/x
3 pox expect example explore perplex explain complex
4 Tex picked six apples for a pie for Rex and Pedro.

v/m
5 move vase mean veal make vice mark very comb above
6 Mavis came to visit Mark, Vivian, Val, and Marvin.

easy
7 Their maid may pay for all the land by the chapel.
8 The auditor may do the work for the big city firm.

alphabet
9 Glenn saw a quick red fox jump over the lazy cubs.
10 Gavin quickly explained what Joby made for prizes.

Block Paragraphs

1. Key each paragraph (¶) once SS; DS between ¶s; then key them again faster.
2. Key a 1' timing on each ¶; determine your *gwam*.

For additional practice:
MicroType 5
Alphabetic Keyboarding
Lesson 18

Paragraph 1

gwam 1'

A good team member is honest, does a fair share of | 10
the work, and is eager to help another team member | 20
if there is a need to do so. Quite often the best | 30
team member must be a superb follower as well as a | 40
good leader. | 43

Paragraph 2

There are several other skills that a person ought | 10
to acquire in order to become a good leader. Such | 20
skills as the ability to think, listen, speak, and | 30
write are essential for a good leader to possess. | 40

gwam 1' | 1 | 2 | 3 | 4 | 5 | 6 | 7 | 8 | 9 | 10 |

Enrichment

Key each line twice SS; DS between 2-line groups.

Technique cue

- Keep fingers upright.
- Keep hands/arms steady.

x/:
1 To: Rex Cox, Tex Oxley|From: Max Saxe|A:B as C:D
2 Spelling words: extra, extract, exam, and explain

q/,
3 square square|quick quick|equip equip|squad squad;
4 Spelling words: quartz, quiet, quote, and quickly

p/z
5 Lopez Lopez|pizza pizza|zephyr zephyr|Perez Perez;
6 Spelling words: utilize, appeal, cozy, and pepper

m/v
7 velvet velvet|move move|remove remove|movie movie;
8 Spelling words: Vermont, Vermillion, and Vermeil.

Lesson 7   REVIEW LETTER KEYS (q, comma, z, AND colon)

OBJECTIVE

• To review reach technique for **q**, **comma**, **z**, and **colon**.

7A

Conditioning Practice

Key each line twice SS;
DS between 2-line groups.
If time permits, rekey the
lines.

m/x   1   extra room; exact amount; exciting menu; six exams

p/v   2   every paper; very poor; vivid picture; vital part;

all letters
learned   3   Jane Oka will place my bid for the ugly vase next.

7B

Q and , (Comma) Review

Key each line twice SS;
DS between 2-line groups.

Spacing Cue

Space once after , (comma)
used as punctuation.

Learn q

1   a q|aqua aqua|quiet quiet|quake quake|equal equal;

2   equip equip|query query|quote quote|equity equity;

3   require a quote; quite a sequel; requested a quote

Learn , (comma)

4   k ,|k, k,|Jill, Mary, Dick, and Juan rode the bus.

5   Javier hit a single, double, triple, and home run.

6   Three, four, five, and eight are my lucky numbers.

7C

Keyboard Reinforcement

Key each line twice SS;
DS between 2-line groups.

Technique Goals

• Reach up without
moving hands away
from your body.
• Reach down without
moving hands toward
your body.

reach
review   1   rf mj nj tf p; xs ,k ol cd ik vf ed hj bf qu .l ws

  2   yj gf hj for vow got quote cute known mixer invite

3rd/1st
rows   3   cute muck just pick sixty maybe coyote wince turns

  4   to win|to give|my voice|a peck|come back|next time

key
words   5   got sit man for fix jam via oak the wash bark code

  6   buy lay apt mix pay when rope give just stub quick

key
phrases   7   of all|golf game|if he is|it is due next|to pay us

  8   if we pay|is of age|up to you|so we own|she saw me

all letters
learned   9   Jevon will fix my pool deck if the big rain quits.

  10   Rex did fly quick jets to map the seven big towns.

Lesson 18

NEW KEYS: z AND COLON (:)

• To learn reach technique for **z** and **:** (colon).

18A

Conditioning Practice

Key each line twice SS; then key a 1' timing on line 3; determine *gwam*.

all letters learned	1 Jack quickly helped Mary Newton fix the big stove.
spacing	2 it is│if you can│by the end│when will he│to be the
easy	3 Helen may go to the city to buy the girls a shake.

gwam 1' │ 1 │ 2 │ 3 │ 4 │ 5 │ 6 │ 7 │ 8 │ 9 │ 10 │

18B

New Keys: z and : (colon)

Key each line twice SS; DS between 2-line groups. If time permits, key lines 7–10 again.

z *Left little* finger

: *Left Shift* and tap : key

Spacing cue

Space twice after : used as punctuation.

Capitalization cue

Capitalize the first word of a complete sentence following a colon.

Learn z

1 a z a z│az az│zap zap│zip zip│raze raze│size size;

2 daze daze│maze maze│lazy lazy│hazy hazy│zest zest;

3 Utah Jazz; hazel eyes; loud buzz; zoology quizzes;

Learn : (colon)

4 ; : ; :│a:A b:B c:C d:D e:E f:F g:G h:H i:I j:J kK1L

5 M:m N:n O:o P;p Q:q R:r S:s T:t U:u V: w: X: y: Z:

6 Dear Mr. Baker: Dear Dr. Finn: Dear Mrs. Fedder:

Combine z and :

7 Liz invited the following: Hazel, Inez, and Zach.

8 Use these headings: Zip Code: Zone: Zoo: Jazz:

9 Buzz, spell these words: size, fizzle, and razor.

10 Dear Mr. Perez: Dear Ms. Ruiz: Dear Mrs. Mendez:

7D

Z and : (Colon) Review

Key each line twice SS;
DS between 2-line groups.

Review z

1 a z|az az|zone zone|raze raze|lazy lazy|zone zone;

2 ozone ozone|razor razor|amaze amaze|fizzle fizzle;

3 too lazy; a dozen zigzags; dozen sizes; he quizzed

Review : (colon)

4 ; :|::|:; Date: Time: Name: Room: From: File:

5 Subject: File: Reply to: Dear Sue: Shift for :

6 Dear Mr. Smith: Dear Mr. Perez: Dear Mr. Mendez:

7E

Keyboard Reinforcement

Key each line twice SS;
DS between 2-line groups.

Technique Goals

- curved, upright fingers
- steady keystroking pace

q/z
1 zinc quiz zero quota kazoo dazzle inquire equalize
2 Zelda and Quinn amazed us all on the zoology quiz.

p/x
3 except expect expel export explore explain express
4 Expect Roxanne to fix pizza for the next six days.

v/m
5 Vim man van dim have move vamp more dive time five
6 Val drove them to the mall in my vivid maroon van.

easy
7 Their sick dog slept by the oak chair in the hall.
8 Nancy may go with us to the city; Jane may go too.

alphabet
9 Nate will vex the judge if he bucks my quiz group.
10 Quig just fixed prize vases he won at my key club.

7F

Block Paragraphs

1. Read the note at the
   right below the
   paragraphs (¶s).
2. Key each ¶ twice (slowly,
   then faster).
3. If your instructor directs,
   key a 1' writing on each
   ¶; determine your *gwam*.

Paragraph 1   gwam 1'

The space bar is a vital tool, for every fifth or   10

sixth stroke is a space when you key. If you use   20

it with good form, it will aid you to build speed. 30

Paragraph 2

Just keep the thumb low over the space bar. Move   10

the thumb down and in quickly toward your palm to   20

get the prized stroke you need to build top skill. 30

gwam 1' | 1 | 2 | 3 | 4 | 5 | 6 | 7 | 8 | 9 | 10 |

Note: At the end of a full line, the insertion point goes to the next line automatically. This is called **wordwrap**. Use wordwrap when you key a ¶. At the end of a ¶, tap the **ENTER** key twice to place a DS between the ¶s.

Lesson 17   REVIEW

• To improve keying technique and speed.

17A

Improve Keyboarding Skill

Key each line twice SS; DS between 2-line groups.

1 Vivian may make their formal gowns for the social.
2 It may be a problem if both men work for the city.
3 The antique box is in the big field by the chapel.
4 The man paid a visit to the firm to sign the form.
5 He works with the men at the dock to fix problems.
6 The rich man may work with Jan to fix the bicycle.

17B

Speed Check

Key three 20" timings on each line. Try to go faster on each timing.

1 You will need to buy the book.
2 Jana will have to pay the late fee.
3 Scott and James left for Utah yesterday.
4 Reed has not set a date for the next meeting.
5 I will not be able to finish the book before then.
6 Enrique took the final exam before he left for Georgia.

| gwam 20" | 3 | 6 | 9 | 12 | 15 | 18 | 21 | 24 | 27 | 30 | 33 |

17C

Increase Keying Speed

Key each line twice SS; DS between 2-line groups. Key a 30" timing on each line.

1 It is a civic duty to handle the problem for them.
2 Six of the city firms may handle the fuel problem.
3 Jay may make an authentic map for the title firms.
4 Hal and Orlando work at the store by the big lake.
5 I may make a shelf for the neighbor on the island.
6 Rick and I may go to town to make the eight signs.
7 He may blame the boy for the problem with the bus.
8 Jan Burns is the chair of the big sorority social.
9 A box with the bugle is on the mantle by the bowl.

| gwam 30" | 2 | 4 | 6 | 8 | 10 | 12 | 14 | 16 | 18 | 20 |

For additional practice:
MicroType 5
Alphabetic Keyboarding
Lesson 17

OBJECTIVE

• To review reach technique for **CAPS LOCK, ?** (question mark), **TAB** key, ' (apostrophe), - (hyphen), and " (quotation mark).

8A

Conditioning Practice

Key each line twice SS; then key a 1' timing on line 3. Determine *gwam* using the scale below line 3.

alphabet 1 Gus Javon quickly baked extra pizza for the women.
z/: 2 To: Ms. Zachary Zeman; From: Dr. Liza J. Zitzer.
easy 3 Rick kept busy with the work he did on the mantle.

| gwam | 1' | 1 | 2 | 3 | 4 | 5 | 6 | 7 | 8 | 9 | 10 | |

Note: Your *gwam* (gross words a minute) is the figure under the last letter keyed. If you keyed more than a line, add 10 for each additional line keyed.

8B

Review CAPS LOCK and ? (Question Mark)

Key each line twice SS; DS between 2-line groups.

Note: To key a series of capital letters, tap CAPS LOCK using the left little finger. To release CAPS LOCK, tap it again.

Spacing Cue

Space twice after a ? at the end of a sentence.

Review CAPS LOCK

1 The book, A NEW START, was written by JACK SPENCE.
2 JEFFERSON drafted THE DECLARATION OF INDEPENDENCE.
3 INDEPENDENCE HALL is situated in PHILADELPHIA, PA.

Review ? (question mark)

4 ; ? ;? ;? Who? What? When? Where? Why? Is it?
5 Where is it? When is it? Did he stay? May I go?
6 Do I space twice? Did you key all the lines once?

8C

Review TAB

Indent and key each ¶ once SS; DS between ¶s.

Note: To indent the first line of a ¶, tap TAB using the left little finger. Tabs are usually set every .5" to the right of the left margin.

Tab ⟶ The Tab key is used to indent lines of copy such as these. It can also be used for tables to arrange data quickly and neatly into columns.
Tab ⟶ Learn now to use the Tab key by touch. Tap the Tab key firmly and release it very quickly. Begin the line without a pause.
Tab ⟶ If you hold the Tab key down, the insertion point will move from tab to tab across the line.

8D

Review TAB

Key each line twice SS; DS between 2-line groups.

Tab ⟶ the   Tab ⟶ and   Tab ⟶ can   Tab ⟶ did
         sea   fan   eat   not
         tea   sat   lot   hat

New-Key Mastery

Key each line twice SS; DS between 2-line groups. If time permits, key lines 9–10 again.

Technique cues

- Reach up without moving hands away from your body.
- Use quick-snap key-strokes.

Goal: finger-action keystrokes; quiet hands and arms

reach review

1 jh fg l. o. k, I, ft sw aq de ;p fr jn jb fv jn jm
2 We can leave now. Take Nancy, Michael, and Jorge.

3rd/1st rows

3 nice bond many when oxen come vent quit very prom;
4 drive a truck|know how to|not now|when will you be

key words

5 have jail wept quit desk from goes cave yarn boxer
6 brand extra cycle event equip know fight made show

key phrases

7 when will you|may be able to|if you can|he will be
8 ask about the|need to be|where will|as you can see

all letters learned

9 The quaint old maypole was fixed by Jackie Groves.
10 Very fixed the job growth plans quickly on Monday.

16D

Technique: Spacing with Punctuation

Key each twice; DS between 2-line groups.

Spacing cue

Space once after , (comma) or ; (semicolon) used as punctuation.

1 Jay asked the question; Tim answered the question.
2 Ann, Joe, and I saw the bus; Mark and Ted did not.
3 I had ibid., op. cit., and loc. cit. in the paper.
4 The Mets, Dodgers, Cardinals, and Padres competed.

16E

Enrichment

Key each line twice SS; DS between 2-line groups.

Adjacent keys

1 ew mn vb tr op iu ty bv xc fg jh df ;l as kj qw er
2 week oily free join dash very true wash tree rash;
3 union point extra river tracks water cover weapon;

Long direct reaches

4 ny many ce rice my myself mu mute gr grand hy hype
5 lunch hatch vouch newsy bossy yearn beyond crabby;
6 gabby bridge muggy venture machine beauty luncheon

Double letters

7 book feet eggs seek cell jeer keep mall adds occur
8 class little sheep effort needle assist happy seem
9 Tennessee Minnesota Illinois Mississippi Missouri;

For additional practice:
MicroType 5
Alphabetic Keyboarding
Lesson 16

**Review ' (apostrophe),
- (hyphen), and
" (quotation mark)**

Key each line twice SS; DS between 2-line groups.

Note: On your screen, apostrophes and quotation marks may look different from those shown in these lines.

Review ' (apostrophe)

1 ;' ;' ;' '; I didn't say Jen's keys weren't taken.
2 Didn't Jack's friend Mary say she'll be here soon?
3 I've been told she'll quit; I'm not sure how soon.

Review - (hyphen)

4 ; - ;- ;- up-to-date computer; hit-or-miss effort;
5 sister-in-law; do-or-die effort; first-rate report
6 Their high-priced player had a do-or-die attitude.

Review " (quotation mark)

7 ;" '" "They won." "I can't believe it." "I did."
8 "John Adams," he said, "was the second President."
9 "James Monroe," I said, "was the fifth President."

Keyboard Reinforcement

1. Key lines twice SS; DS between 2-line groups.
2. Key a 1' writing on lines 10–12.

Reach review (Keep on home keys the fingers not used for reaching.)

1 sixth jay bark wren quit truck open give team zero
2 pro quo|is just|my firm|was then|may grow|must try
3 Olga sews aqua and red silk to make six big kites.

Space Bar emphasis (Think, say, and key the words.)

4 to and but the men pay with land field visit girls
5 She may|on the|go to the|by the man|on a lake|I do
6 He is to go to the city hall for the forms for us.

Shift key emphasis (Reach up and reach down without moving the hands.)

7 Jan and I are to see Ms. Cey. May Lana come, too?
8 Denver, Colorado; Chicago, Illinois; New York City
9 Oates and Co. has a branch office in Boise, Idaho.

Easy sentences (Think, say, and key the words at a steady pace.)

10 Jake paid the six firms for all the work they did.
11 Chris is to pay the six men for the work they did.
12 Keith is to work with us to fix the big dock sign.

For additional practice:
MicroType 5
New Key Review, Alphabetic
Lesson 8

| gwam | 1' | 1 | 2 | 3 | 4 | 5 | 6 | 7 | 8 | 9 | 10 |

OBJECTIVE

• To learn reach technique for **q** and **,** (comma).

16A

Conditioning Practice

Key each line twice SS; DS between 2-line groups. If time permits, key the lines again.

all letters learned 1 dash give wind true flop comb yolk joke hunt gain;

p/v 2 prove vapor above apple voted super cover preview;

all letters learned 3 Mary forced Jack to help move six big water units.

16B

New Keys: q and , (comma)

Key each line twice SS; DS between 2-line groups.

q *Left little* finger

, (comma) *Right middle* finger

Spacing cue

Space once after **,** (comma) used as punctuation.

Learn q

1 a q aq|quit quit|aqua aqua|quick quick|quote quote

2 quest quest|quart quart|quite quite|liquid liquid;

3 quite quiet; quick squirrel; chi square; a quarter

Learn , (comma)

4 , k ,k ,k one, two, three, four, five, six, seven,

5 Akio, Baiko, Niou, and Joji are exchange students.

6 Juan, Rico, and Mike voted; however, Jane did not.

Combine q and , (comma)

7 Quota, square, quiche, and quite were on the exam.

8 Quin can spell Quebec, Nicaragua, Iraq, and Qatar.

9 Joaquin, Jacque, and Javier sailed for Martinique.

10 Quin, Jacqueline, and Paque quickly took the exam.

11 Rob quickly won my squad over quip by brainy quip.

12 Quit, quiet, and quaint were on the spelling exam.

Lesson 9   SKILL BUILDING

OBJECTIVE

- To learn proper response patterns to gain speed.

9A

Conditioning Practice

Key each line twice SS; then key a 1' timing on line 3. Determine *gwam*.

alphabet	1	Wusov amazed them by jumping quickly from the box.
spacing	2	am to|is an|by it|of us|an oak|is to pay|all of us
easy	3	The sorority may do the work for the city auditor.
gwam	1' |	1 | 2 | 3 | 4 | 5 | 6 | 7 | 8 | 9 | 10 |

9B

Speed Check: Sentences

Key each line three times SS at the speed level (see blue box at the right); DS between 3-line groups.

Technique Cue

- After keying the last letter of a word, quickly tap the Space Bar and immediately begin keying the next word.
- After keying the period or question mark at the end of each line, quickly tap **ENTER** and immediately begin keying the next line.

1 She has three more games left.

2 When will he make the payment?

3 Felipe left for school an hour ago.

4 Mary has four more puppies to sell.

5 The girls won the game by eleven points.

6 Taisho finished the report on Wednesday.

7 Their runner fell with less than a lap to go.

8 Inez will finish the project by the deadline.

9 You can register for classes starting next Friday.

10 Jessica was elected president by just three votes.

Speed Level of Practice

When the purpose of practice is to reach a new speed, use the **speed level**. Take the brakes off your fingers and experiment with new stroking patterns and new speeds. Do this by:

- reading two or three letters ahead of your keying to foresee stroking patterns;

- getting the fingers ready for the combinations of letters to be keyed;

- keeping your eyes on the copy in the book;

- keying at the word level rather than letter by letter.

15C

New-Key Mastery

Key each line twice SS; DS between 2-line groups.

Technique cues

- Reach up without moving hands away from your body.
- Reach down without moving hands toward your body.

Goal: finger-action keystrokes; quiet hands and arms

reach review

1 fv fr ft fg fb jn jm jh jy ju l. lo sx sw dc de ;p
2 free kind junk swim loan link half golf very plain

3rd/1st rows

3 oven cove oxen went been nice more home rice phone
4 not item river their newer price voice point crime

key words

5 pair pays pens vigor vivid vogue panel proxy opens
6 jam kept right shake shelf shape soap visit visual

key phrases

7 pay them|their signs|vote for|when will|if they go
8 you will be|much of the|when did they|to see their

all letters learned

9 Crew had seven of the votes; Brooks had only five.
10 They just left the park and went to see Dr. Nixon.

15D

Technique: SHIFT and ENTER Keys

1. Key each line once SS; at the end of each line, quickly tap the **ENTER** key, and immediately start the next line.
2. On lines 7 and 8, see how many words you can key in 30".

Eyes on copy as you shift and as you tap ENTER key

1 Mary was told to buy the coat.
2 Vern is to choose a high goal.

3 Jay and Livan did not like to golf.
4 Ramon Mota took the test on Monday.

5 Lexi told Scott to set his goals higher.
6 Eric and I keyed each line of the drill.

7 Roberto excels in most of the things he does.
8 Vivian can key much faster than Jack or Kate.

| gwam | 1' | | 1 | 2 | 3 | 4 | 5 | 6 | 7 | 8 | 9 | |

15E

Enrichment

Key each line twice SS; DS between 2-line groups.

Technique cues

- keep fingers upright
- keep hands/arms steady

m/p

1 plum bump push mark jump limp camp same post maple
2 Pete sampled the plums; Mark sampled the apricots.

b/x

3 box exact able except abide job expand debt extend
4 Dr. Nixon placed the six textbooks in the taxicab.

y/v

5 very verb eyes vent layer even days save yard vast
6 Darby Vance may take the gray van to Vivian today.

For additional practice:

MicroType 5
Alphabetic Keyboarding
Lesson 15

Technique: Response Patterns

1. Key each line twice SS; DS between 2-line groups.
2. Key 1' timings on lines 10–12; determine *gwam* on each timing.

Technique Cues

Word response: Key easy (balanced-hand) words as words.

Letter response: Key letters of one-hand words steadily and evenly, letter by letter.

Balanced-hand words

1 us so an by is or it do of go he if to me of ox am
2 an box air wig the and sir map pen men row fix jam
3 girl kept quay town auto busy firm dock held makes

One-hand words

4 be my up we on at no as oh as ax in at my up be we
5 no cat act red tax was you pin oil hip ear fat few
6 milk fast oily hymn base card safe draw pink gates

Balanced-hand phrases

7 to go|it is due|to the end|if it is|to do so|he is
8 pay the|for us|may do the|did he|make a|paid for a
9 he may|when did they|so do they|make a turn|to the

Balanced-hand sentences

10 I am to pay the six men if they do the work right.
11 Title to all of the lake land is held by the city.
12 The small ornament on their door is an ivory duck.

gwam 1' | 1 | 2 | 3 | 4 | 5 | 6 | 7 | 8 | 9 | 10 |

Skill Building

Speed Building

1. Key a 1' timing on each ¶; determine *gwam*.
2. Key two 2' timings on ¶s 1–2 combined; determine *gwam*.

E all letters used (MicroPace) gwam 2'

```
              •        2        •        4        •        6        •        8        •
        To risk your own life for the good of others          5
        10        •        12        •        14        •        16        •        18    •
has always been seen as an admirable thing to do.            10
        20        •        22        •        24        •        26        •        28    •
Harriet Tubman was a slave in the South.  She became         16
30        •        32        •        34        •        36        •        38        •
a free woman when she was able to run away to the            21
40        •        42        •        44        •        46        •        48        •        50
North.  This freedom just did not mean much to her           26
        •        52        •        54        •        56        •
while so many others were still slaves.                      30

              •        2        •        4        •        6        •        8        •
        She quickly put her own life at risk by going        35
        10        •        12        •        14        •        16        •        18    •
back to the South.  She did this to help others get          41
        20        •        22        •        24        •        26        •        28    •        30
free.  She was able to help several hundred.  This is        46
        •        32        •        34        •        36        •        38        •        40
a large number.  During the Civil War she continued          51
•        42        •        44        •        46        •        48        •        50
to exhibit the traits of an amazing hero.  She served        57
52        •        54        •        56        •        58
the Union as a spy and as a scout.                           60
```

For additional practice:

MicroType 5
New Key Review, Alphabetic
Lesson 9

gwam 2' | 1 | 2 | 3 | 4 | 5 |

Lesson 15   NEW KEYS: p AND v

• To learn reach technique for **p** and **v**.

Fingers curved

Fingers upright

Hard return

15A

Conditioning Practice

Key each line twice SS; DS between 2-line groups.

one-hand words
balanced-hand words
all letters learned

1 rare gear seed hill milk lion bare moon base onion
2 town wish corn fork dish held coal owns rich their
3 Gabe Waxon may ask us to join him for lunch today.

15B

New Keys: p and v

Key each line twice SS; DS between 2-line groups. If time permits, key lines 7–9 again.

p *Right little* finger

v *Left index* finger

Learn p

1 ; p ;p ;p|put put|pin pin|pay pay|pop pop|sap sap;
2 pull pull park park open open soap soap hoop hoops
3 a purple puppet; pay plan; plain paper; poor poet;

Learn v

4 f v fv fv|van van|vain vain|very very|value value;
5 over over|vote vote|save save|move move|dove dove;
6 drive over; seven verbs; value driven; viable vote

Combine p and v

7 cave push gave pain oven pick jive keep very river
8 have revised; river view; five to seven; even vote
9 Eva and Paul have to pick papa up to vote at five.

Lesson 10 SKILL BUILDING

OBJECTIVES

- To build straight-copy speed and accuracy.
- To enhance keying technique.

10A

Conditioning Practice

Key each line twice SS; then key a 1' timing on line 3. Determine *gwam*.

alphabet	1	Levi Lentz packed my bag with six quarts of juice.
CAPS LOCK	2	KANSAS is KS; TEXAS is TX; IDAHO is ID; IOWA is IA
easy	3	Jan may name a tutor to work with the eight girls.

gwam 1' | 1 | 2 | 3 | 4 | 5 | 6 | 7 | 8 | 9 | 10 |

10B

Technique: Response Patterns

1. Key each line twice SS; DS between 2-line groups.
2. Key a 1' timing on lines 3, 6, 9, and 12.

letter response

1 pink safe tree face hill look only fact date start
2 red dress|extra milk|union awards|pink car|you are
3 Jim Carter started a car in my garage in Honolulu.

word response

4 with work dock half coal hair both busy city civic
5 when they|fix their|pay the|did she|cut down|to it
6 Diana and Jan may go to the island to do the work.

combination response

7 big cat air act did fat due joy got pin rug was us
8 pink bowl|city street|their jump|extra chair|is at
9 Ed Burns was with Steve when we started the feast.

letter 10 Jim saw a fat cat in a cab as we sat in my garage.

combination 11 Jay was the man you saw up at the lake in the bus.

word 12 I may go to the lake with the men to fix the door.

gwam 1' | 1 | 2 | 3 | 4 | 5 | 6 | 7 | 8 | 9 | 10 |

10C

Speed Check: Sentences

Key two 30" timings on each line. Try to increase your keying speed the second time you key the line. Determine *gwam* for the faster timing of each line.

1 Ben will be ready before noon.
2 Sam will bring his dog to the lake.
3 Jack did not fill the two cars with gas.
4 Jon will take the next test when he is ready.
5 Susan is to bring two or three copies of the play.
6 This may be the last time you will have to take a test.

gwam 30" | 2 | 4 | 6 | 8 | 10 | 12 | 14 | 16 | 18 | 20 | 22 |

Goal: finger-action keystrokes; quiet hands and arms

New-Key Mastery

Key each line twice SS; DS between 2-line groups.

- Reach up without moving hands away from your body.
- Reach down without moving hands toward your body.

3rd/1st rows

1 no cut not toy but cow box men met bit cot net boy
2 torn core much oxen only time next yarn into north

space bar

3 as ox do if go oh no we of is he an to by in it at
4 jar ask you off got hit old box ice ink man was in

key words

5 mend game team card exam back hold join form enjoy
6 were time yarn oxen four dent mask when dark usual

key phrases

7 she can|go to the|if they will|make the|at the end
8 when will|we will be able|need a|take a look|I can

all keys learned

9 Fabio and Jacki said you would need the right mix.
10 Glen said that he would fix my bike for Jacob Cox.

Technique: Spacing with Punctuation

Key each line twice SS; DS between 2-line groups.

Do not space after an internal period in an abbreviation, such as Ed.D.

1 Dr. Smythe and Dr. Ramos left for St. Louis today.
2 Dr. Chen taught us the meaning of f.o.b. and LIFO.
3 Keith got his Ed.D. at NYU; I got my Ed.D. at USU.
4 Sgt. J. Roarke met with Lt. Col. Christina Castro.

Enrichment

Key each line twice SS; DS between 2-line groups.

Keep the insertion point moving steadily across each line (no pauses).

m/x 1 Mary Fox and Maxine Cox took all six of the exams.
b/y 2 Burly Bryon Beyer barely beat Barb Byrnes in golf.
w/right shift 3 Carlos DeRosa defeated Wade Cey in the last match.
u/c 4 The clumsy ducks caused Lucy Lund to hit the curb.
./left shift 5 Keith and Mike went to St. Louis to see Mr. Owens.
n/g 6 Glen began crying as Ginny began singing the song.
o/t 7 Tom bought a total of two tons of tools yesterday.
i/r 8 Rick and Maria tried to fix the tire for the girl.
h/e 9 Helen Hale heard her tell them to see the hostess.

For additional practice:
MicroType 5
Alphabetic Keyboarding
Lesson 14

New Key Learning   Lesson 14: m and x

Quarter-Minute Checkpoints				
gwam	1/4'	1/2'	3/4'	Time
16	4	8	12	16
20	5	10	15	20
24	6	12	18	24
28	7	14	21	28
32	8	16	24	32
36	9	18	27	36
40	10	20	30	40

Guided (Paced) Timing Procedure

Establish a goal rate

1. Key a 1' timing on ¶ 1 of a set of ¶s that contain superior figures for guided timings, as in 10D below.

2. Using the *gwam* as a base, add 4 *gwam* to set your goal rate.

3. From column 1 of the table at the left, choose the speed nearest your goal rate. In the quarter-minute columns beside that speed, note the points in the copy you must reach to attain your goal rate.

4. Determine the checkpoint for each quarter minute from the word count above the lines in ¶ 1. (*Example:* Checkpoints for 24 *gwam* are 6, 12, 18, and 24.)

Practice procedure

1. Key two 1' timings on ¶ 1 at your goal rate guided by the quarter-minute calls (1/4, 1/2, 3/4, time). Try to reach each checkpoint before the guide is called.

2. Key two 1' timings on ¶ 2 of a set of ¶s in the same way.

3. If time permits, key a 2' writing on the set of ¶s combined, without the guides.

10D

Speed Check: Paragraphs

1. Key a 1' timing on each ¶; determine *gwam* on each timing.

2. Using your better *gwam* as a base rate, set a goal rate and key two 1' guided timings on each ¶ as directed above.

3. Key two 2' unguided timings on ¶s 1–2 combined; determine *gwam*.

 LA   all letters used   (MicroPace)   gwam 2'

		2		4		6		8		
Is it possible for a mouse to make an individual 5
10   •   12   •   14   •   16   •   18   •   20
quite wealthy? Yes, of course it is. If you do not 11
22   •   24   •   26   •   28   •   30
believe it, consider Walt Disney. This individual 16
32   •   34   •   36   •   38   •   40
came from a very humble beginning. But in the end, 21
42   •   44   •   46   •   48   •   50
he was a very wealthy person. He was a person whose 26
52   •   54   •   56   •   58   •   60
work brought great enjoyment to the lives of many 31
62   •
people. 31

•   2   •   4   •   6   •   8   •
A mouse, duck, and dog are just a few of the 36
10   •   12   •   14   •   16   •   18
exquisite personalities he brought to life. After 41
20   •   22   •   24   •   26   •   28
all these years, his work is still a part of our 46
30   •   32   •   34   •   36   •   38
lives. People travel miles to step into the amazing 51
40   •   42   •   44   •   46   •   48   •   50
world of Disney. It would be impossible to picture 56
•   52   •   54   •
this world without his work. 59

gwam 2' | 1 | 2 | 3 | 4 | 5 |

10E

Technique

Key each line twice SS; DS between 2-line groups.

··········

For additional practice:

MicroType 5
New Key Review, Alphabetic
Lesson 10

··········

Double letters

1 took yell meet carrot need cross spoon little loop
2 Dianna has lived in Massachusetts and Mississippi.

Shift keys

3 New Jersey, South Dakota, New Mexico, North Dakota
4 The Padres play the Cubs on Tuesday and Wednesday.

Lesson 14   NEW KEYS: m AND x

OBJECTIVE

• To learn reach technique for **m** and **x**.

14A

Conditioning Practice

Key each line twice SS; DS between 2-line groups.

reach review 1 car hit bus get ice not win boy try wait knit yarn

b/y 2 body obey baby busy bury bully byway beauty subway

all letters learned 3 Jerry will take the four cans of beans to Douglas.

14B

New Keys: m and x

Key each line twice SS; DS between 2-line groups

m *Right index* finger

x *Left ring* finger

Learn m

1 j m|jm jm|jam jam|arm arm|aim aim|man man|ham hams

2 lamb some game firm come dome make warm mark must;

3 more magic; many firms; make money; many mean men;

Learn x

4 s x|sx sx|six six|axe axe|fix fix|box box|tax tax;

5 Lexi Lexi|oxen oxen|exit exit|taxi taxi|axle axle;

6 fix the axle; extra exit; exact tax; excited oxen;

Combine m and x

7 Max Max|mix mix|exam exam|axiom axiom|maxim maxim;

8 tax exams; exact amount; maximum axles; six exams;

9 Max Xiong took the extra exam on the sixth of May.

10 Mary will bike the next day on the mountain roads.

11 Martin and Max took the six boys to the next game.

12 Marty will go with me on the next six rides today.

Lesson 11   SKILL BUILDING

- To build straight-copy speed and control.
- To introduce rough-draft copy.

11A

Conditioning Practice

Key each line twice SS; then a 1' timing on line 3; determine *gwam*.

alphabet	1	J. Fox made five quick plays to win the big prize.
?	2	Where is Helen? Did she call? Is she to go, too?
easy	3	Pam owns the big dock, but they own the lake land.

gwam 1' | 1 | 2 | 3 | 4 | 5 | 6 | 7 | 8 | 9 | 10 |

11B

Speed Building

Key each line twice SS with a DS between 2-line groups.

> ### Technique Cue
> - Reach up without moving hands away from your body.
> - Reach down without moving hands toward your body.

za/az	1	zap lazy lizard pizza hazard bazaar frazzle dazzle
	2	Zack and Hazel zapped the lazy lizard in the maze.
ol/lo	3	old load olive look fold lost bold loan allow told
	4	Olympia told the lonely man to load the long logs.
ws/sw	5	swing cows sweet glows swept mows sword knows swap
	6	He swung the sword over the sweaty cows and swine.
ju/ft	7	often jury draft judge left just hefty juice after
	8	Jud, the fifth juror on my left, just wants juice.
ed/de	9	deal need debit edit deed edge deli used dent desk
	10	Jed needed to edit the deed made by the defendant.
ik/ki	11	kick like kind bike kiln hike kids strike king ski
	12	I like the kind of kids who like to hike and bike.

11C

Rough Draft (Edited Copy)

1. Study the proofreaders' marks shown below.
2. Key each sentence twice SS; DS between 2-line groups. Make all editing (handwritten) changes.

∧ = insert

= add space

∿ = transpose

⤶ = delete

◡ = close up

≡ = capitalize

1 A first rough draft is a preliminary orr tentative one revision.

2 It is where the creator writer gets his/her thoughts on paper.

3 After the rough draft is created, it will be looked over edited.

4 Reviewing Editing is the step where a person writer refines the copy.

5 Proof readers marks are used to edit the original rough copy draft.

6 The edting changes will be then be made to the copy original.

7 After the changes have been made read the copy agian.

8 more changes still may need to be made to the copy.

9 Edting and proof reading does take a lot time and effort.

10 an error free copy message is worth the trouble, however.

Lesson 13 REVIEW

- To improve spacing and shifting.
- To increase keying control and speed.

13A

Keyboard Mastery

Key each line twice SS; DS between 2-line groups.

Space bar (Space immediately after each word.)

1 She will be able to see the show in a week or two.
2 Jack lost the ball; Gary found it behind the door.
3 Kay and Jo went to the beach to look for starfish.

Shift keys (Shift; tap key; release both quickly.)

4 Dick and Allene went with Elaine to New York City.
5 The New York Yankees host the New York Mets today.
6 Don and Jack used the new bats that Jason brought.

13B

Speed Check

Key three 20" timings on each line. Try to go faster on each timing.

1 He can go to town for a shelf.
2 Gary can fish off the dock with us.
3 Jo thanked the girls for doing the work.
4 Becky took the girls to the show on Thursday.
5 Lance and Jared will be there until noon or later.
6 Jose and I should be able to stay for one or two hours.

gwam 20" | 3 | 6 | 9 | 12 | 15 | 18 | 21 | 24 | 27 | 30 | 33 |

13C

Increase Keying Speed

Key each line twice SS; DS between 2-line groups. Key the word the first time at an easy speed; repeat it at a faster speed.

For additional practice:
MicroType 5
Alphabetic Keyboarding
Lesson 13

1 Juan hikes each day on the side roads near school.
2 Taki and I will take the algebra test on Thursday.
3 Fran told the four boys to take the bus to school.
4 Jordan took the dogs for a walk when he got there.
5 Sandra and I went to the store to buy new outfits.
6 Jennifer will buy the food for the January social.

Speed Check: Straight Copy

1. Key one 1' unguided and two 1' guided timings on ¶ 1 and then on ¶ 2, as directed on p. 22.
2. Key two 2' unguided timings on ¶s 1–2 combined; determine *gwam*.

LA   all letters used   MicroPace   gwam 2'

His mother signed her name with an X. His   5
father had no schooling. Could a President come   10
from such a humble background? President Lincoln   14
did. Lincoln was not just a President, he is often   20
recognized as one of the best to ever hold the office. 25
    Honest Abe, as he was often called, always gave   30
the extra effort needed to be a success. Whether the 35
job was splitting logs, being a lawyer, or being   40
President, he always gave it his best. Dealing with   45
the Civil War required a man who gave his best.   50

gwam 2' | 1 | 2 | 3 | 4 | 5 |

Skill Transfer: Straight Copy and Rough Draft

1. Key each ¶ once SS; DS between ¶s.
2. Key two 1' timings on each ¶; determine *gwam* on each timing.

Straight copy   gwam 1'

    Documents free of errors make a good impression.   10
When a document has no errors, readers can focus on   20
the content. Errors distract readers and can cause   31
them to think less of the message.   38

    Therefore, it is important to proofread the   10
final copy of a document several times to make sure   20
it contains no errors before it leaves your desk.   29
Readers of error-free documents form a positive image   40
of the person who wrote the message.   47

Rough draft

    When a ~~negative~~ positive image of the person who wrote the ~~the~~   10
messge is formed the message is ~~less~~ more likely to succeed.   22
rememble, you never get a ~~another~~ second chance to make a good first   34
impression.   36

For additional practice:
MicroType 5
New Key Review, Alphabetic
Lesson 11

New Keys: b and y

Key each line twice SS; DS between 2-line groups.

b *Left index* finger

y *Right index* finger

Learn b

1 f b│fb fb│fob fob│tub tub│bug bug│bat bat│bus bus;

2 bfb bfb│boat boat│boot boot│jobs jobs│habit habit;

3 blue bus; bit bat; brown table; a bug; big hubbub;

Learn y

4 j y│jy jy│yet yet│eye eye│dye dye│say say│day day;

5 yjy yjy│yell yell│stay stay│easy easy│style style;

6 Sunday or Friday; buy or bye; fly away; any jockey

Combine b and y

7 by by│baby baby│bury bury│lobby lobby│gabby gabby;

8 bay bridge│blue eyes│busy body│noisy boys│baby toy

9 Tabby and Barry had a baby boy with big blue eyes.

New-Key Mastery

Key each line twice SS; DS between 2-line groups.

Practice Cue

- Reach up without moving hands away from your body.
- Reach down without moving hands toward your body.

reach review

1 jnj ftf ded kik hjh dcd fgf juj jyj sws lol 1.1 hg

2 how got eat was rat you ice not bat fun done only;

3rd/1st rows

3 nice hit│not now│only twice│were busy│they can be;

4 Cody told both boys before they left for the show.

key words

5 and are the can did was ask far you foil boat note

6 joke dine call ball gold feet hold wash yard flute

key phrases

7 to the│and then│if you want│when will you│you were

8 here is the│this is the│you will be able to│is the

all letters learned

9 Julio and Becky forgot to show Dick their new dog.

10 Barry found two locks by his jacket in the garage.

gwam 1' │ 1 │ 2 │ 3 │ 4 │ 5 │ 6 │ 7 │ 8 │ 9 │ 10 │

For additional practice:

MicroType 5
Alphabetic Keyboarding
Lesson 12

Lesson 12   SKILL BUILDING

OBJECTIVES
- To build straight-copy speed and control.
- To enhance keying technique.

12A

Conditioning Practice

Key each line twice SS; then key a 1' timing on line 3. Determine *gwam*.

alphabet	1	Kevin can fix the unique jade owl as my big prize.
spacing	2	She will be able to see the dogs in a week or two.
easy	3	A box with the form is on the chair by the mantle.

gwam 1' | 1 | 2 | 3 | 4 | 5 | 6 | 7 | 8 | 9 | 10 |

12B

Difficult-Reach Mastery

Key each line twice SS; DS between 2-line groups.

Adjacent keys

1 Her posh party on their new patio was a real bash.
2 Robert knew that we had to pool our points to win.
3 Juan will try to stop a fast break down the court.
4 Bart saw her buy a red suit at a new shop in town.

Long direct reaches

5 Betty is expected to excel in this next long race.
6 My fervor for gym events was once my unique trait.
7 Music as a unique force is no myth in any country.
8 Lynda has since found many facts we must now face.

Reaches with 3rd and 4th fingers

9 Nick said the cash price for gas was up last week.
10 My squad set a quarter quota to equal our request.
11 Zane played a zany tune that amazed the jazz band.
12 The poet will opt for a top spot in our port town.

12C

Speed Check: Sentences

Key two 30" timings on each line. Try to increase your keying speed the second time you key the line. Determine *gwam* for the faster timing of each line.

1 Yizel will take the test soon.
2 Nick will take his turn on Tuesday.
3 Felipe will apply for a job at the bank.
4 Marsha took both computers in to be repaired.
5 Their next ballgame will be in two or three weeks.
6 The repairs ended up costing much more than he thought.

gwam 30" | 2 | 4 | 6 | 8 | 10 | 12 | 14 | 16 | 18 | 20 | 22 |

Lesson 12 NEW KEYS: b AND y

• To learn reach technique for **b** and **y**.

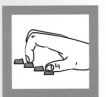

Fingers curved

12A

Conditioning Practice

Key each line twice SS; DS between 2-line groups.

reach review 1 sw ju ft fr ki dc lo .l jh fg ce un jn o. de gu hw

c/n 2 cent neck dance count clean niece concert neglect;

all letters learned 3 Jack and Trish counted the students on the risers.

12B

Technique: Space Bar

Key each line twice.

Technique Cue

Space with a down-and-in motion immediately after each word.

1 Ann has an old car she wants to sell at this sale.
2 Len is to work for us for a week at the lake dock.
3 Gwen is to sign for the auto we set aside for her.
4 Jan is in town for just one week to look for work.
5 Juan said he was in the auto when it hit the tree.

12C

Technique: ENTER Key

1. Key each line twice SS; at the end of each line, quickly tap **ENTER** key, and immediately start new line.

2. On line 4, see how many words you can key in 30 seconds (30").

A **standard word** in keyboarding is five characters or any combination of five characters and spaces, as indicated by the number scale under line 4. The number of standard words keyed in 1' is called **gross words a minute** (gwam).

1 Dot is to go at two.
2 Justin said she will be there.
3 Sarah cooked lunch for all of the girls.
4 Glenda took the left turn at the fork in the road.

gwam 1' | 1 | 2 | 3 | 4 | 5 | 6 | 7 | 8 | 9 | 10 |

To find 1-minute (1') gwam:

1. Note on the scale the number beneath the last word you keyed. That is your 1' gwam if you key the line partially or only once.

2. If you completed the line once and started over, add 10 to the figure determined in step 1. The result is your 1' gwam.

To find 30-second (30") gwam:

1. Find 1' gwam (total words keyed).

2. Multiply 1' gwam by 2. The resulting number is your 30" gwam.

Technique: Response Patterns

1. Key each line twice SS; DS between 2-line groups.
2. Key a 1' timing on lines 10–12; determine *gwam* on each line.

One-hand words (Think and key by letter response.)

1 bear aware data gave edge states race great street

2 ink pin you hook milk moon only join union million

3 were you|up on|are in fact|my taxes are|star gazed

Balanced-hand words (Think and key by word response.)

4 oak box land sign make busy kept foal handle gowns

5 chair disown mantle right world theme towns theory

6 go to the|it may work|did he make|she is|he may go

One-hand sentences (Think and key by letter response.)

7 Jim gazed at a radar gadget we gave him in a case.

8 Dave saved a dazed polo pony as we sat on a knoll.

9 Carter gave him a minimum rate on state oil taxes.

Balanced-hand sentences (Think and key by word response.)

10 Rick may make them turn by the lake by their sign.

11 Jane may go to the city to work for the six firms.

12 Ken may make the girl pay for the keys to the bus.

| gwam | 1' | 1 | 2 | 3 | 4 | 5 | 6 | 7 | 8 | 9 | 10 |

For additional practice:
MicroType 5
New Key Review, Alphabetic
Lesson 12

Speed Building: Guided Writing

1. Key one 1' unguided and two 1' guided timings on each ¶.
2. Key two 2' unguided timings on ¶s 1–2 combined; determine *gwam*.

LA   all letters used   (MicroPace)   gwam 2'

	Quarter-Minute Checkpoints			
gwam	1/4'	1/2'	3/4'	1'
20	5	10	15	20
24	6	12	18	24
28	7	14	21	28
32	8	16	24	32
36	9	18	27	36
40	10	20	30	40
44	11	22	33	44
48	12	24	36	48
52	13	26	39	52
56	14	28	42	56

Laura Ingalls Wilder is a beloved writer of books for   5
children. Most of her books are based on her own experiences   12
as a youth. Her first book was about her life in Wisconsin.   18
From just reading such a book, children fantasize about what   24
it would have been like to live with the pioneers during this   30
time period of our nation.   33

Besides writing about her own life and the lives of her   38
family members, she also wrote about the life of her husband,   45
Almanzo, and his family. Her second book was about the early   51
years of his life growing up on a farm near the Canadian bor-   57
der in the state of New York. Through these exquisite books,   63
this period of time in our history is preserved forever.   69

| gwam | 2' | 1 | 2 | 3 | 4 | 5 | 6 |

New-Key Mastery

Key each line twice SS; DS between 2-line groups.

Practice Cue

Space quickly after keying each word.

Goal: finger action reaches; quiet hands and arms

w and right shift

1 Alaska; Wisconsin; Georgia; Florida; South Dakota.
2 Dr. Wick will work the two weekends for Dr. Woods.

n/g

3 eight or nine|sing the songs again|long length of;
4 Dr. Wong arranged the song for singers in Lansing.

key words

5 wet fun ask hot jar cot got use oil add run are of
6 card nice hold gnaw join knew face stew four feat;

key phrases

7 will see|it is the|as it is|did go|when will|if it
8 I will|where is the|when can|use it|and the|of the

all keys learned

9 Nikko Rodgers was the last one to see Jack Fuller.
10 Alfonso Garcia and I took Taisuke Johns to Newark.

11D

Technique: Spacing with Punctuation

Key each line twice SS; DS between 2-line groups.

Spacing Cue

Do not space after an internal period in an abbreviation; space once after each period following initials.

No space — Space once.

1 Use i.e. for that is; cs. for case; ck. for check.
2 Dr. West said to use wt. for weight; in. for inch.
3 Jason F. Russell used rd. for road in the address.
4 Dr. Tejada got her Ed.D. degree at Colorado State.

11E

Enrichment

Key each line twice SS; DS between 2-line groups.

Technique Cue

- unused fingers curved, upright over home keys
- eyes on copy as you key

u/c

1 cute luck duck dock cure junk clue just cuff ulcer
2 Luci could see the four cute ducks on the counter.

w and right shift

3 Wade and Will; Don W. Wilson and Frank W. Watkins.
4 Dr. Wise will set the wrist of Sgt. Walsh at noon.

left shift and .

5 Julio N. Ortega|Julia T. Santiago|Carlos L. Sillas
6 Lt. Lou Jordan and Lt. Jan Lee left for St. Louis.

n/g

7 gain gown ring long range green grind groan angle;
8 Last night Angie Nagai was walking along the road.

o/t

9 foot other tough total tooth outlet outfit notice;
10 Todd took the two toddlers towards the other road.

i/r

11 ik rf or ore fir fir sir sir ire ire ice ice irons
12 Risa fired the fir log to heat rice for the girls.

h/e

13 hj ed he the the hen hen when when then then their
14 He was with her when she chose her new snow shoes.

Communication & Math
SKILLS 1

ACTIVITY 1

Simple Sentences

1. Study each of the guides for simple sentences shown below.
2. Key *Learn* lines 1–8, noting the subjects and predicates.
3. For *Apply* lines 9–11, combine the two sentences into one simple sentence with two nouns as the subject and one verb as the predicate.
4. Revise sentence 12 by combining the two sentences into one simple sentence with two nouns as the subject and two verbs as the predicate.

Save as: CS1 ACTIVITY1

A simple sentence consists of one independent clause that contains a subject (noun or pronoun) and a predicate (verb).

Learn	1	Stan is at the game.
Learn	2	Felipe went to the game.
Learn	3	Rebecca likes to play computer games.
Learn	4	Laura tried out for the basketball team.

A simple sentence may have as its subject more than one noun or pronoun (compound subject) and as its predicate more than one verb (compound predicate).

Learn	5	He painted the house. (single subject/single predicate)
Learn	6	Steve and I won an award. (compound subject/single predicate)
Learn	7	Jenny washed and polished her car. (single subject/compound predicate)
Learn	8	Jay and I wrote and edited the paper. (compound subject and predicate)
Apply	9	Juan read the book. Juanita read it, also.
Apply	10	Jason keyed his own paper. So did Keith.
Apply	11	Taji rode to the game with Monica. Alisha rode with her, also.
Apply	12	Mary washes and dries her hair every day. Jan also washes and dries hers.

ACTIVITY 2

Compound Sentences

1. Study each of the guides for compound sentences shown below.
2. Key *Learn* lines 13–20, noting the words that make up the subjects and predicates of each sentence.
3. For *Apply* lines 21–24, combine the two sentences into a compound sentence. Choose carefully from the coordinating conjunctions *and, but, for, or, nor, yet,* and *so.*

Save as: CS1 ACTIVITY2

A compound sentence contains two or more independent clauses connected by a coordinating conjunction (*and, but, for, or, nor, yet, so*).

Learn	13	Rhea likes to play softball, and Tara likes to play basketball.
Learn	14	The blue car is sold, but the red one is still available.
Learn	15	You may go with us, or you may stay at home.
Learn	16	Erika plays the flute, Joan plays the drums, and Tim plays the trumpet.

Each clause of a compound sentence may have as its subject more than one noun/pronoun and as its predicate more than one verb.

Learn	17	Jon came and stayed for the entire game, and Jay and Ty left at the half.
Learn	18	Don took biology and chemistry, but the others took only biology.
Learn	19	You can cook dinner, or you and Maria can go out to dinner.
Learn	20	Roberto finished the exam, but Alex and Karl needed more time to finish.
Apply	21	Sasha played video games. Mark read a book.
Apply	22	You may watch television. You and Lynda may go to a movie.
Apply	23	Jorge may play golf or tennis. He may not play both.
Apply	24	Karla went to the University of Iowa. Glen went to the University of Utah.

Lesson 11

NEW KEYS: w AND right shift

OBJECTIVE

• To learn reach technique for **w** and **right shift**.

11A

Conditioning Practice

Key each line twice SS; DS between 2-line groups.

reach review 1 jn de ju fg ki ft lo dc fr l. jtn ft. cde hjg uet.

u/c 2 cut cue duck luck cute success accuse juice secure

all letters learned 3 Jake and Lincoln sold us eight large ears of corn.

11B

New Keys: w and Right Shift

Key each line twice SS ; DS between 2-line groups.

w *Left ring* finger

Right Shift *Right little* finger

Shifting cue

1. Hold down the right shift key with the little finger on the right hand.
2. Tap the letter with the finger on the left hand.
3. Return finger(s) to home key.

Learn w

1 s w sw sw|we we|saw saw|who who|wet wet|show show;

2 will will|wash wash|work work|down down|gown gown;

3 white gown; when will we; wash what; walk with us;

Learn right shift key

4 ;A ;A;|A1; A1;|Dan; Dan;|Gina; Gina;|Frank; Frank;

5 Don saw Seth Green and Alfonso Garcia last August.

6 Trish Fuentes and Carlos Delgado left for Atlanta.

Combine w and right shift

7 Will Wenner went to show the Wilsons the two cars.

8 Wes and Wade want to know who will work this week.

9 Willard West will take Akiko Tanaka to Washington.

10 Rafael and Donna asked to go to the store with us.

11 Walt left us at Winter Green Lake with Will Segui.

12 Ted or Walt will get us tickets for the two shows.

ACTIVITY 3

Complex Sentences

1. Study the guides for complex sentences shown below.
2. Key *Learn* lines 25–32, noting the subject and predicate of the independent clause and of the dependent clause for each sentence.
3. For *Apply* lines 33–36, combine the two sentences into a complex sentence.

Save as: **CS1 ACTIVITY3**

A complex sentence contains only one independent clause but one or more dependent clauses.

Learn 25 The music that you bought for Ashley at the mall is excellent.

Learn 26 If I go on the trip, I will ask Marge to take care of your pets.

Learn 27 Ms. Moore, who chaired the committee last year, took a new job.

Learn 28 Students who do not procrastinate are generally successful.

The subject of a complex sentence may consist of more than one noun or pronoun; the predicate may consist of more than one verb.

Learn 29 All who attended the seminar received a free book and had lunch.

Learn 30 If you are going on the tour, you should call Tim and let him know.

Learn 31 After Jay and I left for the game, Joe and Barb washed and dried the dishes.

Learn 32 Even though they thought they would win, Nick and Phil were not sure.

Apply 33 My interview went really well. I may not get the job.

Apply 34 They attended the game. They went to the party.

Apply 35 Frank is going to take the CPS exam. He should register now.

Apply 36 You are buying the camera. You should also get a memory card.

ACTIVITY 4

Composing

Key each line once
(do not key the figure).
In place of the blank line,
key the word(s) that correctly
complete(s) the sentence.

Save as: **CS1 ACTIVITY4**

1. A small mass of land surrounded by water is a(n) _____.
2. A large mass of land surrounded by water is a(n) _____.
3. The earth rotates on what is called its _____.
4. When the sun comes up over the horizon, we say it _____.
5. When the sun goes down over the horizon, we say it _____.
6. A device used to display temperature is a(n) _____.
7. A device used to display atmospheric pressure is a(n) _____.

ACTIVITY 5

Math: Adding and Subtracting Numbers

1. Open *DF CS1 ACTIVITY5* and print the file.
2. Solve the problems as directed in the file.
3. Submit your answers.

 CAREER **Clusters**

ACTIVITY 1

There are many different career opportunities available to you once you graduate from high school. Some careers require no additional education, while others require many years of additional education. The 14 career exploration activities will help you understand the requirements for some of the careers in which you may have an interest. Begin your exploration by completing the following steps.

1. Access http://www.careerclusters.org.

2. Complete the Career Clusters Interest Survey Activity. Your instructor will provide you with a copy of the survey or you can click on Free Career Clusters Interest Survey Activity and then click on View/Print Now. Print a copy of the survey and the Sixteen Career Clusters pages that follow the Interest Survey.

3. Obtain a folder for your Career Exploration Portfolio from your instructor, write your name and class period on it, place your completed Interest Survey and descriptions of the career clusters in the folder, and file the folder as instructed.

New-Key Mastery

Key each line twice SS; DS between 2-line groups.

Technique Cue

- Reach up without moving hands away from your body.
- Reach down without moving hands toward your body.

3rd/1st rows
1 run car nut nice cute noon touch other clean truck
2 Lincoln coin; strike three; cut the cards; four or

left shift and .
3 Jack and Nicholas are going to Otter Lake in Ohio.
4 Lucille took a truck to Ohio. Janet sold her car.

key words
5 call fund kind race neck golf half just toil lunch
6 cause guide hotel feast alike joins; laugh; judge;

key phrases
7 if she can|he can do the|it is the|and then|all of
8 till the end|tie the knot|faster than|a little red

all keys learned
9 Either Jack or Lance said the four girls are here.
10 Hugh likes to run on the lakefront; Jack does not.

10D

Technique: Space Bar and Left Shift

Key the lines once SS; DS between 3-line groups.

For additional practice:

MicroType 5
Alphabetic Keyboarding
Lesson 10

space bar
1 Lucas asked the girls to get the dogs at the lake.
2 Lance said he can go to Oregon to get the old car.
3 Janice and her three dogs ran along the shoreline.

left shift
4 Jack and Joe Kern just left to go to Lake Ontario.
5 Jo thinks it takes less than an hour to get there.
6 Kanosh and Joliet are cities in Utah and Illinois.

10E

Enrichment

Key each line once SS; DS between 2-line groups.

Practice Cue

Try to reduce hand movement and the tendency of unused fingers to fly out or follow reaching finger.

u/c
1 cut luck such cuff lunch crush touch torch justice
2 Okichi Kinura had juice. Lucius caught the judge.

n/g
3 gone ring fang long eggnog length; sing sang song;
4 Glen thinks Glenda Leung can sing the eight songs.

all keys learned
5 Julian and Hector left a note for Leticia Herrera.
6 Juan and Luisa took Jorge and Leonor to the dance.

all keys learned
7 Jack Lefstad said to take the road through Oregon.
8 Janet and Linda caught eight fish in Lake Ontario.

UNIT 3
Lessons 13-14

Learn/Review Figure-Key Technique

Lesson 13 — LEARN/REVIEW FIGURE KEYS (8, 1, 9, 4, AND 0)

OBJECTIVES

- To review reach technique for **8, 1, 9, 4,** and **0.**
- To improve skill on script and rough-draft copy.

13A

Conditioning Practice
Key each line twice SS.

alphabet 1 Jackie and Zelda's next big purchase may require two favors.

spacing 2 When you get to the game, save two seats for Rob and Felipe.

easy 3 Jan may make a big profit if she owns the title to the land.

gwam 1' | 1 | 2 | 3 | 4 | 5 | 6 | 7 | 8 | 9 | 10 | 11 | 12 |

13B

Learn/Review 8 and 1
Key each line twice.

Learn/Review 8

1 k k 8k 8k kk 88 k8k k8k 88k 88k Reach up for 8, 88, and 888.

2 Key the figures 8, 88, and 888. Please open Room 88 or 888.

Learn/Review 1

3 a a 1a 1a aa 11 a1a a1a 11a 11a Reach up for 1, 11, and 111.

4 Add the figures 1, 11, and 111. Only 1 out of 111 finished.

Combine 8 and 1

5 Key 11, 18, 81, and 88. Just 11 of the 18 skiers have left.

6 Reach with the fingers to key 18 and 188 as well as 1 and 8.

7 The stock person counted 11 coats, 18 slacks, and 88 shirts.

Lesson 10   NEW KEYS: u AND c

OBJECTIVE

• To learn reach technique for **u** and **c**.

10A

Conditioning Practice

Key each line twice SS; DS between 2-line groups.

reach review   1 hjh tft njn gfg iki .l. ede olo rfr it go no or hi

space bar   2 so ask let jet his got ink are and the kid off did

left shift   3 Jason and I looked for Janet and Kate at the lake.

10B

New Keys: u and c

Key each line twice SS; DS between 2-line groups.

u *Right index* finger

c *Left middle* finger

Learn u

1 j u|juj juj|uju uju|us us|due due|jug jug|sun sun;

2 suit suit|dusk dusk|four four|fund fund|huge huge;

3 just for fun; under the rug; unusual urt; found us

Learn c

4 d c|dcd dcd|act act|cash cash|card card|ache ache;

5 Jack Jack|sack sack|lock lock|calf calf|rock rock;

6 acted sick; tic toc goes the clock; catch the cat;

Combine u and c

7 duck duck|accuse accuse|cruel cruel|actual actual;

8 crucial account; cute cousin; chunk of ice; juice;

9 such success; rustic church; no luck; count trucks

10 June and Chuck told us to take four cans of juice.

11 Jack asked us for a list of all the codes he used.

12 Louise has gone to cut the cake on the green cart.

Keyboard Reinforcement

Key each line twice.

Figures

1 May 1-8, May 11-18, June 1-8, and June 11-18 are open dates.

2 The quiz on the 18th will be on pages 11 to 18 and 81 to 88.

3 He said only 11 of us got No. 81 right; 88 got No. 81 wrong.

Home/1st

4 ax jab van gab man call back land calf jazz hack cabana Jack

5 small man|can mask|lava can|jazz band|lack cash|a small lamb

6 Ms. Maas can call a cab, and Jan can call a small black van.

Learn/Review 9, 4, and 0

Key each line twice.

Review 9

1 l l 9l 9l ll 99 l9l l9l 99l 99l Reach up for 9, 99, and 999.

2 The social security number was 919-99-9191, not 191-99-1919.

Review 4

3 f f 4f 4f ff 44 f4f f4f 44f 44f Reach up for 4, 44, and 444.

4 Add the figures 4, 44, and 444.   Please study pages 4 to 44.

Review 0

5 ; ; 0; 0; ;; 00 ;0; ;0; 00; 00; Reach up for 0, 00, and 000.

6 Snap the finger off the 0.   I used 0, 00, and 000 sandpaper.

Combine 9, 4, and 0

7 Flights 904 and 490 left after Flights 409A, 400Z, and 940X.

8 My ZIP Code is 40099, not 44099.   Kim keyed 0909, not 09094.

Speed Check

1. Key three 30" timings on each line. Try to go faster on each timing.
2. Key a 2' timing on 12E, p. 26.

1 The firm kept half of us busy.

2 The girls work for the island firm.

3 Diane may blame the girls for the fight.

4 Pay the man for the work he did on the autos.

5 The social for the maid is to be held in the city.

6 Jake may sign the form if they do an audit of the firm.

30" | 2 | 4 | 6 | 8 | 10 | 12 | 14 | 16 | 18 | 20 | 22 |

OBJECTIVES
- To increase keying speed.
- To improve **Space Bar**, **left shift**, and **ENTER** technique.

9A

Keyboard Mastery

Key each line twice SS; DS between 2-line groups.

Technique Cue

- curved, upright fingers
- eyes on copy
- wrists not touching keyboard

o/t

1 too took foot told hot toes lot dot toil toga torn

2 Otto has lost the list he took to that food store.

n/g

3 gin song sing sign long ring gone green gnat angle

4 Link N. Nagle is going to sing nine songs at noon.

Left shift/.

5 Lake Ontario; Hans N. Linder; Lake Larson; J. Hill

6 Jake left for Indiana; Kathleen left for Illinois.

9B

Improve ENTER Key Technique

Key each line twice SS; DS between 2-line groups. Keep up your pace at the end of the line, tap **ENTER** quickly, and begin the new line immediately.

1 I like the dog.

2 Jan has a red dress.

3 Hal said he left it here.

4 Kate has gone to the ski hill.

5 Lane said he left the dog in Idaho.

6 Kristi and Jennifer are hiking the hill.

9C

Increase Keying Speed

Key each line twice SS; DS between 2-line groups. Key the word the first time at an easy speed; repeat it at a faster speed.

1 add add|ask ask|hot hot|ring ring|eat eat|off off;

2 jar jar|ago ago|feet feet|hotel hotel|other other;

3 sand sand|join join|lake lake|half half|dear dear;

4 Janet said she left three letters on his old desk.

5 Hal and Jan added three things to her latest list.

6 Jen is to go to Illinois to get the old gold ring.

For additional practice:
MicroType 5
Alphabetic Keyboarding
Lesson 9

13F

Speed Building

1. Key a 1' timing on ¶ 1; key three more 1' timings on ¶ 1, trying to go faster each time.
2. Repeat the procedure for ¶ 2.
3. Key a 2' timing on ¶s 1 and 2 combined.

For additional practice:
MicroType 5
New Key Review, Number & Symbol Lesson 1

LA all letters used (MicroPace) gwam 2'

How did music come about? If you enjoy music, you may   6
have thought about this query previously. It is extremely   11
doubtful that any of us has the answer to why, when, where, 17
or how it got its start. It is plausible that the people who 24
started music did not even realize they were creating music. 30

Today music adds a great deal to our lives and defines   35
who we are. Different types of music exist to please each   41
of our personal tastes. Some people think that classical   47
music is the only music worth hearing. Others would vote   53
for country, rap, rock, or another form of music. There is   59
one thing, though, that nearly all of us agree on; music   64
enriches our lives.   66

gwam 2' | 1 | 2 | 3 | 4 | 5 | 6 |

Lesson 14   LEARN/REVIEW FIGURE KEYS (5, 7, 3, 6, AND 2)

OBJECTIVES
• To review reach technique for **5**, **7**, **3**, **6**, and **2**.
• To improve skill transfer and build speed.

14A

Conditioning Practice
Key each line twice.

alphabet 1 Many expect Frank Valdez to quit working on all of the jobs.
spacing 2 Did they say when they will be able to do the work for Stan?
easy 3 Rick and the girls may go downtown to pay for the six signs.
gwam 1' | 1 | 2 | 3 | 4 | 5 | 6 | 7 | 8 | 9 | 10 | 11 | 12 |

14B

Learn/Review 5 and 7
Key each line twice.

Review 5

1 f f 5f 5f ff 55 f5f f5f 55f 55f Reach up for 5, 55, and 555.
2 Reach up to 5 and back to f. Did he say to order 55 or 555?

Review 7

3 j j 7j 7j jj 77 j7j j7j 77j 77j Reach up for 7, 77, and 777.
4 Key the figures 7, 77, and 777. She checked Rooms 7 and 77.

New-Key Mastery

Key each line twice SS; DS between 2-line groups.

Technique Cue

- eyes on copy except when you lose your place
- out-and-down shifting

abbrev./ initials
1 J. Hart and K. Jakes hired Lila J. Norton to sing.
2 Lt. Karen J. Lane took Lt. Jon O. Hall to the jet.

3rd row emphasis
3 I told her to take a look at the three large jets.
4 Iris had three of her oldest friends on the train.

key words
5 if for the and old oak jet for oil has egg jar oar
6 told lake jade gold here noon tear soil goes fade;

key phrases
7 and the|ask for|go to the|not so fast|if he|to see
8 if there is|to go to the|for the last|none of the;

all letters learned
9 Jodi and Kendra Jaeger are in the National finals.
10 Jason Lake did not take Jon Hoag for a train ride.

8D

Technique: Space Bar and ENTER Key

Key each line twice SS; DS between 2-line groups.

Spacing Cue

Immediately tap Space Bar after the last letter in each word.

1 Linda had fish.
2 Jan is on the train.
3 Nat took her to the lake.
4 He is here to see his friends.
5 Kathleen sold the large egg to her.
6 Kate and Jason hired her to do the roof.
7 Lane took all eight of the girls to the lake.

> Tap ENTER quickly and start each new line immediately.

8E

Enrichment

Key each line twice SS; DS between 2-line groups.

Spacing/shifting

1 Kellee and I did see Jed and Jonathan at the lake.
2 Jane and Hal are going to London to see Joe Hanks.
3 Lee left for the lake at noon; Kenneth left later.
4 Jo and Kate Hanson are going to take the test soon.

Keying easy sentences

5 Jessie is going to talk to the girls for the kids.
6 Harold Lett took his friends to the train station.
7 Lon and Jen are going to see friends at the lodge.
8 Natasha and Hansel are taking the train to London.

For additional practice:
MicroType 5
Alphabetic Keyboarding
Lesson 8

14c

Script and Rough-Draft Copy

Key each line twice.

≡ = capitalize

∧ = insert

∼ = transpose

⌿# = delete space

= add space

ℓc = lowercase

⌒ = close up

Script

1 Proofread: Compare copy word for word with the original.
2 Compare all figures digit by digit with your source copy.
3 Be sure to check for spacing and punctuation marks, also.
4 Copy in script or rough draft may not show exact spacing.
5 It is your job to insert correct spacing as you key copy.
6 Soon you will learn how to correct your errors on screen.

Rough draft

7 cap the first word an all proper nouns in every sentence.
8 For example: pablo Mendez is from San juan, Puerto rico.
9 Ami Qwan and parents will return to Taipie this summer.
10 our coffee is from Columbia; tea, from England or china.
11 How many of you have Ethnic origins in a for eign country?
12 did you know which of the states once were part of mexico?

14d

Learn/Review 3, 6, and 2

Key each line twice.

Review 3

1 d d 3d 3d dd 33 d3d d3d 33d 33d Reach up for 3, 33, and 333.
2 Add the figures 3, 33, and 333.   Read pages 3 to 33 tonight.

Review 6

3 j j 6j 6j jj 66 j6j j6j 66j 66j Reach up for 6, 66, and 666.
4 Key the figures 6, 66, and 666.   Did just 6 of 66 finish it?

Review 2

5 s s 2s 2s ss 22 s2s s2s 22s 22s Reach up for 2, 22, and 222.
6 Reach up to 2 and back to s.   Ashley reviewed pages 2 to 22.

Combine 3, 6, and 2

7 Only 263 of the 362 flights left on time on Monday, July 26.
8 Read Chapter 26, pages 263 to 326, for the exam on April 23.

OBJECTIVE

• To learn reach technique for **left shift** and . (period).

8A

Conditioning Practice

Key each line twice SS; DS between 2-line groups.

reach review 1 ft jn fr jh de ki gf lo tf nj rf hj ed ik fg ol ng

space bar 2 so it if at or on is go do ask the and jar art lid

all letters learned 3 join the; like those; ask her to sing; define the;

8B

New Keys: Left shift and . (period)

Key each line twice SS; DS between 2-line groups. If time permits, key lines 7–9.

Left Shift *Left little* finger

. (period) *Right ring* finger

Down-and-in spacing

Quick out-and-tap ENTER

Spacing cue

• Do not space after . within abbreviations.
• Space once after . following abbreviations and initials.
• Space twice after . at end of a sentence except at the end of a line. There, return without spacing.

Shifting Cue

(1) Hold down the left shift key with the little finger on the left hand, (2) tap the letter to be keyed with the finger on the right hand, and (3) return finger(s) to home keys in a quick 1-2-3 count.

Learn left shift key

1 a J|a J|Ja Ja|Jan Jan|a K a K|Kate Kate|Hank Hank;

2 Idaho; Kansas; Ohio: Oregon: Indiana; Illinois; IL

3 Lane and I; Ida and Jane; Hal and Kate; John and I

Learn . (period)

4 l . l .|l. l.|a.l. a.l.|d.l. d.l.|j.l j.l|k.l. k.l

5 hr. hr.|ft. ft.|in. in.|rd. rd.|ea. ea.|ltd. ltd.;

6 fl. fl.|fed. fed.|alt. alt.|ins. ins.|asst. asst.;

Combine left shift and . (period)

7 I took Linda to Lake Harriet. Lt. Kerns is there.

8 I did it. Lana took it. Jett Hill left for Ohio.

9 Karl and Jake got Ida and Janet to go to the fair.

Skill Building

Figure-Key Mastery

Key each line twice.

Straight Copy

1 She moved from 819 Briar Lane to 4057 Park Avenue on May 15.

2 The 50-point quiz on May 17 covers pages 88-94, 97, and 100.

3 The meeting will be held in Room 87 on March 19 at 5:40 p.m.

Script

4 *The 495 representatives met from 7:00 to 8:40 p.m. on May 1.*

5 *Social Security Nos. 519-88-7504 and 798-05-4199 were found.*

6 *My office is at 157 Main, and my home is at 4081 9th Avenue.*

Rough draft

7 Numbers 180, 190, and 5077 were scheduled for August 15.

8 her telephone number was changed to 807-194-5009 on July 1.

9 Review Rules 1-9 on pages 89-90 and rules 15-19 on page 174.

Speed Building

1. Key a 1' timing on ¶ 1; key three more 1' timings on ¶ 1, trying to go faster each time.
2. Repeat the procedure for ¶ 2.
3. Key a 2' timing on ¶s 1 and 2 combined.

For additional practice:

MicroType 5
New Key Review,
Number & Symbol
Lesson 2

LA all letters used **MicroPace**

gwam 2'

As you work for higher skill, remember that how well you | 6

key fast is just as important as how fast you key. How well | 12

you key at any speed depends in major ways upon the technique | 18

or form you use. Bouncing hands and flying fingers lower the | 24

speed, while quiet hands and low finger reaches increase speed. | 31

Few of us ever reach what the experts believe is perfect | 36

technique, but all of us should try to approach it. We must | 42

realize that good form is the secret to higher speed with | 48

fewer errors. We can then focus our practice on the improve- | 54

ment of the features of good form that will bring success. | 60

gwam 2' | 1 | 2 | 3 | 4 | 5 | 6 |

New-Key Mastery

Key each line twice SS; DS between 2-line groups.

Technique Cue

- curved, and upright fingers
- wrists low, but not resting
- down-and-in spacing
- eyes on copy as you key

reach review

1 rf ik hj tf ol ed nj gf; lo fr ft jn de ki jh fgf;
2 it it|oil oil|the the|ink ink|here here|song song;

n/g

3 sing gone night seeing doing going ringing longest
4 sing one song; going along; long night; good angle

space bar

5 if he no as to it is so do at in so of did elk jet
6 It ask and the are let oil oar ill son odd fan sat

all keys learned

7 desk soil lark joke that done find join gold lake;
8 tank logs hand jade free toil seek said like tear;

all keys learned

9 oil free; did join; has half; go get; near the end
10 tell jokes; right here; ask her; fine desk; is it;

Enrichment

Key each line twice; DS between 2-line groups.

Technique Cue

- space immediately after each word; down-and-in motion of thumb
- maintain pace to end of line; tap **ENTER** key quickly and start new line immediately

Reach review

1 jh jh|jn jn|fg fg|fr fr|ft ft|de de|ki ki|lo lo|jh
2 no no|hot hot|oil oil|the the|gold gold|rest rest;
3 hold nest gone that nails there going alert radio;

Space Bar

4 is at if so no do as he of go it to an or is on in
5 of hen got ink and the ask jar let hit jet den far
6 no ink|on the go|hit it|ask her to|did not see the
7 he is to join her at the lake; she is not the one;

ENTER key

8 he is there;
9 ask if it is far;
10 the sign for the lake;
11 she still has three of the;
12 did he join her at the lake the;

Short words and phrases

13 on on|do do|in in|it it|go go|or or|as as|are are;
14 see see|the the|and and|are are|for for|hire hire;
15 jet jet|kid kid|fit fit|ask ask|ton ton|risk risk;
16 he is go to the ski lodge; he lost the three jars;

For additional practice:
MicroType 5
Alphabetic Keyboarding
Lesson 7

New Key Learning   Lesson 7: n and g

UNIT 4
Lessons 15-16

Build Keyboarding Skill

Lesson 15   SKILL BUILDING

OBJECTIVES
- To improve technique on individual letters.
- To improve keying speed on 1' and 2' writings.

15A

Conditioning Practice
Key each line twice SS.

alphabet	1	The exquisite prize, a framed clock, was to be given to Jay.
spacing	2	it has | it will be | to your | by then | in our | it may be | to do the
easy	3	The maid was with the dog and six girls by the field of hay.
gwam	1' |	1 | 2 | 3 | 4 | 5 | 6 | 7 | 8 | 9 | 10 | 11 | 12 |

15B   Skill Building

Technique: Response Patterns
Key each line twice SS.

Technique Cue
Keep keystroking movement limited to the fingers.

Emphasize continuity and rhythm with curved, upright fingers.

A	1	Katrina Karrigan ate the meal of apples, bananas, and pears.
B	2	Bobby bought a beach ball and big balloons for the big bash.
C	3	Cody can serve cake and coffee to the cold campers at lunch.
D	4	David did all he could to dazzle the crowd with wild dances.
E	5	Elaine left her new sled in an old shed near the gray house.
F	6	Frank found a file folder his father had left in the office.
G	7	Gloria got the giggles when the juggler gave Glen his glove.
H	8	Hugh helped his big brother haul in the fishing net for her.
I	9	Inez sings in a trio that is part of a big choir at college.
J	10	Jason just joined the jury to judge the major jazz festival.
K	11	Nikki McKay kept the black kayaks at the dock for Kay Kintz.
L	12	Lola left her doll collection for a village gallery to sell.
M	13	Mona asked her mom to make more malted milk for the mission.
gwam	1' |	1 | 2 | 3 | 4 | 5 | 6 | 7 | 8 | 9 | 10 | 11 | 12 |

For additional practice:
MicroType 5
New Key Review,
Number & Symbol
Lesson 3

OBJECTIVE

• To learn reach technique for **n** and **g**.

7A

Conditioning Practice

Key each line twice SS; DS between 2-line groups.

e/r 1 rare doer fear feet tire hire read ride rest after

o/t 2 toad told took other hotel total tools tooth torte

i/h 3 hits idle hail hiked their fifth faith heist hairs

7B

New Keys: n and g

Key each line twice SS; DS between 2-line groups. If time permits, key lines 7–9 again.

> Follow the *Standard Plan for Learning New Keys* outlined on p. 511.

n *Right index* finger

g *Left index* finger

Learn n

1 j n jn jn|njn njn|an an|on on|no no|in in|and and;

2 kind kind|none none|loan loan|find find|land land;

3 not till noon; not a need; not in; a national need

Learn g

4 f g fg fg|gfg gfg|go go|dog dog|gas gas|goes goes;

5 age age|logs logs|glad glad|eggs eggs|legal legal;

6 great grin; large frog; gold dog; eight large eggs

Combine n and g

7 gone gone|sing sing|king king|gnat gnat|ring rings

8 sing along; a grand song; green signs; long grass;

9 eight rings; a grand king; long gone; sing a song;

7C

Technique: ENTER Key

Key each line twice SS; DS between 2-line groups.

Practice Cue

Keep up your pace to end of line, tap **ENTER** key quickly, and start new line without pausing.

1 large gold jar;

2 take the last train;

3 did he take the last egg;

4 she has to sing the last song;

5 join her for a hike at the lake at;

Reach out and tap ENTER

Technique: TAB Key

Key the title, the author, and the first line(s) of the stories shown at the right. DS after keying the first line of each entry.

Key the copy again at a faster pace.

Save as: 15C TITLES for use in Lesson 25.

"Farmer Boy" by Laura Ingalls Wilder

Tab ⟶ It was January in northern New York State, sixty-seven years ago. Snow lay deep everywhere.

"The Scotty Who Knew Too Much" by James Thurber

Tab ⟶ Several summers ago there was a Scotty who went to the country for a visit.

"Roughing It" by Mark Twain

Tab ⟶ After leaving the Sink, we traveled along the Humboldt River a little way.

"The Chrysanthemums" by John Steinbeck

Tab ⟶ The high grey-flannel fog of winter closed off the Salinas Valley from the sky and from all the rest of the world.

"The Story of My Life" by Helen Keller

Tab ⟶ The most important day I remember in all my life is the one on which my teacher, Anne Mansfield Sullivan, came to me.

Speed Building

1. Key one 1' unguided and two 1' guided timings on each ¶.
2. Key two 2' unguided timings on ¶s 1–2 combined; determine *gwam*.

A all letters used MicroPace gwam 2'

Austria is a rather small country, about three times
the size of Vermont, located between Germany and Italy. The
best known of the cities in this country is Vienna. Over the
years this city has been known for its contributions to the
culture in the region, particularly in the area of performing
arts. Another place that has played an important part in the
exquisite culture of the area is the city of Salzburg.

Salzburg is recognized as a great city for the performing
arts, particularly music. Just as important, however, is that
the city is the birthplace of Wolfgang Amadeus Mozart, one of
the greatest composers of all time. Perhaps no other composer
had an earlier start at his professional endeavors than did
Mozart. It is thought that he began playing at the age of
four and began composing at the age of five.

Quarter-Minute Checkpoints				
gwam	1/4'	1/2'	3/4'	1'
20	5	10	15	20
24	6	12	18	24
28	7	14	21	28
32	8	16	24	32
36	9	18	27	36
40	10	20	30	40
44	11	22	33	44
48	12	24	36	48
52	13	26	39	52
56	14	28	42	56

gwam 2' | 1 | 2 | 3 | 4 | 5 | 6 |

New-Key Mastery

Key each line twice SS; DS between 2-line groups.

Technique Cue

- curved, upright fingers
- down-and-in spacing
- wrists low, but not resting
- eyes on copy as you key

Practice Cue

In lines of repeated words (lines 3, 5, and 7), speed up the second keying of each word.

reach
review

1 ki lo de ft jh fr ei or th olo ere hjh iki edr iro
2 here is; the fort; their old trail; first look at;

h/e

3 the the|hear hear|here here|heat heat|sheet sheet;
4 the sheets; hear her heart; their health; heat the

i/t

5 sit sit|fit fit|silt silt|kites kites|tried tried;
6 a little tire; he tried to tilt it; he tied a tie;

o/r

7 tort tort|tore tore|fort fort|road road|roof roof;
8 a road|a door|a rose|or a rod|a roar|for her offer

space bar

9 to do it he as are hit dot eat air the ask jar let
10 if he|do it|to see|had it|is the|for her|all of it

all keys
learned

11 ask jet art oil old fit hit the sad did soil risk;
12 oil the; the jail; oak door; he said; their forts;

Enrichment

Key each line twice; DS between 2-line groups.

Keying Cue

Keep up your pace to the end of each line, tap the **ENTER** key quickly, and start the new line without a pause.

1 it is
2 the jet is
3 he had the rose
4 ask to hear the joke
5 she took the old shirt to
6 she told her to take the tests
7 at the fort; the lake road; did she
8 take the test; it is the last; he did it
9 the last jar; the old fort; he took the offer
10 take a jet; solid oak door; a red rose; ask her to

For additional practice:
MicroType 5
Alphabetic Keyboarding
Lesson 6

New Key Learning   Lesson 6: o and t

Lesson 16   SKILL BUILDING

OBJECTIVES

- To improve technique on individual letters.
- To improve keying speed on 1' and 2' writings.

16A

Conditioning Practice

Key each line twice.

alphabet	1	Zelda might fix the job growth plans very quickly on Monday.
spacing	2	did go | to the | you can go | has been able | if you can | to see the
easy	3	The six men with the problems may wish to visit the tax man.

gwam 1' | 1 | 2 | 3 | 4 | 5 | 6 | 7 | 8 | 9 | 10 | 11 | 12 |

16B

Technique: Response Patterns

Key each line twice.

Technique Cue

Keep keystroking movement limited to the fingers.

Emphasize continuity and rhythm with curved, upright fingers.

N	1	Nadine knew her aunt made lemonade and sun tea this morning.
O	2	Owen took the book from the shelf to copy his favorite poem.
P	3	Pamela added a pinch of pepper and paprika to a pot of soup.
Q	4	Quent posed quick quiz questions to his quiet croquet squad.
R	5	Risa used a rubber raft to rescue four girls from the river.
S	6	Silas said his sister has won six medals in just four meets.
T	7	Trisha told a tall tale about three little kittens in a tub.
U	8	Ursula asked the usual questions about four issues you face.
V	9	Vinny voted for five very vital issues of value to everyone.
W	10	Wilt wants to walk in the walkathon next week and show well.
X	11	Xania next expects them to fix the extra fax machine by six.
Y	12	Yuri said your yellow yacht was the envy of every yachtsman.
Z	13	Zoella and a zany friend ate a sizzling pizza in the piazza.

gwam 1' | 1 | 2 | 3 | 4 | 5 | 6 | 7 | 8 | 9 | 10 | 11 | 12 |

16C

Skill Building

Key each line twice.

....

For additional practice:

MicroType 5
New Key Review,
Number & Symbol
Lesson 4

....

Space Bar

1 and the see was you she can run ask took turn they were next

2 I will be able to fix the desk and chair for you next month.

Word response

3 the pay and pen make city rush lake both did dock half field

4 I may make a big sign to hang by the door of the civic hall.

Double letters

5 book grass arrow jelly little dollar illness vaccine collect

6 Kelly Pizzaro was a little foolish at the football assembly.

gwam 1' | 1 | 2 | 3 | 4 | 5 | 6 | 7 | 8 | 9 | 10 | 11 | 12 |

Lesson 6

NEW KEYS: o AND t

OBJECTIVE

• To learn reach technique for **o** and **t**.

6A

Conditioning Practice

Key each line twice SS; DS between 2-line groups.

Fingers curved

Fingers upright

h/e 1 her head; has had a; see here; feed her; hire her;

i/r 2 hire a; fire her; his risk; fresh air; a red hair;

all keys learned 3 a lake; ask a lad; a risk; here she is; a red jar;

6B

New Keys: o and t

Key each line twice SS; DS between 2-line groups. If time permits, key lines 7–9 again.

o *Right ring* finger

t *Left index* finger

Follow the *Standard Plan for Learning New Keys* on p. 511.

Learn o

1 l o lo lo|olo olo|fold fold|sold sold|holds holds;

2 of of|do do|oak oak|soil soil|does does|roof roof;

3 load of soil; order food; old oil; solid oak door;

Learn t

4 f t ft ft|tf tf|the the|tea tea|eat eat|talk talk;

5 at at|fit fit|set set|hit hit|talk talk|test tests

6 flat feet; the treats; the first test; take a hike

Combine o and t

7 total total|tooth tooth|toast toast|otters otters;

8 the total look; other tooth; took a toll; too old;

9 those hooks; the oath; old tree fort; took a tool;

Skill Building

1. Key three 1' timings on the ¶; determine *gwam*.
2. Key two 2' timings on ¶; determine *gwam*.

 all letters used (MicroPace) **gwam** 2'

• 2 • 4 • 6 • 8 • 10				

Thomas Jefferson was an excellent persuasive writer. 6

• 12 • 14 • 16 • 18 • 20 • 22
Conceivably his most persuasive piece of writing was the 12

• 24 • 26 • 28 • 30 • 32 •
Declaration of Independence, on which he was asked to col- 18

34 • 36 • 38 • 40 • 42 • 44 •
laborate with John Adams and Benjamin Franklin to justify 23

46 • 48 • 50 • 52 • 54 • 56
the necessity for independence. We all should recognize 29

• 58 • 60 • 62 • 64 • 66 • 68
elements of that document. For example, "We hold these 35

• 70 • 72 • 74 • 76 • 78 •
truths to be self-evident, that all men are created equal, 41

80 • 82 • 84 • 86 • 88 • 90 • 92
that they are endowed by their Creator with certain unalienable 47

• 94 • 96 • 98 • 100 • 102 • 104 •
Rights, that among these are Life, Liberty and the pursuit of 53

106 •
Happiness." 54

gwam 2' | 1 | 2 | 3 | 4 | 5 | 6 |

Skill Building

1. Key one 1' unguided and two 1' guided timings on each ¶; determine *gwam*.
2. Key two 2' unguided timings on ¶s 1–2 combined; determine *gwam*.

Quarter-Minute Checkpoints

gwam	1/4'	1/2'	3/4'	1'
20	5	10	15	20
24	6	12	18	24
28	7	14	21	28
32	8	16	24	32
36	9	18	27	36
40	10	20	30	40
44	11	22	33	44
48	12	24	36	48
52	13	26	39	52
56	14	28	42	56

 all letters used (MicroPace) **gwam** 2'

• 2 • 4 • 6 • 8 • 10 •
Who was Shakespeare? Few would question that he was the 6

12 • 14 • 16 • 18 • 20 • 22 •
greatest individual, or one of the greatest individuals, ever 12

24 • 26 • 28 • 30 • 32 • 34 •
to write a play. His works have endured the test of time. 18

36 • 38 • 40 • 42 • 44 • 46 • 48
Productions of his plays continue to take place on the stages 24

• 50 • 52 • 54 • 56 • 58 •
of theaters all over the world. Shakespeare was an expert 30

60 • 62 • 64 • 66 • 68 • 70 • 72
at creating comedies and tragedies, both of which often leave 36

• 74 • 76 •
the audience in tears. 38

• 2 • 4 • 6 • 8 • 10 •
Few of those who put pen to paper have been as successful 44

12 • 14 • 16 • 18 • 20 • 22 •
at creating prized images for their readers as Shakespeare. 50

24 • 26 • 28 • 30 • 32 • 34
Every character he created has a life of its own. It is 56

• 36 • 38 • 40 • 42 • 44 • 46
entirely possible that more middle school and high school 62

• 48 • 50 • 52 • 54 • 56 • 58
students know about the tragedy that Romeo and Juliet experi- 68

• 60 • 62 • 64 • 66 • 68 • 70
enced than know about the one that took place at Pearl Harbor. 74

gwam 2' | 1 | 2 | 3 | 4 | 5 | 6 |

Lesson 5 REVIEW

OBJECTIVES

- To increase keying speed.
- To improve **Space Bar** and **ENTER** technique.

5A

Improve Space-Bar Technique

Key each line twice SS; DS between 2-line groups. Space quickly after keying a letter or a word; begin keying the next letter or word immediately.

1 a s d f; a s d f; j k l; j k l; as; ask; he; held;
DS
2 ask her; ask her; last sale; last sale; if he asks
DS
3 a red jar; a red jar; she said half; she said half
DS
4 hear a lark; hear a lark; a fire sale; a fire sale
DS
5 he fired her; he fired her; a dark red; a dark red
DS
6 ask her kids; ask her kids; he has had; he has had
TS

5B

Improve ENTER Key Technique

Key each line twice SS; DS between 2-line groups. Keep up your pace at the end of the line, enter quickly, and begin the new line immediately.

1 she said;
2 a red jar is;
3 ask her if she is;
4 he said her ad is here;
5 he asked her if she had it;
6 here is; his last lead; she is;

5C

Increase Keying Speed

Key each line twice SS; DS between 2-line groups. Key the word the first time at an easy speed; repeat it at a faster speed.

1 had had|sad sad|her her|lake lake|dad dad|has has;
2 is is|lad lad|red red|jade jade|lake lake|far far;
3 sad; sad;|ask ask|desk desk|fall fall|hired hired;
4 sir sir|jar jar|like like|ash ash|far far|are are;
5 fair fair|fall fall|read read|risk risk|here here;

For additional practice:

MicroType 5
Alphabetic Keyboarding
Lesson 5

Office Features 1

For each activity, read and learn the feature described, then follow instructions at the left.

Activity 1

Insert, Typeover, Auto-Correct, Underline, Italic, and Bold

 WP • Home/Font/Select Feature

1. Read the information at the right; learn to use the features described.
2. Key lines 1–10. Note how the errors in line 1 are corrected automatically.
3. After keying the lines, make the following changes:

line 2
Change *January* to *October*.
line 9
Insert *new* before *car*.
Insert *for college* after *left*.
line 10
Insert *not* before *know*.
Insert *the* after *know*.

Save as: **OF1 ACTIVITY1**

Note: In lines 8 and 10, the punctuation after a formatted word should NOT be formatted (underlined, bolded, or italicized).

Insert

The **Insert** feature is active when you open a software program. Move the insertion point to where you want to insert text; key the new text.

Typeover

Typeover allows you to replace current text with newly keyed text.

AutoCorrect

The **AutoCorrect** feature detects and corrects *some* typing, spelling, and capitalization errors for you automatically.

Underline

The **Underline** feature underlines text as it is keyed.

Italic

The **Italic** feature prints letters that slope up toward the right.

Bold

The **Bold** feature prints text darker than other copy as it is keyed.

> **Note:** When keying the numbers, key <*number*> <*period*> <*space*> <*space*> <*text*>.

1. would it help if rebecca johnson and i made the boxx for you?

2. His credit card bill for the month of January was $3,988.76.

3. Rebecca read *Little Women* by Louisa May Alcott for the test.

4. Yes, it is acceptable to *italicize* or <u>underline</u> book titles.

5. Patricia used the **bold** feature to **emphasize** her main points.

6. Their cell number was **698 388 0054**, not 698 388 9954.

7. I have read both *The Firm* and *The Rainmaker* by John Grisham.

8. She overemphasized by ***<u>underlining</u>***, ***<u>bolding</u>***, and ***<u>italicizing</u>***.

9. I believe James bought a car before he left.

10. Sarah did know difference between <u>affect</u> and <u>effect</u>.

Activity 2

Select Text/ Select All

1. Read the copy at the right.
2. Learn how to select text.
3. Open *DF OF1 ACTIVITY2*.
4. Use the select text feature to select and change the copy as shown at the right.

Save as: **OF1 ACTIVITY2**

The **Select Text** feature allows you to select (highlight) text to apply formatting changes to after copy has been keyed. Text can be selected by using the mouse or by using the keyboard. As little as one letter of text or as much as the entire document (**Select All**) may be selected.

Once selected, the text can be bolded, italicized, underlined, deleted, copied, moved, printed, saved, etc.

John F. Kennedy: *"And so, my fellow Americans: ask not what your country can do for you—ask what you can do for your country."*

Dwight D. Eisenhower: *"Love of liberty means the guarding of every resource that makes freedom possible—from the sanctity of our families and the wealth of our soil to the genius of our scientists."*

Franklin D. Roosevelt: *"I see a great nation, upon a great continent, blessed with a great wealth of natural resources."*

Abraham Lincoln: *"Both parties deprecated war, but one of them would make war rather than let the nation survive, and the other would accept war rather than let it perish, and the war came."*

New Keys: i and r

Key each line twice SS; DS between 2-line groups. If time permits, key lines 7–9 again.

Technique cue

- curved, upright fingers
- eyes on copy

i *Right middle* finger

r *Left index* finger

Follow the *Standard Plan for Learning New Keys* on p. 511.

Learn i

1 k i|ki ki|ik; ik;|is; is;|lid lid|kid kid|aid aid;

2 ill; ill;|said said|like like|jail jail|file file;

3 he likes; file a lease; a slide; if he is; his kid

Learn r

4 f r|fr fr|far far|red red|are are|ark ark|jar jar;

5 dark dark|real real|rake rake|hear hear|rear rear;

6 a red jar; hear her; dark red; a real rake; read a

Combine i and r

7 ride ride|fire fire|hair hari|hire hire|liar liar;

8 air air|risk risk|fair fair|dire dire|rifle rifle;

9 fire risk; hire a; her side; like air; a fire; sir

New-Key Mastery

Key each line twice SS; DS between 2-line groups.

Technique cue

- wrists low, but not resting on desk
- fingers curved
- eyes on copy

For additional practice:

MicroType 5
Alphabetic Keyboarding
Lesson 4

reach review

1 de ki jh fr ed ik rf ik ki rf jh ed ik fr jh de ki

2 are are|hair hair|hear hear|risk risk|shear shear;

h/e

3 she she|her her|seeks seeks|shed sheds|shelf shelf

4 her shelf; he had; he held a jar; he heard; he has

i/r

5 ir ir|air air|hair hair|hired hired|riddle riddle;

6 hire a kid; ride like; her hair; like her; a fire;

all keys learned

7 jar jar|half half|fire fire|liked liked|lake lake;

8 fire fire|jail jail|hire hire|sake sake|deal deal;

all keys learned

9 if she is; he did ask; he led her; he is her aide;

10 she has had a jak sale; she said he had a red fir;

New Key Learning Lesson 4: i and r

Activity 3

Cut, Copy, and Paste

WP • Home/Clipboard/Select Feature

1. Read the copy at the right. Learn how to cut, copy, and paste text.
2. Open file *DF OF1 ACTVITY3*. Copy the text in this file and paste it a TS below the last line of text.
3. In the second set of steps, use Cut and Paste to arrange the steps in order.

Save as: **OF1 ACTIVITY3**

After you have selected text, you can use the Cut, Copy, and Paste features. The **Cut** feature removes selected text from the current location; the **Paste** feature places it at another location.

The **Copy** feature copies the selected text so it can be placed in another location (pasted), leaving the original text unchanged.

Step 1. Select text to be cut (moved).

Step 2. Click **Cut** to remove text from the current location.

Step 3. Move the insertion point to the desired location.

Step 4. Click **Paste** to place the cut text at the new location.

Activity 4

Undo and Redo

1. Read the copy at the right.
2. Learn how to use the Undo and Redo features.
3. Key the sentence at the right.
4. Delete *San Francisco* and *Tchaikovsky's.*
5. Use the Undo feature to reverse both changes.
6. Use the Redo feature to reverse the last Undo action.

Save as: **OF1 ACTIVITY4**

Use the **Undo** feature to reverse the last change you made in text. Undo restores text to its original location, even if you have moved the insertion point to another position. Use the **Redo** feature to reverse the last Undo action.

The **San Francisco** Symphony Orchestra performed **Tchaikovsky's** 1812 Overture Op. 49 Waltz for their final number.

Activity 5

Zoom and Print Preview

WP • View/Zoom/Select Feature

WP • Office Button/Print/Print Preview

1. Read the copy at the right.
2. Learn how to use the Zoom and Print Preview features of your software.
3. Open the *OF1 ACTIVITY1* file. Complete the steps at the right.
4. Close the file.

Use the **Zoom** feature to increase or decrease the amount of the page appearing on the screen. As you decrease the amount of the page appearing on the screen, the print will be larger. Larger print makes it easier to read and edit. As you increase the amount of the page appearing on the screen, the print becomes smaller. Other options of the Zoom feature include viewing one page, two pages, or multiple pages on the screen.

Quite often you will want to see the whole page on the screen to check the appearance (margins, spacing, graphics, tables, etc.) of the document prior to printing. You can display an entire page by using the Zoom feature or the **Print Preview** feature.

Step 1: View the document as a whole page using the Zoom feature.

Step 2: View the document at 75 percent.

Step 3: View the document at 200 percent.

Step 4: View the document as a whole page using Print Preview.

Lesson 4   NEW KEYS: i AND r

• To learn reach technique for **i** and **r**.

4A

Get Ready to Key

Follow the steps in the *Standard Plan for Getting Ready to Key* on p. 511.

4B

Conditioning Practice

Key each line twice SS; DS between 2-line groups.

Practice cue

• Key the line at a slow, steady pace, tapping and releasing each key quickly.

• Key the line again at a faster pace; move from key to key quickly.

home keys 1 `ll aa ff jj ss kk dd ;; jd f; ls ak sj ;a df kl ak`

Tap ENTER twice to DS.

h/e 2 `he he|she she|held held|heed heed|shed shed|ahead;`

DS

all keys learned 3 `she had a sale; a jade desk; she ask a as he fled;`

Tap ENTER 3 times to TS between lesson parts.

4C

Speed Building

Key each line twice SS; DS between 2-line groups.

Keying cue

Keep up your pace to the end of each line, tap the **ENTER** key quickly, and start the new line without a pause.

1 `had a deal`

2 `see if she did;`

3 `ask if she has read;`

4 `her dad did ask her if he`

5 `a sled ride; half a jar; he is`

6 `ask dad if she has had a real sale;`

7 `her aide asked if he has real dark hair;`

8 `she has a shed; half a flask; she has a desk;`

Activity 6

Customize Status Bar

1. Read the copy at the right.
2. Learn how to customize the status bar.
3. Open the *OF1 ACTIVITY1* file. Complete the steps at the right.
4. Close the file.

There are many options (page number, vertical page position, line number, spelling and grammar check, etc.) that the software can perform. The **status bar** indicates whether the options are turned on or off. The status bar can be customized to meet the needs of the person using the software.

Step 1: Note the options that are available on the status bar.

Step 2: See what additional options are available on the status bar.

Step 3: Turn off one of the options that is currently available. Note the change on the status bar.

Step 4: Turn the option back on. Note the change on the status bar.

Step 5: Turn on the Line Number, Page Number, and Vertical Page Position if they are not already on.

Step 6: Move the insertion point and note how the status bar informs you of the location of the insertion point.

Activity 7

Apply What You Have Learned

1. Key lines 1–6, applying formatting as shown.
2. After keying the lines, make the following changes.

line 1
Change *Kennedy* to *Washington* and *Democrat* to *Federalist.*

line 4
Change *New York Times* to *Washington Post.*

line 6
Delete *frequently.* Insert or **bold** after *italic.*

Save as: **OF1 ACTIVITY7**

1. **Kennedy** was a *Democrat*; **Lincoln** was a *Republican.*

2. Is the correct choice <u>two</u>, <u>too</u>, or <u>to</u>?

3. Is *Harry Potter and the Deathly Hallows* still on the bestseller list?

4. There was an article on her in the *New York Times.*

5. Are the names to be **bolded** or <u>underlined</u> or **<u>bolded and underlined</u>**?

6. The <u>underscore</u> is being used less frequently than *italic.*

Activity 8

Apply What You Have Leaned

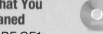

1. Open *DF OF1 ACTIVITY8.*
2. Use the select text feature to select and change the formatting of the copy as shown at the right.
3. Use the copy and paste feature to arrange the Presidents in the order they served: Roosevelt 1901–1909, Wilson 1913–1921, Truman 1945–1953, Reagan 1981–1989

Save as: **OF1 ACTIVITY8**

Harry S. Truman: *"The American people stand firm in the faith which has inspired this Nation from the beginning. We believe that all men have a right to equal justice under law and equal opportunity to share in the common good. We believe that all men have the right to freedom of thought and expression."*

Theodore Roosevelt: *"Much has been given us, and much will rightfully be expected from us. We have duties to others and duties to ourselves; and we can shirk neither."*

Ronald Reagan: *"We are a nation that has a government--not the other way around. And this makes us special among the nations of the Earth. Our government has no power except that granted it by the people. It is time to check and reverse the growth of government, which shows signs of having grown beyond the consent of the governed."*

Woodrow Wilson: *"We have built up, moreover, a great system of government, which has stood through a long age as in many respects a model for those who seek to set liberty upon foundations that will endure against fortuitous change, against storm and accident."*

New Keys: h and e

1. Use the *Standard Plan for Learning New Keys* (p. 511) for each key to be learned. Study the plan now.

2. Relate each step of the plan to the illustrations below and copy at the right. Then key each line twice SS; leave a DS between 2-line groups.

h *Right index* finger

e *Left middle* finger

Do not key the line numbers, the vertical lines separating word groups, or the labels.

Learn h

1 j h jh jh|hj hj|ha ha|has has|dash dash|hall hall;

2 jh jh|had had|ash ash|has has|half half|lash lash;

3 ha ha; a half; a dash; has had; a flash; had half;

Tap ENTER twice to DS after you complete the set of lines.

Learn e

4 d e de de|ed ed|elk elk|elf elf|see see|leak leak;

5 fake fake|deal deal|leaf leaf|fade fade|lake lake;

6 jade desk; see a lake; feel safe; see a safe deal;

Combine h and e

7 he he|she she|shelf shelf|shake shake|shade shade;

8 he has; half ashes; he fed; held a shelf; she has;

9 held a sale; he has a shed; he has a desk; she has

Tap ENTER 3 times to TS between lesson parts.

New-Key Mastery

Key each line twice SS; DS between 2-line groups.

Spacing cue

Space once after ; used as punctuation.

Fingers curved

Fingers upright

home row

1 add add|dad dad|jak jak|ask ask|lad lad|fall falls

2 all fall; as a jak; a sad lad falls; all salad ads

h/e

3 he he|had had|see see|she she|held held|shed shed;

4 half a shelf; a jade sale; she has a jak; he deals

all keys learned

5 jell jell|half half|sale sale|lake lake|held held;

6 a lake; she has half; he held a flask; a jade sale

all keys learned

7 she held a deed; a flash; a jade keel; has a shed;

8 a jak; half a flask; he has a desk; he held a sale

For additional practice:

MicroType 5
Alphabetic Keyboarding
Lesson 3

UNIT 5
Lessons 17-18
Using Help

Lesson 17   HELP BASICS

OBJECTIVES

• To gain an overview of software Help features.
• To learn to use software Help features.

17A

Overview

1. Study the information at the right.
2. Access your Help feature.

Note: The size of the Help box can be adjusted by clicking and dragging the edges of the dialog box. The Help box can also be moved to a different location on the screen (click the title bar at the top of the dialog box and drag to a new location) to allow you to see other parts of the screen.

Help Basics

Application software offers built-in Help features that you can access directly in the software as you work. Help is the equivalent of a user's manual on how to use your software. Listed below are some of the main functions that most software Help features allow you to do.

• Browse a table of contents of Help topics organized by categories.
• Search for topics in an alphabetic index.
• Point to screen items for a concise explanation of their use.
• Access technical resources, free downloads, and other options at the software manufacturer's website.

The Help features work the same way for each software application in the Office suite. For example, the Microsoft Help feature works the same in *Word* or *Excel* as it does in *PowerPoint* or *Access*.

The software's Help features can be accessed by tapping F1 or by clicking on the question mark located in the upper-right corner of the screen.

Access Help Feature

Help Menu

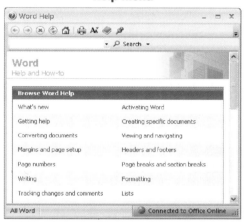

Use the scroll bar to see help features located at the bottom of the Help menu.

Bottom of Help Menu

Lesson 3 NEW KEYS: h AND e

OBJECTIVE

• To learn reach technique for **h** and **e**.

3A

Get Ready to Key

Before starting each lesson, follow the *Standard Plan for Getting Ready to Key* at the right.

Standard Plan for Getting Ready to Key

1. Arrange work area as shown on page 243.
2. Start your word processing software.
3. Align the front of the keyboard with the front edge of the desk.
4. Position the monitor and the textbook for easy reading.

3B

Plan for Learning New Keys

All keys except the home keys (**fdsa jkl;**) require the fingers to reach in order to tap them. Follow the *Standard Plan for Learning New Keys* at the right to learn the proper reach for each new key.

Standard Plan for Learning New Keys

1. Find the new key on the keyboard chart shown on the page where the new key is introduced.
2. Look at your keyboard and find the new key on it.
3. Study the reach-technique picture near the practice lines for the new key. Read the statement below the illustration.
4. Identify the finger to be used to tap the new key.

5. Curve your fingers; place them in home-key position (over asdf jkl;).
6. Watch your finger as you reach to the new key and back to home position a few times (keep it curved).
7. Refer to the set of drill lines near the reach-technique illustration. Key each line twice SS—once slowly to learn the new reach and then again at a faster rate. DS between 2-line groups.

3C

Home-Key Review

Key each line twice SS; DS between 2-line groups.

All keystrokes learned

1 ss jj ff ;; dd ll aa kk jj ff kk ss dd ll ;; aa kk

2 fk ja ld s; aj d; fl sk ka jf ls d; jd kf sl ;a dj

3 a sad lass; all ads; ask a lad; all fall; a flask;

4 a lad ask; a salad; a fall ad; ask a dad; all fall

Tap ENTER 3 times to TS between lesson parts.

Using Help

1. Access Microsoft Office Word Help.
2. Click *What's new;* then click *Introduction to Word 2007.* Scroll down to *What's new in Word 2007?* Change the font size to Largest.
3. Use the Back button to return to the Word Help and How-to screen.
4. Use the Forward button to return to *Introduction to Word 2007.* Scroll down to *What's where in Word?*
5. Use the Home button to return to the Home screen.
6. Click the Keep on Top button. Click outside of the Help dialog box. Click the Keep on Top button again. Click outside the Help dialog box. Notice what happens to the dialog box each time.

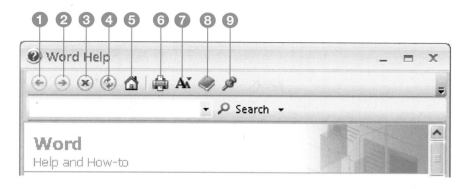

Help Buttons

1. Back
2. Forward
3. Stop
4. Refresh
5. Home

6. Print
7. Change Font Size
8. Show Table of Contents
9. Keep On Top (Not On Top)

Help Table of Contents

1. Read the information at the right.
2. Access the Table of Contents, and open a category that interests you. Open subcategories if necessary. Read the topic information. Go to related topics, if any.
3. Read two other categories that interest you. Print any information you think will be helpful in the future.

Like the table of contents in a book, the Table of Contents feature in Help lets you look for information that is organized by categories. In the Table of Contents shown below in the left-hand pane, a book icon indicates a category.

Click on the book to open it and reveal the topics available on the category.

Some categories have subcategories (see illustration below). The topics available for the subcategories can also be viewed by clicking on the book to open. Click on the desired topic, and information on the topic will be displayed in the right-hand pane.

Help Table of Contents

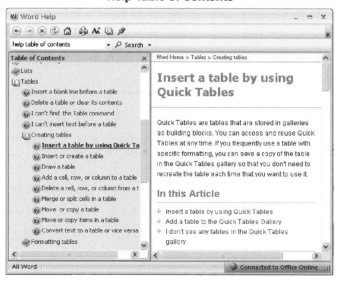

Lesson 2

OBJECTIVES
- To review control of home keys (**fdsa jkl;**).
- To review control of the **Space Bar** and **ENTER**.

2A

Practice Home Keys

Key each line twice SS; DS between 2-line groups. Do not key the numbers.

1 s s ss l l ll d d dd k k kk f f ff j j jj a; a; ;a
DS

2 f f ff j j jj d d s sl fl lf al la ja aj sk ks jj;
DS

3 sa as ld dl af fa ls sl fl lf al la ja aj sk ks jj
DS

4 fj dk sl a; jf kd ls ;a ds kl df kj sd lk sa ;l jj
DS

5 fa ds jk ;f jf kd ls ;a f; dl sk aj sj ak d; fl ad
TS

2B

Improve ENTER Key Technique

Key each line twice SS; DS between 2-line groups.
- fingers curved and upright
- wrists low, but not touching keyboard
- body erect, sitting back in chair
- eyes on copy

1 alj; ksf; dak;

2 sff; ldd; ajj; lkk;

3 jaj; sls; kdk; fjf; sks;

4 ljd; fss; jdj; skj; asj; fdl;

5 afsd klj; fsda lj;k flaj s;dk fj;k

6 akdj ls;f daj; kfls jlja fsdl ;skd ajsa

2C

Improve ENTER Key Technique

Key each line twice SS; DS between 2-line groups.

For additional practice:
MicroType 5
Alphabetic Keyboarding
Lesson 2

1 a fall; a fall; a jak; a jak; asks dad; asks dad;;

2 all ads; all ads; a fad; a fad; as a lad; as a lad

3 a sad lad; a sad lad; a fall; a fall; ask a ask a;

4 a fad a fad; ask a lass; ask a lass; a dad; a dad;

5 all fall ads; all fall ads; a sad fall; a sad fall

6 a lad asks a lass; a lad asks a lass; a lad; a lad

OBJECTIVES

- To learn to use the pop-up description feature.
- To access additional software support on the Internet.

18A

Screen Tips

1. Read the information at the right.
2. Learn how to use the pop-up description feature of your software.
3. Take a pop-up description tour of your screen. Use the feature to learn what unfamiliar screen items do.

A valuable Help feature for new users is the pop-up description box. This feature may be called ScreenTips, Quick Tips, or something similar. It allows you to use the mouse to point to commands or other objects on the screen. After a brief period of time, a pop-up box appears, giving a concise description of the feature.

The illustration below shows what happens when you point at the Format Painter command found in the Clipboard group of the Home tab. For this particular command, the pop-up box tells you:

- The name of the command
- What it is used for
- How to use it

Sometimes the box will offer more information about the command by telling you to *Press F1 for more help.*

When you are finished reading the information, move the pointer away from the command to close the description box.

Screen Tips

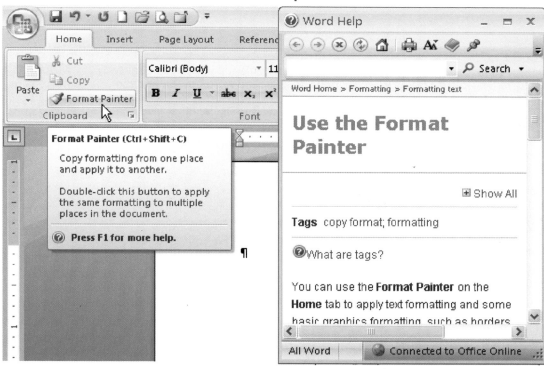

18B

Use Screen Tips

1. Use the pop-up description to learn about each of the features at the right.
2. Key a sentence or two explaining the purpose of each feature.

Thesaurus - Review Tab

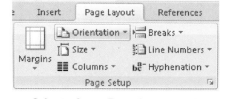

Orientation – Page Layout Tab

Line Spacing – Home Tab

1H

Home-Key Mastery

Key each line twice (without the numbers).

Correct finger alignment

Technique cue

Keep fingers curved and upright over home keys, right thumb just barely touching the Space Bar.

Spacing cue

Space once after ; (semi-colon) used as punctuation.

```
1 j j jk jk l l l; l; a a as as d d df df af kl dsj;
                                                    DS
2 jj kjk kjk ll ;l; ;l; ja ja dk dk ls ls ;f ;f kjd;
                                                    DS
3 sad sad|lad lad|all all|ask ask|jak jak|fall fall;
                                                    DS
4 a sad lass; ask all dads; a lad ask; a salad; as a
                                                    DS
5 as a dad; add a fall; ask all lads; as a fall fad;
                                                    TS
```

1I

End-of-Lesson Routine

Follow the routine shown at the right at the end of each practice session.

1. Save the document if you have not already done so. Use the word Lesson and the lesson number (Lesson 1) for the filename unless directed to use another filename.
2. Exit the software.
3. Remove disk from disk drive.
4. Turn off equipment if directed to do so.
5. Store materials as instructor directs.
6. Clean up your work area and push in your chair before you leave.

1J

Enrichment

Key each line twice SS; DS between 2-line groups.

```
1 ja js jd jf f; fl fk fj ka ks kd kf d; dl dk dj a;
                                                    DS
2 la ls ld lf s; sl sk sj ;a ;s ;d ;f a; al ak aj fj
                                                    DS
3 jj aa kk ss ll dd ;; ff fj dk sl a; jf kd ls ;a a;
                                                    DS
4 as as ask ask ad ad lad lad all all fall fall lass
                                                    DS
5 as a fad; as a dad; ask a lad; as a lass; all lads
                                                    DS
6 a sad dad; all lads fall; ask a lass; a jak salad;
                                                    DS
7 add a jak; a fall ad; all fall ads; ask a sad lass
                                                    TS
```

For additional practice:

MicroType 5
Alphabetic Keyboarding
Lesson 1

Office Online

1. Read the information at the right.
2. Learn how to access the software manufacturer's website.
3. Go to the software manufacturer's website. Spend some time browsing the different options. Take advantage of two or three options. For example, print a helpful article or download clip art or a template (with your instructor's permission).

An abundance of additional help and resources is available from most software manufacturers' websites. These resources include:

- articles on software features
- downloads for templates, clip art, and "patch" files to fix problems
- online training courses

These resources can be accessed (provided you have Internet access) directly from the bottom of the Help menu by clicking on the desired link.

Microsoft Downloads Home Page

Training Home Page

Templates Home Page

Online Training

1. Access Microsoft Online Training from the Help menu.
2. Select the 2007 Office System training course.
3. Complete *Up to Speed with Word 2007*.
4. Complete the online tests.
5. Answer the questions at the right.

Training course evaluation.

1. Was the training course easy to understand?
2. What did you like best about the training course?
3. What suggestions would you give for improving the course?
4. Which of the Help options that were presented in Lessons 17–18 do you think you will use most often? Explain your answer.

1F

Home-Key, Space-Bar, and ENTER-Key Practice

1. Place your hands in home-key position (left-hand fingers on **f d s a** and right-hand fingers on **j k l ;**).

2. Key each line once single-spaced (SS); double-space (DS) between 2-line groups. Do not key line numbers.

Fingers curved and upright

Down-and-in spacing motion

1 a aa s ss d dd f ff

2 a aa s ss d dd f ff
                                        DS

3 j jj k kk l ll ; ;;

4 j jj k kk l ll ; ;;
                                        DS

5 aj lf d; ks ja fl ;d aja

6 aj lf d; ks ja fl ;d aja
                                        DS

7 djd kak s;s flf jal d;k;

8 djd kak s;s flf jal d;k;

Tap the ENTER key 3 times to triple-space (TS)

1G

Technique: ENTER-Key Practice

Key the lines once SS; DS between 2-line groups. Do not key the numbers.

Spacing cue

When lines are SS, tap ENTER twice to insert a DS between 2-line groups.

1 jj ss ll

2 jj ss ll
                DS

3 aa kk dd ;; ff

4 aa kk dd ;; ff
                      DS

5 ll ff jj dd kk ss ;;

6 ll ff jj dd kk ss ;;
                            DS

7 aa aa fd l; kj j; lk af ds

8 aa aa fd l; kj j; lk af ds
                                      DS

9 ;f; ;f; ala ala djd djd ksk ksk;

10 ;f; ;f; ala ala djd djd ksk ksk;
                                      DS

11 kkff kkff jjss jjss aall aall dd;s dd;

12 kkff kkff jjss jjss aall aall dd;s dd;
                                            TS

Reach out with little finger; tap the ENTER key quickly; return finger to home key.

Communication & Math
SKILLS 2

CAPITALIZATION

ACTIVITY 1

Capitalization

1. Study each of the eight rules.
   a. Key Learn line(s) beneath each rule, noting how the rule is applied.
   b. Key Apply line(s), using correct capitalization.

Capitalization

Rule 1: Capitalize the first word of a sentence, personal titles, and names of people.

Learn 1 Ask Ms. King if she and Mr. Valdez will sponsor our book club.

Apply 2 did you see mrs. watts and gloria at the school play?

Rule 2: Capitalize days of the week and months of the year.

Learn 3 He said that school starts on the first Monday in September.

Apply 4 my birthday is on the third thursday of march this year.

Rule 3: Capitalize cities, states, countries, and specific geographic features.

Learn 5 When you were recently in Nevada, did you visit Lake Tahoe?

Apply 6 when in france, we saw paris from atop the eiffel tower.

Rule 4: Capitalize names of clubs, schools, companies, and other organizations.

Learn 7 The Voices of Harmony will perform at Music Hall next week.

Apply 8 lennox corp. operates the hyde park drama club in boston.

Rule 5: Capitalize historic periods, holidays, and events.

Learn 9 The Fourth of July celebrates the signing of the Declaration of Independence.

Apply 10 henri asked if memorial day is an american holiday.

Rule 6: Capitalize streets, buildings, and other specific structures.

Learn 11 Jemel lives at Bay Shores near Golden Gate Bridge.

Apply 12 dubois tower is on fountain square at fifth and walnut.

Rule 7: Capitalize an official title when it precedes a name and elsewhere if it is a title of high distinction.

Learn 13 In what year did Juan Carlos become King of Spain?

Learn 14 Masami Chou, our class president, made the scholastic awards.

Apply 15 did the president speak to the nation from the rose garden?

Apply 16 mr. chavez, our company president, wrote two novels.

Rule 8: Capitalize initials; also, letters in abbreviations if the letters would be capitalized when the words are spelled out.

Learn 17 Does Dr. R. J. Anderson have an Ed.D. or a Ph.D.?

Learn 18 She said that UPS stands for United Parcel Service.

Apply 19 we have a letter from ms. anna m. bucks of washington, d.c.

Apply 20 m.d. means Doctor of Medicine, not medical doctor.

(continued on next page)

1C

Home-Key Position

1. Find the home keys on the keyboard illustration: **f d s a** for left hand and **j k l ;** for right hand.

2. Locate the home keys on your keyboard, and place your fingers, well curved and upright (not slanting), on them.

3. Remove your fingers from the keyboard; then place them in home-key position again, curving and holding them lightly on the keys.

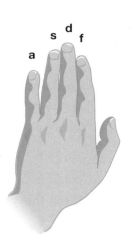

Left Fingers   **Right Fingers**

1D

Technique: Keystroking and Space Bar

1. Read the hints and study the illustrations at the right.

2. Place your fingers in home-key position as directed in 1C above.

3. Key the line beneath the illustration. Tap the Space Bar once at the point of each arrow.

4. Review proper position at the keyboard (1B); key the line again.

Technique Hints

Keystroking: Tap each key with the tip of the finger. Keep your fingers curved as shown.

Spacing: Tap the Space Bar with the right thumb; use a quick down-and-in motion (toward the palm). Avoid pauses before or after spacing.

Space once

f d s a j k l ; ff jj dd kk ss ll aa ;;

1E

Technique: Hard Return at Line Endings

Read the information and study the illustration at the right.

Hard Return

To return the insertion point to the left margin and move it down to the next line, tap **ENTER**.
This is called a hard return. Use a hard return at the end of all drill lines. Use two hard returns when directed to double-space.

Hard Return Technique

Reach the little finger of the right hand to the **ENTER** key, tap the key, and return the finger quickly to home-key position.
Practice the **ENTER** key reach several times.

2. Key Proofread &
Correct, using correct
capitalization.
a. Check answers.
b. Using the rule
number(s) at the left
of each line, study the
rule relating to each
error.
c. Rekey each incorrect
line, using correct
capitalization.

Save as: **CS2 ACTIVITY1**

Proofread & Correct

Rules

1,6	1	has dr. holt visited his studio at the hopewell arts center?
1,3,5	2	pam has made plans to spend thanksgiving day in fort wayne.
1,2,8	3	j. c. hauck will receive a b.a. degree from usc in june.
1,4,6	4	is tech services, inc. located at fifth street and elm?
1,2,7	5	i heard senator dole make his acceptance speech on thursday.
1,3,6	6	did mrs. alma s. banks apply for a job with butler county?
1,3	7	she knew that albany, not new york city, is the capital.
1,3	8	eldon and cindy marks now live in santa fe, new mexico.
1,6	9	are you going to the marx theater in mount adams tonight?
1,2,6	10	on friday, the first of july, we will move to Keystone Plaza.

1. Listen carefully to the sounds around you for 3'.
2. As you listen, key a numbered list of every different sound you hear.
3. Identify with asterisks the three loudest sounds you heard.

ACTIVITY 2

Listening

Complete as directed.

Save as: **CS2 ACTIVITY2**

ACTIVITY 3

Composing

1. Read the quotations.
2. Choose one and make notes of what the quotation means to you.
3. Key a ¶ or two indicating what the quotation means to you.
4. Proofread, revise, and correct.

Save as: **CS2 ACTIVITY3**

1. "A teacher affects eternity; he can never tell, where his influence stops." (Henry B. Adams)

2. "Every man I meet is in some way my superior." (Ralph Waldo Emerson)

3. "I'm a great believer in luck, and I find the harder I work the more I have of it." (Thomas Jefferson)

ACTIVITY 4

Math: Multiplying and Dividing Numbers

1. Open *DF CS2 ACTIVITY4* and print the file.
2. Solve the problems as directed in the file.
3. Submit your answers.

CAREER Clusters

ACTIVITY 2

You must complete Activity 1 on page 28 before completing this activity.

1. Retrieve your completed Career Clusters Interest Survey from your folder.

2. Determine your top three career clusters by adding the number of circled items in each box. Write the total number of items

circled in the small box at the right of each section; then determine the boxes with the highest numbers. The box numbers correspond to the career cluster numbers on the pages you printed earlier. For example, let's say you had 15 circles in Box 6, 11 circles in Box 7, and 12 circles in Box 11. You have shown an interest in Finance (Box 6), Government & Public Administration (Box 7), and Information Technology (Box 11).

3. Return your Career folder to the storage area.

Lessons 1-16

New Key Learning

Lesson 1 HOME KEYS (fdsa jkl;)

OBJECTIVES

- To review control of home keys (**fdsa jkl;**).
- To learn control of the **Space Bar** and **ENTER**.

1A

Work Area Arrangement

Properly arranged work area includes:

- alphanumeric keyboard directly in front of chair
- front edge of keyboard even with edge of desk
- monitor placed for easy viewing
- book at right of keyboard

© CENGAGE LEARNING

Properly arranged work area

1B

Keying Position

Proper position includes:

- fingers curved and upright (not slanted) over home keys
- wrists low, but not touching keyboard
- forearms parallel to slant of keyboard
- body erect, sitting back in chair
- feet on floor for balance
- eyes on copy

© franksiteman.com 2007

Proper position at computer

UNIT 6
Lessons 19-21

Learn/Review Symbol-Key Techniques

Lesson 19   LEARN/REVIEW /, $, %, #, &, (, AND)

OBJECTIVE

• To review control of /, $, %, #, &, (, and).

19A

Conditioning Practice

Key each line twice.

alphabet 1 Quincy just put back five azure gems next to the gold watch.

fig/sym 2 Tim moved from 5142 Troy Lane to 936-123rd Street on 8/7/03.

speed 3 He lent the field auditor a hand with the work for the firm.

gwam 1' | 1 | 2 | 3 | 4 | 5 | 6 | 7 | 8 | 9 | 10 | 11 | 12 |

19B

Learn/Review
/, $, and %

Key each line twice.

The / is the same key
as the ?.
Key the shift of 4 for $.
Key the shift of 5 for %.

Spacing Cue

Do not space between a figure and the / or the $ sign.
Do not space between a
figure and the % sign.

Learn/Review / (diagonal or slash) Reach down with the right little finger.

1 ; /|; /|;/ ;/ |;/; ;/; |2/3 4/5|and/or|We keyed 1/2 and 3/4.

2 Space between a whole number and a fraction: 5 2/3, 14 6/9.

3 Do not space before or after the / in a fraction: 2/3, 7/8.

Learn/Review $ (dollar sign) Reach up with the left index finger.

4 f R $|f R $|F$ F$|F r $ F r $|4$ 4$|f r 4 $|f r 4 $|$f$ f;

5 A period separates dollars and cents: $4.50, $6.25, $19.50.

6 I earned $33.50 on Mon., $23.80 on Tues., and $44.90 on Wed.

Learn/Review % (percent sign) Reach up with the left index finger.

7 fF 5% fF 5%|f 5 % f 5 %|f%f f%f|5f% 5f%|rF5% rF5%|T5f% T5f%.

8 Do not space between a number and %: 5%, 75%, 85%, and 95%.

9 Prices fell 10% on May 1, 15% on June 1, and 20% on July 15.

Slide 2

<HPJ From the Desk of>

HPJ From the Desk of
Helen St. Claire

I've started an electronic slide presentation for the annual meeting (DF HPJ Job16). Please insert slides 2–8. I've attached sketches of slides 2, 3, and 4. Slides 5–8 will be similar to slide 4, showing a description of each of the new seminars. Get the information for the slides from the New Seminar Descriptions table (Job 7) you formatted earlier. Add transitions for slides 2–9.

June 12   **HSC**

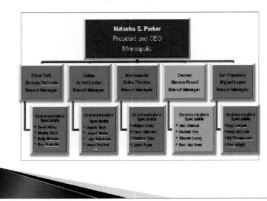

Slide 3

New Seminars

- ▸ Business Etiquette: You Cannot Not Communicate!

- ▸ Gender Communication: "He Says, She Says."

- ▸ International Communication

- ▸ Listen Up!

- ▸ Technology in the Workplace

Slide 4

Business Etiquette: You Cannot Not Communicate!

- ▸ If business etiquette is important to you, don't miss this seminar. Learn what's acceptable—and what's not—in formal business settings.

19c

Speed Building

1. Key three 1' timings; determine *gwam*.
2. Key one 2' timing; determine *gwam*.

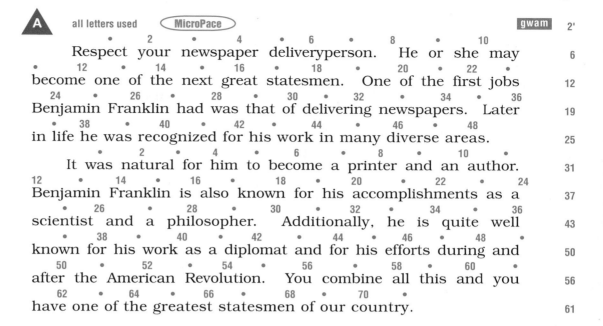

A all letters used MicroPace |gwam| 2'

Respect your newspaper deliveryperson. He or she may 6
become one of the next great statesmen. One of the first jobs 12
Benjamin Franklin had was that of delivering newspapers. Later 19
in life he was recognized for his work in many diverse areas. 25

It was natural for him to become a printer and an author. 31
Benjamin Franklin is also known for his accomplishments as a 37
scientist and a philosopher. Additionally, he is quite well 43
known for his work as a diplomat and for his efforts during and 50
after the American Revolution. You combine all this and you 56
have one of the greatest statesmen of our country. 61

19d

Learn/Review #, &, (, and)

Key each line twice.

> Key the shift of the 3 for #.
> Key the shift of the 7 for &.
> Key the shift of 9 for (.
> Key the shift of 0 for).

Spacing Cue

Do not space between # and a figure; space once before and after & used to join names.

Do not space after a left parenthesis or before a right parenthesis and the copy enclosed.

For additional practice:
MicroType 5
New Key Review,
Number & Symbol
Lesson 5

Learn/Review # (number/pounds) Reach up with the left middle finger.

1 d E # d E #|D e # D e #|3 d # 3 d #|dd #3 dd #3|#d E3 #d E3;
2 Do not space between a number and #: 3# of #633 at $9.35/#.
3 Jerry recorded Check #38 as #39, #39 as #40, and #40 as #41.

Learn/Review & (ampersand) Reach up with the right index finger.

4 j U & j U &|J u & J u &|7 j & 7 j &|jj &7 jj &7|&j U7 &j U7;
5 Do not space before or after & in initials, e.g., CG&E, B&O.
6 She will interview with Johnson & Smith and Jones & Beckett.

Learn/Review ((left parenthesis) Reach up with the right ring finger.

7 l O (l O (|L o (L o (|9 l (9 l (|ll (9 ll (9|(l o9 (l o9.
8 As (is the shift of 9, use the l finger to key 9, (, or (9.

Learn/Review) (right parenthesis) Reach up with the right little finger.

9 ; P) ; P)|: p) : p)|0 ;) 0 ;)|;;)0 ;;)0|); p0); p0.
10 As) is the shift of 0, use the ; finger to key 0,), or 0).

Combine (and)

11 Hints: (1) depress shift key; (2) tap key; (3) release both.
12 Tab steps: (1) clear tabs, (2) set stops, and (3) tabulate.

Job 14 (shown below)   **Job 15** (shown right)

HPJ From the Desk of
Helen St. Claire

Here is the company organization chart we have on file (DF HPJ JOB14). Some of the information is missing or outdated. Each branch's website contains the most up-to-date information. Print a copy of the file; then verify the information against that on the website. Mark the changes on the printed copy; finally, make the changes to the master file. Be sure to change the date to today's date, June 12.

June 12   HSC

HPJ From the Desk of
Helen St. Claire

Prepare (don't send) this message as an e-mail to the communication specialists in the Minneapolis branch from Erika Thomas. You will need to get the e-mail addresses from their Web page. New Communication Specialist is the subject.

June 12   HSC

Stewart Peters will be joining our branch as a Communication Specialist on Monday, July 15.

Stewart grew up in New York, where he completed an undergraduate degree in organizational communication at New York University. He recently completed his master's degree at the University of Minnesota.

Stewart's thesis dealt with interpersonal conflict in the corporate environment. Since we intend to develop a seminar in this area, he will be able to make an immediate contribution.

Please welcome Stewart to HPJ and our branch when he arrives on the 15th.

HPJ COMMUNICATION SPECIALISTS

Organizational Chart

January 2, 20--

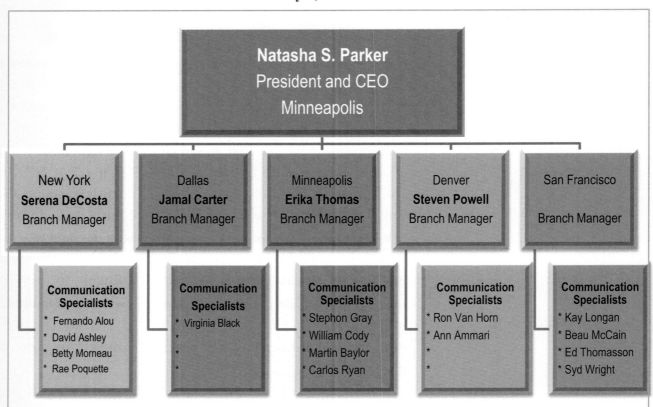

OBJECTIVE

• To review control of _, *, @, +, !, and \.

20A

Conditioning Practice

Key each line twice.

alphabet   1   Joyce Savin fixed the big clock that may win a unique prize.

fig/sym   2   Items marked * are out of stock: #785*, #461A*, and #2093*.

speed   3   The firm paid for the rigid sign by the downtown civic hall.

gwam   1' | 1 | 2 | 3 | 4 | 5 | 6 | 7 | 8 | 9 | 10 | 11 | 12 |

20B

Learn/Review _, *, @, and +

Key each line twice.

> Key the shift of - for _.
> Key the shift of 8 for *.
> Key the shift of 2 for @.
> Key the shift of the key to the right of the hyphen for +.

Learn/Review _ (underline)   Reach up with the right little finger.

1   ; _ ; _|_;_ _;_|;_;- ;_;-|I shifted for the _ as I keyed _-.

2   The _ is used in some Internet locations, i.e., http2_data_2.

Learn/Review * (asterisk)   Reach up with the right middle finger.

3   k I * k I *|K i * K i *|8 k * 8 k *|kk 8* ii *8|*k I8 *k I*;

4   Put an * after Gary*, Jane*, and Joyce* to show high scores.

Learn/Review @ ("at" sign)   Reach up with the left ring finger.

5   s W @ s W @|S w @ S w @|2 s @ 2 s @|ss @2 dd @2|@s W2 @s W2;

6   Change my e-mail address from myers@cs.com to myers@aol.com.

Learn/Review + ("plus" sign)   Reach up with the right little finger.

7   ; + ; +|;+; ;+;|+;+ +;+|7 + 7,|a + b + c < a + b + d,|12 + 3

8   If you add 3 + 4 + 5 + 6 + 7, you will get 25 for an answer.

20C   Skill Building

Guided Timings

1. Review the procedure for setting speed goals (Guided Timing Procedure, p. 22).

2. Use the procedure to key unguided and guided timings on the ¶s of 15D, p. 35.

3. Compare your gwam for the best 2' timing with your previous rate on these ¶s.

Job 13 continued

Internal barriers. Internal barriers are those that deal with the
mental or psychological aspects of listening. The perception of the
importance of the message, the emotional state, and the turn in
and out of the speaker by the listener are examples of internal barriers.

External Barriers. External barriers are barriers other than
those that deal with the mental and psychological makeup of the listener
that tend to keep the listener from devoting full attention to what is
being said. Telephone interruptions, uninvited visitors, noise, and the physical environment are examples of external barriers.

Ways to Improve Listening

Barriers to listening can be overcome. However, it does take a
sincere effort on the part of the listener. Neher and Waite suggest
the following ways to improve listening skills.[3]

- Be aware of the barriers that are especially troublesome for you.
  Listening difficulties are individualistic. Developing awareness
  is an important step in overcoming such barriers.

- Listen as though you will have to paraphrase what is being said.
  Listen for ideas rather than for facts.

- Expect to work at listening. Work at overcoming distractions, such
  as the speaker's delivery or nonverbal mannerisms.

- Concentrate on summarizing the presentation as you listen. If
  possible, think of additional supporting material that would fit
  with the point that the speaker is making. Avoid trying to refute
  the speaker. Try not to be turned off by remarks you disagree with.

---

[1]H. Dan O'Hair, James S. O'Rourke IV, and Mary John O'Hair,
Business Communication: A Framework for Success (Cincinnati:
South-Western Publishing, 2001), p. 211.

[2]Ronald B. Adler and Jeanne Marquardt Elmhorst, *Communicating
at Work* (New York: The McGraw-Hill Companies, 2008), p. 77.

[3]William W. Neher and David H. Waite, *The Business and
Professional Communicator* (Needham Heights, MA: Allyn and Bacon,
1993), p. 28.

Learn/Review ! and \

Key each line twice.

Key the shift of 1 for !.
Key the \ with the key
above the ENTER key.

Spacing Cue

Space twice after an ! at the
end of a sentence.

For additional practice:

MicroType 5
New Key Review,
Number & Symbol
Lesson 6

Learn/Review ! (exclamation point) Reach up with the left little finger.

1 a Q! a Q! |aq! aq! |a! a! |!a! !a! |Qa! Qa! |Felipe won the game!

2 On your mark! Get ready! Get set! Go! Go faster! I won!

3 Great! You made the team! Hurry up! I am late for school!

Learn/Review \ (backslash) Reach up with the right little finger.

4 ;\ ;\ |;\; ;\; |\;\ \;\ |Juan\Mary Juan\Mary |Chan\Kay Chan\Kay

5 Use the \ key to map the drive to access \\sps25\deptdir556.

6 Map the drive to \\global128\coxjg$, not \\global217\coxjg$.

Lesson 21   LEARN/REVIEW =, [ ], AND < >

OBJECTIVE

• To review control of =, [ ], and < >.

21A

Conditioning Practice

Key each line twice.

alphabet 1 Jacques paid a very sizeable sum for the meetings next week.

fig/sym 2 The desk (#539A28) and chair (#61B34) usually sell for $700.

speed 3 Pamela did the work for us, but the neighbor may pay for it.

gwam 1' | 1 | 2 | 3 | 4 | 5 | 6 | 7 | 8 | 9 | 10 | 11 | 12 |

21B

Learn/Review =, [, and]

Key each line twice.

Key the = using the same
key as the +.
Key the [with the key to
the right of p.
Key the] with the key to
the right of [.

Learn/Review = ("equals" sign) Reach up with the right little finger.

1 ; = ; =|;=; ;=;|=;= =;=|a = 5, a = 5,|4 + 6 = 10|4 + 6 = 10;

2 Solve the following: 3a = 15, 5b = 30, 3c = 9, and 2d = 16.

Learn/Review [(left bracket) Reach up with the right little finger.

3 ; [; [|[;[[;[|;[;[;|[a [B [c [D [e [F [g [H [i [J [k [L.

4 [m [N [o [P [q [R [s [T [u [V [w [X [y [Z [1 [2 [3 [4 [5 [6.

Learn/Review] (right bracket) Reach up with the right little finger.

5 ;] ;]|];]];]|;]; ;];|A] b] C] d] E] f] G] h] I] j] K] l.

6 M] n] O] p] Q] r] S] t] U] v] W] x] Y] z] 7] 8] 9] 10] 11]].

Graphic Designer

A graphic artist has been hired to design all of the materials for the new seminar. He will design promotional items as well as content-related items. Currently he is working on the manual cover and divider pages. These items will be coordinated with the emblems used in the slide show portion of the presentation, along with name tags, promotional paraphernalia, and business cards. This should give our seminar a more professional appearance. If it works as well as I think it is going to, we will have the designer work on materials for our existing seminars to add the "professional" look.

Job 13

> **HPJ** From the Desk of
> **Helen St. Claire**
>
> *Format the text as an unbound report with foot-notes (shown at bottom of attached copy). The report will be a handout for the "Listen Up!" seminar.*
>
> *June 12*   HSC

LISTEN UP!

According to Raymond McNulty, "Everyone who expects to succeed *in* life should realize that success ~~only will~~ come if you give careful consideration to other people"[1] To ac**c**omplish this, you must be an excellent listener. One of the most critical skills that an individual acquires is the ability to listen. studies indicate that a person spends 70 percent to 80 percent of ~~their~~ *his or her* time communicating, of which 32.7~~%~~ *spell* is spent listening. Adler and Elmhorst give the following breakdown for the average *an* individual ~~of~~ time spen*ds* communicating.[2]

- Writing 18.8%

- Reading 22.6%

- Speaking 25.8%

- Listening 32.7%

Since *a great deal* ~~most~~ of the time spent communicating is spent listening, it is important to overcome any obstacles that obstruct our ability to listen and to learn new ways to improve our listening ability.

Barriers to Listening

Anything that interferes with our ability to listen is classified as a barrier to listening. *These* ~~B~~arriers ~~that obstruct our ability to listen~~ can be divided into two basic categories--external and internal barriers.

(Report continued on next page)

Speed Building

1. Key three 1' timings; determine *gwam*.
2. Key two 2' timings; determine *gwam*.

 all letters used   MicroPace

gwam 2'

Who lived a more colorful and interesting — 4

existence than this President? He was a rancher in — 9

the west. He participated as a member of the Rough — 14

Riders. He was a historian. He went on an African — 20

safari. He was quite involved in the development of — 25

the Panama Canal. He was the youngest person ever to — 30

become President of the United States; however, he was — 35

not the youngest person that was ever elected to the — 41

office of President. And these are just a few of his — 46

accomplishments. — 48

Theodore Roosevelt was an active and involved — 52

man. He lived life to the fullest and tried to make — 57

the world a better place for others. Today, we still — 63

benefit from some of his many deeds. Some of the — 68

national forests in the West came about as a result of — 73

legislation enacted during the time he was President. — 78

He worked with college leaders to organize the — 83

National Collegiate Athletic Association. — 87

gwam 2' | 1 | 2 | 3 | 4 | 5 | 6 |

Learn/Review < and >

Key each line twice.

Key the shift of comma for <.
Key the shift of period for >.

Learn/Review < ("less than" sign) Reach down with the right middle finger.

1 K< K<|k< k<|,k< ,k<|,i< ,i<|a<b a<b|9<12 9<12|13c<4d 13c<4d;

2 If a < b, and c < d, and e < f, and a < c and e, then a < d.

Learn/Review > ("greater than" sign) Reach down with the right ring finger.

3 L> L>|l> l>|.l> .l>|.o> .o>|d>c d>c|10>8 10>8|5c>17d 5c>17d;

4 If b > a, and d > c, and f > e, and c and e > a, then f > a.

For additional practice:

MicroType 5
New Key Review,
Number & Symbol
Lesson 7

Job 11

Seminar Objectives for:
Technology in the Workplace
Minneapolis Branch

1. *Discuss the role of communication technology in today's business environment and how it has changed over the past ten years.*
2. *Inform participants of various technological communication tools presently available.*
3. *Highlight the advantages/disadvantages of these tools presently available.*
4. *Demonstrate:*
   - *Videoconferencing*
   - *Teleconferencing*
   - *Data conferencing*
   - *GroupSystems*
   - *Internet resources*
5. *Inform participants of various technological communication tools that are in development.*
6. *Discuss Internet resources available to participants.*
7. *Discuss how using high-speed communication in today's business environment can give a firm a competitive advantage in the global marketplace.*

Job 12

Here is an update on recent progress of the Minneapolis Branch.

Seminar Bookings

We are fully booked through April and May. Additional communication specialists are desperately needed if we are going to expand into other states in our region. Most of our current bookings are in Minnesota, Iowa, and Wisconsin. We will be presenting in Illinois for the first time in May. I anticipate this will lead to additional bookings that we won't be able to accommodate. This is a problem that I enjoy having. Michigan, Indiana, and Ohio provide ample opportunities for expansion, when resources are made available.

New Seminar

A lot of progress has been made on the new seminar we are developing, "Technology in the Workplace" (see attachment for seminar objectives). Our branch will be ready to preview the seminar at our annual meeting. Not only will the seminar be a great addition to our seminar offerings, but also I believe HPJ can use it to communicate better internally. I will present my ideas when I preview the seminar. The seminar covers:

- Videoconferencing
- Teleconferencing
- Data conferencing
- GroupSystems
- Internet resources

(Memo continued on next page)

Lesson 22

SKILL BUILDING

OBJECTIVES

- To improve technique on individual letters.
- To improve keying speed on 1' and 2' writings.

22A

Conditioning Practice

Key each line twice.

alphabet 1 Jack liked reviewing the problems on the tax quiz on Friday.
figures 2 Check #365 for $98.47, dated May 31, 2001, was not endorsed.
easy 3 The auditor may work with vigor to form the bus audit panel.

gwam 1' | 1 | 2 | 3 | 4 | 5 | 6 | 7 | 8 | 9 | 10 | 11 | 12 |

22B — Skill Building

Technique Mastery: Individual Letters

Key each line twice.

Technique Goals

- curved, upright fingers
- quick keystrokes

Emphasize continuity and rhythm with curved, upright fingers.

A 1 After Nariaki ate the pancake, he had an apple and a banana.
B 2 Ben Buhl became a better batter by batting big rubber balls.
C 3 Chi Chang from Creek Circle caught a raccoon for Cara Locke.
D 4 Did David and Dick Adams decide to delay the departure date?
E 5 Ed and Eileen were selected to chaperone the evening events.

F 6 Jeff Flores officially failed four of five finals on Friday.
G 7 Garth and Gregg glanced at the gaggle of geese on the grass.
H 8 His haphazard shots helped through half of the hockey match.
I 9 Ida insisted on living in Illinois, Indiana, or Mississippi.
J 10 Jackie objected to taking Jay's jeans and jersey on the jet.

K 11 Ken kept Kay's snack in a knapsack in the back of the kayak.
L 12 Lillian and Layne will fill the two small holes in the lane.
M 13 The minimum amount may make the mission impossible for many.

gwam 1' | 1 | 2 | 3 | 4 | 5 | 6 | 7 | 8 | 9 | 10 | 11 | 12 |

For additional practice:

MicroType 5
New Key Review,
Number & Symbol
Lesson 8

Job 8

Job 9

Job 10

Agenda

I. Greetings
II. Overview of past year
III. Seminars
    a. Enhancement
    b. Expansion
    c. Client base
IV. Leadership
V. Company growth
    a. Regional expansion
    b. International expansion
VI. Employee Incentives
    a. Branch managers
    b. Communication specialists
VII. Technology
VIII. Miscellaneous
IX. Adjournment

Attached is the agenda for the annual meeting. I didn't hear from any of you about additions to the agenda; so if you have items to discuss, we can include them under Miscellaneous.

Your accommodations have been made for the McIntyre Inn. Your confirmation is enclosed. A limousine will pick you up at the Inn at 8:30 a.m. on Monday. Activities have been planned for Monday and Wednesday evenings. Tuesday and Thursday mornings have been left open. You can arrange something on your own, or we can make group arrangements. We'll decide on Monday before adjourning for the day.

I'm looking forward to seeing you on the 26th.

HPJ Communication Specialists
Interview Schedule for **Jamal Carter**
June 29, 20--, Room 101

Time	Name of Interviewee
1:00 – 1:15	Joan Langston
1:20 – 1:35	Tim Wohlers
1:40 – 1:55	Mark Enqvist
2:00 – 2:15	Stewart Peters
2:20 – 2:35	Felipe Valdez
2:40 – 2:55	Katarina Dent
3:00 – 3:15	Jennifer Kent
3:20 – 3:35	Sandra Baylor

Speed Check: Sentences

1. Key a 30" writing on each line. Your rate in *gwam* is shown word-for-word below the lines.
2. Key another 30" writing on each line. Try to increase your keying speed.

1 Dr. Cox is running late today.
2 Ichiro baked Sandy a birthday cake.
3 Kellee will meet us here after the game.
4 Gordon will be leaving for college on Friday.
5 Juan and Jay finished the project late last night.
6 This is the first time that I have been to Los Angeles.

| gwam 30" | 2 | 4 | 6 | 8 | 10 | 12 | 14 | 16 | 18 | 20 | 22 | |

22D Skill Building

Speed Building: Guided Writing

1. Key one 1' unguided and two 1' guided timings on each ¶; determine *gwam*.
2. Key two 2' unguided timings on ¶s 1–2 combined; determine *gwam*.
3. Key one 3' unguided timing on ¶s 1–2 combined; determine *gwam*.

Quarter-Minute Checkpoints				
gwam	1/4'	1/2'	3/4'	Time
16	4	8	12	16
20	5	10	15	20
24	6	12	18	24
28	7	14	21	28
32	8	16	24	32
36	9	18	27	36
40	10	20	30	40

A all letters used (MicroPace) gwam 2' | 3'

	2'	3'
You must be an extra-special individual if you	5	3
are recognized throughout the world. Eleanor Roosevelt	10	7
was such a person. All through her life she took up	15	10
the cause of the less fortunate. Quite often you could	21	14
find her trying to help people out of work.	25	17
Women's issues, racial issues, and youth issues were	30	20
other causes that she spent an amazing amount of time	36	24
working on. Being the first lady gave her a platform	41	27
to further these causes. Serving on the United Nations	46	31
gave her the opportunity to continue to promote these	52	34
just causes on the world level.	55	37

| gwam 2' | 1 | 2 | 3 | 4 | 5 | 6 |
| 3' | | 1 | 2 | 3 | 4 | |

Job 5

SUBJECT: JOB DESCRIPTION FOR COMMUNICATION SPECIALISTS

I've attached a draft of the job description for the communication specialists that we will be hiring for each branch. I wanted to give each of you an opportunity to review it before we advertise for the positions in the newspaper.

If there are additional responsibilities that you would like to see included with the job description before we post it, please let me know by Friday. The advertisement will run in the Star on Sunday and appear on its Job Board website next week. I'm confident that we will have an even greater interest in the positions than we had when we hired a couple of communication specialists last January.

Job 6

New Seminar Descriptions

Seminar Title	Seminar Description	Cost per Person
Business Etiquette: You Cannot Not Communicate!		$99
Gender Communication: "He Says, She Says"		$75
International Communication		$75
Listen Up!		$99
Technology in the Workplace		$125

Job 7

Lesson 23   SKILL BUILDING

- To improve technique on individual letters.
- To improve keying speed on 1' and 2' writings.

23A

Conditioning Practice

Key each line twice.

alphabet	1	Wayne gave Zelda exact requirements for taking the pulp job.
fig/sym	2	Add tax of 5.5% to Sales Slip #86-03 for a total of $142.79.
easy	3	Rick may bicycle to the ancient city chapel by the big lake.

gwam 1' | 1 | 2 | 3 | 4 | 5 | 6 | 7 | 8 | 9 | 10 | 11 | 12 |

23B

Technique Mastery: Individual Letters

Key each line twice.

Technique Cue

- Limit keystroking movement to fingers; keep hands and arms motionless.

Emphasize continuity and rhythm with curved, upright fingers.

N	1	A new nanny can tend Hanna's nephew on Monday and Wednesday.
O	2	Two of the seven women opposed showing more shows on Monday.
P	3	Phil's playful puppy pulled the paper wrapping off the pear.
Q	4	Quincy quickly questioned the adequacy of the quirky quotes.
R	5	Our receiver tried to recover after arm surgery on Thursday.
S	6	Russ said it seems senseless to suggest this to his sisters.
T	7	Ty took title to two cottages the last time he went to town.
U	8	Uko usually rushes uptown to see us unload the sugar trucks.
V	9	Vivian voted to review the vivid videos when she visits Val.
W	10	Will waved wildly when a swimmer went wading into the water.
X	11	Six tax experts explained that Mary was exempt from the tax.
Y	12	Your younger boy yearns to see the Yankees play in New York.
Z	13	Zelda quizzed Zack on the zoology quiz in the sizzling heat.

gwam 1' | 1 | 2 | 3 | 4 | 5 | 6 | 7 | 8 | 9 | 10 | 11 | 12 |

23C

Skill Building

Key each line twice.

Space Bar

1 day son new map cop let kite just the quit year bay vote not
2 She may see me next week to talk about a party for the team.

Word response

3 me dye may bit pen pan cow sir doe form lamb lake busy their
4 The doorman kept the big bushel of corn for the eight girls.

Double letters

5 Neillsville berry dollar trees wheels sheep tomorrow village
6 All three of the village cottonwood trees had green ribbons.

gwam 1' | 1 | 2 | 3 | 4 | 5 | 6 | 7 | 8 | 9 | 10 | 11 | 12 |

For additional practice:

MicroType 5
New Key Review,
Number & Symbol
Lesson 9

Job 3

> **HPJ** From the Desk of
> **Helen St. Claire**
>
> I've started the attached
> letter from Ms. Parker
> to the branch managers.
> It is saved as DF HPJ JOB3.
> Please finish the letter. You
> will need to use your
> textbook to see how to for-
> mat the heading for the
> second page of a letter.
> Save each letter with the
> last name of the addressee,
> e.g., HPJ JOB3 CARTER.
>
> June 6   HSC

Technology. The changed marketplace is demanding that we explore new ways of delivering our seminars. How can we better use technology to deliver our product? This may include putting selected seminars online, inter- and intra-company communication, etc.

Company growth. What steps can we take to increase company growth? Last year revenues grew by 15 percent; our expenses grew by 8 percent.

Employee incentives. Last year we implemented a branch manager profit-sharing plan. Some of you have indicated that we need to expand this profit-sharing plan to include our communication specialists.

Regional expansion. Some of the regions have been very successful. How do we capitalize on that success? Is it time to divide the successful regions?

International expansion. **HPJ** has put on several seminars overseas--at a very high cost. Is it time to start thinking about creating a branch of **HPJ** at a strategic overseas location?

I am proud of what we have been able to accomplish this year. The foundation is in place, and we are ready to grow. Each of you plays a critical role in the success of **HPJ**. Thank you for your dedication and commitment to making our company the "leader in providing corporate and individual communication training." Best wishes for continued success. I'm looking forward to discussing **HPJ**'s future at this year's annual meeting. If you have additional items that you would like included on the agenda, please get them to me before June 15.

Job 4

> **HPJ** From the Desk of
> **Helen St. Claire**
>
> Format the attached Job
> Description. I've included
> some notes. In order to get
> the title on two lines, you
> need to key the entire title
> on one line and then go
> back and tap ENTER after
> Description.
>
> June 6   HSC

> 2" TM—Use 12 pt.
> Calibri for body

Job Description
HPJ Communication Specialist

HPJ Communication Specialists work cooperatively with other branch members to develop and deliver communication seminars throughout the United States.

Position Requirements
 a. College degree
 b. Excellent oral and written communication skills
 c. Excellent interpersonal skills
 d. Technology skills
 e. Knowledge of business concepts

Duties and Responsibilities
 a. Research seminar topics
 b. Develop seminars
 c. Prepare electronic presentations for seminars
 d. Prepare seminar manual
 e. Present seminars

Speed Check: Sentences

1. Key a 30" writing on each line.
2. If time allows, key an additional 30" on selected lines.

1 Tomas   left   just   before   supper.
2 When   will   you   be   able   to   return   it?
3 He   has   two   more   final   exams   to   complete.
4 Their   next   concert   will   be   held   in   September.
5 Jacob   and   Sarah   left   for   San   Francisco   on   Tuesday.
6 Orlando   wanted   to   see   the   last   home   game   of   the   season.

gwam 30" | 2 | 4 | 6 | 8 | 10 | 12 | 14 | 16 | 18 | 20 | 22 |

23E Skill Building

Speed Building

1. Key one 1' unguided and two 1' guided timings on each ¶.
2. Key two 2' unguided timings on ¶s 1–2 combined; determine *gwam*.

Quarter-Minute Checkpoints			
gwam	1/4'	1/2'	3/4'	Time
16	4	8	12	16
20	5	10	15	20
24	6	12	18	24
28	7	14	21	28
32	8	16	24	32
36	9	18	27	36
40	10	20	30	40

  all letters used   MicroPace   gwam 2'

Whether you are an intense lover of music or simply   5
enjoy hearing good music, you are more than likely aware of   11
the work completed by Beethoven, the German composer. He is   17
generally recognized as one of the greatest composers to ever   24
live.   Much of his early work was influenced by those who   29
wrote music in Austria, Haydn and Mozart.   33

   It can be argued whether Beethoven was a classical or   39
romantic composer.   This depends upon which period of time in   45
his life the music was written.   His exquisite music has ele-   51
ments of both.   It has been said that his early works brought   57
to a conclusion the classical age.   It has also been stated   63
that Beethoven's later work started the romantic age of music.   69

gwam 2' | 1 | 2 | 3 | 4 | 5 | 6 |

OBJECTIVES

- To use your decision-making skills to process documents.
- To improve your ability to read and follow directions.

76–80A

Conditioning Practice

Key each line twice.

alphabet 1 Seven complete textbooks were required for the new zoology major.

figures 2 Shipping charges ($35.98) were included on the invoice (#426087).

speed 3 A sick dog slept on the oak chair in the dismal hall of the dorm.

gwam 1' | 1 | 2 | 3 | 4 | 5 | 6 | 7 | 8 | 9 | 10 | 11 | 12 | 13 |

76–80B

Work Assignment

Job 1

HPJ From the Desk of
Helen St. Claire

You will be corresponding with the branch managers frequently. Create an HPJ Branch Managers contact folder and enter contact information for each of the branch managers as shown at the right. You will need to get the information for the other three managers from the company website.

June 5   HSC

Job 2

HPJ From the Desk of
Helen St. Claire

Ms. Parker wants the attached letter sent to each branch manager. Find mailing addresses from your contacts. Save each letter with the last name of the addressee, e.g., HPJ JOB2 CARTER.

June 5   HSC

Dear

Each of you has indicated a need for additional personnel. I've heard your requests. With this quarter's increase in seminar revenues, I am now in a position to respond to them. Five new communication specialist positions, one for each branch, have been added.

Since training for the positions takes place here at the home office, it is more cost effective to hire communication specialists from this area. I will take care of recruitment and preliminary screening. However, since each of you will work closely with the individual hired, I think you should make the final selection.

When you are here for the annual meeting, I'll schedule time for you to interview eight individuals. If you are not satisfied with any of the eight, we will arrange additional interviews. I should have a job description created within the next week. When it is completed, I'll send it to you for your review.

Office Features 2

For each activity, read and learn the feature described, then follow instructions at the left.

Activity 1

Margins

WP • Page Layout/Page Setup/Margins

1. Key the ¶s using the default margins.
2. Change the margins to the Wide margin option.
3. Change the left and right margins to 2.5" and the top margin to 2.0" using the Custom Margins option.

Save as: **OF2 ACTIVITY1**

Use the **Margins** feature to change the amount of blank space at the top, bottom, right, and left edges of the paper.

The default margin settings are not the same for all software.

Margins are the white space left between the edge of the paper and the print. When the right and left margins are increased, the length of the line of text will be decreased. When the top and bottom margins are increased, the number of lines of text that can be placed on a page will be decreased.

Of course, increasing or decreasing the size of the font also changes the amount of text that can appear on a page. Changing the font will also impact the amount of text that is placed on one page. You will understand this concept better when you complete the font activity below.

Activity 2

Line Spacing

WP • Home/Paragraph/Line Spacing

Change the line spacing to DS and key the four lines (include the numbers).

Save as: **OF2 ACTIVITY2**

Use the **Line Spacing** feature to change the amount of white space left between lines of text. Single spacing, one-and-a-half spacing, and double spacing are common to most software.

The default setting for *Word 2007* is 1.15. This allows a little more white space between lines of type than the previous version's default setting of 1.0. The new 1.15 default is treated as single spacing. Also note that there is a default of 10 points after each paragraph. This can be removed.

1. Click the I-beam where you want the line spacing changed.
2. Access the Line Spacing feature.
3. Specify the line spacing.
4. Begin or continue keying.

> When keying the numbers, key *<number> <period> <space> <space> <text>*.

Activity 3

Font

WP • Home/Font

Read each sentence then key it in the font, font size, and font color shown.

Save as: **OF2 ACTIVITY3**

The **Font** is the type, or letters, in which a document is printed. The size of the printed letters can be changed by changing the **Font Size** (measured in points). The font size can also be changed by using **Grow Font** to increase the font size or **Shrink Font** to decrease the font size. The default color of the font is black. Use the **Font Color** feature to change the color.

This is 11-point font size in Calibri font.

This is 11-point font size in Times New Roman font.

This is 14-point font in Lucida Handwriting.

This is 15-point font size in Comic Sans MS font.

This is 16-point font size in Calibri font.

Work Assignment

HPJ Communication Specialists prepares, organizes, and delivers communication training seminars. Three partners—Stewart **Herrick**, Natasha **P**arker, and Spencer **J**orstad—founded the company in 1991. In 1998, Ms. Parker bought out the other two partners. Today the company has five branches located in Dallas, Denver, Minneapolis, New York, and San Francisco.

Because of your skills with *Word, Outlook,* and *PowerPoint,* you have been hired by HPJ to work part-time for the administrative assistant, Helen St. Claire. Ms. St. Claire processes documents for the President and CEO, Natasha S. Parker, as well as for Erika Thomas, the Minneapolis branch manager.

During your training program, you were instructed to use the unbound format for reports and block format for all company letters. Ms. Parker likes all her letters closed as follows:

Sincerely

Natasha S. Parker
President & CEO

When a document has more than one enclosure, format the enclosure notation as follows:

Enclosures: Agenda
             Hotel Confirmation

General processing instructions will be attached to each document you are given to process. Use the date included on the instructions for all documents requiring a date.

As with a real job, you will be expected to learn on your own (using resources that are available to you) how to do some things that you haven't previously been taught.

You will also be expected to use your decision-making skills to arrange documents attractively whenever specific instructions are not provided. Since HPJ has based its word processing manual on the *Century 21* textbook, you can refer to this text in making formatting decisions and learning how to do things that you haven't been taught. In addition to your textbook, you can use the Help feature of your software to review a feature you may have forgotten or to learn new features you may need.

You are expected to produce error-free documents, so check spelling, proofread, and correct your work carefully before presenting it for approval.

Contacts File

Use the Contacts feature of *Outlook* to create an HPJ Branch Managers contact folder with information for each of the branch managers.

HPJ Files and Website

Some jobs will require you to use documents stored in HPJ company files. Some documents will require you to gather information from the company's website at www.cengage.com/school/keyboarding/hpj. All files you create should be named with *HPJ*, followed by the job number (*HPJ JOB1, HPJ JOB2,* etc.).

HPJ Website

HPJ Headquarters

Activity 4

Hyphenation

 WP • Page Layout/Page Setup/Hyphenation

1. Key the ¶ in Courier New 12 pt. with hyphenation off.
2. Turn on the Automatic Hyphenation feature.
3. Change the margin setting to Wide.
4. Change the right and left margins to 2.5".

Save as: **OF2 ACTIVITY4**

The **Hyphenation** feature automatically divides (hyphenates) words that would normally wrap to the next line. This evens the right margin, making the text more attractive.

Use the **Hyphenation** feature to give text a professional appearance. When the **Hyphenation** feature is activated, the software divides long words between syllables at the end of lines. Using hyphenation makes the right margin less ragged. This feature is particularly helpful when keying in narrow columns.

Activity 5

Spelling and Grammar Check

 WP • Review/Proofing/Spelling & Grammar

1. Key the ¶ *exactly* as shown. Some errors are automatically corrected.
2. Use the Spelling and Grammar check to identify errors. Correct all errors.
3. Proofread to find errors not caught.

Save as: **OF2 ACTIVITY5**

Use the **Spelling and Grammar Check** to check for misspellings and grammar errors. The Spelling Check feature compares each word in the document to words in its dictionary (or dictionaries). If a word in a document is not identical to one in its dictionary, the word is flagged by a wavy red underline. Usually the Spelling Check lists words it *thinks* are likely corrections (replacements).

The Grammar Check feature flags potential grammar errors with a wavy green underline. The Grammar Check also lists words it thinks will correct the grammar error.

Note: The Grammar Check may or may not catch incorrect word usage (*too* for *to* or *two*). Even when using these features, it is important to proofread your documents.

Dr. Smith met with the students on Friday to reviiw for for there test. He told the students that their would be three sections to the test. The first secction would be multiplee choice, the second sction would be true/fals, and the last section would be shoot answer. He also said, "If you have spelling errors on you paper, you will have pionts deducted.

Activity 6

Print

WP • Office Button/Print

1. Open *OF2 ACTIVITY4* and preview the document using Print Preview.
2. Close Print Preview and open the Print dialog box to see the options.
3. Cancel the Print dialog box and use Quick Print to print the document. Close the document.

The **Print** feature under the Microsoft Office Button offers three options:

• The **Print** option opens the Print dialog box, where you select the printer, indicate which page(s) and the number of copies to be printed, etc.

• The **Quick Print** option sends the document directly to the default printer.

• The **Print Preview** option allows you to preview the document and make changes before printing it.

Activity 9

Table

Format the table at the right. Center the table horizontally and vertically. Key the main heading in 16-pt. font and the secondary headings in 13-pt. font. Make the main heading row height .5" and the rest of the rows .3"

Save as: CA2 ACTIVITY9

Major United States Rivers

River	Length	
	Miles	Kilometers
Arkansas	1,459	2,348
Colorado	1,450	2,333
Columbia	1,243	2,000
Mississippi	2,348	3,779
Missouri	2,315	3,726
Red	1,290	2,080
Rio Grande	1,900	3,060
Snake	1,038	1,670
Yukon	1,979	3,185

Source: *Time Almanac 2004*, pp. 500–501.

Activity 10

Table

Format the table at the right. Adjust column widths and heights to attractively arrange the text on the page. In cells, use bottom vertical alignment and the horizontal alignment shown. Apply shading in the *Dem.* and *Rep.* columns. Center the table horizontally and vertically.

Save as: CA2 ACTIVITY10

Note: Since 2000, many additional female governors have been elected.

United States Female Governors
1925–2000

Name		Party Affiliation		State	Years Served
Last	First	Dem.	Rep.		
Collins	Martha	X		Kentucky	1984–1987
Ferguson	Miriam	X		Texas	1925–1927 1933–1935
Finney	Joan	X		Kansas	1991–1995
Grasso	Ella	X		Connecticut	1975–1980
Hollister	Nancy		X	Ohio	1998–1999
Hull	Jane		X	Arizona	1997–2003
Kunin	Madeleine	X		Vermont	1985–1991
Mofford	Rose	X		Arizona	1988–1991
Orr	Kay		X	Nebraska	1987–1991
Ray	Dixy Lee	X		Washington	1977–1981
Richards	Ann	X		Texas	1991–1995
Roberts	Barbara	X		Oregon	1991–1995
Ross	Nellie	X		Wyoming	1925–1927
Shaheen	Jeanne	X		New Hampshire	1997–2003
Wallace	Lurleen	X		Alabama	1967–1968
Whitman	Christine		X	New Jersey	1994–2001

Source: http://www.cawp.rutgers.edu/Facts/Officeholders/govhistory.pdf, February 11, 2008.

Activities 7 & 8

Horizontal Alignment: Left, Center, Right, Justify

WP • Home/Paragraph/Select alignment type

1. Key the lines at the right. Right-align the page number, center-align the title, and left-align the last two lines.

Save as: OF2 ACTIVITY7

2. Open *OF2 ACTIVITY4* and justify the text.

Save as: OF2 ACTIVITY8

Horizontal alignment refers to the position of a line of text on the page. Use **left** alignment to start text at the left margin. Use **right** alignment to start text at the right margin.

Use **center** alignment to center lines of text between the left and right margins. Use **justify** alignment to align text to both the right and left margin.

Page 13

THE FINAL ACT

Just before dawn the policeman arrived at the home of Ms. Kennington.

All the lights were shining brightly . . .

Activity 9

Tabs

WP • View Ruler

1. Set a left tab at 1", a right tab at 3", and a decimal tab at 4.5".
2. Key the first four lines using these tab settings. TS after keying the fourth line.
3. Reset tabs: left tab at 1.5", right tab at 4.0", decimal tab at 5.5"; key the last four lines.

Save as: OF2 ACTIVITY9

 Left tab

 Right tab

Decimal tab

Most software has left tabs already set at half-inch (0.5") intervals from the left margin. However, tabs can be set at intervals you determine.

When you set a tab, the preset tabs are automatically cleared up to the point where you set the tab. Most software lets you set **left tabs, right tabs,** and **decimal tabs**.

Left tabs
Left tabs align all text evenly at the left by placing the text you key to the right of the tab setting. Left tabs are commonly used to align words.

Right tabs
Right tabs align all text evenly at the right by placing the text you key to the left of the tab setting. Right tabs are commonly used to align whole numbers.

Decimal tabs
Decimal tabs align all text at the decimal point or other character that you specify. If you key numbers in a column at a decimal tab, the decimal points will line up, regardless of the number of places before or after the decimal point.

Left tab at 1" ↓	Right tab at 3" ↓	Decimal tab at 4.5" ↓
(TAB) James Hill (TAB)	6,750 (TAB)	88.395 (ENTER)
(TAB) Mark Johnson (TAB)	863 (TAB)	1.38 (ENTER)
Sue Chen	30	115.31
Seth Ramirez	1,397	24.6580

Left tab at 1.5" ↓	Right tab at 4.0" ↓	Decimal tab at 5.5" ↓
Juan Ortiz	142,250	0.25
Marsha Black	3,219	13.6
Kay Kent	56,873	297.312
Kay Ichiro	571,490	32.68

Interestingly enough, most of Edison's learning ~took~ place at home under the guidance of his mother. "Nancy Edison's secret: she was more dedicated than any teacher was likely to be, and she had the flexibility to experiment with various ways of nurturing her son's live for learning."²

Benjamin Franklin

Benjamin Franklin was a man of many talents. He was an inventor, printer, diplomat, philosopher, author, postmaster, and leader. A few of his more noteworthy accomplishments included serving on the committee that created the Declaration of Independence; *publishing* Poor Richard's Almanac; and *inventing* the lightning rod, the Franklin stove, the odometer, and bifocal glasses.

Abraham Lincoln

For many Americans the impact of Abraham Lincoln is as great today as it was during his life time.

> Abraham Lincoln is remembered for his vital role as the leader in preserving the Union and beginning the process that led to the end of slavery in the United States. He is also remembered for his character, his speeches and letters, and as a man of humble origins whose determination and perseverance led him to the nation's highest office.³

DS Lincoln is a great example of one who dealt positively with adversity in his personal and professional life. His contributions towards the shaping of America will be long remembered.

Activity 7

References Page

Format a references page from the information shown at the right.

Save as: CA2 ACTIVITY7

Activity 8

Title Page

Format a title page for the report.

Save as: CA2 ACTIVITY8

"An Overview of Abraham Lincoln's Life." March 30, 2004. http://home.att.net/~rjnorton/Lincoln77.html.

Clinton, Susan. The Story of Susan B. Anthony. Chicago: Children's Press, 1986.

Powell, Jim. "The Education of Thomas Edison." April 25, 2000. http://www.self-gov.org/freeman/9502powe.htm.

Activity 10

Text Wrapping Break

1. Key the text in the first box, tapping ENTER at the end of each line.
2. QS and key the text in the second box, holding down the Shift key and tapping ENTER as instructed.
3. Compare the difference.

Save as: OF2 ACTIVITY10

The default settings leave space after a paragraph each time the ENTER key is tapped.

Mr. Ricardo Seanez (Tap ENTER)

1538 Village Square (Tap ENTER)

Altoona, WI 54720 (Tap ENTER)

Dear Ricardo (Tap ENTER)

I will be arriving in Altoona on July 15 for the next meeting.

The space can be removed by using the Text Wrapping Break feature (hold down the Shift key and tap the ENTER key).

Mr. Ricardo Seanez (Hold Shift; Tap ENTER)

1538 Village Square (Hold Shift; Tap ENTER)

Altoona, WI 54720 (Tap ENTER)

Dear Ricardo (Tap ENTER)

I will be arriving in Altoona on July 15 for the next meeting.

Activity 11

Envelope

WP • Mailings/Create/Envelopes

Use the Envelopes feature to format a small envelope (No. 6 3/4) for Envelope 1 and a large envelope (No. 10) for Envelope 2.

Save as: OF2 ACTIVITY11-1 and OF2 ACTIVITY11-2

Use the **Envelopes** feature to format envelopes for the documents you create. This feature allows you to select the size of the envelope, enter the **return address** and the **delivery address**, and print the envelope.

The delivery address can be keyed, inserted automatically from the letter file, or inserted from your Address Book.

Electronic postage software can be used with this feature.

Return address:

Envelope 1

Carson Sanchez
270 Rancho Bauer Drive
Houston, TX 77079-3703

Envelope 2

Victoria Westmont
499 Tulpehocken Avenue
Philadelphia, PA 19117-6741

Delivery address:

Ms. Susan Keane
872 Mayflower Drive
Terre Haute, IN 47803-1199

Mr. Jacob Saunders
396 Hickory Hill Lane
Kalamazoo, MI 49009-0012

Activity 12

Apply What You Have Learned

1. Set top margin at 2.5"; side margins at 2.7".
2. Change the ¶ font to 12 pt. Arial Narrow, black. Change the line spacing to 1.0; remove the space after paragraph.
3. Justify the paragraph alignment. Leave one blank line before and after the list of books.
4. Use Print Preview, then print the document.

Save as: OF2 ACTIVITY12

Center the heading; use Lucida Handwriting, 14 pt., blue, for the font. →

Leave one blank line between the heading and the text. →

Put the titles of the books in italic and bold, using the colors shown. Center-align each book entry. Use 1.5 line spacing for the book listings.

CHILDREN'S BOOKS

There are several older books that have been added to this year's children's book list. With all the new books being written, we often forget about these older books. The books added include:

Little Women by Louisa May Alcott

A Christmas Carol by Charles Dickens

The Jungle Book by Rudyard Kipling

The Adventures of Tom Sawyer by Mark Twain

The Last of the Mohicans by James F. Cooper

Please be sure to present these new additions to our book list at the in-service meeting scheduled for August 29.

Report

Format the text at the right as a bound report with footnotes. Use **Four Outstanding Americans** for the title.

Footnotes

[1]**Susan Clinton,** The Story of Susan B. Anthony **(Chicago: Children's Press, 1986), p. 5.**

[2]**Jim Powell, "The Education of Thomas Edison,"** http://www.self-gov.org/freeman/9502powe.htm, **April 25, 2000.**

[3]**"An Overview of Abraham Lincoln's Life,"** http://home.att.net/~rjnorton/Lincoln77.html, **March 30, 2004.**

Save as: CA2 ACTIVITY6

Many outstanding Americans have influenced the past, and many more will impact the future. Choosing the "Four Greatest Americans" does injustice to the hundreds of others who left their mark on our country and diminishes their contributions. This report simply recognizes four great Americans who helped make America what it is today.

Without these four individuals, America perhaps would be quite different from the country we know. The four individuals included in this report are: Susan B. Anthony, Thomas A. Edison, Benjamin Franklin, and Abraham Lincoln.

Susan B. Anthony

Susan B. Anthony is noted for her advancement of women's rights. She and Elizabeth Cady Stanton organized the national woman suffrage association. The following quotation shows her commitment to the cause.

> At 7 a.m. on November 5, 1872, Susan B. Anthony broke the law by doing something she had never done before. After twenty years of working to win the vote for women, she marched to the polls in Rochester, New York, and voted. Her vote—for Ulysses S. Grant for president—was illegal. In New York state, only men were allowed to vote.[1]

Anthony continued to fight for women's rights, however, for the next 33 years of her life. Even though she died in 1906 and the amendment granting women the right to vote (nineteenth amendment) was not passed until 1920, that amendment is often called the Susan B. Anthony Amendment in honor of Anthony's efforts to advance women's rights.

Thomas Alva Edison

Imagine life without the incandescent light bulb, phonograph, kinetoscope (a small box for viewing moving films), or any of the other 1,090 inventions patented by Edison. Life certainly would be different without these inventions or later inventions that came as a result of Edison's work.

Format Guides: Interoffice Memo

Memos (interoffice memorandums) are written messages used by employees within an organization to communicate with one another. A standard format (arrangement) for memos is presented below and illustrated on p. 61.

Memo heading. The memo heading includes who the memo is being sent to (**TO**), who the memo is from (**FROM:**), the date the memo is being sent (**DATE**), and what the memo is about (**SUBJECT**). Use ALL CAPS for the headings beginning at the left margin, and space as shown below. Use initial caps for subject line.

Note: It is also acceptable to use ALL CAPS for the subject line.

TO: Tab twice to key name. SS
FROM: Tab twice to key name. SS
DATE: Tab twice to key date. SS
SUBJECT: Tab once to key subject. SS

Memo body. The paragraphs of the memo all begin at the left margin and are SS with a SS between paragraphs.

Reference initials. If someone other than the originator of the memo keys it, his/her initials are keyed in lowercase letters at the left margin, a SS below the body.

Attachment/Enclosure notations. If another document is attached to a memo, the word *Attachment* is keyed at the left margin a SS below the reference initials (or below the last line of the body if reference initials are not used). If a document accompanies the memo but is not attached to it, key the word *Enclosure*.

Memo and Letter Margins	
Top margin (TM)	2"
Side margins (SM)	1" or default
Bottom Margin (BM)	At least 1"

Personal-Business Letter, Block Style

A letter written by an individual to deal with business of a personal nature is called a personal-business letter. Block format (see p. 66) is commonly used for formatting personal-business letters. All parts of a letter arranged in block format begin at the left margin. The paragraphs are not indented. The basic parts of the personal-business letter are described below in order of placement.

Return address. The return address (start at 2" from top edge) consists of a line for the street address and one for the city, state, and ZIP Code.

Date. Key the month, day, and year on the line below the city, state, and ZIP Code.

Letter mailing address. Key the first line of the letter mailing (delivery) address a DS below the date. A personal title (Miss, Mr., Mrs., Ms.) or a professional title (Dr., Lt., Senator) is keyed before the receiver's name.

Salutation. Key the salutation a SS below the mailing address.

Body. Begin the letter body (message) a SS below the salutation. SS and block the paragraphs with a SS between them.

Complimentary close. Key the complimentary close a SS below the last line of the body.

Name of the writer. Key the name of the writer a DS below the complimentary close. The name may be preceded by a personal title (Miss, Mrs., Ms.) to indicate how a female prefers to be addressed in a response. If a male has a name that does not clearly indicate his gender (Kim, Leslie, Pat), the title Mr. may precede his name.

Attachment/Enclosure notation. If another document is attached to a letter, the word *Attachment* is keyed at the left margin, a SS below the writer's name. If the additional document is not attached, the word *Enclosure* is used.

Note: The above instructions are based on *Word 2007* default settings. For instructions for the traditional style based on *Word 2003* default settings, see the model document on p. 67.

Activity 4

E-mail

Send the text at the right as an e-mail to your instructor. Send a Bcc notation to yourself and request a delivery receipt. Use **ANSWER TO YOUR QUESTION** for the subject line.

Save as: **CA2 ACTIVITY4**

Your question is a good one. Yes, Nellie Tayloe Ross of Wyoming and Miriam (Ma) Ferguson of Texas were elected on the same day, November 4, 1924. However, Ms. Ross took office 16 days before Ms. Ferguson; therefore, Ms. Ross is considered the first woman governor in the United States, and Ms. Ferguson is considered the second. It should also be noted that Ms. Ross completed her husband's term as governor of Wyoming prior to being elected in 1924.

If you have other questions before the exam on Friday, please let me know. I hope you do well on it.

Activity 5

Electronic Presentations

Create the slides as shown at the right. Use the Foundry design theme with Paper colors.

Slide 1: The picture is in data file *DF CA2 ACTIVITY5*.

Use SmartArt to create slides 2–4.

Slide 2: Vertical Box List—adjust to fit text.

Slide 3: Trapezoid List

Slide 4: Vertical Chevron List

Slide 5: Basic Block List—add two shapes to get the seven blocks.

Apply transitions of your choice between slides. Apply custom animation of your choice so that each shape on the slide comes in *one by one* using *very fast* speed for slides 2–5.

Save as: **CA2 ACTIVITY5**

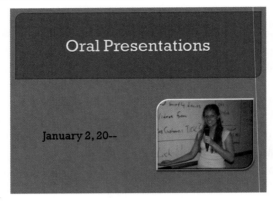

Slide 1

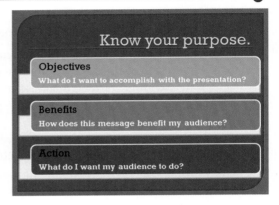

Slide 2

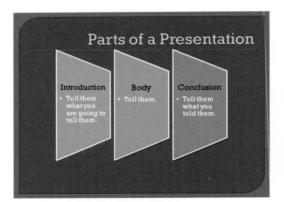

Slide 3

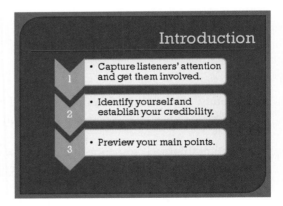

Slide 4

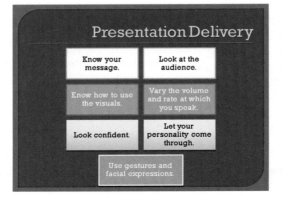

Slide 5

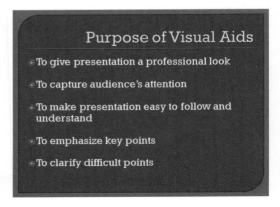

Slide 6

OBJECTIVES

- To learn to format interoffice memos.
- To process memos from arranged and semi-arranged copy.

24A

Conditioning Practice
Key each line twice.

alphabet 1 Zack Gappow saved the job requirement list for the six boys.

figures 2 Jay Par's address is 3856 Ash Place, Houston, TX 77007-2491.

easy 3 I may visit the big chapel in the dismal town on the island.

gwam 1' | 1 | 2 | 3 | 4 | 5 | 6 | 7 | 8 | 9 | 10 | 11 | 12 |

At 2" (3 returns down)

TO: Maria Gutierrez, Secretary ↓1

FROM: Jackson Phipps, President ↓1

DATE: *Current Date* ↓1

SUBJECT: Next FBLA Meeting ↓1

Our next Future Business Leaders of America meeting is scheduled for this Friday at 6:30 p.m. in SSS 400F. Please put up the posters to remind members. ↓1

Default or 1" SM

Based on the attendance at the last meeting, you should have 45 copies of the attached agenda and the minutes to distribute. We will be going over five more competitive event descriptions at the meeting. You can make copies of the descriptions from the FBLA-PBL National Site (www.fbla.org). The events that we will be covering at this meeting are: ↓1

Future Business Leaders
Entrepreneurship
Electronic Career Portfolio
Word Processing 1
Business Communication ↓1

> Hold down the Shift key when you return after the first four items in this list to avoid extra space between lines.

Thank you again for all the time and effort you devote to our organization. You set a great example for other FBLA members at Jefferson High School to follow. ↓1

xx ↓1 *Initials in lower case*

Attachment

> Shown in 11-point Calibri with 2" top margin and 1" side margins, this memo appears smaller than actual size.

Interoffice Memo

Activity 2

Memo

Format the text at the right as a memo to **Kathleen Maloney** from **Miguel Gonzalez**. Date the memo **May 5, 20--**; use **Budget Request** for the subject line. Send a copy of the memo to **Sarah Cambridge** and **Ricardo Castello**.

Save as: **CA2 ACTIVITY2**

As I searched the Internet for teaching resources, I came across some audiocassettes that would be an excellent addition to my World History course. The audiocassette collection, *The World's 100 Greatest People*, currently sells for $295, plus sales tax and shipping and handling charges of $9.95.

According to the advertisement (http://www.4iq.com/iquest16.html), "The 50 tapes included in this collection represent an audio treasury of 100 biographies detailing the life, time, achievement, and impact of some of history's greatest personalities, including philosophers, explorers, inventors, scientists, writers, artists, composers, and religious, political, and military leaders." These tapes could be used in many classes outside the Social Studies Department. Perhaps some of the other departments would be willing to share the cost of the tapes.

When you have a few minutes, I would like to discuss how we should proceed to get these tapes in time for next year.

Activity 3

Letter

Format the text at the right as a letter. Leave 1.5" TM.

Save as: **CA2 ACTIVITY3**

March 3, 20-- | Mr. Michael Kent, President | Quote of the Month Club | 97 Liberty Square | Boston, MA 02109-3625 | Dear Michael

Arrangements for our April **Quote of the Month Club** meeting are progressing nicely. The meeting will be held at the Pilgrims' Inn in Plymouth on Saturday, the 15th.

Members didn't like the format of our last meeting, so I'm proposing this plan: Each person attending will be assigned to a team, and each team will be given four quotes. The team will select one quote and prepare a five-minute presentation explaining the meaning of the quote (their opinion). Each team will select a member to present to the entire group. These are the four quotations I selected:

Person	Quote
Walter Elias Disney	☐ "Our greatest natural resource is the mind of our children."
Ayn Rand	☐ "Throughout the centuries there were men who took first steps down new roads armed with nothing but their own vision."
Wendell Lewis Willkie	☐ "Our way of living together in America is a strong but delicate fabric. It is made up of many threads. It has been woven over many centuries by the patience and sacrifice of countless liberty-loving men and women."
Althea Gibson	☐ "No matter what accomplishments you make, somebody helps you."

These topics provide for excellent discussions leading up to the presentations. When you send the meeting notice, please send the quotes to give members time to think about them prior to the meeting.

Sincerely | Patricia Fermanich | xx | Enclosures

Memos

Study the format guides on p. 60 and the memo format illustration on p. 61. Note the vertical and horizontal placement of memo parts and the spacing between them.

Memo 1

1. Key the model memo on p. 61.
2. Proofread your copy; correct all keying and formatting errors.

Save as: **24B MEM01**

Memo 2

1. Format and key the information at the right as a memo.
2. The memo goes to the Foreign Language Department Students and is from Travel Abroad Coordinator Mary Seville. Date the memo November 2, 20--; supply an appropriate subject line.
3. Use the Speller; proofread and correct all errors.

Save as: **24B MEMO2**

Note: Each time the year is indicated with *20--*, replace it with the current year.

Memo 3

1. Format and key the text at the right in memo format. Use your initials as the keyboard operator (reference initials).
2. Proofread your copy; correct all errors.

Save as: **24B MEMO3**

Are you ready for a summer you will never forget? Then you will want to sign up for this year's Travel Abroad Program. You will travel to the country that famous writers like Virgil, Horace, and Dante called home. The music of Vivaldi, Verdi, and Puccini will come to life. You will visit art museums exhibiting the art of native sons such as Michelangelo Buonarotti and Giovanni Bellini.

By now you have probably guessed that we will be taking a trip to Italy this summer. Touring **Rome, Florence, Venice,** *and* **Naples** *gives you the opportunity to experience firsthand the people, the culture, the history, and the cuisine of Italy.*

If you are interested in learning more about traveling to Italy this summer, attend our open house on <u>November 15</u> *at* <u>3:30</u> *in Room 314.*

TO: Foreign Language Teachers

FROM: Mary Seville, Travel Abroad Coordinator

DATE: November 2, 20--

SUBJECT: OPEN HOUSE

I've enclosed copies of a memo announcing the open house for the Travel Abroad Program. Please distribute the copies to students in your classes.

Last year we had 25 students participate in the trip to England. If you have had the opportunity to talk with them about this experience, you know that the trip was very worthwhile and gave them memories that will last a lifetime. I am confident that the trip to Italy will be just as rewarding to those who participate. As you know, the experiences students gain from traveling abroad cannot be replicated in the classroom.

I appreciate your support of the program and your help in promoting it with your students.

xx

Enclosure

CYCLE 2
Assessment

OBJECTIVE

• To assess Cycle 2 document processing, computer application, and straight-copy skills.

Conditioning Practice

Key each line twice.

alphabet	1	Bugs quickly explained why five of the zoo projects cost so much.
figures	2	Jo's office phone number is 632-0781; her home phone is 832-4859.
speed	3	Pamela may go with us to the city to do the work for the auditor.

gwam 1' | 1 | 2 | 3 | 4 | 5 | 6 | 7 | 8 | 9 | 10 | 11 | 12 | 13 |

Activity 1

Check Keying Skill

Key two 3' timings on ¶s 1–3 combined; determine *gwam* and errors.

A all letters used (MicroPace)

gwam 2' | 3'

The City of Philadelphia is where the roots of 5 | 3
this nation were founded. Independence Hall, which 10 | 7
is located in the center of the city, is often 14 | 10
referred to as the place where the nation was born. 20 | 13
It was here that they met to discuss and agree upon 25 | 16
the Declaration of Independence and the United 30 | 20
States Constitution. It was here that Ben Franklin 35 | 23
said, "If we don't hang together, we shall assuredly 40 | 27
hang separately!" 41 | 27

An easily recognized symbol of our freedom, the 46 | 31
Liberty Bell, can also be seen in the city which is 51 | 34
often called "The City of Brotherly Love." Another 56 | 37
distinction of the city is that it was the first 61 | 41
capital of our new nation. The building where the 66 | 44
Senate and the House met is located right next to 71 | 47
Independence Hall. People can enjoy these and other 76 | 51
exquisite landmarks by spending time in the city. 81 | 54

gwam 2' | 1 | 2 | 3 | 4 | 5 | 6 |
3' | 1 | 2 | 3 | 4 |

OBJECTIVES

- To check knowledge of e-mail and memo formats.
- To check the level of memo processing skills.

25A

Conditioning Practice

Key each line twice.

alphabet	1	Bobby Klun awarded Jayme sixth place for her very high quiz.
figures	2	I had 50 percent of the responses (3,923 of 7,846) by May 1.
easy	3	The haughty man was kept busy with a problem with the docks.

gwam 1' | 1 | 2 | 3 | 4 | 5 | 6 | 7 | 8 | 9 | 10 | 11 | 12 |

25B   Formatting

Memo Processing

Memo 1

1. Format and key the memo at the right. Use your initials as the keyboard operator.
2. Use the Speller; proofread and correct all errors.

Save as: 25B MEMO1

Note: Use italic instead of underline for the play titles.

TO: Drama Students

FROM: Ms. Fairbanks

DATE: November 1, 20--

SUBJECT: Selection of Spring Play

There are three plays that I would like you to consider for next semester's performance. They include:

The Importance of Being Earnest, a comedy written by Oscar Wilde. In the play, Jack Worthing has a complicated courtship with Lady Bracknell's daughter, Gwendolen. His ward, Cecily, has fallen in love with his friend Algernon.

A Delicate Balance, a comedy written by Edward Albee. The play is a funny look at love, compassion, and the bonds of friendship and family.

A Comedy of Errors, a comedy written by William Shakespeare. The play is about mistaken identities of twins.

I have placed copies of the plays on reserve in the library. Please look them over by November 25 so that we can discuss them in class that day. We will need to make a decision before December 1 so that I can order the playbooks.

Format the table at the right. Use the table formatting features you have learned to arrange the information attractively on the page. Include the following source note:

Source: *Fodor's 2000, San Francisco,* and *Fodor's 2000, USA.*

Save as: **CR2 ACTIVITY9**

Places to Explore in San Francisco

Places to Explore	Description	Major Attractions
Union Square	Heart of San Francisco's downtown, major shopping district	❑ Westin St. Francis Hotel ❑ Old San Francisco Mint
Chinatown	Home to one of the largest Chinese communities outside Asia	❑ Chinese Culture Center ❑ Old Chinese Telephone Exchange
Nob Hill	Home of the city's elite and some of its finest hotels	❑ Cable Car Museum ❑ Grace Cathedral ❑ Mark Hopkins Hotel
Civic Center	One of the country's great city, state, and federal building complexes	❑ City Hall ❑ Performing Arts Center ❑ War Memorial Opera House
The Embarcadero	Waterfront promenade great for walking and jogging	❑ Ferry Building ❑ Embarcadero Center ❑ Justin Herman Plaza
Fisherman's Wharf	Hyde cable-car line, waterfront, Ghirardelli Square, Piers 39 and 41	❑ Lombard Street ❑ National Maritime Museum ❑ Museum of the City of San Francisco
Financial District	Cluster of steel-and-glass high-rises and older, more decorative architectural monuments to commerce	❑ Transamerica Pyramid ❑ Bank of America ❑ Pacific Stock Exchange ❑ Stock Exchange Tower

Activity 10

Format the table at the right. Center the table horizontally and vertically. Use a row height of 0.4" for the heading and 0.3" for the body rows.

After you complete the table, shade in red the state where the attraction is located. For example, Arizona is shaded because Hoover Dam is located there.

Save as: **CR2 ACTIVITY10**

Activity 11

Skill Check

1. Key a 1' timing on each ¶ of Activity 7, p. 221; determine *gwam* and errors.
2. Take a 3' timing on ¶s 1–3 of Activity 8, p. 225; determine *gwam* and errors.

Name That State!

Attractions	A	B	C
Hoover Dam	Arizona	California	Colorado
Niagara Falls	Massachusetts	New York	Pennsylvania
Independence Hall	Pennsylvania	Virginia	Washington
Alamo	Arizona	New Mexico	Texas
Zion National Park	Nevada	California	Utah
Jamestown	North Carolina	South Carolina	Virginia
Harvard University	Massachusetts	New Jersey	New York
Mt. Rushmore	Montana	South Dakota	Wyoming
Kennedy Space Center	Florida	Ohio	Texas

Memo 2

1. Format and key the memo at the right.
2. Use the Speller; proofread and correct all errors.

Save as: 25B MEMO2

TO: Office Staff

FROM: Jennifer Green, General Manager

DATE: March 15, 20--

SUBJECT: New Box Office Coordinator

Rebecca Dunwoody has been hired to replace DeWayne Hughes as our box office coordinator. DeWayne has decided to return to school to start work on a Master of Business Administration degree. As you are aware, DeWayne has been a valuable asset to our organization for the past five years.

It was not easy finding a person with similar qualifications to replace DeWayne. His enthusiasm and love of music, combined with a degree in music as well as a minor in business administration, made filling the job particularly difficult. However, we believe we were successful when we were able to hire Ms. Dunwoody. She is a recent graduate of NYC's music program. While completing her degree, she worked as an assistant for the business manager of one of our competitors.

Please extend your appreciation and best wishes to DeWayne before he leaves on March 30 and welcome Rebecca when she arrives on March 25.

Memo 3

1. Format and key the text at the right in memo format. Use your initials as the keyboard operator.
2. Proofread your copy; correct all errors.

Save as: 25B MEMO3

TO: Foreign Language Faculty

FROM: Karla A. Washburn

DATE: December 1, 20--

SUBJECT: Travel Abroad Coordinator

As you may have heard by now, Mary Seville announced her plans to retire at the end of next summer. In addition to hiring a new French teacher, we will need to replace Mary as our Travel Abroad Coordinator. This will be a very difficult task; Mary has done an excellent job.

If you are interested in this position, please let me know before you leave for the winter break. I would like to fill the position early next semester. This will allow the new coordinator to work with Mary as she plans this year's trip. The new coordinator would be expected to travel with Mary and the students to Italy this summer.

We also need to start thinking about a retirement party for Mary. If you are interested in being on a retirement party committee, please let me know.

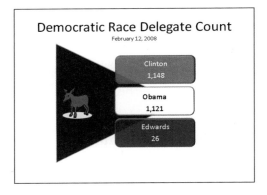

Slide 3

Slide 4

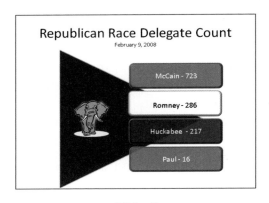

Slide 5

Slide 6

Activity 8

Skill Check

1. Key a 1' timing on each ¶; determine *gwam* and number of errors.

2. Take a 3' timing on ¶s 1–2 combined; determine *gwam* and number of errors.

A all letters used (MicroPace) gwam | 3'

Each President since George Washington has had a — 4

cabinet. The cabinet is a group of men and women selected — 8

by the President. The senate must approve them. It is the — 12

exception rather than the rule for the President's choice — 15

to be rejected by this branch of the government. In — 19

keeping with tradition, most of the cabinet members belong — 23

to the same political party as the President. — 26

The purpose of the cabinet is to provide advice to the — 30

President on matters pertaining to the job of President. — 34

The person holding the office, of course, may or may not — 38

follow the advice. Some Presidents have frequently — 41

utilized their cabinet. Others have used it little or not — 45

at all. For example, President Wilson held no cabinet — 49

meetings at all during World War I. — 51

Lesson 26 PERSONAL-BUSINESS LETTERS

OBJECTIVES
- To learn to format personal-business letters in block format.
- To improve word choice skills.

26A

Conditioning Practice

Key each line twice.

alphabet 1 Jackie will budget for the most expensive zoology equipment.

figures 2 The rate on May 14 was 12.57 percent; it was 8.96 on May 30.

easy 3 The official paid the men for the work they did on the dock.

gwam 1' | 1 | 2 | 3 | 4 | 5 | 6 | 7 | 8 | 9 | 10 | 11 | 12 |

26B Formatting

Personal-Business Letters in Block Format

Letter 1

Study the format guides on p. 60 and the model personal-business letter on p. 66. Note the placement of letter parts and spacing between them.

Format/key the model on p. 66.
Proofread and correct errors.

Save as: **26B LETTER1**

Letter 2

Format/key Letter 2 shown at the right. Refer to the model on p. 66 as needed. Proofread and correct errors.

Save as: **26B LETTER2**

Letter 3 (Optional Activity)

Format/key the model letter on p. 67 in the traditional letter style using the *Office Word 2003* Look Installed Template.

Save as: **26B LETTER3**

2674 Edworthy Road
Dallas, TX 77429-6675
April 15, 20--

Ms. Addilynn Morgan
671 Meadowbank Avenue
Boston, MA 02126-6720

Dear Ms. Morgan

This year's Business Leadership Conference will be held in Dallas on December 8-9. With ethical behavior becoming more and more of an issue in today's society, the main focus of the conference will be on the importance of developing ethical business leaders.

When I was in Boston for another conference earlier this spring, I heard you speak on this topic. I believe you would be the perfect keynote speaker for our conference. Specifically, we would like you to focus your remarks on dealing with others in a fair and honest manner at all times and under all circumstances—not just when it is a matter of convenience. The title of your session would be ***Enhancing Your Company Image through Strong Ethical Leaders.***

We are offering an honorarium of $1,000 and will cover your travel expenses. Please let us know of your availability on the 8th of December. You can reach me at 972-372-8811 if you have questions about this speaking engagement.

We are looking forward to having you share your expertise with our conference participants.

Sincerely

Bella K. Jarvis
Conference Chair

could convince the shameful captain that "Breed's was a logical destination."[2] The performance of the officers at Bunker Hill left much to be desired. After Prescott had repealed the first couple of British attacks on Breed's Hill, his men were running low on ammunition. General Putnam headed over to Bunker Hill to procure reinforcements for the embattled men at Breed's Hill. Wood describes the chaos that was present at Bunker Hill, calling the sight "A disordered mass of milling men moving around the top of the hill . . . through incompetence or inexperience, (the officers) had given up any attempts at rallying and reorganizing their units."[3]

The British assumed, as one of their generals, John Burgoyne, put it, that no number of "untrained rabble" could ever stand up against "trained troops." Under General William Howe, British forces attempted a series of frontal assaults on the American position. These attacks were eventually successful, but only at the terrible cost of 1,000 British casualties.[4]

British Soldiers

Nothing could contrast the chaos on the side of the Americans more sharply than the stoicism of the average British soldiers. Wood explains, "British discipline held fast" even while "whole ranks of light infantry (were being leveled) as though a giant hand had swept them down to the sand."[5] Wave after wave of British soldiers obediently carried out their orders, each being met with the same deadly barrage of bullets the preceding wave had been cut down by. While the Americans were having difficulty maintaining order when they weren't even fighting, the British, like automatons, performed their duty under the harshest of conditions.

Summary

Though the colonists' spirits were buoyed by the massive casualties they inflicted on British forces at Bunker Hill, they could not always hope to have such favorable fighting conditions on their side. The British demonstrated such discipline, resilience, endurance, and indifference to casualties that the colonists surely knew they could not expect to win an easy victory.

When taking into consideration the complete lack of soldiering skills the colonists often demonstrated at Bunker Hill, the success of the battle for the colonists is significantly abated. Indeed, the series of losses the colonists suffered at the hands of the British in the following year made it clear that the initial success at Bunker Hill would not be easily replicated. A single victory under choice conditions is one thing, but to actually win a prolonged war against the mighty British Empire would be another. It speaks volumes of George Washington's leadership that he was able to hold such a force together for such a prolonged period and put together enough success in individual battles to win a war.

Footnotes

[1]W. J. Wood, *Battles of the Revolutionary War, 1775–1781* (Cambridge, MA: Da Capo Press, 2003), p. 33.

[2]Ibid., p. 16.

[3]Ibid., p. 27.

[4]Gordon S. Wood, *The American Revolution* (New York: Modern Library Paperback Edition, 2002), p. 54.

[5]Wood, W. J., op.cit., 20.

Activity 7

Electronic Presentations

Create the six slides as shown at the right and on page 221. Choose appropriate clip art if the art shown at the right isn't available with your software.

Include transitions between each slide. Use your choice of custom animations to create interest in your slide show.

Save as: **CR2 ACTIVITY7**

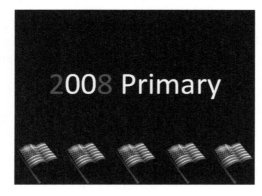

Slide 1

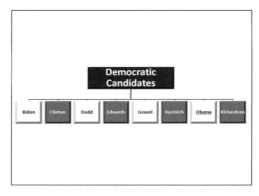

Slide 2

At 2" (3 returns down)

Return address	230 Glendale Court Brooklyn, NY 11234-3721 February 15, 20— ↓2
Letter mailing address	Ms. Julie Hutchinson 1825 Melbourne Avenue Flushing, NY 11367-2351 ↓1
Salutation	Dear Julie ↓1
Body	It seems like years since we were in Ms. Gerhig's keyboarding class. Now I wish I had paid more attention. As I indicated on the phone, I am applying for a position as box office coordinator for one of the theatres on Broadway. Of course, I know the importance o having my letter of application and resume formatted correctly, but I'm not sure that I remember how to do it. ↓1

> Hold down the Shift key when you return after the first two lines of the Return address and the first two lines of the Letter address to avoid having extra space between lines.

Default or 1" SM

Since you just completed your business education degree, I knew where to get the help I needed. Thanks for agreeing to look over my application documents; they are enclosed. Also, if you have any suggestions for changes to the content, please share those with me too. This job is so important to me; it's the one I really want. ↓1

Thanks again for agreeing to help. If I get the job, I'll take you out to one of New York's finest restaurants. ↓1

Default or 1" SM

Complimentary close	Sincerely ↓2
Writer	~~Rebecca Dunworthy~~ ↓1
Enclosure notation	Enclosure

Kelsie Dwyer

> Shown in 11-point Calibri with 2" top margin and 1" side margins, this letter appears smaller than actual size.

Personal-Business Letter in Block Format—Word 2007 defaults

Activity 3

Letter

Format and key the letter at the right.

Proofread your copy; correct all keying and format errors.

Save as: **CR2 ACTIVITY3**

January 16, 20-- | Mr. Caden O'Rourke | 278 Rangeview Drive | Littleton, CO 80120-7611 | Dear Mr. O'Rourke

It was fun visiting with you last week at the Colorado Historical Society's Annual Meeting. It seems impossible that ten years have passed since I was a student in your class.

As I recall, you always start each class off with a trivia question. Since the inauguration is next week, I thought you might like to use some of the following:

- Who was the first President inaugurated in Washington, D.C.? (**Thomas Jefferson in 1801.**)

- Who was the youngest President-elect at the time of his inauguration? (**John F. Kennedy at 43 years, 236 days.**)

- Who was the first inaugurated President to be born outside the original 13 states? (**Abraham Lincoln of Illinois.**)

- Who was the first President inaugurated for a term limited by the Constitution? (**Dwight D. Eisenhower in 1952. The 22nd amendment limits a president to two terms.**)

Thanks for the information on summer school. I'll reserve the week of June 15 for the workshop.

Sincerely | Justin C. Phipps

Report

Activity 4

Report

Format and key the copy below and on p. 224 as a bound report with footnotes.

Save as: **CR2 ACTIVITY4**

Activity 5

Report

Prepare a reference page from the footnotes shown below on a separate sheet. Refer to Rxx for reference page formatting.

Save as: **CR2 ACTIVITY5**

Activity 6

Report

Prepare a title page for the report using a template included with your software. Include the name of the report, the author, and date.

Save as: **CR2 ACTIVITY6**

REVOLUTIONARY WAR
OPPOSING FORCES

By Logan Paul

The Battle of Bunker Hill vividly emphasized the stark contrast between the opposing forces of the Revolutionary War. The English displayed his majesty's finest—highly trained, professional, and obedient troops marching into battle, remaining cool, poised, and confident under fire, and relentlessly pushing forward. On the other hand, the American militia failed to conduct themselves like soldiers and demonstrated a complete lack of "soldiering skills."

American Soldiers

It seems the American militia had an extreme aversion to receiving commands from generals who were from a different colony, and thus not legally their general. This, along with other factors, led to the conspicuous lack of "a higher command structure."[1] This added to the chaos of the situation. An aversion to following orders and the overall fear of the bombardment of cannon fire that was perpetually barraging the Americans made being a general a difficult task.

At one point, a captain retreated from his duty to reinforce Prescott on Breed's Hill. Nothing short of General Putnam putting a pistol muzzle to his head

(continued on next page)

At 2" (Approximately 5 returns down)

Return address
2832 Primrose Street
Eugene, OR 97402-1716
November 20, 20-- ↓4

Letter mailing address
Mr. Andrew Chaney
324 Brookside Avenue NW
Salem, OR 97304-9008 ↓2

Salutation Dear Mr. Chaney ↓2

Body Thank you for taking time out of your busy schedule to speak to our **A**spiring **M**usicians **C**lub. It was great learning more about the "Masters" from you. ↓2

Default or 1" SM I particularly enjoyed learning more about the German composers. It is amazing that so many of the great musicians (Johann Sebastian Bach, Ludwig van Beethoven, Robert Schumann, Felix Mendelssohn, and Richard Wagner) are all from Germany. It is my goal to continue my study of music at the **Staatliche Hochschule fur Musik Rheinland** in Germany once I graduate from college. ↓2

Your insights into what it takes to make it as a professional musician were also enlightening for our members. Those of us who want to become professional musicians know we have to rededicate ourselves to that goal if we are going to be successful. ↓2

Thank you again for sharing your expertise with our club. ↓2

Default or 1" SM

Complimentary close Sincerely ↓4

Writer Stephen R. Knowles
Writer's Title AMC Member

Shown in 12-point Times New Roman with 2" top margin and 1" side margins, this letter appears smaller than actual size.

Personal-Business Letter in Block Format—Word 2003 defaults

OBJECTIVE

• To review Cycle 2 document processing, computer application, and straight-copy skills.

Conditioning Practice

Key each line twice.

alphabet 1 Carl asked to be given just a week to reply to the tax quiz form.

figures 2 Rooms 268 and 397 were cleaned for the 10:45 meetings last night.

speed 3 Vivian burns wood and a small bit of coal to make a dismal flame.

gwam 1' | 1 | 2 | 3 | 4 | 5 | 6 | 7 | 8 | 9 | 10 | 11 | 12 | 13 |

Activity 1 E-mail

Key the text at the right as an e-mail to your instructor. Send a Bcc notation to yourself and request a delivery receipt. Attach the *DF CR2 ACTIVITY1* file. Proofread and correct.

Save as: **CR2 ACTIVITY1**

Subject: Sales Report

The sales figures you requested are attached. This month's sales figures should be available on Friday. As soon as I receive them, I'll update the file to include those figures and e-mail them to you.

If there is any other information I can provide for the meeting next month, let me know. I'm looking forward to seeing you again in San Francisco.

Activity 2 Memo

Format and key the text at the right as a memo to **Investment Club Members** from **Gordon Chandler**. Date the memo **April 20, 20–** and use **Portfolio Update** for the subject line.

Save as: **CR2 ACTIVITY2**

The table below shows the current value of our portfolio. As you are well aware, market results have been mixed this year. The total value of the portfolio increased 12 percent since January 1. Most of this increase is due to additional contributions by members rather than increases in the value of stocks in the portfolio.

Insert table from file:
DF CR2 ACTIVITY2

Stock		Shares Owned	Price Per Share	Value of Stock
Company Name	Symbol			
Citigroup Inc.	C	200	26.03	$ 5,206.00
Coke	KO	250	59.25	14,812.50
Ford	F	100	6.08	608.00
Intel	INTC	175	20.27	3,574.25
J. P. Morgan	JPM	300	43.82	13,146.00
U.S. Bank	USB	200	32.40	6,480.00
Xcel Energy	XEL	250	20.61	5,152.50
Cash				23,495.77
Total Portfolio Value				$ 72,475.02

Our cash balance ($23,495.77) is quite large. We should decide at our next meeting what we want to do with this cash. As I recall, we are scheduled to meet on May 6 and will have potential investment opportunity reports from Catherine Cloninger and Mario Fernandez by then.

If you have questions about the report, please call me.

Language Skills: Word Choice

1. Study the spelling and definitions of the words.
2. Key all *Learn* and *Apply* lines, choosing the correct word in the *Apply* lines.

Save as: 26C CHOICE

hole (n) an opening in or through something	**peak** (n) pointed end; top of a mountain; highest level
whole (adj/n) having all its proper parts; a complete amount or sum	**peek** (vb) to glance or look at for a brief time

Learn 1 The **whole** group helped dig a **hole** to bury the time capsule.

Apply 2 They ate the (hole, whole) cake before going to the water (hole, whole).

Apply 3 He told us, "The (hole, whole) is greater than the sum of its parts."

Learn 1 If you **peek** out the window, you will see the **peak** of the iceberg.

Apply 2 The (peak, peek) of the mountain came into view as they drove around the curve.

Apply 3 Students were told not to (peak, peek) at the keyboard in order to reach (peak, peek) skill.

Lesson 27   PERSONAL-BUSINESS LETTERS

OBJECTIVES

- To review format of personal-business letters in block format.
- To learn to format/key envelopes.

Conditioning Practice

Key each line twice.

alphabet 1 Even Jack will be taking part of a history quiz next Monday.

fig/sym 2 Out-of-stock items (#7850*, #461A*, and #2093*) are in blue.

speed 3 Jake may sign the big form by the antique door of city hall.

gwam 1' | 1 | 2 | 3 | 4 | 5 | 6 | 7 | 8 | 9 | 10 | 11 | 12 |

Personal-Business Letters in Block Format

Letter 1

Format/key the letter at the right. Refer to the model on p. 66 as needed. Proofread and correct errors.

Save as: 27B LETTER1

Note: Line endings for opening and closing lines are indicated by color verticals. Insert a hard return at these points.

	words
610 Grand Avenue	Laramie, WY 82070-1423	October 10, 20--		12
Elegant Treasures	388 Stonegate Drive	Longview, TX 75601-	25
0132	Dear Armani Dealer	29

Last week when I was in Longview visiting relatives, I noticed that — 43
you had Giuseppe Armani figurines displayed in your window. You — 56
had already closed for the day, so I was not able to see if you had — 70
other figurines. — 73

I am interested in three sculptures that Armani had created to — 85
celebrate the new millennium. They are called **Stardust, Silver** — 99
Moon, and **Comet.** I want to buy all three sculptures. Do you — 113
have them in stock, or could you order them? If not, could you — 127
refer me to a nearby dealer? — 129

I am looking forward to adding these exquisite pieces of art to my — 143
collection. — 145

Sincerely | Cynthia A. Maustin — 151

Design Tips

As you create the slide show, consider the following design Do's and Don't's:

- Do use bulleted lists to present concepts one at a time.

- Do use key words and phrases rather than complete sentences.

- Do use contrasting background colors that make text stand out. Use light text against a dark background or dark text against a light background.

- Do choose a font size that the audience can read—even in the back of the room.

- Do use sound and animation to make a point, but not to distract from your message.

- Don't overcrowd slides. Two slides might be better than one.

- Don't overuse clip art. Photos have more impact.

Sites of Washington D. C.

- Washington Monument
- Lincoln Memorial
- Jefferson Memorial
- The White House
- The Treasury Building
- U.S. Capitol Building
- Eleanor Roosevelt Memorial
- Arlington National Cemetery
- World War II Memorial

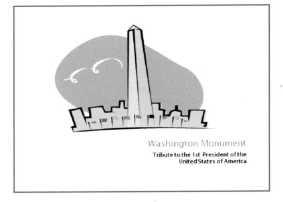

Washington Monument
Tribute to the 1st President of the United States of America

Our Nation's Capitol

Washington Monument
Tribute to the 1st President of the United States of America

Lincoln Memorial

Tribute to the 16th President of the United States of America

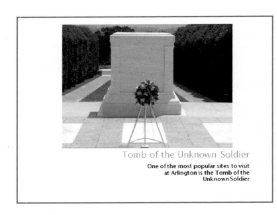

Tomb of the Unknown Soldier

One of the most popular sites to visit at Arlington is the Tomb of the Unknown Soldier

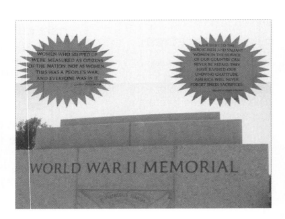

WORLD WAR II MEMORIAL

Letter 2

Format and key the text at the right as a personal-business letter in block format.

Save as: **27B LETTER2**

117 Whitman Avenue	Hartford, CT 06107-4518	July 2, 20--	Ms.	13

117 Whitman Avenue | Hartford, CT 06107-4518 | July 2, 20-- | Ms. Geneva Everett | 880 Honeysuckle Drive | Athens, GA 30606-9231 | Dear Geneva

13
25
28

Last week at the Educational Theatre Association National Convention, you mentioned that your teaching assignment for next year included an Introduction to Shakespeare class. I find the Internet to be a very useful supplement for creating interest in many of the classes I teach. Here are four websites dealing with Shakespeare that you may find helpful for your new class.

42
55
69
84
99
105

http://www.shakespeares-globe.org/Default.htm
http://www.shakespeare-online.com/
http://www.shakespeare.mit.edu/
http://www.albemarle-london.com/map-globe.html

114
122
130
140

Another resource that I use is a booklet published by Cengage Learning: *Introducing Shakespeare*. A copy of the title page is attached. The booklet contains scenes from some of Shakespeare's best-known works. Scenes from my favorites (*Romeo and Juliet*, *A Midsummer Night's Dream*, and *Julius Caesar*) are included.

152
165
178
191
203

As I come across other resources, I will forward them to you. Enjoy the rest of the summer; another school year will be upon us before we know it.

217
231
232

Sincerely | Marshall W. Cline | Attachment

241

27C Formatting

Envelopes

Format a small (No. 6 3/4) envelope for Letter 1 of 27B and a large (No. 10) envelope for Letter 2 of 27B.

Save as: **27C ENVELOPE1**
and 27C ENVELOPE2

117 Whitman Avenue
Hartford, CT 06107-4518
July 2, 20--

Ms. Geneva Everett
880 Honeysuckle Drive
Athens, GA 30606-9231

Dear Geneva

Last week at the Educational T
teaching assignment for next
be a very useful supplement fo
dealing with Shakespeare that

http://www.shakespeares-glo
http://www.wfu.edu/~tedfor
http://www.jetlink.net/~mass
http://www.albemarle-londor

Another resource that I use is a
copy of the title page is attach
works. Scenes from my favori
included.

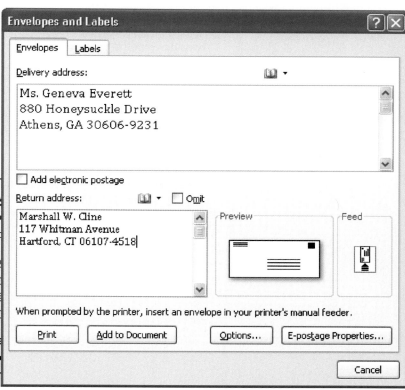

Envelopes and Labels

Envelopes | Labels

Delivery address:

Ms. Geneva Everett
880 Honeysuckle Drive
Athens, GA 30606-9231

☐ Add electronic postage

Return address: ☐ Omit

Marshall W. Cline
117 Whitman Avenue
Hartford, CT 06107-4518

Preview   Feed

When prompted by the printer, insert an envelope in your printer's manual feeder.

Print | Add to Document | Options... | E-postage Properties...

Cancel

• To deliver a presentation using electronic slides.

75B

Practice Presenting

1. Read the information at the right.
2. Review the suggestions for presentation delivery on p. 124.
3. Practice giving the *Government of the United States of America* presentation that you created in Lessons 72 and 73.

Speaker notes. The notes that you created for the *Government of the United States of America* presentation should only be used as an aid when you are practicing your presentation. They should remind you of what you want to say during your practice sessions.

You will know when you have practiced the presentation enough, because you will be able to give the presentation by simply looking at the slides as they appear on the screen. The words on the slides will act as an outline to remind you of the key points you want to make.

Don't be concerned about giving the presentation word for word as it appears in the notes. If you do, it sounds memorized. Memorized speeches come across as unnatural; the speaker is not able to develop a rapport with the audience.

However, experts generally advise speakers to have the first sentence memorized. This allows the speaker to have a strong opening and come across as knowledgeable and confident. If the speaker does memorize the first sentence, he/she should practice it so that it seems natural. This can be done by pausing in appropriate places and using vocal variety—speed, volume.

Definitely don't make the mistake that is often made by beginning presenters—bringing the speaker notes to the podium and then reading to, rather than presenting to, the audience. Speakers who read to their audience are not as credible.

By being well prepared and only glancing at the screen as the next slide comes up, the speaker comes across as natural. This also allows the speaker to focus on the audience rather than on his/her notes.

75C

Give a Presentation

1. Review the evaluation sheet on p. 125.
2. Break up into groups of three. Each student in your group will give the presentation that was developed in Lessons 72–73. While one

student is giving the presentation, the other two will evaluate it using the form shown on p. 125.

3. The evaluation form is available in the data files: *DF 75C EvalForm*.

SOMETHING EXTRA

Planning, Preparing, and Delivering A Presentation

APPLY WHAT YOU HAVE LEARNED

Use the report prepared for 61C (pp. 182–183) and the photos from *DF 75 Photos* as a basis for preparing a presentation that you will be giving on the sites of Washington D.C. If you need more information, use other sources. The presentation will be two to three minutes in length. Develop a slide show to aid you in delivering the presentation to your classmates. Some ideas are shown on the next page.

Plan and organize the presentation:

1. Create an outline of what you want to include.
2. Review the file photos (*DF 75 Photos*) and illustrations and Design Tips on p. 221. Plan and create the slides to be included.
3. Prepare notes and practice the presentation.
4. Give the presentation to two or three of your classmates.

Save as: 75 Sites of DC

OBJECTIVE

• To format personal-business letters in block format.

28A

Conditioning Practice
Key each line twice.

alphabet 1 Peter was amazed at just how quickly you fixed the big vans.

fig/sym 2 Of 34,198 citizens, 25,648 (75%) voted in the 2004 election.

speed 3 Orlando may make a big map to hang by the door of city hall.

gwam 1' | 1 | 2 | 3 | 4 | 5 | 6 | 7 | 8 | 9 | 10 | 11 | 12 |

28B   Formatting

Personal-Business Letters in Block Format

Letter 1

Format and key the letter at the right in block format; check spelling, proofread, and correct the letter before you save it.

Save as: 28B LETTER1

	words
1245 Park Avenue	3
New York, NY 10128-2231	8
October 28, 20--	11

Mrs. Tara Cruz	14
4221 Beekman Street	18
New York, NY 10038-8326	22

Dear Mrs. Cruz — 25

Mrs. Kenningston's fifth-grade class will be attending a production of (40) the Broadway musical *The Lion King* on March 25 to conclude their (53) study of the theatre. As you are probably aware, the play is based on (67) the 1994 Disney film about a young lion's coming-of-age struggles. (80)

Attending the play will give the fifth-graders a real sense of New York (95) theatre. The production will be at the New Amsterdam Theatre, built (109) in 1903 and for years considered the most majestic on 42nd Street. (122) With its recent renovation, it has been restored almost to its original (136) grandeur. The theatre is best known as the home of the Ziegfeld (149) Follies (1913 through 1927) and George M. Cohan's *Forty-Five Minutes* (163) *from Broadway.* (166)

This will be a great experience for the fifth-graders. Mrs. Kenningston (181) would like four parents to help chaperone on the day of the (193) production. Are you interested and willing to assist? I will call you (207) next week to determine your availability and discuss details. (220)

Sincerely — 222

Marsha Rhodes — 224
Parent Volunteer — 228

74C (continued)

Script for the Gettysburg
Address by Abraham
Lincoln slide presentation

Slide 2

Abraham Lincoln is one of the best-known presidents of the United States. He
was our sixteenth president and held office from 1861 until 1865, when he was
assassinated.

Slide 3

The Gettysburg Address is a speech delivered by President Lincoln at the
dedication of the Gettysburg National Cemetery to honor those who died in
the Battle of Gettysburg during the Civil War.

Slide 4

Four score and seven years ago our fathers brought forth on this continent, a
new nation, conceived in Liberty, and dedicated to the proposition that all men
are created equal.

Slide 5

Now we are engaged in a great civil war, testing whether that nation, or any
nation so conceived and so dedicated, can long endure. We are met on a great
battlefield of that war.

Slide 6

We have come to dedicate a portion of that field, as a final resting place for those
who here gave their lives that that nation might live. It is altogether fitting and
proper that we should do this.

Slide 7

But, in a larger sense, we cannot dedicate—we cannot consecrate—we cannot
hallow—this ground. The brave men, living and dead, who struggled here, have
consecrated it, far above our poor power to add or detract.

Slide 8

The world will little note, nor long remember what we say here, but it can never
forget what they did here. It is for us the living, rather, to be dedicated here
to the unfinished work which they who fought here have thus far so nobly
advanced.

Slide 9

It is rather for us to be here dedicated to the great task remaining before us—that
from these honored dead we take increased devotion to that cause for which they
gave the last full measure of devotion—that we here highly resolve that these
dead shall not have died in vain—that this nation, under God, shall have a new
birth of freedom—and that government of the people, by the people, for the people,
shall not perish from the earth.

Letter 2

Format and key the letter at the right in block format; check spelling, proofread, and correct the letter.

Save as: 28B LETTER2

1245 Park Avenue | New York, NY 10128-2231 | January 5, 20-- | 11
Ticket Manager | New Amsterdam Theatre | 214 West 42nd Street | 23
New York, NY 10036 | Dear Ticket Manager   31

Mrs. Kenningston's fifth-grade class from Washington Elementary   44
School will be studying theatre during the month of March. To   56
conclude their study, Mrs. Kenningston would like for them to attend   70
a Broadway production of *The Lion King* on March 25.   81

Approximately twenty children would attend the performance along   94
with five chaperones. Does your theatre offer educational discounts   108
for the matinee performance?   114

One of our students needs wheelchair accessibility. What facilities do   128
you have to accommodate this student?   136

The students are very excited about the possibility of attending a live   150
Broadway production. Please provide me with the requested information   164
as soon as possible so that the necessary arrangements can be made.   178

Sincerely | Marsha Rhodes | Parent Volunteer   186

Letter 3

Format and key the letter at the right in block format; check spelling, proofread, and correct the letter.

Save as: 28B LETTER3

OPTIONAL WORD PROCESSING ACTIVITY

Prepare letters for the other three parents who helped chaperone the field trip. Their addresses are:

**Mr. Charles Chan
389 Wadsworth Avenue
New York, NY 10040-0025**

**Ms. Alesha Ramirez
175 Morningside Avenue
New York, NY 10027-8735**

**Ms. Gwendolyn Maas
1615 Henry Hudson Parkway
New York, NY 10034-6721**

Save as: 28B LETTER-3CHAN, 28B LETTER-3RAMIREZ, and 28B LETTER3MAAS

1245 Park Avenue | New York, NY 10128-2231 | April 1, 20-- | Mrs.   13
Tara Cruz | 4221 Beekman Street | New York, NY 10038-8326 | Dear   26
Mrs. Cruz   28

Thank you for helping chaperone the fifth-grade class on their   41
field trip to Broadway. When I visited Mrs. Kenningston's classroom   54
yesterday, the children were still excited about having attended the play.   70
Their thank-you note is enclosed.   76

Because of parents like you, educational experiences outside the   89
classroom are possible. These experiences bring to life what the students   101
learn in school. I'm glad our children have this enrichment.   117

Thank you again for accepting the challenge of watching over   129
the fifth-graders on their exciting trip to Broadway. I know the task   143
wasn't easy, but I felt it was well worth our time.   154

Sincerely | Marsha Rhodes | Parent Volunteer | Enclosure   165

Record Sound

1. Create the slides shown at the right. *DF 75 Photos* includes a picture of the Lincoln Monument.

2. Enhance the slide presentation with appropriate animation and transitions.

3. Learn how to use the Record Sound feature of your software.

4. The script for slides 2 through 9 is on p. 219. Read through the script and practice it several times. Using the script, record the narration for the slide show.

5. Learn how to play a CD audio track during a slide show presentation.

6. Select music that would be appropriate to play during the slide presentation. Specify where you want the music to start and where you want it to stop. Consider whether you will need to have the music loop.

7. Learn how to program the Slide Timing feature.

8. Set the Slide Timing feature so that the slide show will run automatically.

Save as: 74C PP

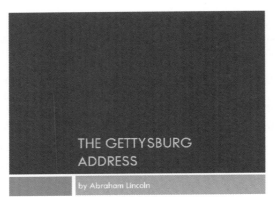

Slide 1

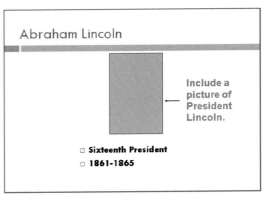

Slide 2

Slide 3

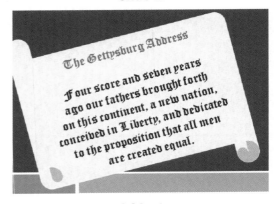

Slide 4

Slide 5

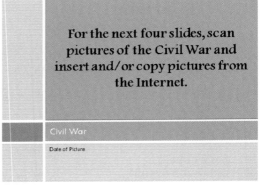

Slide 6–9

Slide 10

(continued on next page)

Skill 1 Builder

Keyboard Review

Key each line twice.

A/Z	1	Zack had a pizza at the plaza by the zoo on a hazy day.
B/Y	2	Bobby may be too busy to buy me a bag for my boat trip.
C/X	3	Ricky caught six cod to fix for the six excited scouts.
D/W	4	Wilda would like to own the doe she found in the woods.
E/V	5	Evan will give us the van to move the five heavy boxes.
F/U	6	All four of us bought coats with fur collars and cuffs.
G/T	7	Eight men tugged the boat into deep water to get going.
H/S	8	Marsha wishes to show how to make charts on a computer.
I/R	9	Ira can rise above his ire to rid the firm of a crisis.
J/Q	10	Josh quietly quit the squad after a major joint injury.
K/P	11	Kip packed a backpack and put it on a box on the porch.
L/O	12	Lola is to wear the royal blue skirt and a gold blouse.
M/N	13	Many of the men met in the hall to see the new manager.
figures	14	I worked 8:30 to 5 at 1964 Lake Blvd. from May 7 to 26.
fig/sym	15	I said, "ISBN #0-651-24879-3 was not assigned to them."

Timed Writings

1. Key two 1' timings on each ¶; determine *gwam*.
2. Key two 2' timings on ¶s 1–2 combined; determine *gwam*.
3. If time permits, key 1' guided timings on each ¶. To set a goal, add 2 to the *gwam* achieved in step 1.

LA all letters used (MicroPace) gwam 2'

One of the best-known inaugural addresses was given by President John F. Kennedy. The exact words of this President are permanently imprinted into the minds of numerous Americans. If you were to say, "Ask not what your country can do for you but what you can do for your country," quite a few Americans would know the individual you were quoting.

These words alone make an impression. However, the way John F. Kennedy delivered them with such zealousness made them have an even greater impact. What do you think he meant by these words? Do you think it is more or less important for Americans to try and live by these words today than when Kennedy delivered them in his inaugural address?

gwam 2' | 1 | 2 | 3 | 4 | 5 | 6 |

Quarter-Minute Checkpoints				
gwam	1/4'	1/2'	3/4'	1'
24	6	12	18	24
28	7	14	21	28
32	8	16	24	32
36	9	18	27	36
40	10	20	30	40
44	11	22	33	44
48	12	24	36	48
52	13	26	39	52
56	14	28	42	56

73C (continued)

The House of Representatives, on the other hand, is based on the population of each state. As the population changes within states, the number of representatives allocated to that state may also change.

14. The third branch of our government is called the Judicial Branch.

15. The Judicial Branch hears cases that challenge or require interpretation of the laws passed by Congress. The Judicial Branch has the responsibility of protecting the rights of all Americans that were granted by the Constitution.

16. The judicial system is three-tiered; the first tier is the U.S. District Courts. Trials take place in these courts. If a person loses in a district court, he/she can usually appeal the decision. These appeals are heard in U.S. Courts of Appeals. Finally, there is the U.S. Supreme Court.

17. The Supreme Court consists of nine justices who have been nominated by the President and confirmed by the Senate. Even though there are many cases submitted to the Supreme Court, very few cases are ever acted upon by this court.

18. This is a very brief overview of our government. You will learn much more about it during the time you spend here. And we hope to learn about your country as well. Welcome to the United States.

Lesson 74 — ENHANCING PRESENTATIONS WITH SOUND

OBJECTIVES
- To insert sound from the Clip Organizer.
- To record sound.
- To play a CD audio track during parts of the slide show.

74B

Insert Sound

1. Read the information at the right.
2. Learn how to insert sound from the Clip Organizer for your software.
3. Insert "America the Beautiful" from the sound Clip Organizer on the first and last slide of the presentation created for Lessons 72 and 73. Have the sound start automatically for slide 1 and manually for slide 18.

Save as: **74B PP**

There are several different types of sounds that can be added to your presentation. These include:

- Sounds from the Clip Organizer
- Sounds from a file
- Sounds from a CD audio track
- Sounds that you record—Recorded Sounds

Sounds from Clip Organizer—Prerecorded sounds available with the software.

Sounds from a file—Sounds that you have recorded and saved as a file that can be linked to the presentation.

Sounds from a CD audio track—Music that is played directly from a CD. Particular parts of the CD can be specified for playing.

Recorded sounds—With recording capability, words (using your voice or the voice of someone else), sounds, or music can be recorded to specific slides.

Communication & Math
SKILLS 3

ACTIVITY 1

Number Expression

1. Study each of the eight rules shown at the right.
   a. Key the *Learn* line(s) beneath each rule, noting how the rule is applied.
   b. Key the *Apply* line(s), expressing numbers correctly.

Rule 1: Spell a number that begins a sentence even when other numbers in the sentence are shown in figures.

Learn 1 Twelve of the new shrubs have died; 48 are doing quite well.

Apply 2 14 musicians have paid their dues, but 89 have not done so.

Rule 2: Use figures for numbers above ten, and for numbers from one to ten when they are used with numbers above ten.

Learn 3 She ordered 8 word processors, 14 computers, and 4 printers.

Apply 4 Did he say they need ten or 14 sets of Z18 and Z19 diskettes?

Rule 3: Use figures to express date and time (unless followed by o'clock).

Learn 5 He will arrive on Paygo Flight 418 at 9:48 a.m. on March 14.

Apply 6 Exhibitors must be in Ivy Hall at eight forty a.m. on May one.

Rule 4: Use figures for house numbers except house number One.

Learn 7 My home is at 8 Vernon Drive; my office, at One Weber Plaza.

Apply 8 The Nelsons moved from 4059 Pyle Avenue to 1 Maple Circle.

Rule 5: Use figures to express measures and weights.

Learn 9 Glenda Redford is 5 ft. 4 in. tall and weighs 118 lbs. 9 oz.

Apply 10 This carton measures one ft. by nine in. and weighs five lbs.

Rule 6: Use figures for numbers following nouns.

Learn 11 Review Rules 1 to 18 in Chapter 5, pages 149 and 150, today.

Apply 12 Case 1849 is reviewed in Volume five, pages nine and ten.

Rule 7: Spell (and capitalize) names of small-numbered streets (ten and under).

Learn 13 I walked several blocks along Third Avenue to 54th Street.

Apply 14 At 7th Street she took a taxi to the theater on 43rd Avenue.

Rule 8: Spell indefinite numbers.

Learn 15 Joe owns one acre of Parcel A; that is almost fifty percent.

Learn 16 Nearly seventy members voted; that is nearly a fourth.

Apply 17 Over 20 percent of the students auditioned for the play.

Apply 18 Just under 1/2 of the voters cast ballots for the best musician.

(continued on next page)

Add Notes

You will be giving the slide show you just created to foreign exchange students at your school. Learn how to create notes pages, and key the notes shown at the right and on the next page for each slide.

Copy the first slide and insert it at the end of your presentation as slide 18.

Print copies of your notes pages to have available for Lesson 75.

Save as: 73C PP

1. The government of the United States as we know it today has evolved over time. Its beginnings date back prior to the U.S. gaining its independence from England.

2. Today we have three branches of government. They include:

   the Executive Branch

   the Legislative Branch, and

   the Judicial Branch

3. Let's start by talking about the Executive Branch.

4. As you can see, the President of the United States is in charge of the Executive Branch. He serves as Commander in Chief of the Armed Forces, appoints cabinet members, and oversees various executive (government) agencies that we will be discussing later on in the presentation.

5. The first Commander in Chief of the Armed Forces was our first President, George Washington. Interestingly enough, he was named the army's Commander in Chief by the Second Continental Congress before he was ever elected president.

6. This slide shows a diagram of the 15 Executive Agencies.

7. The Executive Agencies include: the Department of Agriculture, the Department of Commerce, the Department of Defense, the Department of Education, the Department of Energy,

8. the Department of Health and Human Services, the Department of Homeland Security, the Department of Housing and Urban Development, the Department of the Interior, the Department of Justice,

9. the Department of Labor, the Department of State, the Department of Transportation, the Department of the Treasury, and the Department of Veterans Affairs.

10. Let's take a look at the President's Cabinet.

11. Now that we know a little about the Executive Branch, let's talk briefly about the Legislative Branch of government.

12. The Legislative Branch consists of Congress. Congress has two parts—the Senate and the House of Representatives.

13. As shown on this slide, there are two senators elected from each state. They are elected for a term of six years. The terms of the senators are staggered so that one-third of the Senate seats are up for election every two years. With each state having two senators, each state is given equal representation regardless of size or population.

2. Key Proofread & Correct, expressing numbers correctly. Then follow the steps below.
   a. Check answers.
   b. Using the rule number at the left of each line, study the rule relating to each error you made.
   c. Rekey each incorrect line, expressing numbers correctly.

Save as: **CS3 ACTIVITY1**

ACTIVITY 2

Reading

1. Open *DF CS3 ACTIVITY2*.
2. Read the document; close the file.
3. Key answers to the questions at the right.

Save as: **CS3 ACTIVITY2**

ACTIVITY 3

Composing

1. Read the quotations.
2. Choose one and make notes of what the quotation means to you.
3. Key a ¶ or two indicating what the quotation means to you.
4. Proofread, revise, and correct.

Save as: **CS3 ACTIVITY3**

ACTIVITY 4

Math: Working with Decimals, Fractions, and Percents

Proofread & Correct

Rules

1	1	20 members have already voted, but 15 have yet to do so.
2	2	Only twelve of the dancers are here; six have not returned.
3	3	Do you know if the eight fifteen Klondike flight is on time?
3, 4	4	We should be at 1 Brooks Road no later than eleven thirty a.m.
5	5	This oriental mural measures eight ft. by 10 ft.
5	6	The box of books is two ft. square and weighs six lbs. eight oz.
6	7	Have you read pages 45 to 62 of Chapter two that he assigned?
7	8	She usually rides the bus from 6th Street to 1st Avenue.
8	9	Nearly 1/2 of the cast is here; that is about 15.
8	10	A late fee of over 15 percent is charged after the 30th day.

1. Will at least one member of the cast not return for the next season?
2. Has a studio been contracted to produce the show for next season?
3. Does each cast member earn the same amount per episode?
4. Is the television show a news magazine or comedy?
5. How many seasons has the show been aired, not counting next season?
6. Do all cast members' contracts expire at the same time?
7. What did the cast do three years ago to get raises?

1. "Man does not live by words alone, despite the fact that sometimes he has to eat them." (Adlai Stevenson)

2. "No man is rich enough to buy back his past." (Oscar Wilde)

3. "It is not fair to ask of others what you are unwilling to do yourself." (Eleanor Roosevelt)

1. Open *DF CS3 ACTIVITY4* and print the file.
2. Solve the problems as directed in the file.
3. Submit your answers.

ENHANCING PRESENTATIONS WITH GRAPHICS AND ANIMATION/TRANSITIONS

OBJECTIVES

- To copy and insert graphics from the Internet.
- To use the transition and animation features to enhance a slide show.
- To create and print slide show notes pages.

73B

Slide Show Enhancement

1. Learn how to copy and insert graphics from the Internet.
2. Review the information on transitions and animation on p. 212.
3. Learn how to add transitions and animation to your slide show.
4. Make the changes outlined at the right and insert pictures as shown. *DF 73B Washington* has a picture of the Washington Monument.
5. In Slide Sorter view, add a transition to all slides except the first. Include at least three types of transitions.
6. Animate the bulleted items so they appear one at a time for slides 2 and 16.
7. Use the Wedge animation effect for the illustration for slide 16. Use the Effects option to group graphics One by one.
8. Insert a slide following slide 9 (3rd Executive Agencies slide). Select Section Headers layout. Use **President's Cabinet** for the main heading.
9. Learn how to insert a hyperlink.
10. On the newly inserted slide, include a hyperlink to: http://www .whitehouse.gov/ government/cabinet .html

Save as: **73B PP**

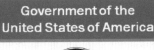

Government of the
United States of America

Student's Name
Current Date

Do an Internet search for the Seal of the United States. Copy and paste the seal on slide 1.

Branches of U.S. Government

 • Executive Branch

 • Judicial Branch

 • Legislative Branch

Revise slide 2 so that it looks like this. Use animation so that the branches appear one at a time. After each branch appears, have its picture appear using the wheel animation.

Add the pictures beneath the branch name to the three branch slides created in 72C.

Include pictures similar to these. These were found on the Internet.
http://www.whitehouse.gov/government/

George Washington

- First President of the U.S.
- 1789-1797

Have bulleted items appear one at a time.

Include a picture of the Washington Monument (from *DF 73B Washington*)

You must complete Career Exploration Activities 1 and 2 before completing this activity.

1. Retrieve your completed Career Clusters Interest Survey from your folder.

2. Review the Career Cluster Plans of Study for your top three career clusters. Do this by returning to http://www.careerclusters.org and clicking the **Free Career Cluster — Plans of Study** link. This will take you to a screen where you can establish a login address and password

(be sure to record your login information in a safe place for future use). Select your top three career clusters. Click your first choice and open and print the file. Click the Back button to return to the career clusters and open and print the second career cluster. Repeat the procedure for the third career cluster.

3. Place your printed files in your folder and file it in the storage area.

Communicating
YOUR PERSPECTIVE | 1

Ethics: The Right Thing to Do

Ethics is a set of moral principles and values. Ethical issues confront us every day. They occur in our community, nation, and world. They also arise in our personal and professional lives.

- A banker makes concealed loans to a company, helping that company inflate its profits by $1.5 billion during a four-year period. The company ends up in bankruptcy; the company stock is worthless.
- An executive of a charitable organization uses funds to remodel the executive suite rather than to support the needy.
- A teenager takes a DVD from a store without paying for it.

Deciding what to do in ethical situations isn't always easy. What is a good way to think them through? What is a good way to make an ethical decision?

1. **Get the facts.** Learn as much as possible about the situation before jumping to a conclusion. Make an intelligent decision rather than an emotional one.

2. **Don't let assumptions get in the way of the facts.** As the actor and comedian Will Rogers said, "It isn't what we don't know that gives us trouble[;] it's what we know that ain't so." You don't like it when people make assumptions about you. Make sure your judgment isn't colored by preconceptions or stereotypes.

3. **Consider the consequences for everyone.** Try to see the situation from the point of view of each party involved. What is each person or group likely to lose or gain as a result of your decision?

4. **Consider your personal values.** Apply your own beliefs and standards to the problem.

5. **Make your decision.**

Situation: In a grocery store, you see your best friend putting items under her coat.

ACTIVITIES

1. Read the material at the left.

2. Think about the situation described at the bottom of the page.

3. Key a ¶ telling how you would use the five-step process at the left to make a decision on how to handle the situation.

4. Form a group with some other students. Discuss an ethical issue in your community. Make sure everyone contributes. Did everyone in the group agree?

5. In an e-mail to your teacher, briefly explain the issue chosen in step 4 and state your point of view. Include your reasons. Always present your viewpoint in a professional and respectful manner.

72B (continued)

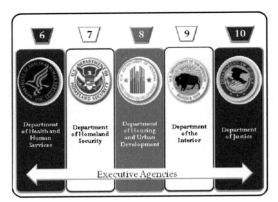

Slide 7

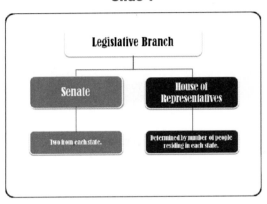

- The legislative branch of the federal government consists of the Congress, which is divided into two chambers—the Senate and the House of Representatives.

Slide 8

Source for slide 8:
http://www.whitehouse.gov/government/legi.html

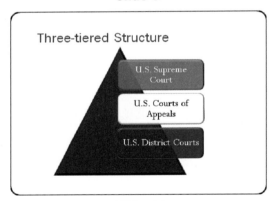

Slide 9

Judicial Branch

- The judicial branch hears cases that challenge or require interpretation of the legislation passed by Congress and signed by the President.

Slide 10

Source for slide 10:
http://www.whitehouse.gov/government/judg.html

Three-tiered Structure

U.S. Supreme Court

U.S. Courts of Appeals

U.S. District Courts

Slide 11

U.S. Supreme Court
- The Supreme Court consists of nine justices.
- Justices are nominated by the President and confirmed by the Senate.

U.S. Supreme Court

Justice #1 Justice #2 Justice #3 Justice #4 Justice #5 Justice #6 Justice #7 Justice #8 Justice #9

Slide 12

72C

Insert Slides

Learn how to insert new slides. Create the two slides shown at the right and insert them as instructed.

Create a similar one for the Legislative Branch (insert it before the Legislative Branch description) and one for the Judicial Branch (insert it before the Judicial Branch description).

Save as: **72C PP**

Executive Branch

Insert between Slides 2 and 3

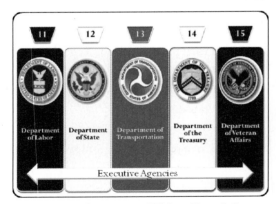

Insert between Slides 7 and 8

Format Guides: E-mail

E-mail (electronic mail) is used in most business organizations. Because of the ease of creating and the speed of sending, e-mail messages have partially replaced the memo and the letter. Generally, delivery of an e-mail message takes place within minutes, whether the receiver is in the same building or in a location anywhere in the world. An e-mail message is illustrated below.

E-mail heading. The format used for the e-mail heading may vary slightly, depending on the program used for creating e-mail. The heading generally includes who the e-mail is being sent to (**To**), what the e-mail is about (**Subject**), and who copies of the e-mail are being sent to (**Cc**). The name of the person sending the e-mail and the date the e-mail is sent are automatically included by the software. If you don't want the person receiving the e-mail to know that you are sending a copy of the e-mail to another person, the **Bcc** feature can be used.

E-mail body. The paragraphs of an e-mail message all begin at the left margin and are SS with a DS between paragraphs.

E-mail attachments. Attachments can be included with your e-mail by using the Attachment feature of the software. Common types of attachments include word processing, database, and spreadsheet files.

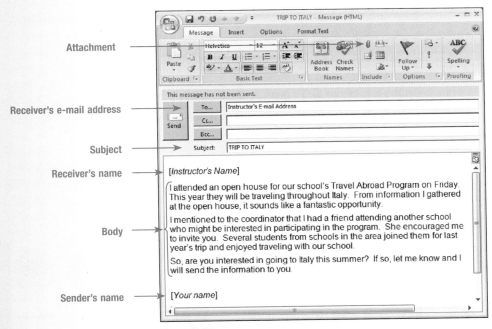

E-mail Message

OBJECTIVES
- To review how to create an electronic presentation.
- To create an electronic presentation with graphics and pictures.
- To add slides to an existing electronic presentation.

72A-75A

Conditioning Practice

Key each line twice SS.

alphabet | 1 | Zachary James always purchased five or six large antique baskets.

figures | 2 | Only 1,548 of the 1,967 expected guests had arrived by 12:30 p.m.

speed | 3 | The neighbor may fix the problem with the turn signal on the bus.

gwam | 1' | 1 | 2 | 3 | 4 | 5 | 6 | 7 | 8 | 9 | 10 | 11 | 12 | 13 |

72B

Create a Presentation

1. Review Unit 12, pp. 110–125.
2. Learn how to copy pictures and graphics from the Internet.
3. Create the 12 slides shown at the right and on the next page. The slides will be used again in Lessons 73–75. The illustrations at the right use the Equity design theme with Office colors.

Save as: **72B PP**

Source for slide 3:
http://www.whitehouse.gov/government/exec.html

Source for slides 6–7 and 72B slide 2:
http://www.whitehouse.gov/government/cabinet.html

Government of the
United States of America

Student's Name
Current Date

Slide 1

Branches of U.S. Government

- Executive Branch
- Judicial Branch
- Legislative Branch

Slide 2

Executive Branch

- The power of the executive branch is vested in the President, who also serves as Commander in Chief of the Armed Forces.

Slide 3

George Washington

- First President of the U.S.
- 1789-1797

Slide 4

Slide 5

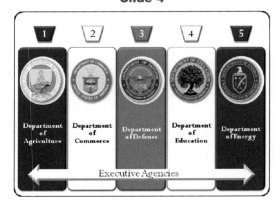

Slide 6

(continued on next page)

What Is Personal Information Management Software?

We live in a fast-paced world. Our schedules are filled with school, work, family, and extracurricular activities. We are constantly communicating with others. The latest technological advances allow us to exchange more information faster than ever before. We are inundated with information. We schedule appointments and exchange addresses, telephone numbers, cell phone numbers, fax numbers, e-mail addresses, etc.

It is critical to be organized if we are to survive in this fast-paced world. Today's personal information manager software (PIMS) provides the solution for individuals to manage this abundance of information and to be personally and professionally organized. Most PIMS have:

- an *E-mail* feature to send, receive, and manage e-mails
- a *Calendar* feature to keep track of schedules
- a *Contacts* feature to maintain information needed to contact others
- a *Tasks* feature to record items that need to be done
- a *Notes* feature to provide reminders

E-mail Inbox—Searches and Sorts

The e-mail inbox receives all incoming e-mail messages. Two features that are used to manage e-mail messages are Search and Sort. The Search feature finds specific messages based on a word, phrase, or other text.

For example, you may want to see only the messages that are from a specific person. The Inbox (Search Results) screen below shows all the messages that were received from *Parker* or that had the name *Parker* in the e-mail. Notice that the search results shown below included messages from Carter. These messages were also included in the search results because they had the word *Parker* in them.

The results of a search are normally shown by date. However, the Sort feature can be used to organize e-mail messages in a variety of ways. The more common sorts arrange e-mail messages by date, by subject, or by name of the person sending the message. The sort shown below organizes them by sender (from), thus placing all the messages from Parker together and all messages from Carter together.

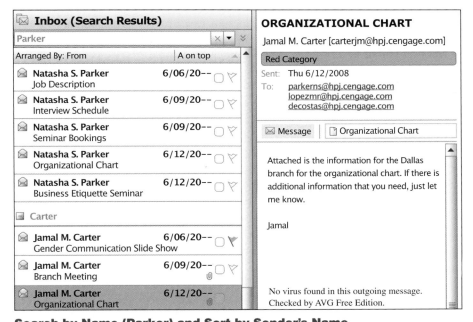

Search by Name (Parker) and Sort by Sender's Name

Electronic presentations can be enhanced by using the capabilities of the presentation software. Enhancements, however, should not be overdone.

Slide Animations

Rather than have a slide appear in its entirety, animations can be used to make text, graphics, and other objects appear one at a time. This allows control of how the information is presented as well as adding interest to the presentation.

A variety of animations are available to choose from. For example, text and objects on a slide can be animated to fade in, spin, float, ascend, or descend. **Animation schemes** are options that are preset. They range from very subtle to very glitzy. The scheme chosen should add interest without taking away from the message. **Custom animation** allows several different animations to be included on each slide.

Slide Transitions

Slide transition is the term used to describe how the display changes from one slide to the next. When no transition is applied, slides go from one directly to the next. Transition effects can make it appear as though the next slide dissolves in or appears through a circle, for example. There are numerous transitions to choose from.

Hyperlinks

A hyperlink is text that is colored and underlined that you click to take you from the current location in the electronic file to another location.

This means that a presenter can create hyperlinks to move from the current slide in a presentation to an Internet site that relates to what he/she is talking about.

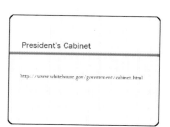

Slide with Hyperlink

Timing

The Slide Timing feature controls the speed with which one slide replaces another. Setting times tells the software how long each slide will remain on the screen.

Pictures

In addition to clip art, pictures can be inserted in an electronic presentation from a number of different sources such as scanners, cameras, files, and the Internet. Care must be taken not to violate copyright laws. Movies can also be inserted into a presentation.

Example of Slide with Picture

SmartArt Graphics

Graphics are used to visually communicate information. SmartArt graphics include list, process, cycle, hierarchy, relationship, matrix, and pyramid.

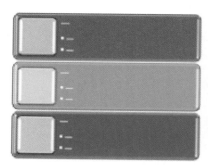

Example of SmartArt

Sound

Sound is another way to enhance a presentation. When people hear something as well as see it, they are much more likely to retain it.

Most electronic presentation software allows you to insert sound from a prerecorded clip organizer or from a sound file, play music from a CD, or record sound directly into the presentation.

The sound capability allows a presenter to bring variety and credibility to a presentation. Hearing John F. Kennedy say "Ask not what your country can do for you, ask what you can do for your country" has much more of an impact than if the presenter reads the quote. Having background music play as you show pictures has more of an impact than just showing the pictures.

Calendar

The Calendar feature is used to record and display appointments electronically. The calendar can be displayed and printed in a variety of ways (daily, weekly, or monthly), depending on how it will be used. The daily display is illustrated at the right.

Appointments can be scheduled by using the Appointment dialog box (**CTRL + N** for *Outlook* users) or by selecting the day and then clicking in the location where you want to key the information. Recurring appointments (those that occur repeatedly) can also be scheduled. For example, if you had a music lesson every Monday at 4 p.m, you could use the Recurrence feature to automatically place the music lesson on the calendar each Monday at 4 p.m.

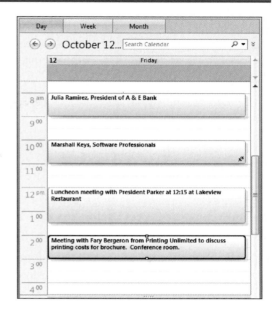

Contacts

The Contacts feature is used to store information about your associates. Generally, the person's name, business address, phone number, and e-mail address are recorded. Some software allows for recording more detailed information.

Once information has been recorded in Contacts, it can be viewed electronically or a hard copy can be printed. Hard copies can be printed in a variety of formats (card style, booklet style, phone directory style, etc.).

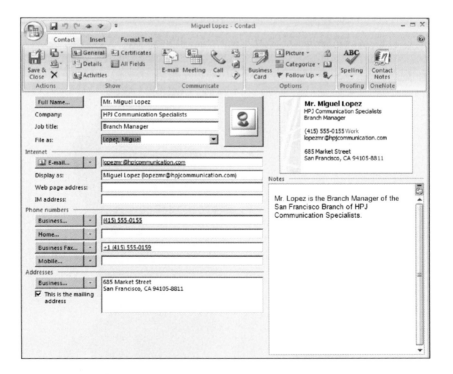

Math: Working with Percents of Change

1. Open *DF CS7 ACTIVITY4* and print the file.
2. Solve the problems as directed in the file.
3. Submit your answers.

CAREER Clusters

ACTIVITY 7

You must complete Career Exploration Activities 1–3 before completing this activity.

1. Retrieve your Career folder and the information in it that relates to the career cluster that is your first choice.

2. Reflect on the skills and knowledge you have gained in the courses you have taken and the extracurricular activities in which you are involved that will be beneficial in the career you selected as your first choice. Then compose a paragraph or two describing the connection between what you have learned and/or your activities and this career. Print your file, save it as Career7, and keep it open.

3. Exchange papers with a classmate and have the classmate offer suggestions for improving the content and correcting any errors he or she finds in your paragraph(s). Make the changes that you agree with and print a copy to turn in to your instructor. Save your file as Career7 and close the file.

4. Return your folder to the storage area. When your instructor returns your paper, file it in your Career folder.

© STOCKBYTE/GETTY IMAGES

Tasks

The Tasks feature allows you to record tasks that you are responsible for completing. When a task is recorded, it is less likely to be forgotten. Completion dates and reminders can be set for each task. If no completion date is recorded, the task will appear on the TaskPad below the calendar (see below illustration). Once the task has been completed, it can be checked off as shown below.

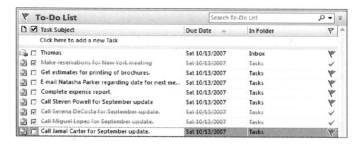

Notes

The Notes feature allows you to write yourself a reminder. The note may remain on the screen as an immediate reminder, or it may be stored for later use. Once the note is no longer needed, it can be deleted. Notes can be used for anything that a paper note could be used for.

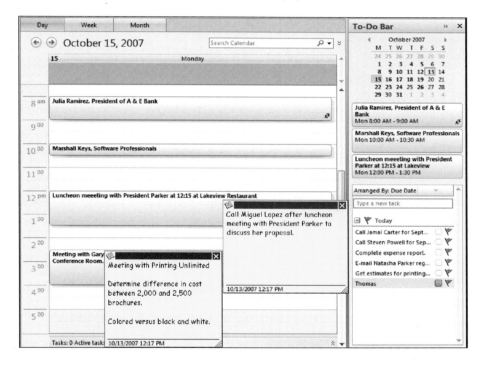

Lesson 29   FORMAT E-MAIL MESSAGES

• To learn to format e-mail messages.

29A

Conditioning Practice

Key each line twice.

alphabet 1 Jordan placed first by solving the complex quiz in one week.

figures   2 The 389 members met on June 21, 2004, from 6:15 to 7:30 p.m.

speed   3 Jan paid the big man for the field work he did for the firm.

gwam 1' | 1 | 2 | 3 | 4 | 5 | 6 | 7 | 8 | 9 | 10 | 11 | 12 |

Activity 1 (continued)

2. Key Proofread & Correct, inserting commas correctly.
   a. Check answers.
   b. Using the rule number(s) at the left of each line, study the rule relating to each error you made.
   c. Rekey each incorrect line, inserting commas correctly.

Save as: **CS7 ACTIVITY1**

Rules

Rules		
1	1	My favorite sports are college football basketball and soccer.
1	2	If you finish your history report before noon please give me a call.
1,2	3	I snacked on milk and cookies granola and some raisins.
3	4	Miss Qwan said "I was born in Taiwan."
4	5	Mr. Sheldon the historian will speak to our students today.
5	6	Why do you persist Kermit in moving your hands to the top row?
6	7	The report which Ted wrote is well organized and informative.
6	8	Only students who use their time wisely are likely to succeed.
3	9	Dr. Sachs said "Take two of these and call me in the morning."
6	10	Yolanda who is from Cuba intends to become a U.S. citizen.

ACTIVITY 2

Reading

1. Open *DF CS7 ACTIVITY2*.
2. Read the document; close the file.
3. Key answers to the questions, using complete sentences.

Save as: **CS7 ACTIVITY2**

1. What was the final score of yesterday's soccer match?
2. Was the winning goal scored in the first or second half?
3. Will last year's City League champion be playing in this year's championship match?
4. Will the top-ranked team in the state be playing in this year's championship match?
5. Will the top-ranked team in the city be playing in the championship match?
6. Is the championship game to be played during the day or the evening?
7. Has one or both of the teams playing in the championship match won a City League championship before?

ACTIVITY 3

Composing

1. Key the ¶, correcting word-choice errors. (Every line contains at least one error.)
2. Compose a 2nd ¶ to accomplish these goals:
   • Define what respect means to you.
   • Identify kinds of behavior that help earn your respect.
   • Identify kinds of behavior that cause you to lose respect.
3. Proofread, revise, and correct.

Save as: **CS7 ACTIVITY3**

That all individuals want others too respect them is not surprising. What is surprising is that sum people think their do respect even when there own behavior has been unacceptable or even illegal. Key two the issue is that we respect others because of certain behavior, rather then in spite of it. Its vital, than, to no that what people due and say determines the level of respect there given buy others. In that regard, than, respect has to be earned; its not hour unquestioned right to demand it. All of you hear and now should begin to chose behaviors that will led others to respect you. Its you're choice.

E-mail Messages

Study the model that illustrates e-mail on p. 75.

E-mail Message 1

1. Key the model e-mail on p. 76.
2. Proofread your copy; correct all errors.

Save as: 29B EMAIL1*

*E-mail can be saved automatically in e-mail software. Use this filename only if your instructor directs you to save the message on disk.

E-mail Messages 2 and 3

1. Format and key the e-mail messages at the right; send to your instructor's e-mail address.
2. Proofread your copy; correct all errors.

Save as: 29B EMAIL2 and 29B EMAIL3

INTERNET ACTIVITY

Using an Internet search engine, gather information about a play, symphony, or concert you would like to attend. Send an e-mail inviting a friend to go with you. Include all the necessary details.

E-mail Message 2

Subject: HELP!!!

Hopefully, my sister told you that I would be e-mailing you. I'm writing a report on Mark Twain for my English class. Last weekend when Katherine was home, we were talking about this assignment. She mentioned that you were an English major and seemed to think that you had completed a course that focused on Mark Twain. She suggested that I contact you to see if you would be able to suggest some sources that I might use for this assignment.

As part of the report project, we have to read two of his books. I've already started reading *Life on the Mississippi*. Could you offer a suggestion as to what other book I should read for this assignment?

Katherine said that you are planning on coming home with her during spring break. I'll look forward to meeting you.

E-mail Message 3

Subject: WEB PAGE CREATION

As we develop our Web page, we may want to review some of those developed by other symphonies. I have already looked at several on the Web. San Francisco's was one that I felt we could model ours after.

Theirs is clear, concise, and easy to navigate. In addition to the normal sections, they have a section called "More about the San Francisco Symphony." Here they include such things as:

1. A brief history
2. The mission statement
3. Community programs
4. News items about the Symphony

To view their Web page, go to http://www.sfsymphony.org. I'll look forward to working with you at our next committee meeting.

Lesson 30   CALENDARING, CONTACTS, TASKS, AND NOTES

OBJECTIVE

• To learn to use the Calendaring, Contacts, Tasks, and Notes features.

Conditioning Practice

Key each line twice.

alphabet	1	Jack next placed my winning bid for the prized antique vase.
fig/sym	2	I deposited Lund & Lutz's $937.46 check (#2408) on April 15.
speed	3	Jan is to go to the city hall to sign the land forms for us.

gwam 1' | 1 | 2 | 3 | 4 | 5 | 6 | 7 | 8 | 9 | 10 | 11 | 12 |

Communication & Math
SKILLS 7

COMMA USAGE

ACTIVITY 1

Internal Punctuation: Comma

1. Study each of the 6 rules.
   a. Key the *Learn* line(s) beneath each rule, noting how the rule is applied.
   b. Key the *Apply* lines, inserting commas correctly.

Internal Punctuation: Comma

Rule 1: Use a comma after long (five or more words) introductory phrases, after clauses, or after words in a series.

Learn 1 When you finish keying the report, please give it to Mr. Kent.

Learn 2 We will play the Mets, Expos, and Cubs in our next home stand.

Apply 3 If you attend the play take Mary Jack and Tim with you.

Apply 4 The last exam covered memos simple tables and unbound reports.

Rule 2: Do not use a comma to separate two items treated as a single unit within a series.

Learn 5 Her favorite breakfast was bacon and eggs, muffins, and juice.

Apply 6 My choices are peaches and cream brownies or ice cream.

Apply 7 Trays of fresh fruit nuts and cheese and crackers awaited guests.

Rule 3: Use a comma before short direct quotations.

Learn 8 The man asked, "When does Flight 787 depart?"

Apply 9 Mrs. Ramirez replied "No, the report on patriotism is not finished."

Apply 10 Dr. Feit said "Please make an appointment for next week."

Rule 4: Use a comma before and after a word or words in apposition (words that come together and refer to the same person or thing).

Learn 11 Coleta, the assistant manager, will chair the next meeting.

Apply 12 Greg Mathews a pitcher for the Braves will sign autographs.

Apply 13 The personnel director Marge Wilson will be the presenter.

Rule 5: Use a comma to set off words of direct address (the name of a person spoken to).

Learn 14 I believe, Tom, that you should fly to San Francisco.

Apply 15 Finish this assignment Mary before you start on the next one.

Apply 16 Please call me Erika if I can be of further assistance.

Rule 6: Use a comma to set off nonrestrictive clauses (not necessary to the meaning of the sentence); however, do not use commas to set off restrictive clauses (necessary to the meaning of the sentence).

Learn 17 The manuscript, which I prepared, needs to be revised.

Learn 18 The manuscript that presents voting alternatives is complete.

Apply 19 The movie which won top awards dealt with human rights.

Apply 20 The student who scores highest on the exam will win the award.

(continued on next page)

30B

Calendar

Using the Calendar feature, record the appointments shown at the right.

Save as: 30B CALENDAR

1. Jamison Russell, Vice President of Riley Manufacturing Company, on June 5 from 10:30 to 11:30 a.m.
2. Vivian Bloomfield, Manager of Garnett Enterprises, on June 9 from 3:30 to 4:30 p.m.
3. Department meeting from 9 to 11:30 a.m. on June 9.
4. Chamber of Commerce meeting on June 5 from 3:30 to 5 p.m.

30C

Contacts

In your contacts create a new file folder called 30C Contacts. Record the information at the right in the folder. Print a copy of the file in Business Cards view.

Save as: 30C CONTACTS

Old Home Studio

Maria Santos
Proprietor

381 Hilltop Drive
Longmont, CO 80501

Phone: 970-923-1655
Fax: 970-923-1600
Email: msantos@microsoft.com

Jason Fennimore
Director of Human Resources

713 Chadwick Circle
Kissimmee, FL 34746

Global Technologies

Phone: 407-382-1832
Fax: 407-382-1838
Email: jpfennim@microsoft.com

30D

Tasks

Record the tasks shown at the right using the Tasks feature.

Save as: 30D TASKS

1. Schedule an appointment with Jack Mason to discuss photo shoot.
2. Schedule a meeting with Marketing to discuss new products.
3. Turn in May expense report.
4. Meet with Erin Hollingsworth to discuss layout of annual report.

30E

Notes

Use the Notes feature to create notes for the items shown at the right.

Save as: 30E NOTES

1. Get the sales figures ready for the 3 p.m. department meeting.
2. Call Brookstone Travel Agency to change reservations.
3. Check with Paul to see if he is ready for the meeting on Friday.

Reading/Keying Response Patterns

1. Key each line three times (slowly, faster, top speed).
2. Key two 1' timings on lines 7–9; determine *gwam* on each timing.

Emphasize quick finger reaches, wrists low and relaxed.

balanced-hand words

1 is by do if go he so us to me of jam row rug she bus air but city
2 both also busy held duck dial form make rush sick soap when towns
3 visit widow theme title ivory proxy quake shape amend burnt chair

Emphasize high-speed phrase responses.

balanced-hand phrases

4 He owns it | make the signs | paid the man | go to work | if they fix the
5 Go to the | they may make | to the problem | with the sign | and the maps
6 With the city | the eighth neighbor | social problem | the big ornament

Emphasize high-speed, word-level response; quick spacing.

balanced-hand sentences

7 Pamela paid the man by the city dock for the six bushels of corn.
8 Keith may keep the food for the fish by the big antique fishbowl.
9 The haughty girls paid for their own gowns for the island social.

gwam 1' | 1 | 2 | 3 | 4 | 5 | 6 | 7 | 8 | 9 | 10 | 11 | 12 | 13 |

Techniques: Figures

1. Set 0.5" side margins.
2. Clear all tabs; then set tabs 2", 4", and 6" from the left margin.
3. Key the lines, tabbing from column to column; key the lines again at a faster rate.

Keep eyes on copy.

$17.84	638-38-4911	(389) 392-8256	11/20/86
$65.67	832-17-0647	(465) 709-7294	05/25/49
$91.03	541-78-0924	(513) 330-5760	06/20/59

Timed Writings

1. Key two 1' timings on each ¶; determine *gwam*.
2. Key three 2' timings on ¶s 1–2 combined; determine *gwam*.

A all letters used MicroPace

gwam 1' | 2'

A business is in business to make a profit. They do 11 | 5
this by employing individuals who help the organization 22 | 11
achieve its goals. In the past, various styles of 32 | 16
leadership were used. Today, however, one of the most 42 | 21
common styles used is the democratic style. This is where 54 | 27
decisions are made by a team of individuals rather than 65 | 33
by just one person. 69 | 34

Because more and more companies are operating as a 79 | 40
team, it is important for you to learn to participate as 90 | 45
part of a team. This requires an effort on your part. 101 | 51
Good team members listen to the opinions of other individuals 113 | 57
on the team. Good team members are considerate of others. 125 | 62
Good team members respect the rights of others. Good team 136 | 68
members are excellent communicators. 144 | 72

gwam 1' | 1 | 2 | 3 | 4 | 5 | 6 | 7 | 8 | 9 | 10 | 11 | 12 |
2' | 1 | 2 | 3 | 4 | 5 | 6 |

Office Features 3

For each activity, read and learn the feature described, then follow instructions at the left.

Activity 1

Format Painter

WP • Home/Clipboard/Format Painter

Open *DF OF3 ACTIVITY1*. Use Format Painter to copy the formatting for University of Wisconsin—Eau Claire from line 1 and apply the formatting to lines 2–4.

Save as: OF3 ACTIVITY1

Use the **Format Painter** feature to copy formatting from one place and apply it in another. Click the paintbrush once to apply the formatting to one place in a document; double-click to apply it to multiple places.

[handwritten: use format painter   highlight then click format painter then high- ligh]

1. The University of Wisconsin—Eau Claire was founded in 1916.
2. The University of Wisconsin—Eau Claire has over 10,000 students.
3. The University of Wisconsin—Eau Claire was rated as a "Best Midwestern College" for 2008 in *The Princeton Review*.
4. The University of Wisconsin—Eau Claire was rated No. 5 among the top regional public universities in the Midwest in the 2008 edition of *America's Best Colleges* (*U.S. News & World Report magazine*).

Activity 2

Sort

WP • Home/Paragraph/Sort

Open *DF OF3 ACTIVITY2*. Use the Sort feature to alphabetize the names in ascending order and the numbers in descending order.

Save as: OF3 ACTIVITY2

Use the **Sort** feature to arrange text in alphabetical order and numbers in numerical order. Ascending order is from A to Z and 0 to 9; descending order is Z to A and 9 to 0.

Entire lists can be sorted, or parts of a list can be selected and sorted.

Ascending Order

Barrett, James
Benavides, Eduardo
Buza, Margaret
Clemens, Nancy
Flannigan, Marsha
George, Theodore

Activity 3

Center Page

WP • Page Layout/Page Setup Dialog Box/Layout

1. Key the copy DS; center the copy horizontally and vertically.
2. Use Print Preview to see how the copy looks on the page.

Save as: OF3 ACTIVITY3

Use the **Center Page** feature to center lines of text between the top and bottom margins of the page. This feature leaves an equal (or nearly equal) amount of white space above and below the text. Inserting one hard return below the last keyed line gives the document a more centered look.

Pot of Gold

by Dianna Vermillion

Together we chased after the rainbow

To find the pot of gold; but in each other,

We found our own treasure to unfold.

[Insert one hard return]

Table 2

Format and key one table that includes all the information shown at the right. Use **INFORMATION ABOUT SELECTED STATES** as a title. Data about each state should make up one row of the table. Alphabetize the rows by state. Include this source note:

Source: James R. Giese, et al. *The American Century,* **New York: West Educational Publishing, 1999, pp. 922–925.**

Place a border around each cell that has a **1** and color the cell light green. Place a border around each cell with a **50** and color the cell light purple.

Save as: **71B TABLE2**

Alaska	Idaho	Montana
Rank Entering Union: 49	Rank Entering Union: 43	Rank Entering Union: 41
Rank Land Area: 1	Rank Land Area: 13	Rank Land Area: 4
Rank Population: 49	Rank Population: 42	Rank Population: 44
California	**Illinois**	**Nebraska**
Rank Entering Union: 31	Rank Entering Union: 21	Rank Entering Union: 37
Rank Land Area: 3	Rank Land Area: 24	Rank Land Area: 15
Rank Population: 1	Rank Population: 6	Rank Population: 36
Delaware	**Kansas**	**Rhode Island**
Rank Entering Union: 1	Rank Entering Union: 34	Rank Entering Union: 13
Rank Land Area: 49	Rank Land Area: 14	Rank Land Area: 50
Rank Population: 46	Rank Population: 32	Rank Population: 43
Hawaii	**Michigan**	**Wyoming**
Rank Entering Union: 50	Rank Entering Union: 26	Rank Entering Union: 44
Rank Land Area: 47	Rank Land Area: 23	Rank Land Area: 9
Rank Population: 41	Rank Population: 8	Rank Population: 50

Table 3

1. Open *DF 71B TABLE3 2007.*
2. Change the page orientation to landscape. Insert the new columns and make the changes to the headings as shown at the right.
3. Open *DF 71B TABLE3 2003* to get the information for the new columns.
4. Key the data for the new columns.
5. The *Inquirer* had a circulation of **365,154** and was ranked **19** in 2003; the *Rocky Mountain News* had a circulation of **390,938** and was ranked **27** in 2003.
6. Change the source note to include both 2007 and 2003.

Save as: **71B TABLE3**

CHANGES IN TOP TEN U. S. DAILY NEWSPAPERS
Comparison of 2007 to 2003

2007 Rank	2003 Rank	Newspaper	Location	2007 Circulation	2003 Circulation
1		*USA Today*	Arlington, VA	2,528,437	
2		*Wall Street Journal*	New York, NY	2,058,342	
3		*Times*	New York, NY	1,683,855	
4		*Times*	Los Angeles, CA	1,231,318	
5		*Post*	Washington, D.C.	960,684	
6		*Tribune*	Chicago, IL	957,212	
7		*Daily News*	New York, NY	795,153	
8		*Inquirer*	Philadelphia, PA	705,965	
9		*Post/Rocky Mountain News*	Denver, CO	704,806	
10		*Chronicle*	Houston, TX	692,557	

Source: *Time Almanac and Information Please 2007* (Upper Saddle River, NJ: Pearson Education, 2006).

Activity 4

Thesaurus

 WP • Review/Proofing/Thesaurus

Key the ¶ at the right DS. After keying the ¶, use the Thesaurus to replace each word in blue with one suggested in the Thesaurus.

Save as: OF3 ACTIVITY4

Use the **Thesaurus** to find words that have a similar meaning to a word in your document.

Review → Thesaurus

If you are writing and can't think of the right word to use or are not quite content with the word you presently have down, you can use the Thesaurus to find words that have a comparable meaning (synonym). This can be a very important tool if you do a lot of writing for your occupation.

Activity 5

Hard Page Break

 WP • Insert/Pages/Page Break

1. Key the roster signup sheet for the Red Sox shown at the right. Leave a 2" top margin on each page. Use 14-pt. Comic Sans for the font; 1.15" spacing below the title and between the numbers; 12 players will be signing up for the team.
2. Insert a hard page break at the end of the Red Sox Roster page. Create sign-up sheets for the Mets, the Dodgers, and the Cubs.

Save as: OF3 ACTIVITY5

Word processing software has two types of page breaks: **soft** and **hard**. Both kinds signal the end of a page and the beginning of a new page. The software inserts a soft page break automatically when the current page is full. You insert hard page breaks manually when you want a new page to begin before the current one is full. When a hard page break is inserted, the wp software adjusts any following soft page breaks so that those pages will be full before a new one is started. Hard page breaks do not move unless you move them. To move a hard page break, you can (1) delete it and let the software insert soft page breaks, or (2) insert a new hard page break where you want it.

RED SOX ROSTER

1.

2.

11.

12.

Activity 6

Widow/Orphan

 WP • Page Layout/Paragraph Dialog Box/Line and Page Breaks

1. Open *DF OF3 ACTIVITY6*. An orphan line appears at the top of p. 4.
2. Turn on the Widow/Orphan feature at the beginning of that line. The line is automatically reformatted to prevent an orphan line.

Save as: OF3 ACTIVITY6

The **Widow/Orphan** feature ensures that the first line of a paragraph does not appear by itself at the bottom of a page (**orphan line**) or the last line of a paragraph does not appear by itself at the top of a page (**widow line**).

2

well organized, and easy to read.

Finally, support your report with a list of references from which you paraphrased or directly quoted. Quoting or paraphras-

Example of widow line

- To improve table formatting skills.
- To format tables with enhanced borders and shading.

71B

Table Formatting

Table 1

Combine the information shown in the two tables at the right into one table as shown in the illustration below. Using the data from July 2005, rank the most populated states in descending order and the least populated states in ascending order.

Main Heading: MOST AND LEAST POPULATED STATES

Secondary Heading: 1990 Compared to 2005

Orientation: landscape

Source Note: *Time Almanac 2007*, p. 122.

Save as: **71B TABLE1**

SELECTED STATE POPULATIONS

July 1990

Most Populated States		Least Populated States	
State	Population	State	Population
California	29,760,021	Wyoming	453,588
Texas	16,986,510	Vermont	562,758
Illinois	11,430,602	South Dakota	696,004
New York	17,990,455	North Dakota	638,800
Ohio	10,847,115	Montana	799,065
Pennsylvania	11,881,643	Delaware	666,168
Florida	12,937,926	Alaska	550,043

SELECTED STATE POPULATIONS

July 2005

Most Populated States		Least Populated States	
State	Population	State	Population
California	36,132,147	Wyoming	509,294
Texas	22,859,968	Vermont	623,050
New York	19,254,630	North Dakota	636,677
Florida	17,789,864	Alaska	663,661
Illinois	12,763,371	South Dakota	775,933
Pennsylvania	12,429,615	Delaware	843,524
Ohio	11,464,042	Montana	935,670

Most Populated States					Least Populated States				
State	1990		2005		State	1990		2005	
	Ranking	Population	Ranking	Population		Ranking	Population	Ranking	Population

Activity 7

Page Numbers

WP • Insert/Header & Footer/
Page Number

1. Open *OF3 ACTIVITY6*.
2. Number all five pages with the page number at the bottom center of the page. Hide the number on p. 1.
3. Use Print Preview to verify that the page numbers have been added (pp. 2–5) or hidden (p. 1).

Save as: OF3 ACTIVITY7

Use the **Page Number** feature to place page numbers in specific locations on the printed page. Most software allows you to select the style of number (Arabic numerals—1, 2, 3; lowercase Roman numerals—i, ii, iii; uppercase Roman numerals—I, II, III).

You can place numbers at the top or bottom of the page, aligned at the left margin, center, or right margin. Use the Different First Page feature to keep the page number from appearing on the first page.

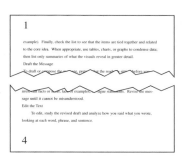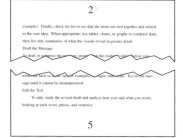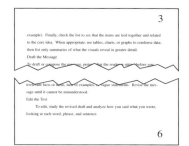

Page numbering positions

Activity 8

Indentations

WP • Home/Paragraph Dialog
Box/Indents and Spacing

1. Set margins at Wide. Use Century Gothic, 14-pt. font.
2. Key the three ¶s, indenting them as indicated.

Save as: OF3 ACTIVITY8

Use the **Indent** feature to move text away from the margin. A **left indent (paragraph indent)** moves the text one tab stop to the right, away from the left margin. A **hanging indent** moves all but the first line of a paragraph one tab stop to the right.

No indent — This example shows text that is not indented from the left margin. All lines begin at the left margin. DS

Left (paragraph) indent 0.5" — This example shows text that is indented from the left margin. Notice that each line begins at the indentation point. DS

Hanging indent 0.5" — This example shows hanging indent. Notice that the first line begins at the left margin, but the remaining lines begin at the indentation point.

Activity 9

Styles

WP • Home/Styles/select style

1. Open *DF OF3 ACTIVITY9*.
2. Select the text for the first line (Title).
3. Click on the Title style feature.
4. Select the next line of text and click on the corresponding style (Subtitle).

Repeat for each of the remaining lines of text.

Save as: OF3 ACTIVITY9

The **Styles** feature provides a collection of preset formats for titles, subtitles, headings, etc. It is easy to format text using the Styles feature. Simply select the text to be formatted and click on the style with the desired formatting.

Before Style Applied	After Style Applied
Title	Title
Subtitle	*Subtitle*
Heading 1	**Heading 1**
Heading 2	**Heading 2**
Intense Quote	*Intense Quote*
Intense Reference	INTENSE REFERENCE

Table 2

Key the table at the right. Use the table format features that you have learned to arrange the information attractively on the page. Use a border and shading similar to the illustration. DS between each data entry.

Include the following source note outside the table:

Source: Matthew T. Downey, et al. _United States History_ (New York: National Textbook Company, 1997), p. 158.

Save as: **70B TABLE2**

THE CONSTITUTION		
The Executive Branch	**The Legislative Branch**	**The Judicial Branch**
• President administers and enforces federal laws • President chosen by electors who have been chosen by the states	• A bicameral or two-house legislature • Each state has equal number of representatives in the Senate • Representation in the House determined by state population • Simple majority required to enact legislation	• National court system directed by the Supreme Court • Courts to hear cases related to national laws, treaties, the Constitution; cases between states, between citizens of different states, or between a state and citizens of another state

Table 3

Key the table at the right. Use the table format features that you have learned to arrange the information attractively on the page. Use a border and shading similar to the illustration. Use landscape orientation and AutoFit Window.

Include the following source note outside the table:

Source: http://www.pollingreport.com/prioriti.htm, August 6, 2007.

Save as: **70B TABLE3**

CNN/OPINION RESEARCH CORPORATION POLL
May 4-6, 2007

"How important will each of the following issues be to your vote for president next year?"				
Issue	**Extremely Important %**	**Very Important %**	**Moderately Important %**	**Not That Important %**	**Unsure %**
The situation in Iraq	51	37	9	2	-
Terrorism	45	35	14	6	-
Education	44	37	16	3	-
Health care	43	35	18	4	-
Gas prices	43	31	16	10	1
Corruption and ethical standards in government	41	36	17	7	-
The situation in Iran	38	39	17	5	1
Social Security and Medicare	38	37	20	4	-
The economy	33	46	16	4	-
Illegal immigration	31	32	26	10	1

Activity 10

Apply What You Have Learned

1. Set spacing for DS—no space before or after ¶; set top margin for 2".
2. Key headings in Title style; key text in 12 pt. font.
3. SS the second ¶; indent the ¶ 0.5" from the left.
4. Place the References on a separate page. Use the Hanging Indent feature to key the reference lines SS.
5. Use the Spelling and Grammar checker; then proofread.

Save as: **OF3 ACTIVITY10**

Famous Speeches

Many famous speeches have been delivered over the years. The content of these speeches continues to be used to inspire, motivate, and unify us today. Winston Churchill and Abraham Lincoln delivered two great examples of such speeches.

Winston Churchill served his country as soldier, statesman, historian, and journalist. His military career and work as a reporter took him to India, Cuba, and the Sudan. He was elected to Parliament in 1900, again from 1906–1908, and from 1924–1945. He held dozens of other key posts, including that of Prime Minister. (LaRocco and Johnson, 1997, 49)

Reference

LaRocco, Christine B., and Elaine B. Johnson. *British & World Literature for Life and Work*. Cincinnati: South-Western, Cengage Learning, 1997.

Activity 11

Apply What You Have Learned

1. Open file *DF OF3 ACTIVITY11*.
2. **Bold** the names of the states and change the font size to 14pt. *Italicize* the names of the state flowers.
3. At the end of each line, key (bold and italicize) the state nickname in blue.
4. Sort the lines alphabetically in ascending order by state.
5. Center the text vertically and horizontally on the page.

Save as: **OF3 ACTIVITY11**

Michigan, Lansing - *Apple Blossom* - *The Great Lakes State*

Florida, Tallahassee - *Orange Blossom* - *The Sunshine State*

Massachusetts, Boston - *Mayflower* - *Bay State*

North Carolina, Raleigh - *Dogwood* - *The Tar Heel State*

California, Sacramento - *Golden Poppy* - *The Golden State*

Washington, Olympia - *Rhododendron* - *Evergreen State*

New York, Albany - *Rose* - *Empire State*

New Jersey, Trenton - *Purple Violet* - *Garden State*

Texas, Austin - *Bluebonnet* - *Lone Star State*

Illinois, Springfield - *Violet* - *Prairie State*

Hint: After making the formatting changes to Michigan, place the insertion point on Michigan, double-click the Format Painter, and then click on each state.

Activity 12

Apply What You Have Learned

1. Set the left and right margins at 1.7"; set the top margin at 2".
2. Key each quote on a separate page using the Title style for the name and date and the Subtitle style for the quote.
3. Place page numbers at bottom center of each page.

Save as: **OF3 ACTIVITY12**

Albert Einstein (1879–1955)

"Every day I remind myself that my inner and outer life are based on the labors of other men, living and dead, and that I must exert myself in order to give in the same measure as I have received and am still receiving."

Abraham Lincoln (1809–1865)

"Nearly all men can stand adversity, but if you want to test a man's character, give him power."

Helen Keller (1880–1968)

"Character cannot be developed in ease and quiet. Only through experience of trial and suffering can the soul be strengthened, ambition inspired, and success achieved."

Winston Churchill (1874–1965)

"All great things are simple, and many can be expressed in single words: freedom, justice, honor, duty, mercy, hope."

- To improve table formatting skills.
- To format tables with enhanced borders and shading.

70B   Formatting

Table Formatting

Table 1

Key the table at the right; insert each of the following three names next to the individual's accomplishments.

Alex Haley
Thurgood Marshall
Colin Powell

Use the table format features that you have learned to arrange the information attractively on the page. Use a border similar to the one shown.

Save as: 70B TABLE1

FAMOUS AMERICANS

Name	Significant Accomplishments
Charles Drew	Developed a means for preserving blood plasma for transfusion.
	First black officer to hold the highest military post in the U.S., Chairman of the U.S. Joint Chiefs of Staff.
Shirley Chisholm	First black woman to be elected to the U.S. Congress.
	First black member of the U.S. Supreme Court.
Booker T. Washington	Organized a teaching and industrial school for African Americans—Tuskegee Institute.
Benjamin Banneker	First African American to receive a presidential appointment. Famous for his role as a planner for Washington, D.C.
W.E.B. DuBois	Cofounder of the organization that became the National Association for the Advancement of Colored People (NAACP).
Alice Walker	Pulitzer Prize-winning writer and poet. Novels include *The Color Purple* and *In Love and Trouble*.
	Pulitzer Prize-winning author. Wrote *Roots*, which was made into the highest-rated television miniseries of all time.
Frederick Douglass	Eminent human rights leader of the 19th century; the first black citizen to hold a high rank in the U.S. government.

Source: "Black History Innovators," *USA Today*, February 15, 2000, http://www.usatoday.com.

UNIT 10
Lessons 31-34

Learn to Format Unbound Reports

Format Guides: Unbound Reports

Short reports are often prepared without covers or binders. If they consist of more than one page, the pages are usually fastened together in the upper-left corner by a staple or paper clip. Such reports are called unbound reports.

Standard Margins

The standard margins for unbound reports are presented below.

	First Page	Second page and subsequent pages
Side Margins (SM)	1"	1"
Top Margin (TM)	2"	1"
Bottom Margin (BM)	Approximately 1"	Approximately 1"
Page number	Optional; bottom at center if used	Top; right-aligned

Internal Spacing of Reports

All parts of the report are SS using the 1.15 default line spacing.

Page Numbers

The first page of an unbound report may or may not include a page number. *The reports keyed for this unit will not include a page number on the first page.* On the second and subsequent pages, the page number should be right-aligned at the top of the page. The Page Number feature of your software can be used to automatically place the page number in the location you specify.

Titles and Headings

The title of the report is formatted using the Title style. The default Title style is 26-point Cambria font (Dark Blue, Text 2) with a bottom border. The default Title style will be used in this unit.

Side headings are keyed at the left margin and formatted using Heading 1 style. The default Heading 1 style is 14-pt. Cambria font (Blue, Accent 1). Capitalize the first letters of all words except prepositions in titles and side headings.

Textual (Within Text) Citations

References used to give credit for paraphrased or quoted material—called textual citations—are keyed in parentheses in the body of the report. *The textual citation method of documentation will be used for this unit.* Textual citations include the names(s) of the author(s), year of publication, and page number(s) of the material cited. *Note*: For electronic (Internet) references, textual citations include the name(s) of the author(s) and the year of publication. When there are two articles by the same author, the title of the article will also be included, as shown on p. 89.

Quotations of up to three keyed lines are enclosed in quotation marks. Long quotations (four lines or more) are indented 0.5" from the left margin. Paraphrased material is not enclosed in quotation marks, nor is it indented.

An ellipsis (. . .) is used to indicate material omitted from a quotation. An ellipsis is three periods, each preceded and followed by a space. If the omitted material occurs at the end of a sentence, include the period or other punctuation before the ellipsis.

> In ancient Greece, plays were performed only a few times a year. . . . The festivals were held to honor Dionysius in the hope that he would bless the Greeks. . . . (Prince and Jackson, 1997, 35)

Reference Lists

All references used in a report are listed alphabetically by author's last name at the end of the report on a separate page under the title References (or Bibliography or Works Cited). The References section is formatted with the same margins as the first page of the report.

The page number for the References page is placed at the top right of the page. *References* is keyed 2" from the top margin using the Title style. Begin the first line of each reference at the left margin; indent other lines 0.5" (hanging indent format).

• To improve table formatting skills.
• To format tables with enhanced borders and shading.

69B Formatting

Table Formatting

Table 1

Key the table at the right using the Arial font and landscape orientation. Use the table format features that you have learned to arrange the information attractively on the page. Use a table border and shading similar to the illustration. Adjust column width so that each entry fits on a single line.

Save as: 69B TABLE1

Table 2

Update the table to include information about Presidents since 2009. Use the Internet site shown in the source note.

Save as: 69B TABLE2

PRESIDENTS 1953–2009			
President	**Dates in Office**	**State of Birth**	**Undergraduate Degree**
Dwight D. Eisenhower	1953–1961	Texas	West Point
John F. Kennedy	1961–1963	Massachusetts	Harvard
Lyndon B. Johnson	1963–1969	Texas	Texas State University-San Marcos
Richard M. Nixon	1969–1974	California	Whittier College
Gerald R. Ford	1974–1977	Nebraska	University of Michigan
James E. Carter, Jr.	1977–1981	Georgia	Naval Academy
Ronald W. Reagan	1981–1989	Illinois	Eureka College
George H. W. Bush	1989–1993	Massachusetts	Yale University
William J. Clinton	1993–2001	Arkansas	Georgetown University
G. W. Bush	2001–2009	Connecticut	Yale University
Blue = Republican Party Affiliation		Red = Democratic Party Affiliation	

Source: http://www.whitehouse.gov/history/presidents/, August 6, 2007.

Table 3

Create a table with the information shown at right. Use **PRESIDENT BUSH'S CABINET** for the main heading and **August 4, 2007** for the secondary heading. Use **Executive Department** and **Head of Department** for the column headings. Apply an appropriate border.

Save as: 69B TABLE3

Table 4

Using the source shown at the right, update the table with the current President's cabinet information.

Save as: 69B TABLE4

Department of Agriculture - Secretary Mike Johanns

Department of Commerce - Secretary Carlos Gutierrez

Department of Defense - Secretary Robert M. Gates

Department of Education - Secretary Margaret Spellings

Department of Energy - Secretary Samuel W. Bodman

Department of Health & Human Services - Secretary Michael O. Leavitt

Department of Homeland Security - Secretary Michael Chertoff

Department of Housing & Urban Development - Secretary Alphonso Jackson

Department of the Interior - Secretary Dirk Kempthorne

Department of Justice - Attorney General Alberto Gonzales

Department of Labor - Secretary Elaine Chao

Department of State - Secretary Condoleezza Rice

Department of Transportation - Secretary Mary E. Peters

Department of the Treasury - Secretary Henry M. Paulson, Jr.

Department of Veterans Affairs - Secretary Jim Nicholson

Source: http://www.whitehouse.gov/government/cabinet.html, August 8, 2007.

Shown in 11-point Calibri with 2" top margin and 1" side margins, this report appears smaller than actual size.

Title **Effective Communicators** (Title style)

1" SM Communication is the thread that binds our society together. Effective communicators are able to use the thread (communication skills) to shape the future. To be an effective communicator, one must know how to put words together that communicate thoughts, ideas, and feelings. These thoughts, ideas, and feelings are then expressed in writing or delivered orally. Some individuals are immortalized because of their ability to put words together. A few examples of those who have been immortalized are Patrick Henry, Nathan Hale, Abraham Lincoln, and Susan B. Anthony.

Side heading **Patrick Henry** (Heading 1 style)

Words move people to action. Patrick Henry's words ("I know not what course others may take; but as for me, give me liberty or give me death!") helped bring about the Revolutionary War in 1775.

Side heading **Nathan Hale** (Heading 1 style)

Words show an individual's commitment. Who can question Nathan Hale's commitment when he said, "I only regret that I have but one life to lose for my country."

Side heading **Abraham Lincoln** (Heading 1 style)

Words can inspire. The Gettysburg Address, delivered in 1863 by Abraham Lincoln, inspired the Union to carry on its cause. Today many Americans, still inspired by Lincoln's words, have committed to memory at least part of his address. "Four score and seven years ago, our fathers brought forth on this continent a new nation, conceived in liberty, and dedicated to the proposition that all men are created equal. Now we are engaged in a great civil war . . ."

Side heading **Susan B. Anthony** (Heading 1 style)

Words bring about change. "The only question left to be settled now is: Are women persons? And I hardly believe any of our opponents will have the hardihood to say they are not. Being persons, then, women are citizens; and no state has a right to make any law, or to enforce any old law, that shall abridge their privileges or immunities."

at least 1"

Unbound Report – Word 2007

Table 2

Column headings: Row height 0.4"; Center alignment; bold text.

Data rows: Row height 0.4"; Bottom Left alignment.

Table placement: Center the table horizontally and vertically.

Save as: **68C TABLE2**

WHAT AMERICANS REMEMBER

Top Five Events

Rank	**Age Group**			
	18–34	**35–54**	**55–64**	**65 and Over**
1	Oklahoma City Bombing	Oklahoma City Bombing	JFK Death	JFK Death
2	Challenger	JFK Death	Moon Walk	Pearl Harbor
3	Gulf War Begins	Challenger	Oklahoma City Bombing	WWII Ends
4	Reagan Shot	Moon Walk	Challenger	Moon Walk
5	Berlin Wall Falls	Gulf War Begins	MLK Death	FDR Death

Source: The Pew Research Center, "America's Collective Memory," July 28, 2007, http://people-press.org/reports/display.php3?PageID=283.

Table 3

Column headings: Row height 0.4"; Center alignment; bold text; 15% shading.

Data rows: Row height 0.4"; Bottom alignment.

Table placement: Center horizontally and vertically.

Save as: **68C TABLE3**

Table 4

Note how Table 3 contains the same information as Table 2, but arranged in a different way. Use your decision-making skills to create a third table from the information, arranging it in still another way.

Save as: **68C TABLE4**

WHAT AMERICANS REMEMBER

Top Five Events

Event	**Age Group**			
	18–34	**35–54**	**55–64**	**65+**
■ Berlin Wall Falls	5	*	*	*
■ Challenger	2	3	4	*
■ Franklin D. Roosevelt Death	*	*	*	5
■ Gulf War Begins	3	5	*	*
■ John F. Kennedy Death	*	2	1	1
■ Martin Luther King Death	*	*	5	*
■ Moon Walk	*	4	2	4
■ Oklahoma City Bombing	1	1	3	*
■ Pearl Harbor	*	*	*	2
■ Reagan Shot	4	*	*	*
■ World War II Ends	*	*	*	3
1 = Ranked First, 2 = Ranked Second, etc.; * = Not ranked in top five by this age group.				

Source: The Pew Research Center, "America's Collective Memory," July 28, 2007, http://people-press.org/reports/display.php3?PageID=283.

Lesson 31   UNBOUND REPORT MODEL

- To learn format features of unbound reports.
- To process a one-page unbound report in proper format.

31A

Conditioning Practice
Key each line twice.

alphabet 1 Jack will help Mary fix the quaint old stove at the big zoo.

figures 2 Check Numbers 197, 267, 304, and 315 were cashed on June 28.

easy 3 Jan and Sydney may wish to make gowns for the civic socials.

gwam 1' | 1 | 2 | 3 | 4 | 5 | 6 | 7 | 8 | 9 | 10 | 11 | 12 |

31B

Report Formatting/Editing
Open *15C TITLES*. For each of the five stories, reformat the title, author, and first sentence in report format as shown at the right. Each entry should appear on a separate page.

Save as: **31B REPORT**

2" TM

(Title) **Farmer Boy** Title style

(Author) *by Laura Ingalls Wilder* Subtitle style ↓ 2

(First sentence) It was January in northern New York State, sixty-seven years ago. Snow lay deep everywhere.

Page number centered at the bottom of the page.

1

31C ── Formatting

Unbound Report

Save as: **31C REPORT**

1. Read the format guides on p. 86; study the model report on p. 87.

2. Key the model report; proofread and correct errors.

Lesson 32   UNBOUND REPORT MODEL

- To process a two-page unbound report in proper format.
- To format textual citations in a report.
- To process references.

32A

Conditioning Practice
Key each line twice.

alphabet 1 Jessica moved quickly to her left to win the next big prize.

figures 2 Kevin used a comma in 3,209 and 4,146 but not in 769 or 805.

easy 3 The key is to name the right six goals and to work for them.

gwam 1' | 1 | 2 | 3 | 4 | 5 | 6 | 7 | 8 | 9 | 10 | 11 | 12 |

Table Editing

Open *67C TABLE3* and make the following changes.

1. Delete *John Wilkes Booth* and *Thomas Jefferson* from the table.
2. Add the three names shown at right (in alphabetical order).
3. Make any adjustments necessary to make the table fit on one page.

Save as: 68B TABLE1

Tisquantum	Taught the Pilgrims farming techniques; helped them establish treaties with native tribes.	1580–1622 (approx.)
Sir Walter Raleigh	English adventurer who settled the region from South Carolina north to present-day New York City under a charter from Queen Elizabeth I of England.	1554–1618
John D. Rockefeller	Oil magnate and philanthropist; founded Standard Oil Company in 1870.	1839–1937

Formatting

Table Formatting

Key Tables 1–4 using the information given below.

Table 1

Table Style: Medium Shading 2 - Accent 4; make adjustments to alignment of rows as shown at right; increase size of last column to fit date on one line.

Font Size: Main heading 14 pt.; column headings 12 pt.; column A 11 pt. columns B, C, D, E 10 pt.

Row Height: Column heading row 0.5"; all other rows 0.4".

Save as: 68C TABLE1

KNOW YOUR COUNTRIES

Country	Term for Citizens	Capital	Largest City	Independence
Australia	Australian(s)	Canberra	Sydney 4.2 million	January 1, 1901
China	Chinese	Beijing	Chongqing 30.5 million	February 12, 1912
Kenya	Kenyan(s)	Nairobi	Nairobi 1.3 million	December 12, 1963
Vietnam	Vietnamese	Hanoi	Ho Chi Minh City 5.6 million	September 2, 1945
Mexico	Mexican(s)	Mexico City	Mexico City *16 million	September 16, 1810
India	Indian(s)	New Delhi	Mumbai 16.4 million	August 15, 1947
Germany	German(s)	Berlin	Berlin 3.4 million	October 3, 1990 Reunification Date
France	French	Paris	Paris *11.3 million	July 14, 1789
Morocco	Moroccan(s)	Rabat	Casablanca 3.5 million	March 2, 1956
Jordan	Jordanian(s)	Amman	Amman 2 million	May 25, 1946
Colombia	Colombian(s)	Bogota	Bogota 4.3 million	July 20, 1810
South Korea	Korean(s)	Seoul	Seoul 11 million	August 15, 1945

*Denotes Greater Metropolitan Population.
Source: http://lcweb2.loc.gov/frd/cs/profiles.html, August 6, 2007.

Title
Samuel Clemens ("Mark Twain")

Report
body
Samuel Clemens was one of America's most renowned authors. The colorful life he led was the basis for his writing. Although his formal education ended when he was 12 years old with the death of his father, his varied career interests provided an informal education, not unlike many others of his generation. Clemens brings these rich experiences to life in his writing.

Textual
citation

Textual
citation
Sam Clemens was recognized for his fiction as well as for his humor. It has been said that " . . . next to sunshine and fresh air Mark Twain's humor has done more for the welfare of mankind than any other agency" (Railton, "Your Mark Twain," 2003). By cleverly weaving fiction and humor, he developed many literary masterpieces. Some say his greatest masterpiece was "Mark Twain," a pen name (pseudonym) Clemens first used in the Nevada Territory in 1863. This fictitious name became a kind of mythic hero to the American public (Railton, "Sam Clemens as Mark Twain," 2003).

1" SM
Mark Twain was brought to national prominence when his first book, *The Celebrated Jumping Frog of Calaveras County and other Sketches*, was published in 1867. The book was comprised of 27 sketches, some of which had previously been published in newspapers. Some of his masterpieces that are among his most widely read books are *The Adventures of Tom Sawyer, Adventures of Huckleberry Finn*, and *The Prince and the Pauper*.

Side
heading
The Adventures of Tom Sawyer
The Adventures of Tom Sawyer was first published in 1876. Such characters as Tom Sawyer, Aunt Polly, Becky Thatcher, and Huck Finn have captured the attention of readers for generations. Boys and girls, young and old, enjoy Tom Sawyer's mischievousness. Who can forget how Tom shared the privilege of whitewashing Aunt Polly's fence? What child isn't fascinated by the episode of Tom and Becky lost in the cave?

Side
heading
Adventures of Huckleberry Finn
Adventures of Huckleberry Finn, the story about a boy who runs away from home and lives in the wild, has appealed to young and old alike since it was first published in 1885. Many of the characters included in *The Adventures of Tom Sawyer* surface again in *Huckleberry Finn*. The widow Douglas and the widow's sister, Miss Watson, provide formidable foes for Huckleberry despite their good intentions.

Children are able to live vicariously through Huck. What child hasn't dreamed of sneaking out of the house at night and running away to live a lifestyle of their own making?

About
1" BM

Unbound Report with Textual Citations, page 1 – Word 2007   *(continued on next page)*

Table 3

Key the table at the right and insert the following three names beside the individual's accomplishments.

Albert Einstein
Thomas Alva Edison
Andrew Carnegie

Use the table format features that you have learned to arrange the information attractively on the page.

Save as: 67C TABLE3

Table 4

Open *66C TABLE1*. Shade the cells with gray shading for the Confederate officers' names and light blue for the Union officers' names.

Save as: 67C TABLE4

INTERNET ACTIVITY

Select one of the names listed in the table at right. Use the Internet to find out more about the individual you select. Compose a ¶ or two telling about his or her contribution to American history.

Save as: 67C INTERNET

KEY PEOPLE IN
AMERICAN HISTORY

Name	Accomplishment	Life
Alexander Grayam Bell	Invented the telephone in 1977.	1847–1922
John Wilkes Boothe	Actor; Assassin of President Lincoln, April 14, 1865	1838–1865
	Scotish immigrant who built a fortune by building steel mills.	1835–1919
Crazy Horse	Sioux Indian chief who resisted government demands for his tribe to leave the Black Hills.	1842 1877
Jefferson David	President of the confederate States of America.	1808–1889
	American physicist; Theory of Relativity led to harnessing nuclear energy.	1879–1955
Thomas Jefferson	Third president of the United States; author of the Declaration of Independence.	1743–1826
Martin Luther King	Civil rights leader; belief in nonviolence was patterned after Mohandas Gandi.	1929–1968
Eleanor Roosevelt	Franklin D. Roosevelt's wife and a major champoin for civil rights and humanitarian issues.	1884–1962
Elizabeth stanton	American social reformer; led the struggle for women's sufferage with Susan B. Anthony.	1815–1902
	American inventor of the incandescent light bulb and the phonograph.	*1847–1931*

Source: James R. Giese, *The American Century* (New York: West Educational Publishing, 1999), pp. 929–935.

Lesson 68   PRESENT INFORMATION IN TABLES

OBJECTIVES

• To improve table formatting skills
• To use decision-making skills to organize information in a table.

Textual
citation

Perhaps the greatest testimony to this book was given by Ernest Hemingway when he said, "All modern American literature comes from one book by Mark Twain called Huckleberry Finn . . . . There was nothing before. There had been nothing as good since" (Waisman, "About Mark Twain," 2003).

Unbound Report with Textual Citations, page 2 – Word 2007

Title

References

List of
references

Railton, Stephen. "Your Mark Twain." http://etext.lib.virginia.edu/railton/sc_as_mt/yourmt13.html (accessed October 23, 2007).

Railton, Stephen. "Sam Clemens as Mark Twain." http://etext.virginia.edu/railton/sc_as_mt/cathompg.html (accessed October 14, 2007).

Waisman, Michael. "About Mark Twain." http://www.geocities.com/swaisman/huckfinn.htm (accessed October 18, 2007).

References Page – Word 2007

Lesson 67

OBJECTIVES
- To improve table formatting skills.
- To enhance tables with shading.

67B

Table Editing

1. Open *66C TABLE1*. Include the information shown at the right at the end of the table.
2. Sort the table to arrange the new entries alphabetically with the rest of the entries.

Save as: **67B TABLE1**

McClellan, George B.	Union Army General
Forrest, Nathan Bedford	Confederate Army General
Johnston, Albert Sidney	Confederate Army General
McDowell, Irvin	Union Army General

67C

Formatting

Table Formatting

Table 1

Format and key Table 1 (shown below) attractively on the page. Adjust row height, column width, alignment, placement, etc. Shade the column headings as shown. Use a 12-pt. font for headings and a 10-pt. font for body and source note of table.

Save as: **67C TABLE1**

Table 2

Open *67C TABLE1*. Change orientation to landscape; apply AutoFit Window. Change main heading to 16 pt. font; secondary headings to 14 pt. font; body and source note to 12 pt. font. Alphabetize columns 1, 3, and 5 of Table 1 by last name in ascending order.

Save as: **67C TABLE2**

FAMOUS AMERICANS					
Thinkers and Innovators		**Politics**		**Arts and Entertainment**	
Name	**Life**	**Name**	**Life**	**Name**	**Life**
George W. Carver	1864–1943	Frederick Douglass	1817–1895	Louis Armstrong	1901–1971
W. E. B. DuBois	1868–1963	Rosa Parks	1913–	Billie Holiday	1915–1959
Madam C. J. Walker	1867–1919	Harriet Tubman	1823–1913	Duke Ellington	1899–1974
Booker T. Washington	1856–1915	Thurgood Marshall	1908–1993	Ella Fitzgerald	1917–1996
Benjamin Banneker	1731–1806	Colin Powell	1937–	Bill Cosby	1937–
Mary McLeod Bethune	1875–1955	Shirley Chisholm	1924–	Alex Haley	1921–1992
Charles Drew	1904–1950	Martin Luther King, Jr.	1929–1968	Oprah Winfrey	1954–
Source: "Black History Innovators," *USA Today*, February 15, 2000, http://www.usatoday.com (accessed June 28, 2008).					

Unbound Report

Save as: **32B REPORT**

1. Review the format guides on p. 86; study the model report on pp. 89–90.
2. Key the model report. Proofread and correct errors.

Optional Internet Activity

Search the Internet for more information about Samuel Clemens and his literary works. Be prepared to present orally what you found.

32C ▬ **Language Skills** ▬

Language Skills: Word Choice

1. Study the spelling and definitions of the words.
2. Key all *Learn* and *Apply* lines, choosing the correct words in the *Apply* lines.

Save as: **32C CHOICE**

know (vb) to be aware of the truth of; to have understanding of	**your (adj)** of or relating to you or yourself as possessor
no (adv/adj/n) in no respect or degree; not so; indicates denial or refusal	**you're** (contr) you are

Learn 1 Did she **know** that there are **no** exceptions to the rule?

Apply 2 I just (know, no) that this is going to be a great year.

Apply 3 (Know, no), she didn't (know, no) that she was late.

Learn 1 When **you're** on campus, be sure to pick up **your** schedule.

Apply 2 (Your, You're) mother left (your, you're) keys on the table.

Apply 3 When (your, you're) out of the office, notify (your, you're) supervisor.

Lesson 33   UNBOUND REPORT MODEL

OBJECTIVES
- To process a poem.
- To process a two-page unbound report and references page in proper format.

33A

Conditioning Practice

Key each line twice.

alphabet 1 Jacob Lutz made the very quick trip to France six weeks ago.

figures 2 Only 1,359 of the 6,487 members were at the 2004 convention.

easy 3 They may turn down the lane by the shanty to their big lake.

| gwam | 1' | 1 | 2 | 3 | 4 | 5 | 6 | 7 | 8 | 9 | 10 | 11 | 12 |

33B

WP Enrichment Activity

Format the poem shown at the right. Leave a 2" TM; center-align the body. Key the title in 14 pt. (bold), the subtitle in 12 pt. (bold blue, Accent 1), and italicize the body.

Save as: **33B POEM**

Note: This poem will be used in Unit 12.

Source: *Encyclopedia Americana*, Vol. 25 (Danbury, CT: Grolier Incorporated, 2001), p. 637.

THE NEW COLOSSUS
By Emma Lazarus

Not like the brazen giant of Greek fame,
With conquering limbs astride from land to land;
Here at our sea-washed, sunset gates shall stand
A mighty woman with a torch, whose flame
Is the imprisoned lightning, and her name
Mother of Exiles. From her beacon-hand
Glows world-wide welcome; her mild eyes command
The air-bridged harbor that twin cities frame.
"Keep ancient lands, your storied pomp!" cries she
With silent lips. "Give me your tired, your poor,
Your huddled masses yearning to breathe free,
The wretched refuse of your teeming shore.
Send these, the homeless, tempest-tost to me,
I lift my lamp beside the golden door!"

Create Tables 2 and 3 using the information given below.

Table 2

Main Title: Row height 0.9"; Center alignment; bold text.

Column headings: Row height 0.4"; Center alignment; bold text.

Data Rows: Row height 0.3"; column A Bottom Left align; column B Bottom Center align.

Table placement: Center the table on the page.

Save as: **66C TABLE2**

MAJOR LAND BATTLES of the CIVIL WAR	
Battle	**Dates**
Fort Sumter	April 12–14, 1861
First Bull Run (Manassas)	July 21, 1861
Harpers Ferry	September 12–15, 1862
Second Bull Run (Manassas)	August 28–30, 1862
Antietam	September 17, 1862
Fredericksburg	December 11–15, 1862
Chancellorsville	April 30–May 6, 1863
Gettysburg	July 1–3, 1863
Wilderness	May 5–7, 1864
Spotsylvania	May 8–21, 1864
Siege & Battles around Petersburg	June 8, 1864–April 2, 1865
Appomattox	April 2–9, 1865
Battles for Atlanta	July 20–September 1, 1864

Source: Margaret E. Wagner, *The Library of Congress Civil War Desk Reference* (New York: Simon & Schuster, 2002), p. 241.

Table 3

Main Title: Row height 0.7"; center vertical alignment; bold text.

Column Titles: Row height 0.4"; Center align; bold text.

Data Rows: Row height 0.35"; column A Bottom Left align; columns B and C Bottom Center align.

Save as: **66C TABLE3**

THE CONFEDERATE STATES OF AMERICA		
State	**Seceded from Union**	**Readmitted to Union**[1]
South Carolina	December 20, 1860	July 9, 1868
Mississippi	January 9, 1861	February 23, 1870
Florida	January 10, 1861	June 25, 1868
Alabama	January 11, 1861	July 13, 1868
Georgia	January 19, 1861	July 21, 1868
Louisiana	January 26, 1861	July 9, 1868
Texas	March 2, 1861	March 30, 1870
Virginia	April 17, 1861	January 26, 1870
Arkansas	May 6, 1861	June 22, 1868
North Carolina	May 20, 1861	July 4, 1868
Tennessee	June 8, 1861	July 24, 1866

[1]Date of readmission to representation in U.S. House of Representatives.

Source: *Time Almanac and Information Please 2007* (Upper Saddle River, NJ: Pearson Education, 2006), p. 104.

Unbound Reports

Report 1

Open *DF 33C REPORT* and finish keying the report from the text at the right. Refer to the guidelines on p. 86 as needed.

After you are done keying, use the format painter to copy the formatting for the *Statue of Liberty* heading and apply it to *Central Park* and *Yankee Stadium* headings. Copy the formatting for the *New York City Today* heading and apply it to *Summary* heading.

Prepare a References page from the information below.

Fodor's New York City, 2nd Edition. New York City: Fodor's Travel Publications, 2006.

"History of New York City," http://en.wikipedia.org/wiki/History_of_New_York_City (accessed 24 October 2007).

Save as: **33C REPORT**

Note: This report will be used in Unit 12.

Statue of Liberty. The Statue of Liberty, located in New York Harbor, is a symbol of political freedom. The statue was given to the United States by the people of France in 1886. The statue was often what the immigrants first saw as they came to the United States from Europe.

Central Park. Central Park provides an opportunity to get away from the hectic pace of New York City and relax. A terrific view of the skyscrapers is always available as a backdrop to the park. The park is perfect for biking, jogging, and rollerblading. Statues throughout the park memorialize famous individuals such as Beethoven and Shakespeare.

Yankee Stadium. New York has many sports teams. The Yankees, however, with their rich tradition, is the team that brings so much attention to New York City. Yankee Stadium, "The House That Ruth Built," is a landmark in the city. When you think of baseball, you think of the Yankees, winners of 26 World Series.

Summary

New York City is like no other city in the United States. It is a hub of activity, offering something for everyone—shopping, entertainment, dining. The city is well known for its extraordinary cultural activities, numerous landmarks, and variety of sporting activities. New York has it all!

Lesson 34   UNBOUND REPORT MODEL

OBJECTIVES
• To process a two-page unbound report in *Word 2003* format (traditional style).
• To process a references page.

34A

Conditioning Practice

Key each line twice.

alphabet 1 Opal Weber made five or six quick flights to Zurich in July.

figures 2 The firm had 15 accountants in 1987 and 134 in 2006 or 2007.

easy 3 Orlando made the panel suspend the pay of the six officials.

gwam 1' | 1 | 2 | 3 | 4 | 5 | 6 | 7 | 8 | 9 | 10 | 11 | 12 |

Lesson 66   IMPROVE TABLE FORMATTING SKILLS

OBJECTIVES
- To improve table formatting skills.
- To improve language skills.

66A–71A

Conditioning Practice

Key each line twice.

alphabet	1	Karla justified a very low quiz score by explaining her problems.
fig/sym	2	My property tax increased by 12.7% ($486); I paid $3,590 in 2001.
speed	3	They may work with us to make a profit for the eighty auto firms.

gwam 1' | 1 | 2 | 3 | 4 | 5 | 6 | 7 | 8 | 9 | 10 | 11 | 12 | 13 |

66B   Language Skills

Language Skills: Word Choice

1. Study the spelling and definitions of the words.
2. Key all *Learn* and *Apply* lines, choosing the correct word in the apply lines.

Save as: 66B CHOICE

do (vb) to bring about; to carry out

due (adj) owed or owing as a debt; having reached the date for payment

for (prep/conj) used to indicate purpose; on behalf of; because; because of

four (n) the fourth in a set or series

Learn 1 **Do** you know when the three library books are **due**?
Apply 2 The next payment will be (do, due) on Tuesday, March 24.
Apply 3 I (do, due) not know when I will be available to meet again.

Learn 1 The **four** men asked **for** a salary increase **for** the next **four** years.
Apply 2 The manager left (for, four) an hour just before (for, four) o'clock.
Apply 3 The (for, four) coaches were mad after waiting (for, four) an hour.

66C   Formatting

Review Table Formatting

Key Tables 1–3 shown at right and on p. 198.

Table 1

1. Determine the number of rows and columns needed.
2. Create a table and fill in the information. Adjust column widths as needed.
3. Center and bold the main title and column headings.
4. Change the row height to 0.35" for all rows.
5. Change alignment to *Center* for the column headings and to *Bottom Left* for all other rows.
6. Center the table on the page.

Save as: 66C TABLE1

CIVIL WAR PERSONALITIES

Name	Position
Davis, Jefferson	Confederate Commander in Chief
Grant, Ulysses S.	Union Army Commanding General
Jackson, Stonewall	Confederate Army General
Johnston, Joseph E.	Confederate Army General
Lee, Robert E.	Confederate Army Commanding General
Lincoln, Abraham	Union Commander in Chief
Longstreet, James	Confederate Army General
Mead, George	Union Army General
Sheridan, Philip H.	Union Army General
Sherman, William T.	Union Army General
Stuart, J. E. B. (Jeb)	Confederate Army General
Thomas, George H.	Union Army General

Source: *Encyclopedia Americana, Vol. 6* (Danbury, CT: Grolier Incorporated, 2001), pp. 789–790.

2" TM

Title –
14pt. Bold,
ALL CAPS

0.5" ¶ Indent;
DS Body

1" SM

Bold side
headings

IMMIGRATION TO AMERICA ↓2

America has often been called the "melting pot." The name is derived from America's rich tradition of opening its doors to immigrants from all over the world. These immigrants came to the United States looking for something better. Most of them did not possess wealth or power in their home countries. Most were not highly educated. Other than these few commonalities of what they didn't possess, their backgrounds were vastly different. The thread, however, that bound these immigrants together was their vision of improving their current situation.

Emma Lazarus, in a poem entitled "The New Colossus," which is inscribed on the pedestal of the Statue of Liberty, tells of the invitation extended to those wanting to make America their home. " . . . 'Give me your tired, your poor, your huddled masses yearning to breathe free,' . . ." (*Encyclopedia Americana*, 2001, Vol. 25, 637).

Immigration Before 1780

Many have accepted the invitation to make America their home. Most of the immigrants before 1780 were from Europe.

The "melting pot" concept can be better understood by the following quote. "I could point out to you a family whose grandfather was an Englishman, whose wife was Dutch, whose son married a French woman, and whose four sons have wives of different nations" (Luedtke, 1992, 3).

Recent Immigration

Recent immigration patterns have changed; the reasons have not. Individuals and families still come to the United States with a vision of improving their lives. The backgrounds of

Unbound Report with Textual Citations, page 1 – Word 2003   *(continued on next page)*

Format Guide: Tables

Tables are used to organize and present information in a concise, logical way to make it easy for the reader to understand and analyze it. The table format can make information easier or more difficult to understand.

You will be required to use the Table word processing features presented in OF 4 (pp. 95–98) and OF 7 (pp. 193–195) to format the tables in this unit. Most of the tables are already organized; you simply need to create them to look like the examples in the text. However, some of the tables will require you to use your decision-making skills to organize the information before formatting and keying them. To complete this unit, you will need to understand the format features given below.

Table Format Features

Landscape orientation. When tables contain a large number of columns and are too wide to fit on the page, the page orientation can be changed from portrait (vertical – 8½" × 11") to landscape (horizontal – 11" × 8½").

Vertical placement. Center tables vertically. The top and bottom margins will be equal.

Horizontal placement. Center tables horizontally. The left and right margins will be equal.

Column width and row height. Adjust column width and row height to put more white space around data in the rows and columns. Additional white space makes data easier to read.

Vertical alignment. Within rows, data may be aligned at the top, center, or bottom. Title rows most often use center alignment. Data rows usually are either center- or bottom-aligned.

Horizontal alignment. Within columns, words may be left-aligned or center-aligned. Whole numbers are right-aligned if a column total is shown; decimal numbers are decimal-aligned. Other figures may be center-aligned.

Delete/Insert rows and/or columns. Delete empty rows or columns wherever they occur in a table. Also, insert a row(s) as needed above or below an existing row. Insert a column(s) to the left or right of an existing column as needed.

Merge/Split cells. To make a table attractive and easy to read, merge (join) two or more cells into one cell for the main title, source note, and other data as needed. Any existing cell can be split (divided) into two or more smaller cells if necessary.

AutoFit Contents. To save space, resize the columns to the size of the longest entry in the column automatically with the AutoFit Contents feature.

AutoFit Window. To use the entire page to attractively display information, resize the columns to maximum width automatically with the AutoFit Window feature.

Shading. Use shading (colors) to enhance table appearance and to highlight selected columns, rows, or individual cells.

Borders. Borders may be applied around an entire table or around cells, rows, or columns within a table. Borders improve appearance as well as highlight the data within them.

Sort. In a table column, text can be sorted alphabetically in ascending (A to Z) or descending (Z to A) order. Also, numbers and dates can be sorted numerically (chronologically), in either ascending or descending order.

Note: When you complete a table in this unit, check your work. Correct all spelling, keying, and formatting errors before closing or printing the file.

today's immigrants expand beyond the European borders. Today they come from all over the world. At a 1984 oath-taking ceremony in Los Angeles, there were nearly a thousand individuals from the Philippines, 890 from Mexico, 704 from Vietnam, 110 from Lebanon, 126 from the United Kingdom, and 62 from Israel. Although not as large a number, there were also individuals from Lithuania, Zimbabwe, and Tanzania (Luedtke, 1992, 3).

Unbound Report with Textual Citations, page 2 – Word 2003

3

Word 2003. The REFERENCES title is bolded, centered, and keyed in ALL CAPS in 14 pt. 2" from TM.

REFERENCES

Encyclopedia Americana, Vol. 25. "Statue of Liberty." Danbury, CT: Grolier Incorporated, 2001.

Luedtke, Luther S., ed. *Making America*. Chapel Hill: University of North Carolina Press, 1992.

References Page – Word 2003

34B Formatting

Unbound Report

Save as: **34B REPORT**

Note: This report will be used in Unit 12.

1. Review the notes on the top of p. 93. Study the model report on pp. 93–94.
2. Key the model report using the *Office Word 2003* Look template. Access the template by opening a new document, clicking on Installed Templates, and clicking on Office Word 2003.
3. Correct errors as you key

Note: Poem shown in its entirety on p. 91.

Internet Activity
Search the Web for additional information about immigration.
Be prepared to make a few comments to your classmates about what you found.

Activity 6

Borders

WP • TableTools/Design/Table Styles/Borders/Select Border

1. Open file *DF OF7 ACTIVITY6* from the data files. Complete the table so that it appears as shown at the right.
2. Increase the row height of the heading rows to enhance the appearance.
3. Bold team names and put a bolder border around the 5th grade Altoona games.

Save as: OF7 ACTIVITY6A

4. Open *OF7 ACTIVITY6A*. Change the orientation to landscape and apply AutoFit Window. Change margins to Narrow to fit table on page.

Save as: OF7 ACTIVITY6B

Use the Borders feature to enhance the appearance and readability of tables. The Borders feature allows a border to be added around an entire table or selected parts of it.

FIFTH & SIXTH GRADE TOURNAMENT SCHEDULE **Altoona** February 26					
Middle School Gym 5th Grade		**Time**	**High School Gym 6th Grade**		
Score	Teams		Teams	Score	
	Bruce Somerset	9:00	Bruce Somerset		
	St. Croix Central St. Croix Falls		St. Croix Central St. Croix Falls		
	Menomonie Rice Lake	10:10	Menomonie Rice Lake		
	Altoona **Eau Claire**		Altoona Eau Claire		
	St. Croix Falls Bruce	11:20	St. Croix Falls Bruce		
	St. Croix Central Somerset		St. Croix Central Somerset		
	Rice Lake Eau Claire	12:30	Rice Lake Eau Claire		
	Menomonie **Altoona**		Menomonie Altoona		
	St. Croix Falls Somerset	1:40	St. Croix Falls Somerset		
	St. Croix Central Bruce		ST. Croix Central Bruce		
	Rice Lake **Altoona**	2:50	Rice Lake Altoona		
	Menomonie Eau Claire		Menomonie Eau Claire		

Activity 7

Gridlines

WP • TableTools/Layout/Table/View Gridlines

Open *OF7 ACTIVITY5A*; apply the No border setting; then hide the gridlines.

Save as: OF7 ACTIVITY7

When you remove table borders (No Border or None), light blue lines, called gridlines, replace the borders. These gridlines give you a visual guide as you work with the table; they do not print. The blue gridlines can be turned off by activating the **Hide Gridlines** option. This allows you to see what the table will look like when it is printed.

Office Features 4

For each activity, read and learn the feature described, then follow instructions at the left.

Activity 1

Insert Table

WP • Insert/Tables/Table

1. Create and key the table shown at the right.
2. Key the main heading in ALL CAPS, bold, and centered above the table.

Main Heading: AMERICAN LEAGUE MOST VALUABLE PLAYERS

Save as: **OF4 ACTIVITY1**

Use the **Insert Table** command to create a grid for arranging information into rows and columns. Tables consist of vertical columns and horizontal rows. **Columns** are labeled alphabetically from left to right; **rows** are labeled numerically from top to bottom. The crossing of columns and rows makes **cells**.

When text is keyed in a cell, it wraps around in that cell—instead of wrapping around to the next row. A line space is added to the cell each time the text wraps around.

To fill in cells, use the TAB key or right arrow key to move from cell to cell in a row and from row to row. (Tapping ENTER will simply insert a blank line space in the cell.) To move around in a filled-in table, use the arrow keys, TAB, or the mouse (click the desired cell).

Year	Player	Team
2003	Alex Rodriguez	Rangers
2002	Miguel Tejada	Athletics
2001	Ichiro Suzuki	Mariners
2000	Jason Giambi	Athletics
1999	Ivan Rodriguez	Rangers
1998	Juan Gonzalez	Rangers
1997	Ken Griffey, Jr.	Mariners

Activity 2

Insert and Delete Rows and Columns

WP • Table Tools/Layout/Rows & Columns/Insert or Delete

1. Open the table you created for Activity 1 (*OF4 ACTIVITY1*).
2. Insert the information for 2004–2006.
3. Delete the 1997–1999 award winners.
4. Delete the column showing the team the award winner played for.
5. Undo the last change made to restore the deleted column.

Save as: **OF4 ACTIVITY2**

The **Table Tools Layout** tab can be used to edit or modify existing tables. The commands found in the **Rows & Columns** group are used to insert and delete rows in an existing table.

A cell, row, column, or entire table can be deleted using the Delete command. Use the Insert commands to place rows above or below existing rows and columns to the right or left of existing columns.

AMERICAN LEAGUE MOST VALUABLE PLAYERS

Year	Player	Team
2006	Justin Morneau	Twins
2005	Alex Rodriguez	Yankees
2004	Vladimir Guerrero	Angels
2003	Alex Rodriguez	Rangers
2002	Miguel Tejada	Athletics
2001	Ichiro Suzuki	Mariners
2000	Jason Giambi	Athletics

Activity 4

Split Cells/Merge Cells

WP
- TableTools/Layout/ Merge/Merge or Split Cells

1. Open the *DF OF7 ACTIVITY4* file.
2. Finish keying any columns that are incomplete.
3. Use the Split Cells and Merge Cells features to complete the formatting. (You will shade the table as part of Activity 5.)
4. Center the table vertically and horizontally.

Save as: OF7 ACTIVITY4

Use the Split Cells table feature to split (divide) cells horizontally or vertically.

Use the Merge Cells table feature to merge (join) cells horizontally or vertically.

ACCOUNTING MAJOR						
General Electives (40 credits)					Business Core (32 credits)	Accounting Requirements (28 credits)
Category I (9 Credits)	**Category II** (9 Credits)	**Category III** (11 Credits)	**Category IV** (11 Credits)		Acct 201 Acct 202 Bcom 206 Bcom 207 MIS 240 Bsad 300 Bsad 305 Fin 320 Mktg 330 Mgmt 340 Mgmt 341 Mgmt 449	Acct 301 Acct 302 Acct 314 Acct 315 Acct 317 Acct 321 Acct 450 Acct 460 Fin 326 Fin 327
CJ 202 Math 111 Math 245	Biol 102 Chem 101 Geog 104	Econ 103 Econ 104 Psyc 100 Soc 101	No specific courses required.			
Category I – Communications and Analytical Skills Category II – Natural Sciences Category III – Social Sciences Category IV – Humanities						

Activity 5

Shading

WP
- TableTools/Design/Table Styles/Shading/Select Color

1. Open *DF OF7 ACTIVITY5*. Shade lines of the table as shown.

Save as: OF7 ACTIVITY5A

2. Open *OF7 ACTIVITY3* (Activity 3 file). Shade *National League* red. Shade *American League* blue.
3. For both the National and American Leagues; shade *East* yellow, *West* green, and *Central* purple.

Save as: OF7 ACTIVITY5B

4. Open the Activity 4 file (*OF7 ACTIVITY4*). Apply shading as shown in Activity 4, above.

Save as: OF7 ACTIVITY5C

Use the Shading feature to enhance the appearance of tables to make them easier to read. The Shading feature allows you to fill in areas of the table with varying shades of color.

Shading covers the selected area. It may be the entire table or a single cell, column, or row within a table.

SEVEN WONDERS OF THE WORLD		
Ancient	New	
	Wonder	Location
Colossus of Rhodes	Chichen Itza Pyramid	Mexico
Great Pyramid of Giza	Colosseum	Italy
Hanging Gardens of Babylon	Great Wall of China	China
Lighthouse of Alexandria	Machu Picchu	Peru
Mausoleum at Halicarnassus	Petra	Jordan
Statue of Zeus at Olympia	Statue of Christ Redeemer	Brazil
Temple of Artemis at Ephesus	Taj Mahal	India

Source: http://www.new7wonders.com

Activity 3

Table Styles and Heading Styles

WP • Table Tools/Design/Table Styles/Select Style

WP • Home/Styles/Select Style

1. Open the table you created for Activity 2 (*OF4 ACTIVITY2*).
2. Format the table in the table style Light Shading — Accent 1.
3. Use Heading 2 style for the main heading for the table.
4. Center the main heading above the table.

Save as: **OF4 ACTIVITY3**

After a table has been created, the commands found on the **Table Tools Design** tab can be used to change the table style.

Before or after text has been keyed, the **Styles** group on the **Home** tab can be used to enhance the appearance of the title or other text within the table.

AMERICAN LEAGUE MOST VALUABLE PLAYERS

Year	Player	Team
2006	Justin Morneau	Twins
2005	Alex Rodriguez	Yankees
2004	Vladimir Guerrero	Angels
2003	Alex Rodriguez	Rangers
2002	Miguel Tejada	Athletics
2001	Ichiro Suzuki	Mariners
2000	Jason Giambi	Athletics

Activity 4

Merging Cells and Changing Column Width

WP • Table Tools/Layout/Merge/Merge Cells

1. Open the file *DF OF4 ACTIVITY4*.
2. Merge the cells of row 1.
3. Adjust the column widths so that the name of the sales representative fits on one line. Adjust the width of other columns as needed.

Save as: **OF4 ACTIVITY4**

Use the **Merge Cells** command to join two or more cells into one cell. This feature is useful when information in the table spans more than one column or row. The main title, for example, spans all columns.

In a newly created table, all columns are the same width. You can change the width of one or more columns to accommodate entries of unequal widths.

SALES REPORT				
Sales Rep.	Territory	Jan.	Feb.	March
Juan Ramirez	Washington	12,325	13,870	12,005
Shawn Hewitt	Oregon	15,680	17,305	7,950
Maria Hernandez	Idaho	9,480	16,780	14,600
Cheryl Updike	Washington	10,054	8,500	17,085
Tanya Goodman	Washington	19,230	11,230	15,780
Jason Graham	Oregon	15,900	16,730	9,290
Carolyn Plummer	Idaho	20,370	13,558	12,654
Scott Bowe	Idaho	15,750	14,560	16,218
Brandon Olson	Oregon	14,371	11,073	19,301
Laura Chen	Washington	17,320	9,108	18,730

Office Features 7

For each activity, read and learn the feature described, then follow instructions at the left.

Activity 1

Review Table Formatting Features

Open the file *DF OF7 ACTIVITY1* and change the table format to make it appear as shown at the right. Center the table on the page.

Save as: **OF7 ACTIVITY1**

MAJOR LEAGUE BASEBALL					
National League			American League		
East	West	Central	East	West	Central
Atlanta Florida Montreal New York Philadelphia	Arizona Colorado Los Angeles San Diego San Francisco	Chicago Cincinnati Houston Milwaukee Pittsburgh St. Louis	Baltimore Boston New York Tampa Bay Toronto	Anaheim Oakland Seattle Texas	Chicago Cleveland Detroit Kansas City Minnesota

Activity 2

Portrait/Landscape Orientation

WP • Page Layout/Page Setup/Orientation

1. Open *OF7 ACTIVITY1*.
2. Change the page orientation to landscape.

Save as: **OF7 ACTIVITY2**

Portrait orientation. The way text is printed on a page determines what type of orientation is used. Portrait orientation, sometimes referred to as vertical – 8 ½" x 11", has the short edge of the paper at the top of the page.

Landscape orientation. Landscape orientation, sometimes referred to as horizontal – 11" x 8 ½", has the wider edge of the paper at the top of the page. When a table is too wide to fit on the page in portrait orientation, switching to the landscape orientation gives 2 ½" more inches to fit the table.

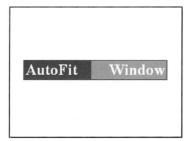

Activity 3

AutoFit Contents/AutoFit Window

 WP • Table Tools/Layout/Cell Size/AutoFit

1. Open *OF7 ACTIVITY2*.
2. Change the page orientation to portrait.
3. Apply AutoFit Contents.
4. Change the page orientation to landscape.
5. Apply AutoFit Window.

Save as: **OF7 ACTIVITY3**

AutoFit Contents. Automatically resizes the column widths based on the text in each column. AutoFit Contents leaves less white space in the columns, but more white space in the margins.

AutoFit Window. Automatically resizes the column widths to give maximum white space between columns. AutoFit Window leaves more white space in the columns but less in the margins.

Activity 5

Make Table Formatting Changes

1. Open the file *OF4 ACTIVITY4* created in Activity 4.
2. Make the formatting changes given below.
   a. Bold and center the main heading and column headings.
   b. Center-align column B.
   c. Right-align columns C, D, and E.
   d. Bold and italicize the highest sales figure for each month.
   e. Apply an appropriate Table Style design.

Save as: OF4 ACTIVITY5

The formatting changes (bold, italicize, different alignment, etc.) that you have learned to make to text can also be made to the text within a table. You can do this prior to keying the text into the table, or it can be done after the text has been keyed. After the table is complete, make changes by selecting the cell (or row or column) to be changed and then selecting the software command to make the change.

SALES REPORT				
Sales Rep.	**Territory**	**Jan.**	**Feb.**	**March**
Juan Ramirez	Washington	12,325	13,870	12,005
Shawn Hewitt	Oregon	15,680	*17,305*	7,950
Maria Hernandez	Idaho	9,480	16,780	14,600
Cheryl Updike	Washington	10,054	8,500	17,085
Tanya Goodman	Washington	19,230	11,230	15,780
Jason Graham	Oregon	15,900	16,730	9,290
Carolyn Plummer	Idaho	*20,370*	13,558	12,654
Scott Bowe	Idaho	15,750	14,560	16,218
Brandon Olson	Oregon	14,371	11,073	*19,301*
Laura Chen	Washington	17,320	9,108	18,730

Activity 6

Centering Tables

1. Open *OF4 ACTIVITY5*.
2. Center the table vertically and horizontally.

Save as: OF4 ACTIVITY6

Use the **Center alignment** command to center a table horizontally on the page. This will make the side margins (right and left margins) equal. See illustration on p. 99.

Use the **Page Vertical alignment** or **Center Page** feature to center a table vertically on the page. This will make the top and bottom margins equal. See illustration on p. 99.

Activity 7

Change Cell Size & Alignment

WP • Layout/Cell Size/Specify Cell Size

WP • Layout/Alignment/Specify Alignment Type

1. Open *OF4 ACTIVITY6*. Change row height as follows: title row, 0.6"; column headings, 0.5"; other rows, 0.4".
2. Change vertical alignment as follows: main heading and column headings, center; other rows, bottom alignment.

Save as: OF4 ACTIVITY7

Use the **Layout Cell Size** commands to change the height of the rows in a table. The height of all the rows of the table can be changed to the same height, or each row can be a different height.

Use the **Layout Alignment** commands to change the alignment of the text in cells. The text within a cell can be top-aligned, center-aligned, or bottom-aligned.

Cell Alignment and Row Height

Top Left – .3"	Top Center – .3"	Top Right – .3"
Center Left – .4"	Center – .4"	Center Right – .4"
Bottom Left – .5"	Bottom Center – .5"	Bottom Right – .5"

Technique: Number Keys/TAB

1. Set tabs at 2" and 4".
2. Key the copy at the right.

Concentrate on figure location; quick tab spacing; eyes on copy.

910 Ponderosa Drive	301 Princeton Way	608 Peachwood Drive
283 Kincaid Court	201 Neilson Terrace	99 Laura Lee Lane
476 Rio Grande Court	342 Remington Ridge	658 Santiago Road
5132 Grey Stone Court	256 Windsor Gardens	790 Blue Ridge Lane
4765 Cherokee Way	756 Woodward Court	231 Meeker Street
908 Glenridge Lane	809 Greenbriar Drive	106 Hanaford Court
576 Red Rock Avenue	142 Timberline Drive	235 Eagles Nest Road
489 Parkview Avenue	357 Gardenia Drive	498 Hancock Court

Skill Check

1. Key a 1' timing on ¶ 1; determine *gwam*.
2. Add 2–4 *gwam* to the rate attained in step 1, and note quarter-minute checkpoints from the chart below.
3. Key two 1' guided timings on ¶ 1 to increase speed.
4. Practice ¶ 2 in the same way.
5. Take two 3' timings on ¶s 1 and 2 combined; determine *gwam* and number of errors.

A all letters used (MicroPace)

	gwam	3'	5'

One of the great statesmen of our nation was Benjamin — 4 | 2
Franklin. Among other things, the man is quite well known for his — 8 | 5
work as an author, as a philosopher, as a scientist, and as a — 12 | 7
diplomat and representative of our country. Recognized as one of — 16 | 10
the excellent leaders of the Revolution, he is considered a founding — 21 | 13
father of the United States. His name can be seen on the — 25 | 15
Declaration of Independence as well as the United States — 29 | 17
Constitution. — 29 | 18

Some of the things that Franklin is given the credit for — 33 | 20
include the Franklin stove, the lightning rod, bifocals, and many, — 38 | 23
many witty quotes in his almanac. Franklin once said, "If you — 42 | 25
would not be forgotten as soon as you are dead, either write — 46 | 27
something worth reading or do things worth the writing." Because — 50 | 30
of his many personal accomplishments and the written documents — 54 | 33
that his signature appears on, Mr. Franklin will not likely be — 58 | 35
forgotten very soon! He is a role model that all Americans should — 63 | 38
try to model their life after. — 65 | 39

Quarter-Minute Checkpoints

gwam	1/4'	1/2'	3/4'	1'
24	6	12	18	24
28	7	14	21	28
32	8	16	24	32
36	9	18	27	36
40	10	20	30	40
44	11	22	33	44
48	12	24	36	48
52	13	26	39	52
56	14	28	42	56
60	15	30	45	60

gwam	3'	1	2	3	4
	5'	1		2	3

Activity 8

Table Sort

WP • Table Tools/Layout/
Data/Sort

1. Open *OF4 ACTIVITY7*.
2. Sort the table by Territory in descending order as shown.
3. Sort the table again by March sales in ascending order.

Save as: OF4 ACTIVITY8

Activity 9

Converting Tables to Text

WP • Table Tools/Layout/Data/
Convert to Text/Tabs

1. Open *OF4 ACTIVITY8*.
2. Convert the table to text, separating text with tabs.

Save as: OF4 ACTIVITY9

The **Sort** feature arranges text in a table in a specific order. The feature will sort alphabetic or numeric text in ascending (A to Z, 0 to 9) or descending (Z to A, 9 to 0) order.

The **Convert to Text** feature converts a table to regular text.

SALES REPORT				
Sales Rep.	**Territory**	**Jan.**	**Feb.**	**March**
Juan Ramirez	Washington	12,325	13,870	12,005
Cheryl Updike	Washington	10,054	8,500	17,085
Tanya Goodman	Washington	19,230	11,230	15,780
Laura Chen	Washington	17,320	9,108	18,730
Shawn Hewitt	Oregon	15,680	*17,305*	7,950
Jason Graham	Oregon	15,900	16,730	9,290
Brandon Olson	Oregon	14,371	11,073	*19,301*
Maria Hernandez	Idaho	9,480	16,780	14,600
Carolyn Plummer	Idaho	*20,370*	13,558	12,654
Scott Bowe	Idaho	15,750	14,560	16,218

*Table shown sorted by **Territory** in descending order.

Activity 10

Apply What You Have Learned

1. Open the file *DF OF4 ACTIVITY10*.
2. Insert a column for the dates; center and key the heading and dates.
3. Merge cells in row 1.
4. Bold and center main heading and column headings.
5. Adjust column widths to fit the information in each cell on one line.
6. Sort the Date column in ascending order.
7. Select a table style to enhance the table.
8. Adjust vertical alignment in cells: main heading and column headings, center; other rows, bottom alignment.
9. Center table on the page.

Save as: OF4 ACTIVITY10

INVENTIONS		
Date	Invention	Inventor
1877	Phonograph	Thomas Edison
1805	Railroad locomotive	Richard Trevithick
1846	Sewing machine	Elias Howe
1867	Revolver	Samuel Colt
1820	Calculating machine	Charles Babbage
1867	Typewriter	Christopher Sholes

Lesson 65 — KEYING TECHNIQUE

- To improve keying techniques.
- To improve keying speed and control.

65B — Skill Building

Technique: Letter Keys
Key each line twice.

One-hand words of 2–5 letters

1 be no up we at in ax my as on add bag car dad war tax sat saw see
2 dad oil egg lip cab joy fee pop art you age him sad mom seat look
3 save milk race pull star pink grade onion grass polio serve pupil

4 as my|at a rate|we are|no war|get set|at my best|you were|a great
5 as few|you set a date|my card|water tax|act on a|tax date|in case
6 my only date|water rate|my tax case|tax fact|my best date|my card

7 No, you are free only after I act on a rate on a state water tax.
8 Get him my extra database only after you set up exact test dates.
9 You set my area tax rate after a great state case on a water tax.

gwam 1' | 1 | 2 | 3 | 4 | 5 | 6 | 7 | 8 | 9 | 10 | 11 | 12 | 13 |

65C — Skill Building

Speed Forcing Drill
Key each line once at top speed. If you finish all lines before time is called, key them again, trying to go faster.

Emphasis: high-frequency balanced-hand words

4| 8| 12| 16| 20| 24| 28| 32| 36| 40| 44| 48| 52|

Jay and I may make a bid for the antique pen.
Clem may make a big profit for the six firms.

Pamela may pay for the eight pens for the auditor.
Nancy bid for the antique chair and antique rifle.

If the pay is right, Sue may make their gowns for them.
When did the auditor sign the audit forms for the city?

Laurie kept the men busy with the work down by the big lake.
Diana may go with us to the city to pay them for their work.

Did the firm bid for the right to the land downtown by city hall?
Jay may suspend the men as a penalty for their work on the docks.

gwam 15" | 4 | 8 | 12 | 16 | 20 | 24 | 28 | 32 | 36 | 40 | 44 | 48 | 52 |

Format Guides: Tables

Although you will use a word processing feature to create tables, you will need these guidelines for making your tables easy to read and attractive.

Parts of a Table

A table is an arrangement of data (words and/or numbers) in rows and columns. Columns are labeled alphabetically from left to right; rows are labeled numerically from top to bottom. Tables range in complexity from those with only two columns and a title to those with several columns and special features. The tables in this unit are limited to those with the following parts:

- Main heading (bold, ALL CAPS, centered in first row or placed above the gridlines of the table).
- Secondary heading (bold, capital and lowercase letters, centered in second row or placed a DS below the main title above the gridlines).
- Column headings (bold, centered over the column).
- Body (data entries).
- Source note (bottom left in last row or may be placed beneath the gridlines of the table. If placed beneath the gridlines, use the Add Space Before Paragraph feature to place space between the gridlines and the source note. (Home/Paragraph/Line Spacing/Add Space Before Paragraph) and set a tab to place the source note at the table's left edge.
- Gridlines (may be hidden).

Table Format Features

The following features (illustrated on p. 100) can be used to make your tables attractive and easy to read.

Vertical placement. A table may be centered vertically (equal top and bottom margins), or it may begin 2" from the top edge of the page.

Horizontal placement. Tables are most attractive when centered horizontally (side to side) on the page.

Column width. Generally, each column should be only slightly wider than the longest data entry in the column. Table columns should be identical widths or markedly different widths. Columns that are only slightly different widths should be avoided.

Row height. All rows, including title rows, may be the same height. To enhance appearance, the main title row height may be slightly more than the secondary title row height, which may be more than the column heading row height. The column heading row height may be more than the data entry rows.

Vertical alignment. Within rows, data entries can be aligned at the top, center, or bottom. Most often you will use center vertical alignment for the headings and bottom vertical alignment for data rows beneath the headings. If a source note is included, it should also be bottom-aligned.

Horizontal alignment. Within columns, words may be left-aligned or center-aligned. Whole numbers may be center-aligned or right-aligned. If a column total is shown, numbers should be right-aligned. Decimal numbers are decimal-aligned.

Table Styles design. The Table Styles feature of the software provides a quick way to enhance the appearance of a table. Table styles can be selected and applied at any time after a table has been inserted into a document. Once the table style has been applied, changes to the format for the selected style can be made such as bolding or removing preset bolding, changing font size, changing alignment, etc., to further enhance the appearance of the table.

64D · Skill Building

Speed Forcing Drill

Key each line once at top speed. If you finish all lines before time is called, key them again, trying to go faster.

Emphasis: high-frequency balanced-hand words

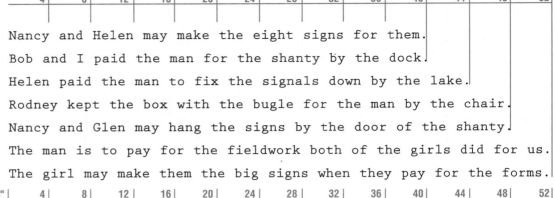

| | 4 | 8 | 12 | 16 | 20 | 24 | 28 | 32 | 36 | 40 | 44 | 48 | 52 |

Nancy and Helen may make the eight signs for them.
Bob and I paid the man for the shanty by the dock.
Helen paid the man to fix the signals down by the lake.
Rodney kept the box with the bugle for the man by the chair.
Nancy and Glen may hang the signs by the door of the shanty.
The man is to pay for the fieldwork both of the girls did for us.
The girl may make them the big signs when they pay for the forms.

gwam 15" | 4 | 8 | 12 | 16 | 20 | 24 | 28 | 32 | 36 | 40 | 44 | 48 | 52 |

64E · Skill Building

Skill Check

1. Key a 1' timing on ¶ 1; determine *gwam*.
2. Add 2–4 *gwam* to the rate attained in step 1, and note quarter-minute checkpoints from the chart below.
3. Key two 1' guided timings on ¶ 1 to increase speed.
4. Practice ¶ 2 in the same way.
5. Key two 3' timings on ¶s 1 and 2 combined; count *gwam* and determine errors.

Quarter-Minute Checkpoints				
gwam	1/4'	1/2'	3/4'	1'
24	6	12	18	24
28	7	14	21	28
32	8	16	24	32
36	9	18	27	36
40	10	20	30	40
44	11	22	33	44
48	12	24	36	48
52	13	26	39	52
56	14	28	42	56
60	15	30	45	60

A   all letters used   (MicroPace)   **gwam**   1' | 3'

When you talk about famous Americans, it doesn't take   4 | 2
long to come up with a long list. However, some individuals would   8 | 5
appear on nearly everyone's list. George Washington would be one   13 | 8
of those on most people's list. He is often referred to as the   17 | 10
Father of our Country because of the role he played in the Ameri-   21 | 13
can Revolution and being our first president.   24 | 15

Abraham Lincoln would also be included on most lists. He is   29 | 17
often referred to as Honest Abe. He always gave the extra ef-   33 | 20
fort. Because of this, he was successful. Whether the job was   37 | 22
splitting logs, being a lawyer, or being president, Lincoln gave   42 | 25
it his best. Dealing with the Civil War required a president who   46 | 28
gave his best.   47 | 28

Harriet Tubman is recognized as another prominent individ-   51 | 31
ual. She risked her own life for the freedom of others. After   55 | 33
becoming a free woman in the North, she returned to the South to   60 | 36
assist several hundred slaves escape. She also took part in the   64 | 38
Civil War, serving the country as a Union spy and scout.   68 | 41

gwam 1' | 1 | 2 | 3 | 4 | 5 | 6 | 7 | 8 | 9 | 10 | 11 | 12 | 13 |
     3' | 1 | 2 | 3 | 4 |

Vertical Centering (equal top and bottom margins)

Main heading

Secondary heading

Column headings

Body

BROADWAY GROSSES		
Week Ending 7/22/2007		
Production	***Gross This Week***	***Gross Last Week***
Wicked	$1,472,649	$1,468,400
The Lion King	1,283,279	1,291,898
Mary Poppins	1,226,944	1,191,101
Jersey Boys	1,197,014	1,211,053
Beauty and the Beast	1,139,499	1,095,124
Legally Blonde	946,840	939,285
Mamma Mia!	935,608	940,187
The Color Purple	926,764	974,904
Hairspray	865,744	809,462
Curtains	837,138	821,457
Totals	$10,831,479	$10,742,871

Horizontal Centering (equal side margins)

Source

Source: http://www.broadwayworld.com/grosses.cfm (24 July 2007).

Three-Column Table Centered Horizontally and Vertically

UNIT 17
Lessons 64-65

Build Keyboarding Skill

Lesson 64   KEYING TECHNIQUE

OBJECTIVES
- To improve keying techniques.
- To improve keying speed and control.

64A-65A

Conditioning Practice
Key each line twice.

alphabet	1	Jack Lopez will attend the quality frog exhibits over the summer.
figures	2	Tim's score was 79 percent; he missed Numbers 18, 26, 30, and 45.
speed	3	Helena may blame the men for the problem with the neighbor's dog.

gwam 1' | 1 | 2 | 3 | 4 | 5 | 6 | 7 | 8 | 9 | 10 | 11 | 12 | 13 |

64B   Skill Building

Keying Skill: Speed
Key each line twice.

Balanced-hand words of 2-5 letters

1 if me go he so us to am or by an of is to row she box air pay the

2 dig got due map jam own she box ant busy when city fish half rush

3 goal down dial firm keys pens rock odor sick soap tubs wish title

4 to do|to us|by the|if they|held a|the pen|their dog|is it|to make

5 a big fox|do the work|the gown is|when is it|he may go|a rich man

6 by the chair|he may make|did he spend|for the girls|for the firms

7 The maid may make the usual visit to the dock to work on the map.

8 Dick and Jay paid the busy man to go to the lake to fix the dock.

9 The girls may visit them when they go to the city to pay the man.

gwam 1' | 1 | 2 | 3 | 4 | 5 | 6 | 7 | 8 | 9 | 10 | 11 | 12 | 13 |

64C   Skill Building

Technique: Number Keys/Tab
Key each line twice (key number, tap TAB, and key next number).

Concentrate on figure location; quick tab spacing; eyes on copy.

264	189	357	509	768	142	642	135	9,607
258	147	630	911	828	376	475	390	1,425
763	905	481	208	913	475	609	173	2,458

gwam 1' | 1 | 2 | 3 | 4 | 5 | 6 | 7 |

Lesson 35 TABLE BASICS

OBJECTIVES

- To learn placement/arrangement of basic table parts.
- To format tables using the Table Format feature.

35A

Conditioning Practice

Key each line twice SS.

alphabet	1	Meg saw an extra big jet zip quickly over the frozen desert.
fig/sym	2	My income tax for 2003 was $4,178.69--up 5% over 2002's tax.
speed	3	Rick may make a bid on the ivory gowns they got in the city.

gwam 1' | 1 | 2 | 3 | 4 | 5 | 6 | 7 | 8 | 9 | 10 | 11 | 12 |

35B Formatting

Format Table

1. Study the format guides for tables on p. 98 and the model table on p. 99.
2. Using the following information, key Tables 1–3 shown at right and on p. 102.
   - Center, bold, and key the main heading in all CAPS.
   - SS after keying the main heading, change the alignment to left, and turn bold off.
   - Create the table and key the data.
   - Center and bold the column headings.
   - Center the table vertically.

Table 1

Save as: **35B TABLE1**

Table 2

Save as: **35B TABLE2**

POEMS TO IMPROVE OUR LIVES

Poem	Written By
Great Men	Ralph Waldo Emerson
Success	Henry Wadsworth Longfellow
If	Rudyard Kipling
The Road Not Taken	Robert Frost
Will	Ella Wheeler Wilcox
The Sin of Omission	Margaret E. Sangster
Good and Bad Children	Robert Louis Stevenson
Lady Clare	Alfred Tennyson

THE PHANTOM OF THE OPERA

Character	Cast Member
Christine Daae	Susan Medford
Phantom of the Opera	Ramon DeRosa
Raoul	Martin Selbach
Monsieur Andre	Justin Wyman
Meg Giry	Sarah Henrich
Carlotta Guidicelli	Rebecca Haynes
Madame Giry	Sandra Keller
Ubaldo Piangi	Richard Kummerfeld
Monsieur Firmin	Clark Gerhig
Don Attilio	Anthony Blass

Integrity is having strong moral values and living by those values no matter what the circumstances may be. A person of high integrity has strong ethical standards. He/she always tries to do the right thing.

What Will You Do?

Situation 1: You just cashed your payroll check. As usual, you step away from the bank teller window to let the next person in line be waited on and start counting the money to make sure that you have the right amount. You find that two new fifty dollar bills were stuck together and that you receive fifty dollars more than you should have. What will you do?

Situation 2: You are on the Student Council Election Committee. Your best friend is running for president. She is a very honest person who works very hard at everything she does; she would make an excellent president. She is running against a person you don't like. The person copied your paper last year and then told the teacher you were the one who had copied her paper. You ended up having to write another paper and only getting half credit for it. The person was vice president this year and was very undependable.

You and another member of the Election Committee, Sandra, are counting the votes when she is called to the office. When Sandra leaves for the office, each person has the same number of votes. While she is gone you look at the remaining nine ballots and determine that the other person is going to win the election by one vote. It would be very easy to take two of the ballots and ensure that your friend wins. What will you do?

Situation 3: Steve, a good friend of yours, has always wanted to go to a very prestigious college that has high entrance requirements. He has met all the requirements except the ACT test score requirement. He didn't achieve a high enough score on the math part of the exam and is having to retake the exam. You are retaking the exam because you didn't do very well on the science part, but you did very well on the math part. During the exam you see Steve copying your math answers. Afterwards you confront him about it. He responds: "It was only a few answers. Those few answers could make the difference between my getting accepted and not getting accepted. What's the big deal?" What will you do?

Ethics: The Right Thing to Do

1. Read each situation at the left.

2. Key a brief ¶ explaining how you would handle each situation.

3. Form a group with three other students. Have each one explain how he or she would handle each of the situations.

4. Discuss the responses and see if your group can agree on one answer to each situation.

Table 3

Save as: **35B TABLE3**

FAMOUS PAINTINGS

Artist	Painting
Claude Monet	The Boat Studio
Paul Cezanne	Riverbanks
Rembrandt	The Mill
Michelangelo	The Holy Family
Leonardo da Vinci	The Mona Lisa
Vincent van Gogh	The Starry Night
Raphael	The School of Athens
Berthe Morisot	Little Girl Reading
Pierre-Auguste Renoir	Girls at the Piano
Jan Vermeer	The Milkmaid

Lesson 36   TABLE LAYOUT AND DESIGN

OBJECTIVES

- To use table layout and design features.
- To format two-column tables with main, secondary, and column titles.

36A

Conditioning Practice

Key each line twice SS.

alphabet 1 Jay was amazed at how quickly a proud man fixed the big van.

fig/sym 2 Review reaches: $70, $64, 95%, #20, 5-point, 1/8, B&O 38's.

speed 3 Lane is to fix the big sign by the chapel for the neighbors.

gwam 1' | 1 | 2 | 3 | 4 | 5 | 6 | 7 | 8 | 9 | 10 | 11 | 12 |

36B   Formatting

Format Tables

Table 1

1. Open file *DF 36B TABLE1*.
2. Make the format changes given at the right.

Save as: **36B TABLE1**

1. Change the width of column A to 3.5"; column B to 2".
2. Merge the cells of row 1; center the main heading.
3. Merge the cells of row 2; center the secondary heading.
4. Center column headings.
5. Apply Light Shading – Accent 3 Table Style design to the table.
6. Bold Column B heading.
7. Change the row height of the main heading to 0.5"; the secondary heading to 0.4"; the column headings to 0.35"; the data rows to 0.3".
8. Change the alignment for the first three rows to Center; column A data rows to Bottom Left; column B data rows to Bottom Center.
9. Center the table horizontally and vertically.

Table 2

1. Open file *DF 36B TABLE2*.
2. Make the format changes given at the right.

Save as: **36B TABLE2**

1. Change the row height for all rows to 0.4".
2. Apply Medium Grid 3 – Accent 4 Table Style design to the table.
3. Change alignment for the column headings to Center; the data rows to Bottom Center.
4. Change the width of column A to 2.5"; column B to 2.3".
5. Change the font size for the main heading and column headings to 14 pt.
6. Center the table horizontally and vertically.
7. Insert two new rows at the end of the table and include the following:

Diego Velazquez — Juan de Pareja

Jean-Auguste-Dominique Ingres — Princess de Broglie

Listening

Complete as directed.

Save as: CS6 ACTIVITY2

1. Open sound file *DF CS6 ACTIVITY2*, which is a set of driving directions.

2. Take notes as you listen to the directions to the Mansfield Soccer Field.

3. Close the sound file.

4. Using your notes, key the directions in sentence form.

ACTIVITY 3

Write to Learn

Complete as directed.

Save as: CS6 ACTIVITY3

1. Using word processing or voice recognition software, write a paragraph explaining how you would split a window so you can display a document in two panes.

2. Write a second ¶ explaining what a style is and how you can use the Style feature.

ACTIVITY 4

Composing

1. Read the ¶.
2. Compose a ¶ indicating what you think the results of your poll would be and what your response would be.
3. Proofread, revise, and correct.

Save as: CS6 ACTIVITY4

　　If you were to take a poll of your classmates, what percent of them would believe that current TV and movie fare glamorizes violence and sex without portraying the negative consequences of immoral behavior? What percent would have the opposite belief?

ACTIVITY 5

Finding the Whole of a Number

1. Open *DF CS6 ACTIVITY5* and print the file.
2. Solve the problems as directed in the file.
3. Submit your answers.

⬤ CAREER Clusters

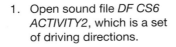

ACTIVITY 6

You must complete Career Exploration Activities 1–3 before completing this activity.

1. Retrieve your Career folder and find the printed Career Cluster Plan of Study for the career cluster that is your third choice.

2. Review the plan and write a paragraph or two about why you would or would not consider a career in this cluster. Print your file, save it as Career6, and keep it open.

3. After composing a paragraph or two, print a copy of your response and exchange papers with a classmate. Have the classmate offer suggestions for improving the content and correcting any errors he or she finds in your paragraph(s). Make the changes that you agree with and print a copy to turn in to your instructor. Save your file as Career6 and close it.

4. Return your folder to the storage area. When your instructor returns your paper, file it in your Career folder.

Tables 3–4

Use the information below to format and key Tables 3 and 4. Complete the steps in this order:

1. Create table.
2. Change the width of column A to 2.4" and column B to 2.1".
3. Change the row height to 0.4" for all rows.
4. Merge the cells in row 1 and in row 2.
5. Key the information—ignore bolding and centering until after applying table style.
6. Use Medium Shading 2 – Accent 1 for the Table Style design for Table 3; use Medium Shading 2 – Accent 2 for Table 4.
7. Change the main heading to 16-pt. font, secondary heading to 12-pt. font, and the column headings to 14-pt. font.
8. Use Center alignment for all heading rows.
9. Use Bottom Left alignment for column A data rows; use Bottom Center alignment for column B data rows.
10. Bold the main heading and the column headings; do not bold the secondary headings.
11. Center the table on the page.

Table 3

Save as: **36B TABLE3**

Table 4

Save as: **36B TABLE4**

CHILDREN'S STORIES	
By Laura Ingalls Wilder	
Book	**Year Published**
Little House in the Big Woods	1932
Little House on the Prairie	1935
On the Banks of Plum Creek	1937
By the Shores of Silver Lake	1939
The Long Winter	1940
Little Town on the Prairie	1941
These Happy Golden Years	1943

LONGEST BROADWAY RUNS	
As of May 25, 2006	
Broadway Show	**No. of Performances**
The Phantom of the Opera	7,637
Cats	7,485
Les Miserables	6,680
A Chorus Line	6,137
Oh! Calcutta (revival)	5,959
Beauty and the Beast	4,964
Rent	4,185
Miss Saigon	4,092
Chicago (revival)	3,963
The Lion King	3,555

Source: *Time Almanac 2007.*

OPTIONAL INTERNET ACTIVITY

Update Table 4 to reflect the most current data available. Use the Internet to search for the *longest running Broadway plays*.

Communication & Math
SKILLS 6

TERMINAL PUNCTUATION

ACTIVITY 1

Terminal Punctuation: Period, Question Mark, Exclamation Point

1. Study each of the five rules.
   a. Key the Learn line(s) beneath each rule, noting how the rule is applied.
   b. Key the *Apply* line(s), using correct terminal punctuation
2. Key Proofread & Correct, using correct terminal punctuation.
   a. Check answers.
   b. Using the rule number(s) at the left of each line, study the rule relating to each error you made.
   c. Rekey each incorrect line, using correct terminal punctuation.

Save as: CS6 ACTIVITY1

Terminal Punctuation: Period

Rule 1: Use a period at the end of a declarative sentence (a sentence that is not regarded as a question or exclamation).

Learn   1   I wonder why *Phantom of the Opera* has always been so popular.

Apply   2   Fran and I saw *Cats* in London We also saw *Sunset Boulevard*

Rule 2: Use a period at the end of a polite request stated in the form of a question but not intended as one.

Learn   3   Matt, will you please collect the papers at the end of each row.

Apply   4   Will you please call me at 555-0140 to set up an appointment

Terminal Punctuation: Question Mark

Rule 3: Use a question mark at the end of a sentence intended as a question.

Learn   5   Did you go to the annual flower show in Ault Park this year?

Apply   6   How many medals did the U.S.A. win in the 1996 Summer Games

Rule 4: For emphasis, a question mark may be used after each item in a series of interrogative expressions.

Learn   7   Can we count on wins in gymnastics? in diving? in soccer?

Apply   8   What grade did you get for history for sociology for civics

Terminal Punctuation: Exclamation Point

Rule 5: Use an exclamation point after emphatic (forceful) exclamations and after phrases and sentences that are clearly exclamatory.

Learn   9   The lady screamed, "Stop that man!"

Learn   10   "Bravo!" many yelled at the end of the Honor America program.

Apply   11   "Yes" her gym coach exclaimed when Kerri stuck the landing.

Apply   12   The burglar stopped when he saw the sign, "Beware, vicious dog"

Proofread & Correct

Rules

5   "Jump" the fireman shouted to the young boy frozen with

1   fear on the window ledge of the burning building "Will you

3   catch me" the young boy cried to the men and women holding a

1, 5, 1   safety net forty feet below "Into the net" they yelled

Mustering his courage, the boy jumped safely into the net and

1   then into his mother's outstretched arms

OBJECTIVES

- To format tables with main, secondary, and column titles.
- To improve language skills (word choice).

37A

Conditioning Practice

Key each line twice SS.

alphabet 1 Eight extra pizzas will be quickly baked for the jovial men.

fig/sym 2 Kaye said, "Can't you touch-key 45, 935, $608, and 17 1/2%?"

speed 3 Orlando and the girls may do the work for the big city firm.

gwam 1' | 1 | 2 | 3 | 4 | 5 | 6 | 7 | 8 | 9 | 10 | 11 | 12 |

37B   Language Skills

**Language Skills:
Word Choice**

1. Study the spelling and definitions of the words.
2. Key all *Learn* and *Apply* lines, choosing the correct words in the *Apply* lines.

Save as: 37B CHOICE

cite (vb) to quote; use as support; to commend; to summon

sight (n/vb) ability to see; something seen; a device to improve aim; to observe or focus

site (n) the place something is, was, or will be located

their (pron) belonging to them

there (adv/pron) in or at that place; word used to introduce a sentence or clause

they're (contr) a contracted form of *they are*

Learn 1 He will **cite** the article from the web**site** about improving your **sight**.

Apply 2 You need to (cite, sight, site) five sources in the report due on Friday.

Apply 3 The (cite, sight, site) he chose for the party was a (cite, sight, site) to be seen.

Learn 1 **There** is the car **they're** going to use in **their** next play production.

Apply 2 (Their, there, they're) making (their, there, they're) school lunches.

Apply 3 (Their, there, they're) is the box of (their, there, they're) tools.

37C   Formatting

Format Tables

Table 1 Format and key the table at the right as directed below.

Main title: 16-pt. font
Secondary title: 12-pt. font
Table Style design: Medium Shading 1 – Accent 3 (do not bold column headings or column A text)
Column headings: row height 0.4"; Center alignment; 14-pt. font
Data rows: row height 0.3"; 12-pt. font
Column A row width 2.3"; Bottom Left alignment
Column B row width 1.0"; Bottom Center alignment
Column C row width 1.2"; Bottom Right alignment
Center table on page

Save as: 37C TABLE1

ALL-TIME TOP MOVIE BOX OFFICE GROSSES
As of May 29, 2006

Movie	Year	Revenue
Titanic	1997	$600,788,188
Star Wars	1977	460,998,007
Shrek 2	2004	436,471,036
E.T. The Extra-Terrestrial	1982	434,949,459
Star Wars: Episode I-The Phantom Menace	1999	431,088,295
Spider-Man	2002	403,706,375

Source: *Time Almanac 2007.*

Document 2 (Cover Page)

Use the Cover Page feature to create a cover page using the Cubicles format. Format and key a title page for "Delivering the Mail" as shown below.

Save as: 63B REPORT2

Document 3 (Table of Contents)

Review the guidelines for formatting a table of contents on p. 173. Format and key a table of contents for "Delivering the Mail." Verify the page numbers with your report page numbers.

Save as: 63B REPORT3

Bound Report

Table of Contents

In previous lessons, you keyed a report titled "Globalization." The headings in that report are shown at the right. Format and key a table of contents for the report.

Open the file (*60B REPORT1*); verify that the page number for each heading is the same as in your report. Change the table of contents as needed.

Save as: 63C REPORT

Table of Contents

Timed Writings

1. Your instructor will provide a timed writing. Key a 3' timing on ¶s 1–3 combined; determine *gwam* and number of errors.
2. Key two 1' timings on each ¶, trying to better the rate achieved in step 1 by three words or more. Don't worry about errors.
3. Key another 3' timing on ¶s 1–3 combined, trying to increase your *gwam* over the 3' timing of step 1.

Table 2

Create the table at the right using the information given below.

Main title: 16-pt. font
Table Style design: Colorful List – Accent 3
Column headings: row height 0.5"; Center alignment; 14-pt. font
Data rows: row height 0.3"
Column A and C: 2.0" wide; Bottom Left alignment
Column B: 1.4" wide; Bottom Center alignment
Center: table on page
Save as: **37C TABLE2**

Table 3

Arrange the information at the right as a table. Use **MOST FREQUENTLY PRODUCED OPERAS** for the main title; **1996–2006** for the secondary title; and **Operas**, **Composer**, and **No. of Productions** for the three column headings. Source: *Time Almanac 2007*.

Save as: **37C TABLE3**

Table 4

Open Table 2 (*37C TABLE2*). Insert the information at the right. Delete the year each author died; change column heading to **Year Born**. Sort the information by Year Born in ascending order.

Save as: **37C TABLE4**

SELECTED WORKS BY AMERICAN AUTHORS

Author	Life	Work
Robert Lee Frost	1874-1963	West-Running Brook
Henry W. Longfellow	1807-1882	Ballads
Carl Sandburg	1878-1967	Smoke and Steel
Louisa May Alcott	1832-1888	Little Women
William Faulkner	1897-1962	The Sound and the Fury
Samuel L. Clemens	1835-1910	Adventures of Tom Sawyer
F. Scott Fitzgerald	1896-1940	All the Sad Young Men

La boheme	Puccini	300
La traviata	Verdi	281
Madama Butterfly	Puccini	272
Carmen	Bizet	250
Tosca	Puccini	204
Don Giovanni	Mozart	201
Rigoletto	Verdi	171

Arthur Miller	1915	Death of a Salesman
Oliver W. Holmes	1809	Old Ironsides

Lesson 38 — TABLE LAYOUT AND DESIGN

OBJECTIVES

- To format tables with main, secondary, and column titles.
- To make independent decisions regarding table format features.

38A

Conditioning Practice
Key each line twice SS.

alphabet	1	David will buy the six unique jackets from Grady for prizes.
fig/sym	2	Glen's 2001 tax was $4,875, almost 7% ($396) less than 2000.
speed	3	Glen works with vigor to dismantle the downtown city chapel.

| gwam | 1' | 1 | 2 | 3 | 4 | 5 | 6 | 7 | 8 | 9 | 10 | 11 | 12 |

Endnotes (cont.)

[5]Albro Martin, *Railroads Triumphant* (New York: Oxford University Press, 1992), p. 94.

[6]Fred Reinfeld, *Pony Express* (Lincoln: University of Nebraska Press, 1973), p. 55.

[7]Carl H. Scheele, *A Short History of the Mail Service* (Washington, D.C.: Smithsonian Institution Press, 1970), p. 117.

[8]Fuller, p. 9.

[9]"Zen and the Art of the Internet," http://www.cs.indiana.edu/docproject/zen/zen-1.0_4.html (accessed February 8, 2004).

Note: You will finish keying the report "Delivering the Mail" in Lesson 63.

April 3, 1860, remains a memorable day in the history of the frontier, for that was the day on which the Pony Express began its operations—westward from St. Joseph and eastward from San Francisco. Even in those days San Francisco had already become the most important city in California.[6]

With the East Coast being connected to the West Coast by railroad in 1869, the Pony Express had a relatively short life span.

Automobiles

The invention of the automobile in the late 1800s brought a new means of delivering mail in the United States.

An automobile was used experimentally for rural delivery as early as 1902 at Adrian, Michigan, and in 1906 the Department gave permission for rural carriers to use their automobiles. The change from horse and wagon to the motor car paralleled improvements in highways and the development of more reliable automotive equipment . . . .[7]

Airplanes

The next major mode of transporting used by the Postal Service was airplanes. Speed was the driving force behind using airplanes. ". . . so closely has speed been associated with the mails that much of the world's postal history can be written around the attempts to send mail faster each day than it went the day before."[8]

Electronic Mail

"People have always wanted to correspond with each other in the fastest way possible . . ."[9] A new way of communicating via the written word became available with the creation of the Internet. The creation of the Internet provides a way of transporting the written word almost instantaneously. Electronic Mail (e-mail) messages generally arrive at their destination within seconds of when they were sent. More and more written messages are being delivered via e-mail.

Lesson 63

COVER PAGE AND TABLE OF CONTENTS

OBJECTIVES

- To complete formatting a bound report.
- To format reference page, title page, and table of contents.

63B Formatting

Bound Report

Document 1 (Report Summary)

Complete the report "Delivering the Mail" that you started in Lesson 62. Insert the file *DF 63B REPORT* at the end of the report and make the corrections shown at the right.

Save as: **63B REPORT1**

Summary

(now the U.S. Postal Service)

The Post Office has been the primary means for transporting written messages for many years. As the information age continues to emerge, technologies will play a significant roll in getting written messages from the sender to the reciever. Again, this change is directly attributable to speed. Instead of talking in terms of months required for delivering a message from the east coast to the west coast, we now talk in terms of it now takes seconds. Today, e-mail and faxes as are just as important to a successful business operation as the Post Office.

Format Tables

Table 1

Format the information at the right as a table. Use **FAMOUS COMPOSERS** for the main title and **1756–1899** for the secondary title. Apply the Medium Grid 3 – Accent 2 Table Style design. Adjust column width and height to attractively arrange the information on the page. Use the Sort feature to arrange the composers in alphabetical order.

Save as: **38B TABLE1**

Composer	Nationality	Life	Music
Mozart	Austrian	1756-1791	Don Giovanni
Beethoven	German	1770-1827	Ninth Symphony
Berlioz	French	1803-1869	Romeo and Juliet
Mendelssohn	German	1809-1847	Reformation
Chopin	Franco-Polish	1810-1849	Sonata in B Minor
Schumann	German	1810-1856	Rhenish Symphony
Wagner	German	1813-1883	Rienzi
Strauss	Austrian	1825-1899	Blue Danube

Table 2

Format the table at the right, arranging the data attractively.

Use **TOP TEN DAILY NEWSPAPERS** for the main title and **United States** for the secondary title. Source: *Time Almanac 2007*.

Apply the Colorful List – Accent 4 Table Style design.

Save as: **38B TABLE2**

Rank	Newspaper	Location	Circulation
1	USA Today	Arlington, VA	2,528,437
2	Wall Street Journal	New York, NY	2,058,342
3	Times	New York, NY	1,683,855
4	Times	Los Angeles, CA	1,231,318
5	Post	Washington, D.C.	960,684
6	Tribune	Chicago, IL	957,212
7	Daily News	New York, NY	795,153
8	Inquirer	Philadelphia, PA	705,965
9	Post/Rocky Mountain News	Denver, CO	704,806
10	Chronicle	Houston, TX	692,557

Table 3

Use **TOP BASEBALL MOVIES** for the main title; **July 27, 2007** for the secondary title; **Rank**, **Movie**, **Year**, and **Percent of Votes** for the column headings.

The tenth movie is **Pride of the Yankees** made in **1942**, **1.9** percent of votes. Include a source note: **Source: ESPN – Page 2 Mailbag.** http://espn.go.com/page2/s/users/baseball/films.html (27 July 2007).

Use the Sort feature to arrange the movies in order by rank; apply an appropriate table style.

Save as: **38B TABLE3**

4	Bull Durham	1988	13.4
9	A League of Their Own	1992	3.1
8	Bad News Bears	1976	3.3
2	Major League	1989	19.2
3	The Natural	1984	15.9
6	For the Love of the Game	1999	4.4
1	Field of Dreams	1989	23.5%
5	The Sandlot	1993	10.8
7	Eight Men Out	1988	4.0

Note: Because of rounding, the amounts do not add up to 100 percent.

- President John F. Kennedy
- Audie Murphy--one of the most decorated WWII soldiers
- Tomb of Unknown Civil War Dead--remains of Union soldiers
- Confederate Monument--remains of many Confederate soldiers
- Iwo Jima--U.S. Marine Corps Memorial
- Anita Newcomb McGee--organizer of Army Nurse Corps

Lesson 62

REPORT WITH ENDNOTES

OBJECTIVES
- To format a bound report.
- To format endnotes.

62B | Formatting

Bound Report

Document 1 (Report Body)

1. Review the format guides on reports on pp. 173–174 as needed.
2. Format the copy at the right as a bound report with endnotes. The endnotes are shown below and on p. 184.
3. When you finish, use the Speller feature and proofread.

Save as: **62B REPORT2**

Document 1 (Endnotes)

[1]Wayne E. Fuller, *The American Mail* (Chicago: University of Chicago Press, 1972), p. ix.

[2]William M. Leary, *Aerial Pioneers* (Washington, D.C.: Smithsonian Institution Press, 1985), p. 238.

[3]Richard Wormser, *The Iron Horse: How Railroads Changed America* (New York: Walker Publishing Company, Inc., 1993), p. 26.

[4]Leary, p. 238.

DELIVERING THE MAIL

For years, people have used written communication as one of their primary means of exchanging information. Those using this form of communicating have depended on the U.S. mail to transport their messages from one place to another.

> For much of American history, the mail was our main form of organized communication. Americans wanting to know the state of the world, the health of a friend, or the fate of their business anxiously awaited the mail. To advise a distant relative, to order goods, to pay a bill, to express views to their congressman or love to their fiancée, they used the mail. No American institution has been more intimately involved in daily hopes and fears.[1]

The history of the U.S. mail is not only interesting but also reflective of the changes in American society, specifically transportation. A variety of modes of transporting mail have been used over the years. Speed, of course, was the driving force behind most of the changes.

Steamboats

Congress used inventions to move the mail from place to place. In 1813, five years after Robert Fulton's first experiments on the Hudson River, Congress authorized the Post Office to transport mail by steamboat.[2] Transporting mail to river cities worked very well. However, the efficiency of using steamboats to transport mail between New York and San Francisco was questionable. "The distance was 19,000 miles and the trip could take as long as six to seven months."[3]

Railroads

Although mail was carried by railroads as early as 1834, it was not until 1838 that Congress declared railroads to be post roads.[4] Trains eventually revolutionized mail delivery. The cost of sending a letter decreased substantially, making it more affordable to the public.

> No aspect of American life was untouched by the revolution that the trains brought in bringing mail service almost to the level of a free good. (For many years--ironically enough, until the Depression called for an increase in the cost of a first-class letter to three cents--an ordinary first-class letter went for two cents.)[5]

Pony Express

The Pony Express was one of the most colorful means of transporting mail. This method of delivery was used to take mail from St. Joseph, Missouri, westward.

(continued on next page)

Skill 2 BUILDER

Speed Building

1. Key each line twice with no pauses between letters or words.
2. Key a 1' timing on lines 2, 4, 6, 8, and 10; determine *gwam* on each timing.

space	1	and the she big city disk held half firm land paid them make
bar	2	Jane and the man may handle the problems with the city firm.
shift	3	Moorcroft, WY; Eau Claire, WI; New York City, NY; Newark, DE
keys	4	M. L. Ramirez left for San Francisco on Tuesday, January 23.
adjacent	5	wire open tire sure ruin said trim quit fire spot lids walks
keys	6	Katrina opened a shop by the stadium to sell sporting goods.
long direct	7	many vice brag stun myth much cents under check juice center
reaches	8	I brought a recorder to the music hall to record my recital.
word	9	their visit signs aisle chapel dials handy shake shelf usual
response	10	Their dog slept by the oak chair in the aisle of the chapel.

gwam 1' | 1 | 2 | 3 | 4 | 5 | 6 | 7 | 8 | 9 | 10 | 11 | 12 |

Timed Writings

1. Key a 1' timing on each ¶; determine *gwam*.
2. Key a 2' timing on ¶s 1–2 combined; determine *gwam*.
3. Key a 3' timing on ¶s 1–2 combined; determine *gwam* and number of errors.

A all letters used (MicroPace)

gwam 2' | 3'

"I left my heart in San Francisco." This expression becomes much easier to understand after an individual has visited the city near the bay. San Francisco is one of the most interesting areas to visit throughout the entire world. The history of this city is unique. Even though people inhabited the area prior to the gold rush, it was the prospect of getting rich that brought about the fast growth of the city.

It is difficult to write about just one thing that this exquisite city is known for. Spectacular views, cable cars, the Golden Gate Bridge, and Fisherman's Wharf are only a few of the many things that are associated with this amazing city. The city is also known for the diversity of its people. In fact, there are three separate cities within the city, Chinatown being the best known.

gwam						
2'	1	2	3	4	5	6
3'	1		2		3	4

2' / 3' column values:
5 | 4
11 | 7
17 | 11
23 | 15
28 | 19
34 | 23
40 | 26
42 | 28
47 | 31
53 | 35
59 | 39
65 | 43
71 | 48
77 | 51
80 | 54

Quarter-Minute Checkpoints

gwam	1/4'	1/2'	3/4'	1'
24	6	12	18	24
28	7	14	21	28
32	8	16	24	32
36	9	18	27	36
40	10	20	30	40
44	11	22	33	44
48	12	24	36	48
52	13	26	39	52
56	14	28	42	56
60	15	30	45	60

Bound Report

Document 1 (Report Body)

1. Format the copy shown at the right as a bound report with endnotes.
2. Information for the endnotes is shown below.

Save as: **61C REPORT1**

Information for Endnotes

[1]W. J. Wood, *Battles of the Revolutionary War* (Cambridge, MA: Da Capo Press, 2003), pp. 63-64.

[2]Lincoln Memorial-- National Park Service, http://www.nps.gov/linc/ (2 November 2007).

[3]The White House, http://www.whitehouse.gov/history/presidents/tj3.html (accessed November 7, 2007).

Document 2 (Reference Page)

Use the endnotes information to prepare a references page. See p. R18 for format.

Save as: **61C REPORT2**

WASHINGTON D.C.

Our nation's capital, Washington D.C., is a magnificent city to visit. It is known for the monuments, memorials, and cemetery that honor those who have given their lives in the cause of freedom and democracy. Some of the more widely recognized tributes to those who have fought for freedom and democracy include:

- Washington Monument
- Lincoln Memorial
- Jefferson Memorial
- Arlington Cemetery

Washington Monument

Few men have impacted the history of this country as much as George Washington. The birth of this nation can in large part be attributed to the Continental Army under the leadership of George Washington. His leadership is easily imagined when reading Wood's book on the Revolutionary War. "He stands on the bank of the stream, wrapped in his cloak, superintending the landing of his troops. He is calm and collected, but very determined. The storm is [again] changing to sleet and cuts like a knife."[i]

Recognized for his leadership abilities, Washington was elected by the American people as the first President following the conclusion of the Revolutionary War. Naming the nation's capital after him and erecting a 555-foot monument in his honor ensure that George Washington's contributions to his country will always be remembered.

Lincoln Memorial

The Lincoln Memorial, another symbol of freedom, is a tribute to the sixteenth President of the United States. While Washington is recognized for fighting for the birth of this nation in the Revolutionary War, Lincoln is recognized for trying to preserve the nation during the Civil war.

The Lincoln Memorial was built to resemble a Greek temple. The 36 columns of the memorial represent the 36 states at the time of Lincoln's death. A sculpture of a seated Lincoln done by Daniel Chester French is the focal point of the memorial. Inscribed above the seated Lincoln are these words, "In this temple, as in the hearts of the people for whom he saved the Union, the memory of Abraham Lincoln is enshrined forever."[ii]

Prominently displayed on the walls of the memorial are the Gettysburg Address (often referred to as Lincoln's most famous speech) and Lincoln's second inaugural address. The words "Four score and seven years ago . . ." and "With malice toward none; with charity for all . . ." need no formal introduction.

Jefferson Memorial

The man recognized as the primary drafter of the Declaration of Independence is memorialized in the Jefferson Memorial. A powerful advocate of liberty and an eloquent correspondent, Jefferson drafted the Declaration of Independence for the Continental Congress in 1776 at the age of 33.[iii] He became the third president in 1801.

Declaration of Independence

We hold these truths to be self-evident, that all men are created equal, that they are endowed by their Creator with certain unalienable Rights, that among these are Life, Liberty and the pursuit of Happiness. — That to secure these rights, Governments are instituted among Men, deriving their just powers from the consent of the governed, —

Arlington Cemetery

The most widely known cemetery in the United States is Arlington Cemetery. Arlington Cemetery is the final resting place of many veterans--every war that the U.S. has been involved in is represented. Perhaps the best known of the memorials at Arlington is the "Tomb of the Unknown Soldier." Other well-known memorials include:

(continued on next page)

Communication & Math
SKILLS 4

PRONOUN AGREEMENT

Pronoun Agreement

1. Study each of the four rules.
   a. Key the Learn lines beneath each rule, noting how the rule is applied.
   b. Key the Apply lines, choosing correct pronouns.

Pronoun Agreement

Rule 1: A personal pronoun (*I, we, you, he, she, it, their*, etc.) agrees in **person** (first, second, or third) with the noun or other pronoun it represents.

Learn 1 We can win the game if we all give each play our best effort. (1st person)

Learn 2 You may practice dancing only after you finish all your homework. (2nd person)

Learn 3 Andrea said that she will drive her car to the antique mall. (3rd person)

Apply 4 Those who saw the exhibit said that (he, she, they) were impressed.

Apply 5 After you run for a few days, (my, your) muscles are less sore.

Apply 6 Before I take the test, I want to review (your, my) class notes.

Rule 2: A personal pronoun agrees in **gender** (feminine, masculine, or neuter) with the noun or other pronoun it represents.

Learn 7 Miss Kimoto will give her talk after the art exhibit. (feminine)

Learn 8 The small boat lost its way in the dense fog. (neuter)

Apply 9 Each winner will get a corsage as she receives (her, its) award.

Apply 10 The ball circled the rim before (he, it) dropped through the hoop.

Rule 3: A personal pronoun agrees in **number** (singular or plural) with the noun or other pronoun it represents.

Learn 11 Celine drove her new car to Del Rio, Texas, last week. (singular)

Learn 12 The club officers made careful plans for their next meeting. (plural)

Apply 13 All workers must submit (his, their) vacation requests.

Apply 14 The sloop lost (its, their) headsail in the windstorm.

Rule 4: A personal pronoun that represents a collective noun (*team, committee, family*, etc.) may be singular or plural, depending on the meaning of the collective noun.

Learn 15 Our men's soccer team played its fifth game today. (acting as a unit)

Learn 16 The drill team took their positions on the field. (acting individually)

Apply 17 The jury will render (its, their) verdict at 1:30 today.

Apply 18 The Social Committee had presented (its, their) written reports.

(continued on next page)

Document 1 cont.

Complete the Globalization report. Format and key the text at the right following the data file *DF 60B GLOBAL* that you inserted.

Footnotes 10–11

[10]"India's Income Per Capita Way Behind China," http:// in.news.yahoo.com /021204/43/1ysk5.html (accessed February 9, 2004).

[11]Pete Engardio, "Third World Leapfrog," *Business Week,* May 18, 1994, p. 47.

Save as: **60B REPORT1**

Document 2 (Cover Page)

Review the Cover Page section of the format guides, p. 173. Prepare a cover page for the Globalization report.

Save as: **60B REPORT2**

Use the Cover Page feature (Puzzle format) to prepare a cover page. Compare the two cover pages.

Save as: **60B REPORT2A**

Document 3 (References Page)

Review the format guides for preparing a references page, p. 174. Use the information from the footnotes and the information shown at the right to prepare a references page for the report. Refer to p. R18 for format of references.

Save as: **60B REPORT3**

Of these emerging markets, the most dramatic increase is in the East Asian countries. India, for example, has been able to achieve higher growth in incomes, longer life expectancy, and better schooling through increased integration into the world economy.[10]

Recent technological developments have also contributed to globalization. Because of these developments, the world is a smaller place; communication is almost instant to many parts of the world. The extent of the technological developments can be sensed in Engardio's comments:[11]

> Places that until recently were incommunicado are rapidly acquiring state-of-the-art telecommunications that will let them foster both internal and foreign investment. It may take a decade for many countries in Asia, Latin America, and Eastern Europe to unclog bottlenecks in transportation and power supplies. But by installing optical fiber, digital switches, and the latest wireless transmission systems, urban centers and industrial zones from Beijing to Budapest are stepping into the Information Age. Videoconferencing, electronic data interchange, and digital mobile-phone services already are reaching most of Asia and parts of Eastern Europe.
>
> All of these developing regions see advanced communications as a way to leapfrog stages of economic development.

Summary

The world continues to become more globalized. The trend will continue because of three main factors: new and improved trade agreements, rapid growth rates of developing countries' economies, and technological advances. All of these factors foster globalization.

Engardio article pp. 47–49   *Jacob article pp. 74–90*
"Fact Sheet" article pp. 87–93   *Richman article p. 14*
Harris article pp. 755–776

Lesson 61   REPORT WITH ENDNOTES

OBJECTIVES

- To format a bound report with endnotes.
- To format a references page.

61B   Skill Building

Timed Writings

1. Your instructor will provide a timed writing. Key a 3' timing on ¶s 1–3 combined; determine *gwam* and number of errors.

2. Key two 1' timings on each ¶, trying to better the rate achieved in step 1 by three words or more. Don't worry about errors.

3. Key another 3' timing on ¶s 1–3 combined, trying to increase your *gwam* over the 3' timing of step 1.

2. Key Proofread & Correct, using correct pronouns.
   a. Check answers.
   b. Using the rule number at the left of each line, study the rule relating to each error you made.
   c. Rekey each incorrect line, using correct pronouns.

Save as: CS4 ACTIVITY1

Proofread & Correct

Rules

2	1	Suzy knew that (he, she, they) should read more novels.
3	2	People who entered the contest say (he, she, they) are confident.
3	3	As soon as art class is over, I like to transcribe (our, my) notes.
2, 3	4	Mrs. Kelso gave (her, his, their) lecture in Royce Hall.
2	5	The yacht moved slowly around (her, his, its) anchor.
1	6	As you practice the lines, (his, your) confidence increases.
1	7	I played my new clarinet in (my, their, your) last recital.
3	8	The editors planned quickly for (its, their) next newsletter.
4	9	The women's volleyball team won (its, their) tenth game today.
4	10	Our family will take (its, their) annual trip in August.

ACTIVITY 2

Listening

1. Open *DF CS4 ACTIVITY2*.
2. Listen to the weather forecast and take notes. Then close the file.
3. Key answers to the questions.

Save as: CS4 ACTIVITY2

1. What were the high and low temperatures for today?
2. What are the predicted high and low temperatures for Tuesday?
3. Is it likely to rain tomorrow?
4. How many days are likely to have rain in the five-day forecast?
5. What is the highest temperature predicted in the five-day forecast?
6. What is the lowest temperature predicted in the five-day forecast?

ACTIVITY 3

Write to Learn

Save as: CS4 ACTIVITY3

1. Using word processing or voice recognition software, write a paragraph explaining how to insert a 3 × 4 table.
2. Write a second paragraph explaining how to change the row height to 0.3".

ACTIVITY 4

Math: Finding the Part of a Whole

1. Open *DF CS4 ACTIVITY4* and print the file.
2. Solve the problems as directed in the file.
3. Submit your answers.

CAREER Clusters

ACTIVITY 4

You must complete Career Exploration Activities 1–3 before completing this activity.

1. Retrieve your Career folder and find the printed Career Cluster Plan of Study for the career cluster that is your first choice.

2. Review the plan and write a paragraph or two about why you would or would not consider a career in this cluster. Print your file, then save it as Career4, and keep it open.

3. Exchange papers with a classmate. Have the classmate offer suggestions for improving the content and correcting any errors he or she finds in your paragraph(s). Make the changes that you agree with and print a copy to turn in to your instructor. Save it as Career4 and close the file.

4. Return your folder to the storage area. When your instructor returns your paper, file it in your Career folder.

OBJECTIVES

- To format a bound report with footnotes.
- To format a references page and a title page.

60B   Formatting

Bound Report

Document 1

Finish the Globalization report started in Lesson 59. Insert the file *DF 60B GLOBAL* after the last sentence in *59C REPORT*. Make the changes shown at the right.

Footnotes 7–9

[7]"Fact Sheet: European Community," Vol. 4, No. 7, Washington, D.C.: *U.S. Department of State Dispatch*, February 15, 1994, p. 89.

[8]Mario Bognanno and Kathryn J. Ready, eds., *North American Free Trade Agreement* (Westport, CT: Quorum Books, 1993), p. xiii.

[9]Rahul Jacob, "The Big Rise," *Fortune*, May 30, 1994, pp. 74–75.

The first step was ~~done~~ accomplished by the Paris and Rome treaties, which established the european community and consequently removed the economic barriers. The treaties called for members to establish a common market; a common customs tariff; and common economic, agricultural, transport, and nuclear policies.[7]

NAFTA. A trade agreement that will have a significant impact on the way business is conducted in the United States is the North American Free Trade Agreement. This trade agreement involves Canada, the United States, and Mexico. Proponents of NAFTA claim that the accord will not only increase trade throughout the Americas, but it will also moderate product prices and create jobs in all three of the countries.[8]

Over the years a number of trade agreements have been enacted that promote trade. The result of these agreements has been an ~~bet-ter~~ enhanced quality of life because of the increased access to goods and services produced in other countries.

Growth in Developing Countries' Economies

The growth in developing countries' economies is another major reason for globalizaiton. According to Jacob, the global surge means more consumers who need goods and services.[9] These needs appear because of the increase in per capita incomes of the developing countries. According to the U.S. Department of Commerce, the world's ten biggest emerging markets include:

- Argentina
- Brazil
- China
- India
- Indonesia
- Mexico
- Poland
- South Africa
- South Korea
- Turkey

UNIT 12
Lessons 39-45

Learn Electronic Presentation Basics

What Is an Electronic Presentation?

Electronic presentations are computer-generated visual aids (usually slide shows) that can be used to help communicate information. Electronic presentations can combine text, graphics, audio, video, and animation to deliver and support key points. With the powerful features of presentation software such as *Microsoft PowerPoint*, attractive and engaging presentations can be created with ease.

Presentations are an important part of communication in business. Presentations are given to inform, to persuade, and/or to entertain. Visual aids generally make a speaker more effective in delivering his/her message. That is because the speaker is using two senses (hearing and sight)

rather than just one. The probability of a person understanding and retaining something seen as well as heard is much greater than if it is just heard. For example, if you had never heard of a giraffe before, you would have a better idea of what a giraffe was if the speaker talked about a giraffe and showed pictures of one than if the speaker only talked about what a giraffe was.

With presentation software, visuals (slides) can be created that can be projected on a large screen for a larger audience to view, or viewed directly on a computer by a smaller audience. Web pages, color or black-and-white overheads, audience handouts, and speaker notes can be created using electronic presentation software.

What Are the Key Features of Electronic Presentation Software?

Learning how to use **PowerPoint** is quite easy for individuals who have had experience with **Word.** *PowerPoint* has many of the same features as *Word* and is set up the same way, using ribbons, groups, and tabs. However, you will learn new features unique to *PowerPoint*.

In this unit you will learn how to:

- Create text slides
- Insert illustrations on a slide
- Create diagrams and tables
- Create charts and graphs
- Create and deliver a presentation

What Is a Design Theme?

PowerPoint comes with files containing design themes (see examples on next page). A theme has everything set up. All the person creating the presentation has to do is select the slide layout and key in their information. The font and font size, places for keying information, background design, and

color schemes are preset for each design theme. Even though these themes are preset, they can be changed to better fit the needs of the user. Using design themes gives your presentations a professional appearance.

Bound Report

1. Review the report format guides on pp. 173–174; study the model report on p. 178. Note the format of the footnotes.

2. Key the first page of the "Globalization" report from the model on p. 178; continue keying the report from the rough-draft copy shown at the right. The information for footnotes 4–6 is given below.

3. Proofread your copy and correct errors.

Footnotes 4–6

[4]Harris, p. 763.

[5]*Encyclopedia Americana*, Vol. 26, "Trade Policy" (Danbury, CT: Grolier Incorporated, 2001), p. 915.

[6]Louis S. Richman, "Dangerous Times for Trade Treaties," *Fortune*, September 20, 1993, p. 14.

Save as: **59C REPORT**

Note: You will finish keying the report in Lesson 60.

- The reduction in trade and investment barriers in the post-world war II period.

- The rapid growth and increase in the size of developing countries' economies.

- Changes in technologies.[4]

Trade Agreements

Originally, each nation established its own rules governing foreign trade. Unfair Regulations and tariffs were often the outcome, leading to the tariff wars of the 1930s. However, Not a long quote, don't Indent

"During the 1950's a concerted effort was made to reduce these artificial barriers to trade, and as a result the quotas and other controls limiting foreign trade were gradually dismantled."[5]

Many trade agreements exist in the world today. Three of those agreements (General Agreement on Tariffs and Trade [GATT], the European Community, and the North American Free Trade Agreement [NAFTA]) have had or will have a significant impact on the United States. #

GATT. The first trade agreement of major significance was the General Agreement on Tariffs and Trade. The purpose of GATT was aimed at to lowering tariff barriers among its members. The success of the organization is evidenced by its membership. Originally signed by 23 countries in 1947, the number of participating countries continues to grow.

The Uruguay Round of GATT is the most ambitious trade agreement ever attempted. Some 108 nations would lower tariff and other barriers on textiles and agriculture goods; protect one another's intellectual property; and open their borders to banks, insurance companies, and purveyors of other services.[6]

The European Community. The European Community is another example of how trade agreements impact the production, distribution, and marketing of goods and services. The 12 member nations of the European Community have dismantled the internal borders of its members to enhance trade relations.

Dismantling the borders was only the first step toward an even greater purpose--the peaceful union of European countries.

What Is Slide Layout?

Layout refers to the way text and graphics are arranged on the slide. Presentation software allows the user to select a slide layout for each slide that is created. Some of the more common layouts (see examples below) include:

- Title Slide layout
- Title and Content layout
- Section header layout
- Two Content layout
- Comparison layout
- Title Only layout
- Blank layout
- Content with Caption
- Picture with Caption layout

Illustrations of Design Themes with Common Slide Layouts

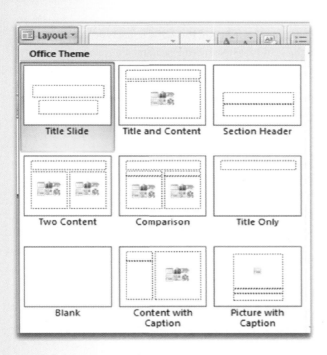

Slide Layout

Title Slide Layout

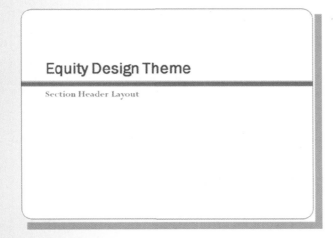

Section Header Layout

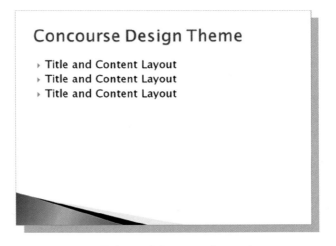

Title and Content Layout

Globalization

We live in a time of worldwide change. What happens in one part of the world impacts people on the other side of the world. People around the world are influenced by common developments.[1]

The term "globalization" is used to describe this phenomenon. According to Harris, the term is being used in a variety of contexts.[2] However, in the broadest context globalization can be defined as:

> . . . a process of interaction and integration among the people, companies, and governments of different nations, a process driven by international trade and investment and aided by information technology. This process has effects on the environment, on culture, on political systems, on economic development and prosperity, and on human physical well-being in societies around the world.[3]

The business world uses this term in a narrower context to refer to the production, distribution, and marketing of goods and services at an international level. Everyone is impacted by the continued increase of globalization in a variety of ways. The types of food we eat, the kinds of clothes we wear, the variety of technologies we utilize, the modes of transportation available to us, and the types of jobs we pursue are directly linked to globalization. Globalization is changing the world we live in.

Causes of Globalization

Harris indicates that there are three main factors contributing to globalization. These factors include:

---

[1] Robert K. Schaeffer, *Understanding Globalization* (Lanham, MD: Rowman & Littlefield Publishers, Inc., 1977), p. 1.

[2] Richard G. Harris, "Globalization, Trade, and Income," *Canadian Journal of Economics*, November 1993, p. 755.

[3] "Globalization 101.org," http://www.globalization101.org/What_is_Globalization.html (accessed November 1, 2007).

Side labels: Footnote Superscript · Long Quote · 1.5" LM · 1.0" RM · Side Heading · Footnotes

Bound Report with Footnotes

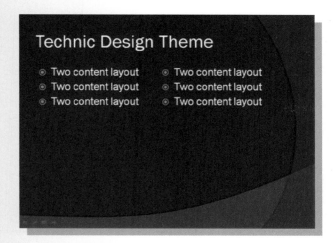

Two Content Layout

Two Content Layout

**Picture with Caption
Shown with Three Design Themes**

What View Options Are Available to View Slides?

As you create a presentation, there are different view options available. Each view serves a distinct purpose for creating, editing, and viewing slides.

View Options:
- Normal View
- Slide Sorter View
- Slide Show View

These views are explained and illustrated on the next page.

Insert *DF 58B SPOTTED TAIL* text file. Make the corrections shown at the right.

Document 2 (Reference Page)

Prepare a separate reference page from the information at the right. Proofread; correct errors.

Save as: **58B REPORT2**

INTERNET ACTIVITY

Use the Internet to learn more about a person named in the report. Compose a ¶ about the person.

Save as: **58B INTERNET**

Spotted Tail

Spotted Tail (?1833-1881) was born along the White River ^either in present-day South Dakota or near present-day Laramie, Wyoming. He be⌣came the leader of the Brulé Sioux and was one of the signers of the Fort Laramie Treaty of 1868. Eventually, he became the government-appointed chief of the agency Sioux and # made frequent trips to Washington, D.C. ^in that capacity (Bowman, 1995, 688). Starting in 1870 ẹpotted Tail became the statesman that made him the greatest chief the Brulés ever k^new (Fielder, 1975, ₤. 29).

Bowman, John S. (ed). *The Cambridge Dictionary of American Biography*. Cambridge: Cambridge University Press, 1995.

Encarta, http://encarta.msn.com/encyclopedia_761578750/sittingbull.html (5 February 2004).

Fielder, Mildred. *Sioux Indian Leaders*. Seattle: Superior Publishing Company, 1975.

Utley, Robert M. *The Lance and the Shield: The Life and Times of Sitting Bull*. New York: Henry Holt and Company, 1993. (accessed February 5, 2004)

Language Skills: Word Choice

1. Study the spelling and definitions of the words.
2. Key all *Learn* and *Apply* lines, choosing the correct word in the apply lines.

Save as: **58C CHOICE**

some (n/adv) unknown or unspecified unit or thing; to a degree or extent	**hour** (n) the 24th part of a day; a particular time
sum (n/vb) the whole amount; the total; to find a total; summary of points	**our** (adj) of or relating to ourselves as possessors

Learn 1 The total **sum** awarded did not satisfy **some** of the people.
Apply 2 The first grader said, "The (some, sum) of five and two is seven."
Apply 3 (Some, sum) of the students were able to find the correct (some, sum) for the problem.

Learn 1 The first **hour** of **our** class will be used for going over the next assignment.
Apply 2 What (hour, our) of the day would you like to have (hour, our) group perform?
Apply 3 Minutes turned into (hours, ours) as we waited for (hour, our) turn to perform.

Lesson 59   REPORT WITH FOOTNOTES

OBJECTIVES
• To format a bound report with footnotes.
• To format a reference page.

Timed Writing

1. Your instructor will provide a timed writing. Key a 3' timing on ¶s 1–3 combined; determine *gwam* and number of errors.

2. Key two 1' timings on each ¶, trying to better the rate achieved in step 1 by three words or more. Don't worry about errors.

3. Key another 3' timing on ¶s 1–3 combined, trying to increase your *gwam* over the 3' timing of step 1.

Lesson 59   Report with Footnotes   **177**

Illustrations of View Options

Normal View (Outline) – The Normal View with outline is used for creating and editing individual slides, outlining, and creating notes.

Normal View (Slides) – The Normal View with slides is used for creating and editing individual slides, viewing miniatures of slides that have already been created, and creating notes.

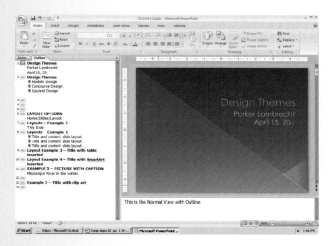

Normal View - Outline

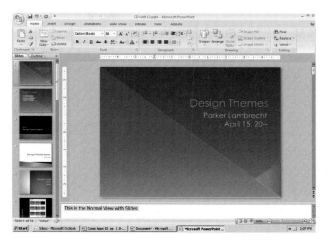

Normal View - Slides

Slide Sorter View – The Slide Sorter View shows all the slides in miniature. This is helpful for rearranging slides and for applying features to several slides at a time.

Slide Show View – The Slide Show View is used to see how the slides will look on the screen. This view is helpful for rehearsing and presenting your slide show.

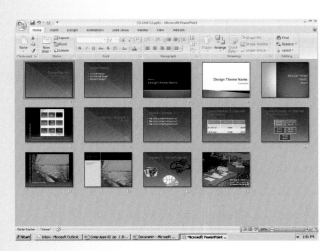

Slide Sorter View

Slide Show View

Crazy Horse

Crazy Horse (?1842–1877) was also born near the Black Hills. His father was a medicine man; his mother was the sister of Spotted Tail. He was recognized as a skilled hunter and fighter. Crazy Horse believed he was immune from battle injury and took part in all the major Sioux battles to protect the Black Hills against white intrusion. He was named war supreme and peace chief of the Oglalas in 1876 and led the Sioux and Cheyenne to victory at the battle of Rosebud in January that year. Perhaps he is remembered most for leading the Sioux and Cheyenne in the battle of the Little Bighorn where his warriors defeated Custer's forces. Crazy Horse is regarded as the greatest leader of the Sioux and a symbol of their heroic resistance (Bowman, 1995, 160–161).

Red Cloud

WP Activity

Insert *DF 58B RED CLOUD* text file. Make the corrections shown at the right.

Red Cloud (1822–1909) was born near the Platte River in present-day Nebraska. Because of his intelligence, strength, and bravery, he became the chief of the Oglala Sioux. "Red Cloud's War" took place between 1865 and 1868. These battles forced the closing of the Bozeman trail and the signing of the Fort Laramie Treaty in 1868. In exchange for peace, the U.S. government accepted the territorial claims of the Sioux (Bowman, 1995, 601).

Sitting Bull

Sitting Bull (?1831–1890) a leader of the Sioux, was born in the region of the Grand River in South Dakota (Encarta, 2004). He was known among the Sioux as a warrior even during his youth. He was bitterly opposed to white encroachment but made peace in 1868 when the U.S. government guaranteed him a large reservation free of white settlers. When gold was discovered in the Black Hills, he joined the Arapaho and Cheyenne to fight the invaders (Bowman, 1995, 673). According to fellow tribesmen, the name Sitting Bull suggested an animal possessed of great endurance that planted immovably on its haunches to fight on to the death (Utley, 1993, 15).

(continued on next page)

OBJECTIVES

- To navigate through an existing electronic presentation.
- To create a title slide.
- To create a bulleted list slide.

39A–45A

Conditioning Practice

Key each line twice SS.

alphabet	1	Jake Lopez may give a few more racquetball exhibitions in Dallas.
figures	2	Ray quickly found the total of 8.16, 9.43, and 10.25 to be 27.84.
speed	3	Bob's neighbor may dismantle the ancient shanty in the big field.

gwam 1' | 1 | 2 | 3 | 4 | 5 | 6 | 7 | 8 | 9 | 10 | 11 | 12 |

39B

View Presentation

1. Open *DF 39B PP*. The file will open in Normal View (Slides).
2. Click the Slide Show View button at the bottom of the screen and view the slide show, noting the design themes and layout options. Click the mouse button to advance to the next slide.
3. When you are done viewing the slide show, click Slide Sorter View.
4. Click Normal View; read the notes beneath each slide, then use the down arrow key to go to the next slide.
5. Close without saving.

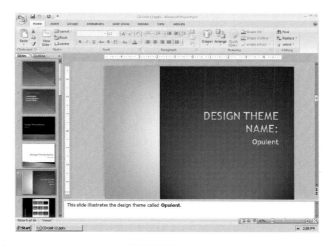

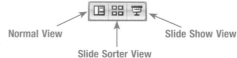

Normal View   Slide Sorter View   Slide Show View

39C

Create Title Slide

P • Design/Themes/Module

P • Home/Slides/Layout/ Title Slide

1. Start a new presentation.
2. Select the Module design theme (or another if Module is not available).
3. Select Title Slide layout.
4. Create the title slide as shown.
5. Increase the font size for the name of the presenter and the company name to 24 pt.

Save as: 39C PP

Title slide. A presentation should begin with a title slide. Include the presentation title, presenter name, and other relevant information.

Slide 1 – Title Slide

OBJECTIVES

- To format a bound report with textual citations and references.
- To improve word choice skills.

58A-63A

Conditioning Practice

Key each line twice.

alphabet 1 Zack and our equipment manager will exchange jobs for seven days.

figures 2 If you call after 12:30 on Friday, you can reach him at 297-6854.

speed 3 The eight men in the shanty paid for a big bus to go to the city.

gwam 1' | 1 | 2 | 3 | 4 | 5 | 6 | 7 | 8 | 9 | 10 | 11 | 12 | 13 |

58B Formatting

Bound Report

Document 1
(Report Body)

1. Review the format guides on pp. 173–174.
2. Format the text at the right and on pp. 176–177 as a bound report with textual citations. Insert text files as noted.
3. Proofread your copy and correct any errors.

Save as: 58B REPORT1

PLAINS INDIANS

The ^American Plains Indians are among the ^best known of all Native Americans. These ^Indians played a ^significant role in shaping the history of the West. Some of the more noteworthy Plains Indians were big Foot, ^Black Kettle, Crazy Horse, Red Cloud, Sitting Bull, and Spotted Tail.

Big Foot

Big Foot (?1825-1890) was also known as Spotted Elk. Born in the northern Great Plains, he eventually became a Minneconjou Teton Sioux chief. He was part of a ^tribal delegation that traveled to Washington, D.C., and worked to establish schools throughout the Sioux territory. He was one of those massacred at Wounded Knee in December 1890 (Bowman, 1995, 63).

Black Kettle

Black Kettle (?1803-1868) was born near the Black Hills in present-day South Dakota. He was recognized as a ^Southern Cheyenne peace chief for his efforts to bring peace to the region. However, his attempts at accommodation ^were not successful and his band was massacred at sand creek in 1864. Even though he continued to seek peace, he was killed with the remainder of his tribe in ^the Washita Valley of Oklahoma in 1868 (Bowman, 1995, 67).

(continued on next page)

Create Title and Content Slide

- Home/Slides/Layout/ Title and Content

1. Read the information at the right.
2. Open *39C PP* and insert two new slides with the Title and Content (bulleted list) layout after the slide you created in 39C.
3. Create the slides as shown below.

Save as: **39D PP**

Title and Content (bulleted list). Use the Title and Content layout for lists to guide discussion and help the audience follow a speaker's ideas. If too much information is placed on a single slide, the text becomes difficult to read. Keep the information on the slide brief—do not write complete sentences. Be concise.

When creating lists, be sure to:
- focus on one main idea.
- add several supporting items.
- limit the number of lines on one slide to six.
- limit long wraparound lines of text.

Presentation Planning
- Consider the audience.
- Consider the subject.
- Consider the equipment.
- Consider the facilities.

Slide 2 - Bulleted List 1

Message Development
- Introduction
- Body
- Summary and/or Conclusion

Slide 3 - Bulleted List 2

Change Template Design

- Design/Themes/Aspect (Concourse, Solstice, Opulent)

Open *39D PP*; change the template design to two other designs, and see how the appearance of the different layouts changes with each template. Close the file without saving.

Professional Electronic Presentations
Denise Strait
Multimedia Design Services

Aspect Design Theme

Professional Electronic Presentations
Denise Strait
Multimedia Design Services

Concourse Design Theme

Presentation Planning
- Consider the audience.
- Consider the subject.
- Consider the equipment.
- Consider the facilities.

Solstice Design Theme

PRESENTATION PLANNING
- Consider the audience.
- Consider the subject.
- Consider the equipment.
- Consider the facilities.

Opulent Design Theme

Table of Contents

A table of contents lists the headings of a report and the page numbers where those headings can be found in the report. The side and top margins for the table of contents are the same as those used for the first page of the report. Include Table of Contents (using the Title style, 2" from top). Then list side and paragraph headings (if included). Side headings are started at left margin; paragraph headings are indented 0.5". Page numbers for each entry are keyed at the right margin; use a right dot leader tab to insert page numbers. Space once before inserting the dot leader and once after inserting the dot leader to leave a space after the heading and before the page number.

Documentation

Documentation is used to give credit for published material (electronic as well as printed) that is quoted or closely paraphrased (slightly changed). Three types of documentation will be used in this unit: textual citation, footnotes, and endnotes.

Textual citation. The textual citation method of documentation was used in Unit 10. This method includes the name(s) of the author(s), the date of the referenced publication, and the page number(s) of the material cited as part of the actual text:

`(McWilliams, 2009, 138)`

When the author's name is used in the text introducing the quotation, only the year of publication and the page number(s) appear in parentheses:

`McWilliams (2009, 138) said that . . .`

For electronic references, include the author's name and the year.

Footnotes. The footnotes method of documentation identifies the reference cited by a superscript number . . . .[1]

The complete documentation for the reference is placed at the bottom of the same page and is identified with the same superscript number (see model on p. 178).

`[1]Richard G. Harris, "Globalization, Trade, and Income," Canadian Journal of Economics, November 1993, p. 755.`

Each footnote is SS, with a DS between footnotes. Footnotes should be numbered consecutively throughout the report.

Endnotes. The endnotes method of documentation identifies the reference cited by a superscript Roman numeral . . . .[1]

The complete documentation for the reference is placed at the end of the report. The references listed in the endnotes section appear in the same order they appear in the report. A corresponding superscript number identifies the reference in the text.

`[1]W. J. Wood, Battles of the Revolutionary War (Cambridge, MA: Da Capo Press, 2003), pp. 63-64.`

Each endnote is SS with a DS between endnotes.

References Page. Each of these three types of documentation (textual citation, footnotes, and endnotes) requires a reference page. All references cited in the report are listed alphabetically by author surnames at the end of a report under the heading References (Title style). The References page can also be called Works Cited or Bibliography.

Use the same margins as for the first page of the report, and include a page number. SS each reference; DS between references. Begin the first line of each reference at the left margin; indent other lines 0.5" (hanging indent).

**Bound Report with
Long Quotation, Footnotes**

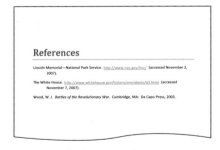

References Page

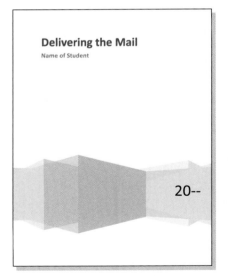

**Bound Report Title Page
using Cubicles Style**

Table of Contents

Lesson 40 INSERTING ART AND DRAWING OBJECTS

- To understand how to use appropriate graphic images, lines, and shapes.
- To insert, position, and size graphic images, photos, lines, and shapes.
- To create slides with graphic enhancements.

40B

Insert Clip Art

P • Insert/Illustrations/Clip Art

1. Read the information at the right.
2. Learn how to insert clip art in a slide and how to size and position graphics.
3. Open *39D PP*. Insert an appropriate piece of clip art from your software or from Clip Art on Office Online on slides 2 and 3. If clip art isn't available, use the clip art from *DF 40B&40F PP*. Size and position the clip art attractively. See slide 2 illustration below.

Save as: 40B PP

Art, or graphics, can enhance a message and help convey ideas. Graphic images might include clip art from your software collection or other sources such as the Internet. Graphic images could also include photo images or even original artwork scanned and converted to a digitized image.

Use graphics only when they are relevant to your topic and contribute to your presentation. Choose graphics that will not distract the audience. Clip art can often be used to add humor. Be creative, but use images in good taste. An image isn't necessary on every slide in a presentation.

40C

Insert Photo

P • Home/Copy
    • Home/Paste

1. Learn how to insert photos in a slide and how to size and position the picture.
2. Open *39D PP.*
3. Open *DF 40C PP.* Copy photo 1 shown at the right and insert on slide 2 as shown below. Copy photo 2 and insert on slide 3. Size and position the picture attractively.

Save as: 40C PP

Photo 1

Photo 2

Slide 2 - Bulleted List with Clip Art

Slide 3 - Bulleted List with Photo

In Unit 10, you learned to format short, **unbound** reports using the textual citation method of documentation. In this unit, you will learn to format longer, **bound** reports. The endnote and footnote methods of documentation are used in this unit.

Bound Reports

Longer reports are generally bound at the left margin. The binding takes about one-half inch (0.5") of space. To accommodate the binding, the left margin is increased to 1.5" on all pages.

Standard Margins

The standard margins for bound reports are presented below.

	First Page	Second page and subsequent pages
Left Margin (LM)	1.5"	1.5"
Right Margin (RM)	1"	1"
Top Margin (TM)	2"	1"
Bottom Margin (BM)	Approximately 1"	Approximately 1"
Page number	Optional, bottom at center if used	Top; right-aligned

Because an exact 1" bottom margin is not always possible, the bottom margin may be adjusted to prevent a side heading or first line of a paragraph from printing as the last line on a page (orphan); or to prevent the last line of a paragraph from occurring at the top of a new page (widow). The Widow/Orphan software feature (p. 83) also may be used to prevent these problems.

Page Numbering

The first page of a report is usually not numbered. However, if a page number is used on the first page, position it at the bottom of the page using center alignment. On the second and subsequent pages, position the page number at the top of the page using right alignment.

Internal Spacing

All parts of the report are SS using the 1.15 default line spacing.

Long quotes. Quoted material of four or more lines should be indented 0.5" from the left margin.

Enumerated items. To format numbers and bullets, the default 0.25" indentation should be used.

Titles and Headings

Title. The title of the report is formatted using the Title style (26-pt. Cambria, Dark Blue, Text 2 font).

Side headings. Side headings are keyed at the left margin and formatted using Heading 1 style (14-pt. Cambria, Blue, Accent 1 font). Capitalize the first letters of all words except prepositions in titles and side headings.

Paragraph headings. Paragraph headings are keyed at the left margin in 11-pt. Cambria and are bolded and italicized. Capitalize only the first letter of the first word and any proper nouns. Place a period after the heading.

Cover/Title Page

A cover or title page is prepared for most bound reports. To format a title page, center and bold the title (14-pt.) in ALL CAPS 2" from the top. Change to 11-pt. type and center the writer's name in capital and lowercase letters 5" from the top. The school name is centered a DS below the writer's name. The date should be centered 9" from the top. Margin settings are the same as the report body. The Cover Page feature of the software can also be used to format professional-looking cover pages.

Insert Shapes

• Insert/Illustrations/Shapes

1. Read the information at the right.
2. Learn how to use the Shapes features of your software.
3. Open *40C PP*. Create a simple logo for Multimedia Design Services. Use a circle, box, or other shape and add a fill to it. Put clip art or text on or around the shape. Place your logo attractively on the title slide.

Save as: 40D PP

Ready-made shapes can be inserted into your PowerPoint presentation. These shapes include:

• Lines
• Basic shapes
• Block arrows
• Equation shapes
• Flowchart
• Stars and banners
• Callouts

• Shapes like arrows can focus an audience's attention on important points.
• Lines can be used to separate sections of a visual, to emphasize key words, or to connect elements.
• Boxes, too, can separate elements and provide a distinctive background for text.
• Decorative borders can call attention to the contents of a box.

Lines

Equation Shapes

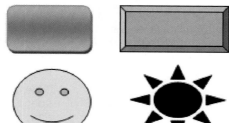

Basic Shapes

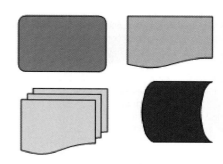

Flowchart Shapes

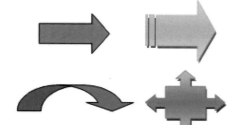

Block Arrows

Stars, Banners, and Callouts

Create a Slide with Shapes

1. Open *40D PP*. Insert a fourth slide with a Title Only layout.
2. Use the Draw Shapes feature to create the slide at the right. Use the Arial font (24-pt. bold and 18-pt. bold) for the text boxes.

Save as: 40E PP

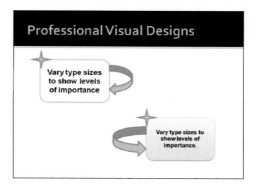

Professional Visual Designs

Vary type sizes to show levels of importance

Vary type sizes to show levels of importance.

Slide 4

Activity 7

Bullets and Numbering

1. Key Activity A at the right using the ✓ Bullet style; TS after keying.
2. Key Activity B using the Numbering feature.

Save as: **OF6 ACTIVITY7**

Bullets (special characters) are used to enhance the appearance of text. Bullets are often used to add visual interest or emphasis. Examples of bullets: ❖ ➤ ✓ •

Numbering is used to show the proper order of a series of steps. Use numbers instead of bullets whenever the order of items is important.

Activity A

Please be sure to bring the following:

- ✓ Paper
- ✓ Pencil
- ✓ CD-R
- ✓ Keyboarding book

Activity B

The standings in the American League East as of September 8, 2007, are:

1. Red Sox
2. Yankees
3. Blue Jays
4. Orioles
5. Devil Rays

Activity 8

Leader

 • Home/Paragraph dialogue box/Tabs/ Select Leader Style

Format and key the copy at the right, leaving a 2" TM and setting a right dot leader tab at the right margin. Leave a space before and after inserting the dot leader tab to enhance the appearance of the text. Use the Title style for the heading.

Save as: **OF6 ACTIVITY8**

The Leader feature automatically places leaders (. . . . .) between columns of text. The leaders lead the eyes from the text in the first column to the text in the second column. A *right* leader tab inserts the text to the left of the tab setting; a *left* leader tab inserts the text to the right of the tab setting.

In the illustration below, a right tab was set at the right margin using the Leader feature. Several type of leaders are available, such as periods, broken lines, and solid lines.

To leave a space before and after the leader, space once before tapping TAB and once after tapping TAB.

TELEPHONE EXTENSIONS

Javier Pizzaro	9458
Mark Cortez	6351
Helen Etheridge	4187
Rachel LaBonte	3067

Activity 9

Text from File

 • Insert/Text/Object/Text from file/file name

1. Leaving a 2" TM, key the copy at the right (except words printed in red). Use the Title style for the heading.
2. Insert the files where indicated at the right.

Save as: **OF6 ACTIVITY9**

To insert text from an existing file into a file that you are currently working on, use the Text from File feature.

TABLE EXAMS

Here is a list of the software features you will need to know for the first exam on tables.

Insert **DF OF6 ACTIVITY9A** file.

For the second exam on tables, you will need to know the following table formatting software features.

Insert **DF OF6 ACTIVITY9B** file.

Create Slides with Clip Art

1. Open *40E PP*.
2. Insert two slides with Two Content layout after slide 4.
3. Create the slides as shown at the right. Insert an appropriate piece of clip art from your software, or use the Clip Art from Office Online or from *DF 40B&40F PP*.

Save as: 40F PP

Clip Art

- Use clip art on slides when appropriate.
- Images should relate to topic.

Slide 5

Presenter Tips

- Dress professionally
- Speak clearly
- Maintain eye contact
- Use natural gestures
- Smile

Slide 6

Lesson 41-42   CREATING DIAGRAMS AND TABLES

OBJECTIVES

- To learn how diagrams and tables can portray processes and ideas.
- To create diagrams using the choice, stair steps, cluster, and flowchart designs.
- To create tables to enhance a presentation.

Create a Choice Diagram

P • Design/Background/ Background Styles/ Format Background

1. Start a new presentation using the Solstice design theme.
2. Choose the Title and Content layout.
3. Learn how to change the background of the slide. Change the slide background to Texture fill —Stationery.
4. Move the box in which you will key the bulleted text to the bottom of the slide.
5. Use the Shapes feature to create the choice diagram in the space above the bulleted list.
6. Key the bulleted list.

Save as: 41-42B PP

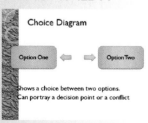

A diagram is a drawing that explains a process or idea. Diagrams can help an audience understand relationships or a sequence of events. Text can be arranged in boxes that are connected with lines or arrows to help the audience visualize the individual steps in a process or the parts of an idea.

The diagram below indicates that a choice must be made between two options. The arrows pointing in opposite directions indicate an either/or situation. This same technique can be used to represent conflict.

Presentation software allows you to use different backgrounds for the entire slide or parts of the slide. The backgrounds fill effects include:

- Solid Fill
- Gradient Fill
- Picture or Texture Fill

Notice the difference in the background of the strip down the side of the slides below.

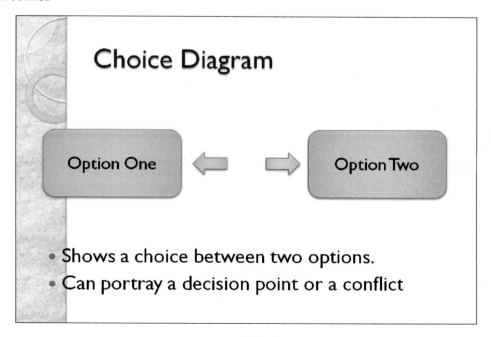

Slide 1

Activity 4

Cover Page

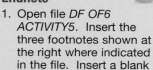

WP
• Insert/Pages/Cover Page

1. Key a cover page using the Tiles style with the following information.
   Title: Plains Indians
   Author: Your Name
   Date: Current Date
2. *Note*: For placeholders not used, click on the placeholder and tap the Space Bar to remove the placeholder from the page.
3. Apply a different style to the cover page you created.
4. Change the style back to Tiles Style.

Save as: OF6 ACTIVITY4

The Cover Page feature inserts a fully-formatted cover page. Placeholders are provided for keying the title, author, and date information.

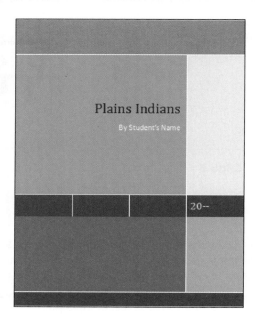

Tiles Style

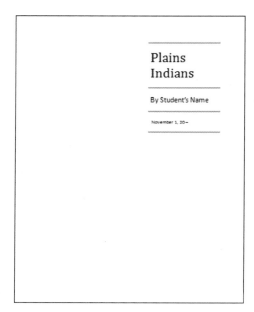

Stacks Style

Activity 5

Footnote and Endnote

1. Open file *DF OF6 ACTIVITY5*. Insert the three footnotes shown at the right where indicated in the file. Insert a blank line between footnotes.
2. Delete (*Insert footnote No*. x) from the copy.

Save as: OF6 ACTIVITY5

Use the **Footnote and Endnote** feature to identify sources quoted in your text. Footnotes are automatically positioned at the bottom of the same page as the reference. Endnotes are automatically placed on a separate page at the end of the report. As you edit, add, or delete footnotes and endnotes, changes in numbering and formatting are automatically made.

[1]David J. Rachman and Michael H. Mescon, *Business Today* (New York: Random House, 1987), p. 529.

[2]Greg Anrig, Jr., "Making the Most of 1988's Low Tax Rate," *Money*, February 1988, pp. 56–57.

[3]Andrew Chamberlain, "Twenty Years Later: The Tax Reform Act of 1986," http://www.taxfoundation.org/blog/show/1951.html (accessed September 7, 2007).

Activity 6

Superscript

1. Open file *DF OF6 ACTIVITY6*. Change the three endnote numbers to superscripts.
2. Delete (*Apply superscript . . .*) from the copy.
3. Format endnotes 2 and 3 (at the right) on p. 4 of the file, below endnote 1.

Save as: OF6 ACTIVITY6

Text may be placed slightly higher than other text on a line by using the Superscript feature. The superscript is commonly used for footnotes and endnotes *not* inserted with the Footnote and Endnote feature, and for mathematical formulas and equations.

[1]Edmund Morgan, *American Slavery, American Freedom* (London: W. W. Norton & Company, 2003), p. 368.

[2]Steven Mintz and Susan Kellogg, *Domestic Revolutions: A Social History of American Family Life* (New York: The Free Press, 1988), p. 4.

[3]Gordon S. Wood, *The Americanization of Benjamin Franklin* (New York: Penguin, 2004), pp. 23–24.

Create a Stair Steps Diagram

1. Read the information at the right.
2. Open *41-42B PP* and insert a slide for slide 2. Create slide 2 using the Title and Content layout.
3. Use the Shapes features to create the stair steps diagram for slides 3–6.

Hint: Use the following steps to create the boxes:
1. Create the bottom box.
2. After creating the first box, copy and paste it to make the remaining boxes (steps).
3. Edit the text and color of the pasted boxes.

Save as: 41-42C PP

The diagram below shows a series of ideas. The stair steps diagram begins with a box at the bottom containing the text for the first idea being explained. Additional boxes with text are positioned to look like stairs going up. For a slide show, you could prepare four separate slides so that the stair steps appear one at a time as the discussion progresses. After completing the first slide, copy and paste it. Make the changes for the second slide; then copy and paste it to make the third slide, etc.

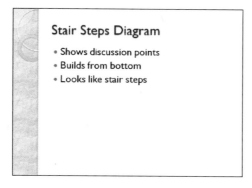

Slide 2

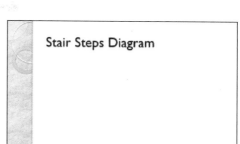

Slide 3

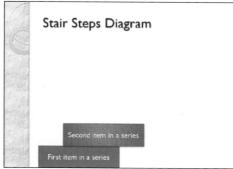

Slide 4

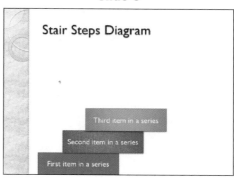

Slide 5

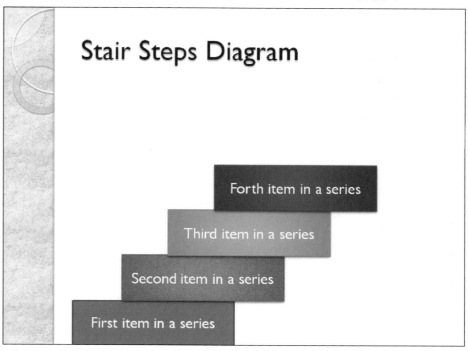

Slide 6

Office Features 6

Activity 1

Review Office Features

1. Format and key the copy at the right, using a 1.5" left margin and a 1" right margin. DS ¶ 1; SS ¶ 2.
2. Use the Left (Paragraph) Indent feature to indent the long quote (¶ 2) 0.5" from the left margin.

Save as: OF6 ACTIVITY1

Another speech of significant magnitude was delivered by Winston Churchill (1940, 572). His words not only lifted the spirits of the British but also were motivational to those committed to the Allied cause.

> We shall go on to the end, we shall fight in France, we shall fight on the seas and oceans, we shall fight with growing confidence and growing strength in the air, we shall defend our island, whatever the cost may be, we shall fight on the beaches, we shall fight on the landing grounds, we . . . .

Activity 2

Review Office Features

1. Set a 1.5" left margin and a 1" right margin. Use the Page Number feature to place the page number (**6**) in the upper-right corner.
2. Key **References** 2" from the top of the page, using Title style. Use the Hanging Indent feature to format and key the references at the right.
3. SS references; DS between references.

Save as: OF6 ACTIVITY2

6

REFERENCES

Churchill, Winston. "We Shall Fight in the Fields and in the Streets." London, June 4, 1940. Quoted by William J. Bennett, *The Book of Virtues*. New York: Simon & Schuster, 1993.

Henry, Patrick. "Liberty or Death." Richmond, VA, March 23, 1775. Quoted in *North American Biographies*, Vol. 6. Danbury, CT: Grolier Education Corporation, 1994.

Lincoln, Abraham. "The Gettysburg Address." *Wikipedia*, "Gettysburg Address," http://en.wikipedia.org/wiki/Gettysburg_Address (accessed September 3, 2007).

Activity 3

Review Office Features

The text shown at the right completes the quote by Winston Churchill in Activity 1.

1. Open *Microsoft Word*.
2. Open file *DF OF6 ACTIVITY3A* and copy the text.
3. Open *DF OF6 ACTIVITY3B*.
4. Paste the copied text at the ellipsis; then delete the ellipsis.

Save as: OF6 ACTIVITY3

shall fight in the fields and in the streets, we shall fight in the hills; we shall never surrender, and even if, which I do not for a moment believe, this island or a large part of it were subjugated and starving, then our Empire beyond the seas, armed and guarded by the British fleet, would carry on the struggle, until in God's good time, the New World, with all its power and might, steps forth to the rescue and the liberation of the old.

Create a Flowchart

P
• Insert/Illustrations/Shapes/
Flowchart symbol

1. Read the information at the right.
2. Start a **new** presentation using the **Median** design theme.
3. Create a title slide using **Flowchart** for the title. Use your name for the subtitle. Use **Stationery** for the slide background.
4. For slides 2–5, use Title Only layout; change the **slide** background to **Stationery**. Create four additional slides using the Shapes feature. The last of the slides is shown at the right. The first slide would only include *Start*. The next slide would include *Start* and *Step*. The third slide would include *Start*, *Step*, and *Input*.

Note: This is a horizontal flowchart. Flowcharts may also be shown vertically.

Save as: 41-42D PP

The flowchart below shows steps in a process, connected by arrows. Flowcharts can use pictures or shapes. In a flowchart with shapes, each shape has a certain meaning. An oval shows the beginning or end of a process. A parallelogram shows input or output. A diamond shows a decision to be made, worded as a question. Two arrows, one marked *Yes* and one marked *No*, extend from the diamond to the flowchart step that results from the decision. A rectangle shows a step that does not require a decision.

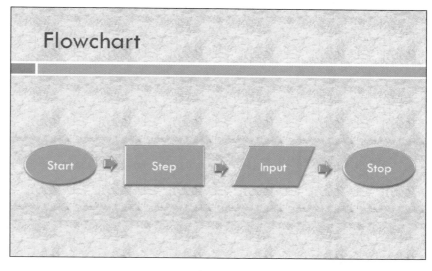

Slide 5

Create a Table

P
• Home/Slides/New Slide/
Layout/Title and Content/
Insert Table

1. Read the information at the right.
2. Create a new presentation using the Technic design theme.
3. Using the Title and Content layout, insert a table to include the information shown at the right.
4. Create the slide.

Save as: 41-42E PP

Tables can be used to organize information that can be displayed in presentations to compare and contrast facts or figures and to list data.

Tables can be created in *PowerPoint*, or they can be created in *Word* or *Excel* and inserted into *PowerPoint*.

FBLA Membership by Year

Year	Members	+/- from Previous Year
2005	20	-
2006	28	8
2007	39	11
2008	56	17
2009	75	19

Signature

Using the E-mail Signature feature, create a signature block that will go out with all your e-mails. Include the information shown at the right. Choose a quote that reflects your personality. If you don't have a favorite quote, use an Internet search engine to search for famous quotes and select one from those you find.

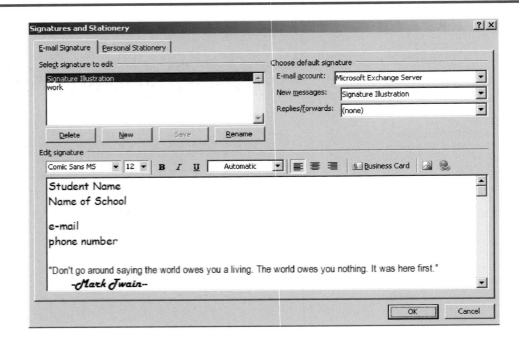

57C — Language Skills

Language Skills: Word Choice

1. Study the spelling and definitions of the words.
2. Key all *Learn* and *Apply* lines, choosing the correct word in the *Apply* lines.

Save as: 57C CHOICE

---

hole (n) an opening in or through something
whole (adj/n) having all its proper parts; a complete amount or sum

peak (n) pointed end; top of a mountain; highest level
peek (vb) to glance or look at for a brief time

Learn 1 The **whole** team is responsible for the **hole** in the wall.

Apply 2 The (hole, whole) team dug a (hole, whole) in which to put the doughnut (holes, wholes).

Apply 3 The (hole, whole) project is just getting to be too much to handle.

Learn 1 If you **peek** out the door, you can see the **peak** of the new building.

Apply 2 The clouds covered the (peak, peek) of the mountain.

Apply 3 Did you get a chance to take a (peak, peek) at your exam after it was graded?

57D

E-Mail

Choose the three e-mail features that you think you will use most often from those listed at the right. Send an e-mail to your teacher explaining why you chose the three features.

Send a copy of the e-mail to the student in front of you. Request a Read Receipt and delay delivery for 2 hours.

- E-mail copies
- Attachments/Inserts
- Request Delivery Receipt/Read Receipt
- Delay Delivery
- E-mail Distribution List
- Out of Office Assistant
- Signature

- To learn which graph or chart to use for particular situations.
- To learn to create graphs.
- To learn various graph elements.

43B

Learn Graph Elements

1. Read the information at the right.
2. Locate the various graph elements in bar chart below.
3. Learn how to create charts and graphs in your software.

Numeric information can be easier to understand when shown as **a graph** or **chart** rather than in text or a table. The relationship between data sets or trends can be compared with bar graphs, line graphs, area graphs, or pie charts. Each type of graph or chart is best suited for a particular situation.

- **Bar graph**—comparison of item quantities
- **Line and area graphs**—quantity changes over time or distance
- **Pie chart**—parts of a whole

Elements common to most graphs are identified on the bar graph shown below. They include:

- **X-axis**—the horizontal axis; usually for categories
- **Y-axis**—the vertical axis; usually for values

- **Scale**—numbers on the Y- or X-axis representing quantities
- **Tick marks**—coordinate marks on the graph to help guide the reader
- **Grids**—lines that extend from tick marks to make it easier to see data values
- **Labels**—names used to identity parts of the graph
- **Legend**—the key that identifies the shading, coloring, or patterns used for the information shown in the graph

To change the design of the graph, click on the graph. This activates the Chart Tools. The Chart Styles under the Design tab allow you to select from a variety of preset designs. Notice the difference between the appearance of the two graphs shown below.

43C

Create Bar Graph

P
- Home/Slides/New Slide/ Layout/Title andContent/ Insert Chart/Column

1. Read the information at the right.
2. Open *41-42E PP* and create the bar graph as shown below for slide 2. Use the data from 41-42E in the previous lesson.
3. Change the Chart Style design to Style 34 (Design/Chart Style/Style 34).

Save as: 43C PP

Bar graphs compare one or more sets of data that are plotted on the horizontal X-axis and the vertical Y-axis. The X-axis usually contains category information (such as years or months); the Y-axis usually contains measured quantity values (numbers).

Vertical bars (columns) are easy to interpret; the baseline on the Y-axis should begin at zero for consistent comparisons when several graphs are used. Special effects can be added, but a simple graph is effective for showing relationships.

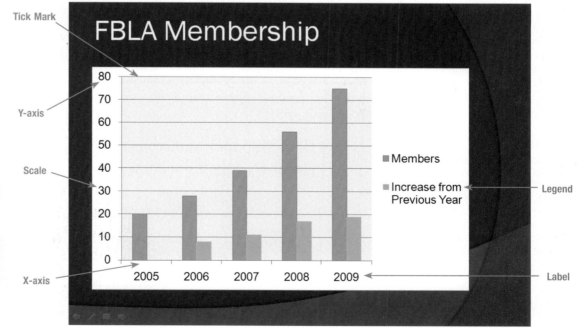

Graph Elements

E-mail 4

Format and key the text at the right as an e-mail message to Professor Perry (use your instructor's e-mail address). Attach the business card for Troy McNeil (created in 56C above) to your e-mail.

Save as: 56D EMAIL4

Professor Perry,

I've talked with Mr. McNeil, a communication specialist from HPJ Communications, about the possibility of his presenting to our class. He would like you to contact him to discuss the specifics of what you would like him to present. He is interested in discussing the communication styles of our most successful Presidents.

I've attached his business contact information. If there is anything else you would like me to do, please let me know.

Lesson 57   SPECIAL E-MAIL FEATURES

OBJECTIVES
- To increase proficiency in formatting and keying e-mails.
- To learn special e-mail features.
- To improve language skills.

57B

E-mail Special Features

Request a Read Receipt

Format and key the text at the right as an e-mail message to the distribution list created in 55B. Request a Read Receipt.

Save as: 57B EMAIL1

Out of Office Assistant

Use the Out of Office Assistant to have the message shown at the right sent to incoming e-mail messages for the next two days.

Send a message to yourself to see if it works (you should get the message you send plus the Out of Office Message). Forward the message to your instructor.

Cancel the Out of Office Message.

Delay Delivery

Send yourself two e-mails with the messages shown at the right using the Delay Delivery feature. The first one should be delivered tomorrow at 3:30 p.m.; the second should be delivered tomorrow at 11:30 p.m.

I know this is very short notice, but I think that we should meet one more time before we turn in the report on Friday. I've combined each of our parts into one report. However, we need to work on the transitions between the parts and proofread the report one more time to make sure there are no additional keying, formatting, spelling, or grammar errors.

We could meet in the library this evening. Does 6:30 work for you?

I will not be reading my e-mails until next Tuesday, (include the date). If you would like to contact me before then, please call me at (include your telephone number).

Remember:
- English paper due tomorrow.
- Algebra quiz tomorrow.

Remember:
- Piano lesson at 4:30 p.m.
- Play practice on Saturday – 3:30 to 5:30.

Create Line Graph

P
• Home/New Slide/Layout/
Title and Content/Insert
Chart/Column

1. Start a new presentation
using the Paper design
theme with Title and
Content layout. Create
a line graph showing the
number of employees
using the following data:
   • 1980   30   • 2000   40
   • 1985   38   • 2005   47
   • 1990   45   • 2010   60
   • 1995   42
2. Display the data labels
above the line.

Save as: 43D PP

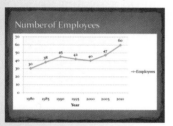

**Same slide with different
chart style**

Line graphs display changes in quantities over
time or distance. Usually the X-axis shows a
particular period of time or distance. The Y-axis
shows measurements of quantity at different
times or distances. The baseline of the Y-axis
should be zero to provide a consistent reference point when several graphs are used in a
presentation.

When the numbers for the X-axis are entered,
lines appear connecting the values on the graph
to reflect the changes in amounts. A grid with
vertical lines helps the viewer interpret quantities.

Several sets of data can be displayed by using
lines in different colors. Various options are available for placing titles, legends, and labels on line
graphs.

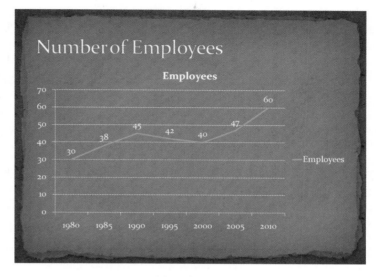

Line Graph

Create an Area Graph

P
• Design/Type/Change Chart
Type/Area

1. Open *43D PP*.
2. Change the Chart Type
from line graph to area
graph.
3. Do not display the data
values.

Save as: 43E PP

**Same slide with different
chart style**

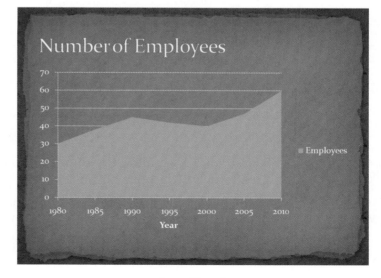

Area Graph

E-mails

E-mail 1

Send the text at the right as an e-mail to the American history distribution list created in 55B. Attach Document 3 (*55C ATTACHMENT2*).

When you receive this e-mail message from one of your class-mates, forward one message to your instructor.

Save as: 56D EMAIL1

E-mail 2

Format and key the text at the right as an e-mail message for Professor Perry (use your instructor's e-mail address).

Save as: 56D EMAIL2

E-mail 3

Format and key the text at the right as an e-mail message to Professor Perry (use your instructor's e-mail address). Attach the calendar you created for 56B.

Save as: 56D EMAIL3

Subject: Meeting Reminder

Don't forget our meeting tomorrow. Since the librarian wouldn't give me a specific room ahead of time, let's plan on meeting at the front desk at 3:00 p.m. ¶ I went ahead and created a combined list of all the names you sent me via e-mail. A total of 19 individuals were named at least once. The alphabetical list is attached. ¶ See you tomorrow at 3 p.m.

Subject: Next Exam

Here is the information about next week's exam. The exam will cover Chapter 22, pages 702–727, and Chapter 23, pages 740–769.

The main emphasis of Chapter 22 is the New Deal. You will be expected to explain what the New Deal was, why some people criticized it while others praised it, and the impact of the New Deal on the U.S. economy.

Between 1933 and 1937, many pieces of legislation associated with the New Deal were passed. Make sure you know the purpose of each of the following acts.

* Emergency Banking Act
* Agricultural Adjustment Act
* Federal Emergency Relief Act
* Home Owners Refinancing Act
* National Industrial Recovery Act
* Emergency Relief Appropriation Act
* National Labor Relations Act
* Social Security Act

Chapter 23 covers World War II. We thoroughly discussed this chapter in class. Make sure you review your notes carefully.

If you are knowledgeable about these topics, you should do well on the exam.

Professor Perry,

Thank you for sending the information on next week's exam. I have several questions on Chapter 22 that I would like to discuss with you.

Would you be available to meet with me on January 23? I have attached my schedule for that day. I would be available any time that is shown as "Free" on my calendar. Let me know if any of the times will work with your schedule.

Create Pie Charts

P • Home/ New Slide/Layout/ Title and Content/Insert Chart/Pie

Pie Chart 1

1. Read the information at the right.
2. Open *43C PP*.
3. Create the pie chart shown at right as slide 3.

   Chart data:

   2005   20
   2006   28
   2007   39
   2008   56
   2009   75

Save as: 43F PP

Pie charts are best used to display parts of a whole. They show clearly the proportional relationship of only one set of values. Without any numbers displayed, the chart shows only general relationships. In the examples shown below, the different colors used for the pie slices are identified in a legend. Colors used on the pie chart should provide adequate contrast between the slices. Consider also the color scheme of your entire presentation so that the pie chart will coordinate with other visuals.

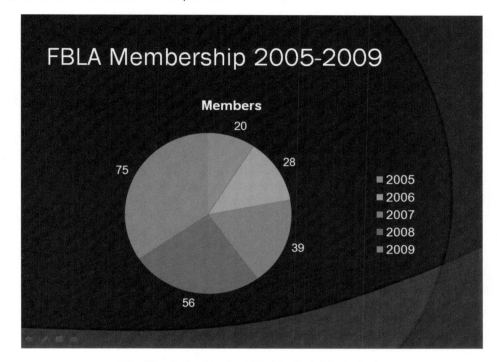

Pie Chart, Legend at Right, Outside Labels

Pie Chart 2

P • Insert/Type/Change Chart Type/Pie/Explode

P • Layout/Labels/Legend/ None

P • Layout/Labels/Data labels/ More Label Options/Cat. Name, Percent

1. Change Pie Chart 1 to give it a 3D appearance and to emphasize the pie slices by exploding them.
2. Remove the legend.
3. Display Category Name labels and percentages with each slice.

Save as: 43F-2 PP

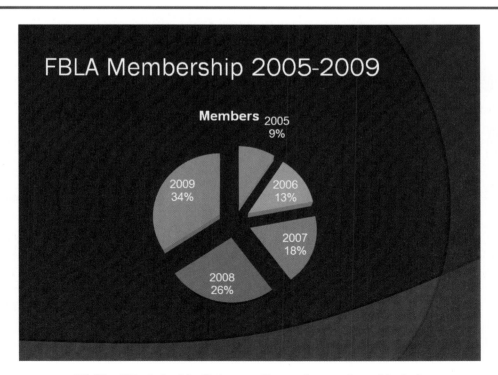

3D Pie Chart, Inside Category Name, Legend, and Labels

Document 3 (Attachment)

Key the list centered horizontally on the page. Leave a 1.5" TM.

Title: **Suggestions for American History Report**

Use the Title style for the heading. Key the names in Calibri 14 pt.

Save as: **55C**
ATTACHMENT2

Susan B. Anthony
Neil Armstrong
Alexander Graham Bell
Thomas Alva Edison
Albert Einstein
Benjamin Franklin
Ulysses S. Grant
Patrick Henry
Thomas Jefferson
Martin Luther King, Jr.

Abraham Lincoln
Douglas MacArthur
Thomas Paine
Sir Walter Raleigh
Eleanor Roosevelt
Franklin Roosevelt
Harriet Beecher Stowe
Henry David Thoreau
George Washington

Lesson 56   IMPROVE E-MAIL FORMATTING SKILLS

OBJECTIVES

- To increase proficiency at formatting e-mails.
- To use the Attachment feature to attach calendars and business cards to e-mails.

56B

Calendars

Using the Calendar feature, record the class and lab hours shown at the right for January 23.

January 23

1. English 110 (8 to 8:50 a.m.)

2. Biology 101 (10 to 10:50 a.m.)

3. Math 246 (1 to 1:50 p.m.)

4. Biology Lab (3 to 5:00 p.m.)

56C

Contacts

Record the information on the business card at the right in your *Outlook* contacts file.

HPJ Communications

Troy McNeil
Communication Specialist

142 Colebrooke Lane
Louisville, KY 40219-1221
Phone: 502.555.0105
Fax: 502.555.0102
TMCNEIL@hpj.com

• To create an electronic presentation

44B

Create an Electronic Presentation

Open *DF 44B PP* and review the pictures of New York City. Read the poem and reports you keyed for 33B, 33C, and 34B on the city. Use the Internet to learn more about it.

Using these pictures and the information from the reports and the Internet, prepare an electronic presentation to give to your classmates on the sights of New York City.

Shown at the right are a few examples of what can be done with the pictures. Use your creativity to make the presentation interesting as well as informative.

Save as: **44B PP**

Display inside the Empire State Building

View of New York City from Central Park

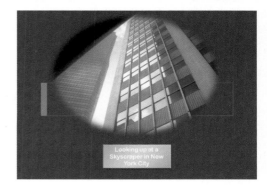

Looking up at a Skyscraper in New York City

Send/Receive E-mail and Attachments

Document 1 (Attachment)

1. Format and key the text at the right. Leave a 2" top margin; SS paragraphs. Use the Title style for the heading and Heading 1 style for your name and the date.
2. Use 12-pt. Calibri for the text beneath the heading. Bold all names.
3. Correct all spelling, keying, and formatting errors.

Save as: **55C ATTACHMENT1**

INTERNET ACTIVITY

Search the Web to learn more about one of the individuals whose names appear at the right or one of those listed in Document 3 (p. 164). Compose a ¶ or two about the individual.

Document 2 (E-mail)

Key the text at the right as an e-mail and send to your American history project distribution list; copy your instructor. Use **American History Project** for the subject line and attach Document 1 (*55C ATTACHMENT1*).

When you receive the message from one of your classmates, reply indicating that you will be there.

Save as: **55C EMAIL1**

American History

Your Name

March 18, 20--

Albert Einstein: American physicist whose theory of relativity led to the harnessing of nuclear energy.

Benjamin Franklin: A leading American statesman, inventor, philanthropist, publisher, author, revolutionary, and thinker.

Abraham Lincoln: The sixteenth President of the United States; helped keep the Union together during the Civil War, which led to the abolishment of slavery; recognized for his honesty and compassion.

Franklin Roosevelt: Thirty-second President of the United States; led the country during two critical periods in United States history (the Great Depression and World War II).

George Washington: Commander in Chief of the Continental Army during the American Revolution; first President of the United States.

Attached is the list of the five Americans who I feel had the greatest impact on our history. A few notes about the individuals are provided after each name. Narrowing the list to five was very difficult. ¶ I've reserved a room in the library for us to meet on Thursday, March 25, at 3 p.m. By then we should have received and reviewed each other's lists. Be prepared to decide on the final ten individuals to include in the report for Ms. Graham. ¶ I look forward to receiving each of your lists.

OBJECTIVE

• To give a presentation using electronic slides.

45B

Practice Presenting

1. Read the information about delivering a presentation.

2. Practice giving the presentation that you created in 44B.

Presenting Delivery

Planning and preparing a presentation is only half the task of giving a good presentation. The other half is the delivery. Positive thinking is a must for a good presenter. Prepare and practice before the presentation. This will help you be confident that you can do a good job. Don't worry that the presentation will not be perfect. Set a goal of being a better speaker each time you give a speech, not of being a perfect speaker each time. Practice these tips to improve your presentation skills.

• **Know your message.** Knowing the message well allows you to talk with the audience rather than read to them.

• **Look at the audience.** Make eye contact with one person briefly (for two to three seconds). Then move on to another person.

• **Look confident.** Stand erect and show that you want to communicate with the audience.

• **Let your personality come through.** Be natural; let the audience know who you are. Show your enthusiasm for the topic you are presenting.

• **Vary the volume and rate at which you speak.** Slow down to emphasize points. Speed up on points that you are sure your audience is familiar with.

• **Use gestures and facial expressions.** A smile, frown, or puzzled look, when appropriate, can help communicate your message. Make sure your gestures are natural.

• **Know how to use the visuals.** Practice using the visual aids you have chosen for the presentation. Glance at each visual as you display it. Then focus on the audience.

45C

Give a Presentation

1. Review the evaluation at the right.

2. Break up into groups of three. Each student in your group will give the presentation that was developed in Lesson 44. While one student is giving the presentation, the other two will evaluate it using the form shown at the right.

The evaluation form is available in the data files: *DF 45C Eval Form*.

	Excellent	Good	Need(s) Improvement	Comments
The introduction to the topic is				
The body of the presentation is				
The visual aids are				
The speaker's ability to use the visual aids is				
The speaker's enthusiasm is				
The speaker's eye contact is				
The speaker's gestures are				
The speaker's confidence is				
The speaker's vocal variation is				
The speaker's facial expressions are				
The closing is				

**Out of Office Assistant
Message Illustration**

Lesson 55   IMPROVE E-MAIL FORMATTING SKILLS

- To create a distribution list.
- To process e-mail messages with attachments and copy notations.

55A–57A

Conditioning Practice

Key each line twice.

alphabet	1	Tom saw Jo leave quickly for her job after my dog won six prizes.
fig/sym	2	Check No. 203 ($1,486.17) and Check No. 219 ($57.98) are missing.
speed	3	Did their auditor sign the key element of the forms for the firm?

gwam 1' | 1 | 2 | 3 | 4 | 5 | 6 | 7 | 8 | 9 | 10 | 11 | 12 | 13 |

55B

Create a Distribution List

Create a distribution list following the instructions at the right.

1. Create a folder for your contacts for your American history project. (Your instructor will assign four students to be part of your group.) See the illustrations on p. 160 and below.

2. Create a contact card for each student assigned to your group. For this project, you only need to include their names and e-mail addresses.

3. Create a distribution list that includes the students in your group.

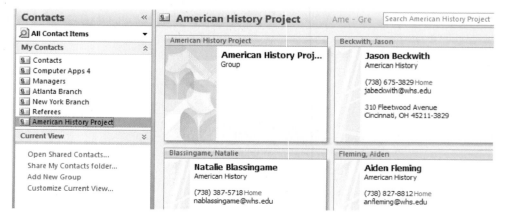

CYCLE 1
Review

• To review Cycle 1 formatting skills, *Office Suite* features, and straight-copy skills.

Conditioning Practice

Key each line twice SS.

alphabet	1	Quincy just put back five azure gems next to the gold watch.
fig/sym	2	Tim moved from 5142 Troy Lane to 936--123rd Street on 8/7/03.
speed	3	He lent the field auditor a hand with the work for the firm.

gwam 1' | 1 | 2 | 3 | 4 | 5 | 6 | 7 | 8 | 9 | 10 | 11 | 12 |

Activity 1

Memo

Format and key the text at the right as a memo. Proofread your copy; correct all keying and format errors.

Save as: CR1 ACTIVITY1

TO: Marguerite Mercedes, Director

FROM: Justin Mathews, Administrative Assistant

DATE: March 5, 20--

SUBJECT: BALLET COMPANY ADDRESSES

Attached is the address list for the ballet companies that you requested. I was unable to secure an address for the Bolshoi Ballet in Moscow.

I have seen the Royal Swedish Ballet, the American Ballet Theatre, and the Paris Opera Ballet perform. They were all excellent. The patrons of our Artist Series would be extremely pleased with any of the three performances.

Even though I have not personally seen performances by any of the other groups on the list, I have heard excellent comments by others who have been fortunate enough to see them perform. I don't think we can go wrong by inviting any of those on the list to be a part of next year's Artist Series.

xx

Attachment

Attach a Calendar to an E-mail Illustration

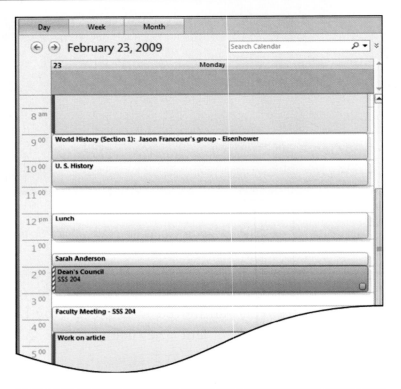

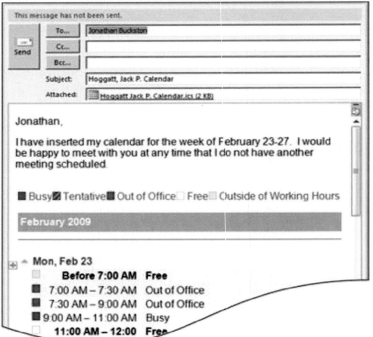

The Out of Office Assistant automatically sends your out-of-the-office message to those who send you an e-mail message. Use this feature when you are not going to be checking your e-mail messages for an extended period of time to let individuals know when they can expect to hear from you or who to contact in your absence. An example is shown on the next page.

Activity 2

Letter

Format and key the text at the right as a personal-business letter. Proofread your copy; correct all keying and format errors.

Save as: CR1 ACTIVITY2

810 Lake Grove Court | San Diego, CA 92131-8112 | March 30, 20-- | Ms. Barbara Knight | 2010 Rosewood Place | Riverside, CA 92506-6528 | Dear Barbara

Can you believe that we will be in London in less than three months? London is one of my favorite places to visit.

I've done some checking on London's theatres. Do any of the three plays I've listed below interest you? If so, let me know, and I'll make the arrangements.

Les Miserables: Story revolves around nineteenth-century French Revolution with its struggles, passion, and love.

Amadeus: Story about the life of Mozart in eighteenth-century Vienna and his rivalry with composer Sallieri.

Starlight Express: Musical by Andrew Lloyd Weber with lyrics by Richard Stilgoe.

Les Miserables is being performed at the Palace Theatre, *Amadeus* at The Old Vic, and *Starlight Express* at the Apollo Victoria. The Palace Theatre and The Old Vic were both built in the 1800s.

I've confirmed our reservations at the Copthorne Tara. If there is anything else that you would like me to check, let me know.

Sincerely | Jessica C. Holloway

xx

Activity 3

E-mail

Key the e-mail message at the right to your instructor. If you do not have access to e-mail, format and key the text as an interoffice memo using the following information:

TO: Jessica Holloway
FROM: Barbara Knight
DATE: March 15, 20—
SUBJECT: LONDON EXCURSION

Proofread your message; correct all errors.

Save as: CR1 ACTIVITY3

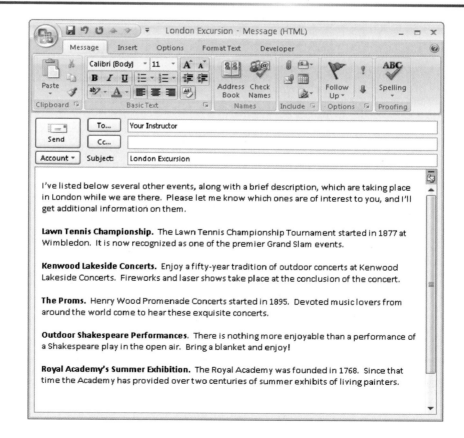

Distribution List Illustrations

A distribution list is created with the e-mail addresses of those you want included from the contacts list.

A distribution list is used to send the same e-mail to all those on the list (see below).

To see who is on the list and to delete any one you don't want to receive the e-mail, click on the + (see below).

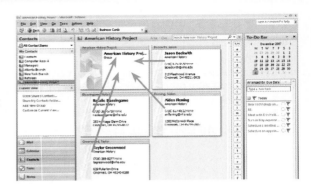

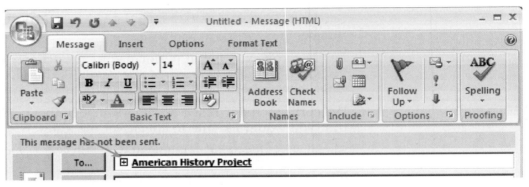

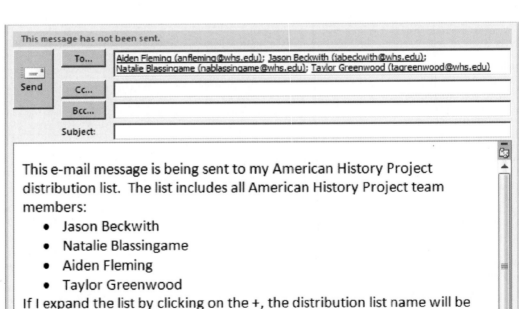

This e-mail message is being sent to my American History Project distribution list. The list includes all American History Project team members:

- Jason Beckwith
- Natalie Blassingame
- Aiden Fleming
- Taylor Greenwood

If I expand the list by clicking on the +, the distribution list name will be replaced with the e-mail address of all team members.

Attachments/Inserts

Various items may be sent with your e-mails including files, previously sent or received e-mails, business cards, calendars, etc. An example of a calendar being attached to an e-mail is shown on the next page. You can choose to show availability only, limited details as shown below, or full details of your calendar in the e-mail.

Activity 4

Timed Writings

1. Key a 1' timing on each ¶; determine *gwam*.
2. Key a 2' timing on ¶s 1–2 combined; determine *gwam*.
3. Key a 3' timing on ¶s 1–2 combined; determine *gwam* and number of errors.

Quarter-Minute Checkpoints				
gwam	1/4'	1/2'	3/4'	1'
24	6	12	18	24
28	7	14	21	28
32	8	16	24	32
36	9	18	27	36
40	10	20	30	40
44	11	22	33	44
48	12	24	36	48
52	13	26	39	52
56	14	28	42	56

A all letters used (MicroPace)

	gwam	2'	3'

In deciding upon a career, learn as much as possible about 5 | 4

what individuals in that career do. For each job class, there are 11 | 7

job requirements and qualifications that must be met. Analyze 17 | 11

these tasks very critically in terms of your personality and what 23 | 15

you like to do. 28 | 19

A high percentage of jobs in major careers demand education or 34 | 23

training after high school. The training may be very specialized, 40 | 26

requiring intensive study or interning for two or more years. You 42 | 28

must decide if you are willing to expend so much time and effort. 47 | 31

After you have decided upon a career to pursue, discuss the 53 | 35

choice with parents, teachers, and others. Such people can help 59 | 39

you design a plan to guide you along the series of steps required 65 | 43

in pursuing your goal. Keep the plan flexible and change it when- 71 | 48

ever necessary. 77 | 51

gwam 2' | 1 | 2 | 3 | 4 | 5 | 6 |
3' | 1 | 2 | 3 | 4 |

Activity 5

Unbound Report

Format and key the text at the right as an unbound report. Use **Theatre** for the title of the report. Proofread and correct all keying and format errors.

Save as: **CR1 ACTIVITY5**

Tonight the house lights will dim, and another performance will begin on Broadway. Perhaps it will be another performance of *The Phantom of the Opera*, the longest-running show in the history of Broadway with 8,251 performances as of November 25, 2007 (Hernandez). Or perhaps it will be the play that replaces *The Phantom of the Opera*.

Somewhere, sometime today, another enactment of one of Shakespeare's plays will take place. It may be in a high school auditorium, or it may be at a professional Shakespearean playhouse.

Theatre has enriched the lives of people for many years. No one really knows when the first play production was performed. However, historians say, "Theatre is as old as mankind. There have been primitive forms of it since man's beginnings" (Berthold, 1991, 1). The more commonly recognized form of theatre, the play, dates back to what is referred to as "Greek Theatre" and "Roman Theatre."

Special E-mail Features

E-mail Address List. Names and e-mail addresses of persons (contacts) you correspond with often may be kept in an address list. An address can be entered on the TO line by selecting it from the list.

E-mail Copies. Copies of e-mail can be sent to additional addresses at the same time you send the original message. The **Cc:** (courtesy copy) and **Bcc:** (blind courtesy copy) features of e-mail software are used to send copies.

Reply and Forward. The Reply feature automatically puts the e-mail address of the person you are replying to in the TO area of the e-mail heading. The Forward feature allows you to send a copy of an e-mail message you received to other individuals.

Request Delivery Receipt. Request Delivery Receipt notifies you when an e-mail has been delivered successfully.

Request a Read Receipt. Request a Read Receipt notifies you when an e-mail has been read.

Signature. Signatures are a way of personalizing your e-mail messages and making them appear more professional. For business, a signature usually includes your name, your professional title, the company name, the company address, and the company phone number.

Delay Delivery. The Delay Delivery features allows you to specify a date and time for an e-mail message to be sent. This allows a message to be created early but not sent until the specified date and time. For example, your teacher may give you an assignment that is due in two weeks and may automatically remind you two days before the assignment is due by creating a reminder message today with a delayed delivery date.

E-mail Distribution List. When e-mail is regularly sent to the same group of contacts, use a distribution list. A distribution list is a collection of contacts. For example, if you are part of a team in your American History class, you can create a distribution list called *American History Project* that includes the names of all team members. When you want to e-mail them, you can use the distribution list rather than listing each individual separately. This feature is very helpful when you send e-mails frequently to the same people, especially when there is a large number.

When a distribution list is selected and it appears in the TO area of the e-mail heading, a + appears in front of the name of the distribution list. By clicking the +, all of the names and address of the individuals who are part of the distribution list appear in the TO area. If you do not want an individual included, highlight the name and tap DELETE.

Activity 6

References List

Use the information below to create a references list on a separate page. Proofread and correct all keying and format errors.

References

Berthold, Margot. *The History of World Theatre*. New York: The Continuum Publishing Company, 1991.

Hernandez, Ernio. "Playbill News: Long Runs on Broadway." http://www.playbill.com/celebritybuzz/article/ 75222.html (accessed November 25, 2007).

Prince, Nancy, and Jeanie Jackson. *Exploring Theatre*. Minneapolis/St. Paul: West Publishing Company, 1997.

Save as: CR1 ACTIVITY6

Greek Theatre

Greek Theatre started around 500 B.C. Sophocles and Aristophanes are two of the well-known Greek playwrights whose works are still being performed today.

Religious festivals that honored the Greek god of wine and fertility (Dionysus) were part of the culture of Greece around this time. The Greeks felt that if they honored Dionysus, he would in turn bless them with many children, rich land, and abundant crops. Plays were performed as part of these festivals.

To accommodate the large number of people who attended the plays (as many as 14,000 to 17,000 people, according to historians), theatres were built into a hillside. The plays were staged in the morning and lasted until sunset, since there was no electricity for lighting (Prince and Jackson, 1997, 35).

Roman Theatre

Roman Theatre was the next widely recognized form of the theatre. The first Roman theatrical performance, historians believe, was performed around 365 B.C. Seneca, Plautus, and Terence are the best known of the early Roman playwrights. Seneca was known for his tragedies, while the other two were known for their comedies.

The Roman plays were similar to those of the Greeks. Unlike the Greeks, however, the Romans did not limit the number of actors in each play. Another major difference between the Greek and Roman theatres was the theatre buildings. The Romans were great engineers and architects. They built theatres that were unified, free-standing structures several stories in height (Prince and Jackson, 1997, 44).

Activity 7

Table 1

Create the table at the right.
- Table Styles – Medium Shading 1 – Accent 4
- Center the table horizontally and vertically.
- **Main title:** row height 0.5"; align center; 14-pt. font
- **Column headings:** row height 0.4"; align center
- **Data rows:** row height 0.3"; bottom vertical alignment
- Adjust column widths to arrange material attractively on the page.

Save as: CR1 ACTIVITY7

American Literature – 1900s	
Literature	Author
A Rose for Emily (1930)	William Faulkner
The Grapes of Wrath (1939)	John Steinbeck
The Scotty Who Knew Too Much (1940)	James Thurber
House Made of Dawn (1968)	N. Scott Momaday
Everyday Use (1973)	Alice Walker
I Ask My Mother to Sing (1986)	Li-Young Lee
The Phone Booth at the Corner (1989)	Juan Delgado

Letter Editing

Open the file *53B LETTER1* and make the changes shown at the right. Include a subject line: **KEYNOTE SPEAKERS**. Leave the rest of the letter as it is.

Save as: 54C LETTER

...When you contact them, please ~~share with~~ *tell* them the theme of our convention and determine what they ~~would~~ propose as an opening or closing session ~~for our convention.~~ ~~Of course, we need to be concerned with the budget; please determine what they would charge.~~ ¶ As I am sure you are aware, we have a very limited budget. The budget often determines whom we invite. As you discuss fees with them, make sure they are aware that we are an educational institution. Oftentimes, professional presenters are willing to give "educational discounts."

¶ The information will be needed before June 15 for our meeting. ...
speaker

Enrichment Activities
Editing Business Letters

Open *54B LETTER1*; revise and send it to the Massachusetts and Arizona state presidents with the information shown at the right. Make sure you change the state at the very end of the letter.

Save as: 54B LETTER1-R and 54B LETTER1-R2

Letter Address:
Ms. Judith Austin, President
711 Colonial Way
New Bedford, MA 02747-0071

Massachusetts
Capital: Boston
State Nickname: The Bay State
Admitted to the Union: No. 6 on
February 6, 1788

Letter Address:
Mr. Scott Mathews, President
55 Rio Cancion, N.
Tucson, AZ 85718-3399

Arizona
Capital: Phoenix
State Nickname: The Grand
Canyon State
Admitted to the Union: No. 48 on
February 14, 1912

Timed Writings

1. Key a 1' timing on each ¶; determine *gwam*.
2. Key two 2'timings on ¶s 1–2 combined; determine *gwam*.

LA all letters used MicroPace   gwam 2'

The Bill of Rights includes the changes to the — 4
constitution that deal with human rights of all people. — 10
The changes or amendments were to improve and correct the — 16
original document. They were made to assure the quality of — 22
life and to protect the rights of all citizens. — 27

One of the changes provides for the right to religious — 32
choice, free speech, and free press. Another addresses the — 38
right to keep and bear firearms. Another deals with the — 44
rights of the people with regard to unreasonable search and — 50
seizure of person or property. Two others deal with the — 55
right to an immediate and public trial by a jury and the — 61
prevention of excessive bail and fines. — 65

gwam 2' | 1 | 2 | 3 | 4 | 5 | 6 |

Activity 8

Table 2

Create the table shown at the right using the information given for Activity 7, Table 1.

Use Medium Shading 2 – Accent 1 for the Table Style.

Save as: **CR1 ACTIVITY8**

WILLIAM SHAKESPEARE		
Play	Year Written	Category
The Comedy of Errors	1590	Comedy
Richard II	1595	History
Romeo and Juliet	1595	Tragedy
Much Ado About Nothing	1599	Comedy
Julius Caesar	1599	Tragedy
Hamlet	1601	Tragedy
King Lear	1605	Tragedy
The Tempest	1611	Comedy

Activity 9

Electronic Presentations

Create the slides as shown at the right. Choose appropriate clip art if the art shown at the right isn't available with your software.

Slide 1: Title slide

Slide 2: Section Header

Slide 3-6: Title and Content slides

Save as: **CR1 ACTIVITY9**

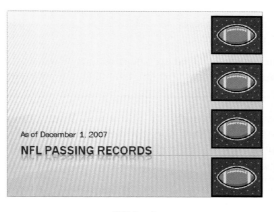

Slide 1

Slide 2

Slide 3

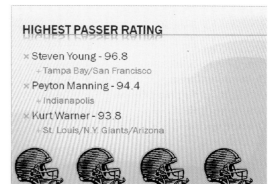

Slide 4

(continued on next page)

- To increase skill at formatting business letters with special features.

54B   Formatting

Business Letters

Key in block format the business letters shown at the right.

Letter 1

Date: **March 14, 20--**
Letter Address:
Ms. Gwen English, President
3801 Wedgewood Road
Wilmington, DE 19805-9921

Letter 1 is from **Marsha J. Johnson, Display Coordinator**. Supply all missing letter parts.

Save as: 54B LETTER1

Letter 2

Revise Letter 1; address it to the Florida State President:

Ms. Sandra Ortiz, President
723 Majestic Pines Court
Orlando, FL 32819-3487

Change the letter to reflect this Florida information:

Capital: Tallahassee
Nickname: The Sunshine State
Admitted to the Union: No. 27 on March 3, 1845

Save as: 54B LETTER2

Letter 3

Use the Insert Date feature to insert the current date.

Letter address:
Attention Special Collections Director University of Virginia Library Alderman, 2 East Charlottesville, VA 22903-0011

Supply a salutation, complimentary closing, and reference initials. The letter is from **Gregg G. Elway, Doctoral Candidate**.

Save as: 54B LETTER3

At last year's national convention, our displays highlighted the U.S. Presidents. This year's exhibits will spotlight the states. Each delegation will have a table to display items relating to their state. Exhibits will be in the order the states were admitted to the Union. State presidents are being asked to coordinate the display for their state.

Each display area will include a backdrop, a table, and two chairs for representatives from your state. The table (2' x 6') will be covered with a white cloth. Your state flag will be displayed in front of the backdrop on the far right. The 10-foot-wide backdrop will have a cutout of your state, along with the following information.

Delaware
Capital: Dover
State Nickname: The Diamond State
Admitted to the Union: No. 1 on December 7, 1787

Each delegation can decide what they want to exhibit on the table. We hope that you will include something to give to the people attending the convention. You know how attendees like freebies. We anticipate about eight hundred people at the convention.

We are excited about the state exhibits and hope that you and your officers will make **Delaware's** display the best one at the convention.

I'm doing my dissertation on the Civil War generals and their families. Of course, it is easy to gather the needed information on U. S. Grant and Robert E. Lee. So much has been written about these icons of the Civil War that the problem is deciding what to include.

However, I'm not having as much luck with some of the other generals. I'm particularly interested in Galusha Pennypacker, who was claimed to be the youngest general of the Civil War, and in John E. Wool, who was claimed to be the oldest Civil War general. I believe Pennypacker was from Pennsylvania and Wool from New York. From the little I've been able to gather, I believe Pennypacker didn't reach voting age until after the war and Wool was on active duty at the age of 77 when the war began.

I'm going to be in Washington, D.C., next month. Would it be worth my time to drive to Charlottesville to have access to the archives at the University of Virginia? Since I have very limited time on this trip, I want to use it in the best way possible. If you don't feel that your library would be the best place to visit, could you suggest where my time might be better spent?

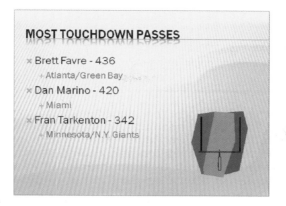

MOST TOUCHDOWN PASSES

× Brett Favre - 436
  + Atlanta/Green Bay
× Dan Marino - 420
  + Miami
× Fran Tarkenton - 342
  + Minnesota/N.Y. Giants

Slide 5

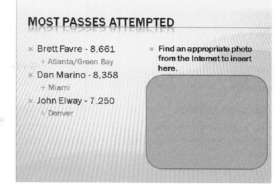

MOST PASSES ATTEMPTED

× Brett Favre - 8,661
  + Atlanta/Green Bay
× Dan Marino - 8,358
  + Miami
× John Elway - 7,250
  + Denver

× Find an appropriate photo from the Internet to insert here.

Slide 6

Activity 10

Timed Writings

1. Key a 1' timing on each ¶; determine *gwam*.
2. Key a 2' timing on ¶s 1–2 combined; determine *gwam*.
3. Key a 3' timing on ¶s 1–2 combined; determine *gwam* and number of errors.

A all letters used   (MicroPace)   gwam   2' | 3'

Atlanta, the capital of Georgia, is a gem of the South. 6 | 4
It is the largest city in the state and exists because of 12 | 8
railroads. The original site was selected as the end of the 18 | 12
line for the railroad to be built northward. Eight years 23 | 16
later, the area became known as Atlanta. Because of the 29 | 19
railroad, Atlanta was the key supply center for the Confederacy 36 | 24
and was virtually destroyed during the Civil War. 40 | 27

One of the more famous Atlanta citizens was Margaret 46 | 30
Mitchell. The book she wrote exquisitely portrays the area 52 | 34
during the Civil War period. During the war, much of the city 58 | 39
was destroyed. However, a few of the elegant southern homes 64 | 43
of this time period have been restored and are open for the 70 | 47
public to see. Today, Atlanta is recognized as a modern city 76 | 51
that gives those who visit as well as the residents of the city 83 | 55
a variety of cultural and sporting events for their enjoyment. 89 | 59

gwam 2' | 1 | 2 | 3 | 4 | 5 | 6
      3' | 1 | 2 | 3 | 4

OBJECTIVES

- To format business letters.
- To increase straight-copy keying skill.

53B   Formatting

Business Letters

Key in block format the business letters shown at the right.

Letter 1

Date: **May 23, 20--**

Letter address:

Mr. Jamison Cooper
882 Elderberry Drive
Fayetteville, NC 28311-0065

Letter 1 is from **Susanne J. Warrens** who is the **Program Chair**. Supply an appropriate salutation, complimentary closing, and reference initials. Send a copy of the letter to **Marsha Edinburgh, President**.

Save as: **53B LETTER1**

Letters 2 & 3

Date (Letter 2):   **June 4, 20--**
Date (Letter 3):   **June 10, 20--**

Letter Address:

Ms. Susanne J. Warrens
Program Chair
8367 Brookstone Court
Raleigh, NC 27615-1661

The letters are from **Jamison R. Cooper**, who is a **Program Committee Member**. Supply an appropriate salutation and complimentary closing. Be sure to include an Enclosure notation and reference initials on each letter.

Save as: **53B LETTER2**
and 53B LETTER3

Last week at our meeting, you mentioned several individuals you thought would be excellent presenters for the opening and closing sessions of next year's convention. I accept your offer to contact them. When you contact them, please share with them the theme of our convention and determine what they would propose as an opening or closing session for our convention. Of course, we need to be concerned with the budget; please determine the fee they would charge.

The information will be needed before June 15 for our meeting. Your willingness to serve on this committee is greatly appreciated. I'll look forward to seeing you in a couple of weeks.

Here is the information you requested. The presenter's name, the title of the presentation, a brief description of the presentation, and the fees charged are included. I've heard Kai Westmoreland and Steve Harmon present; they were excellent.

Kai Westmoreland--*The Great Depression.* Dr. Westmoreland explores the Great Depression in terms of the stock market crash, the economy, income distribution, and international and federal factors. The suffering that millions of American families endured during the depression is brought to life by Dr. Westmoreland's captivating style of presenting. ($500 plus expenses)

Steve Harmon--*World War II.* What better person to have speak about World War II than one of the 156,000 Allied soldiers who crossed the English Channel in the D-Day invasion of France in June of 1944? Harmon's presentation depicts the grim realities of a world war through the eyes of a young soldier. ($350 plus expenses)

Members who attended this year's convention recommended two other presenters--Tayt McCauley and Judith Earnhardt. McCauley's presentations deal with the Kennedy years; Earnhardt is well known for her presentations on women's suffrage. I have contacted them, but I've not yet heard from them. As soon as I do, I will get the information to you.

Here is the information on Judith Earnhardt and Tayt McCauley that I said I would   send to you. Only a brief sketch on each person is given below; their complete resumes (enclosed) arevery impressive. Evidently these two as well as the two I previously sent would all be excellent choices for our convention. It's just a matter of deciding which two we want to go with and then contacting them to make surethey are available. We will want to do that as quickly as possible, as I'm sure all four are in high demand.

Judith Earnhardt--*Women's Suffrage.* Dr. Earnhardt explores the women's movement and the impact of such organizations as the American Woman Suffrage Association and the National Woman Suffrage Association. The presentation brings to life the early advocates of women's rights--Elizabeth Cady Stanton, Susan B. Anthony, Lucy Stone, and Julia Ward Howe. ($500 plus expenses)

Tayt McCauley--*The Kennedy Years.* Dr. McCauley recounts the events that touched the nation during the years of John F. Kennedy's administration. Included in the presentation are the Bay of Pigs, the Cuban Missile Crisis, the Moon Landing, Civil Rights, and the Kennedy Assassination. ($450 plus expenses)

If you think we need to identify additional presenters, I will be happy to do so. Please let me know if you want me to take care of anything else before our next meeting.

CYCLE 1
Assessment

• To assess Cycle 1 document processing, computer application, and straight-copy skills.

Conditioning Practice

Key each line twice SS.

alphabet 1 John was quite amazed by his blocking of seven extra points.

fig/sym 2 In 1994, we had only 345 computers; as of 2004 we owned 876.

speed 3 Rick and Jan may pay for the antique box for their neighbor.

gwam 1' | 1 | 2 | 3 | 4 | 5 | 6 | 7 | 8 | 9 | 10 | 11 | 12 |

Activity 1

Memo

Format and key the text at the right as a memo to **Suzanne Hamlin** from **Elizabeth A. Ross**. Date the memo **May 6, 20--**; use **Summer Trip** for the subject line. Correct all errors.

Save as: CA1 ACTIVITY1

Here are some of the costs that our group will incur on our trip to The Breakers.

The admission fee for The Breakers is $10. I'll check on group rates this week. Round-trip airfare from Portland to T. F. Green Airport is $235. Of course, you know that rates vary considerably during the summer months. My travel agent will inform me of any summer specials.

I'm still waiting for rates for the hotel accommodations. I've narrowed the list to Castle Hill Inn and Resort, Vanderbilt Hall, and Hotel Viking. Any of the three would provide excellent accommodations. As soon as they send the rates, I'll forward them to you.

Activity 2

E-mail

Format and key the text at the right as an e-mail message to your instructor. Use **MACBETH QUOTE** for the subject line.

Correct all spelling, keying, and formatting errors.

Save as: CA1 ACTIVITY2

I enjoyed our visit last week at the class reunion. How quickly time passes; it seems like only yesterday that we graduated. Of course, a class reunion is a quick reminder that it *wasn't* yesterday.

I was able to find the quote that we discussed with the group on Friday. Your memory definitely serves you better than mine; it was a quote from George Bernard Shaw. However, he was referring to Shakespeare's *Macbeth*. Here is the exact quote by Shaw: "Life is not a 'brief candle.' It is a splendid torch that I want to make burn as brightly as possible before handing it on to future generations."

I was glad to see that so many of our classmates are living lives as "splendid torches" rather than as "brief candles."

OBJECTIVE

• To learn to format business letters.

52B Formatting

Letters

Letter 1

Key the model business letter on p. 154.

Save as: 52B LETTER1

Letter 2

Format and key the text at the right as a business letter in block format.

Save as: 52B LETTER2

February 20, 20-- | Mr. and Mrs. Eric Russell | P.O. Box 215 | Moorcroft, WY 82721-2152 | Dear Mr. and Mrs. Russell

Wyoming women were the first women in the United States to have the right to vote (1869). Ester Morris of South Pass City became the first woman judge in 1870. Wyoming was the first state to elect a woman to state office when Estelle Reel was elected State Superintendent of Public Instruction in 1894. Nellie Tayloe Ross became the first female governor in the United States when she was elected governor of Wyoming in 1925.

It is time to honor women such as these for the role they played in shaping Wyoming and U.S. history. A Wyoming Women's Historical Museum is being planned. With your help, the museum can become a reality.

Our community would benefit from the increased tourist activity. Thousands of tourists visit the nation's first national monument, Devil's Tower, each year. Since Moorcroft is only 30 miles from Devil's Tower, a museum would draw many of them to our city as they travel to and from the Tower.

National and state funds for the project are being solicited; however, additional funding from the private sector will be required. Please look over the enclosed brochure and join the Wyoming Women's Historical Museum Foundation by making a contribution.

Sincerely | William P. Shea | xx | Enclosure

Letter 3

Format and key the text at the right as a business letter in block format.

Save as: 52B LETTER3

August 10, 20-- | Ms. Dorothy Shepard | P.O. Box 275 | Moorcroft, WY 82721-2342

Dear Ms. Shepard

GROUNDBREAKING CEREMONY

¶The planning committee is thrilled to announce the groundbreaking ceremony for the **Wyoming Women's Historical Museum** will take place on Saturday, August 25.

¶As one who played an important role in reaching this milestone, you are invited to a luncheon before the ceremony. The luncheon will be held at the Mead House at 11:30. The groundbreaking will begin at 1:30.

¶The museum will be a source of great pride for Wyoming residents and will give them a sense of their history. Visitors will be reminded of the part Wyoming women played in the history of the state and nation.

Sincerely | William P. Shea | Committee Chair | xx

Activity 3

Letter

Format and key the text at the right as a personal-business letter from **Elizabeth A. Ross.**

Supply an appropriate salutation and complimentary close. Be sure to include your reference initials and an attachment notation. Correct all errors.

Return Address and Date:

183 Lennox Street
Portland, ME 04103-5282
May 3, 20--

Letter Address:

Ms. Suzanne Hamlin, President
Portland Historical Society
1821 Island View Road
Portland, ME 04107-3712

Save as: CA1 ACTIVITY3

After doing research on possible historical destinations for our Annual Portland Historical Society trip, I narrowed our choices to the Hildene House in Manchester, Vermont, and The Breakers in Newport, Rhode Island. The Hildene House was built in 1902 for Robert Todd Lincoln, the son of Abraham Lincoln; The Breakers was built for Cornelius Vanderbilt II in 1895.

I met with our planning committee yesterday to share the information I was able to obtain. After discussing the merits of both places, our recommendation is The Breakers for this year's trip. Even though we liked both places, the committee felt that many of our members would have already visited the Hildene House since it is so close to Portland.

I've attached some information on The Breakers. As soon as I receive the additional information I requested about expenses, I will send it to you. You should have it in plenty of time for the June meeting.

Activity 4

Timed Writings

1. Key a 1' timing on each ¶; determine *gwam*.
2. Key two 3' timings on ¶s 1–2 combined; determine *gwam* and number of errors.

 A   all letters used   *MicroPace*

	gwam	1'	3'

New York City, a city of many large buildings, is the 11 | 4
largest city in the United States. The city is recognized all 23 | 8
over the world for its theater, finance, fashion, advertising, 36 | 12
and exquisite stores. New York City is said to be a city of 48 | 16
extremes. It is a city with a diverse population, a melting 60 | 20
pot of people from various backgrounds. No individual group 72 | 24
forms a majority. In addition to its wealthy citizens, New 85 | 28
York also has a large number of people living on the street. 97 | 32

Not only is New York the largest city in the United 10 | 36
States, it is also one of the largest cities in the entire 22 | 40
world. Because of its size, the city has many cultural and 34 | 44
sporting activities for an individual to attend. Baseball, 46 | 48
football, and basketball are just a few of those available. 58 | 52
Carnegie Hall, the Lincoln Center, and the New York State 70 | 56
Theater are several of the places where the performing arts 82 | 60
can be taken in throughout the year. The harbor, parks, art 94 | 64
galleries, and museums provide other interesting attractions 106 | 68
for those who live within New York City as well as for those 119 | 72
who go there to visit. 123 | 73

gwam	1'	1	2	3	4	5	6	7	8	9	10	11	12
	3'		1		2			3			4		

2" TM

Date	February 15, 20-- ↓2
Letter mailing address	Ms. Ariel McKenzie, Principal 4608 Delaware Avenue Baltimore, MD 21215-8794 ↓1
Salutation	Dear Ms. McKenzie ↓1
Subject Line	NEW TEXTBOOKS
Body	Thank you for meeting with the history department instructors to discuss our priority list for the next school year. The proposed curriculum revisions are not going to happen without incurring significant costs in terms of textbooks, technology resources, and faculty development. As we agreed, we will start with textbooks. The table below shows the books that are essential for next year. ↓1

Default or 1" Right Margin

Textbook	Author	Copyright
The Glorious Cause: The American Revolution, 1763-1789	Robert Middlekauff	2007
The American Revolution: A History	Gordon S. Wood	2002
The Women of the American Revolution	Elizabeth Ellet	2004

↓1

Default or 1" Left Margin   At our last meeting, the history instructors agreed to develop a tentative budget for the technology resources and faculty development costs. The budget is attached.

I've scheduled the library conference room for our next meeting on February 23. ↓1

Complimentary close	Sincerely ↓2
Writer	Barbara Segee ↓1
Writer's Title	Curriculum Coordinator
Reference Initials	xx
Attachment Notation	Attachment

Copy Notation	c Rebecca Schultz
	   Marshall Woodward
	   Gavin Sanchez

Shown in 11-point Calibri with 2" top margin and 1" side margins, this letter appears smaller than actual size. Change the default bottom margin to .5" to fit copy on the page.

Business Letter with Special Features

Unbound Report

Format and key the text at the right as an unbound report. Correct all spelling, keying, and formatting errors.

Save as: **CA1 ACTIVITY5**

The castles listed on A&E's *America's Castles* belonged to the rich and famous. By looking at the history of some of the families that owned these castles, it is easy to see why people say that America is the land of opportunity.

Cornelius Vanderbilt was a man who took advantage of the opportunities America had to offer. He was born on May 27, 1794, to a family of modest means. Cornelius ended his formal schooling by the age of 11 (*Encyclopedia Americana*, 2001, Vol. 27, 891). He achieved success because he was industrious. He knew how to work, and he knew the value of the money that came from hard work. Other qualities that made him successful were perseverance, enterprise, courage, and trustworthiness. Being trustworthy meant he could command better prices than others doing the same job (Smith, 528, 1886). Because of these qualities, Cornelius Vanderbilt was able to amass one of the largest fortunes ever made in America from his shipping and railroad enterprises.

Three of America's castles were built by descendents of the man who came out of humble beginnings to amass such a large fortune. The Biltmore House, The Breakers, and Marble House were all built by Cornelius Vanderbilt's descendents.

Biltmore House

The Biltmore House, the largest private residence in America, is located on the Biltmore Estate of 8,000 acres near Asheville, North Carolina. The house and grounds are the most visited historic tourist destination in the nation. The mansion, built for George W. Vanderbilt by Richard Morris Hunt (the late nineteenth century's most renowned architect), was styled after a French Renaissance Chateau (*Visitor's Guide to the Biltmore Estate*, 2007).

The Breakers

The Breakers is located in Newport, Rhode Island. It was built for Cornelius Vanderbilt II. The 70-room castle (Italian Renaissance) was started in 1895. Upon its completion, the castle was filled with antiques from France and Italy (A&E, *America's Castles*, "The Breakers," 2000).

Marble House

Marble House is also located in Newport, Rhode Island. During the 1890s, Newport became the summer colony of New England's wealthiest families. Marble House was built by William K. Vanderbilt, a grandson of Cornelius Vanderbilt, for his wife's birthday. The castle cost $11 million; the 500,000 cubic feet of white marble that it took to build it cost $7 million alone (*Architecture*, "Vanderbilt Marble House," 2003).

Language Skills: Word Choice

1. Study the spelling and definitions of the words.
2. Key all *Learn* and *Apply* lines, choosing the correct word in the *Apply* lines.

Save as: 51C CHOICE

to (prep/adj) used to indicate action, relation, distance, direction	**cents** (n) specified portion of a dollar
too (adv) besides; also; to excessive degree	**sense** (n/vb) meaning intended or conveyed; perceive by sense organs; ability to judge
two (pron/adj) one plus one in number	**since** (adv/conj) after a definite time in the past; in view of the fact; because

Learn 1 I plan on going **to** at least **two** of the games if you go **too**.

Apply 2 (To, Too, Two) of the history students are going (to, too, two) take the exam early.

Apply 3 You will need (to, too, two) bring (to, too, two) boxes (to, too, two).

Learn 1 **Since** I changed the dollars and **cents** columns, the figures make **sense**.

Apply 2 (Cents, Sense, Since) you gave me a dollar, you will get 77 (cents, sense, since) back.

Apply 3 (Cents, Sense, Since) he doesn't have common (cents, sense, since), be careful.

Drill: Personal-Business Letter

1. Take a 3' timing on the letter to determine *gwam*.
2. Key two 1' timings on opening lines through first ¶ of letter. If you finish the lines before time is called, QS and start over. Try to key four more words on the second timing.
3. Key two 1' writings on ¶ 3 through closing lines. If you finish before time is called, QS and start ¶ 3 again. Try to key four more words on the second timing.
4. Key another 3' timing on the letter. Try to increase your *gwam* by 4–8 words over your rate in step 1.

	words
622 Main Street | Moorcroft, WY 82721-2342 | January 5, 20--	13
Ms. Dorothy Shepard | P.O. Box 275 | Moorcroft, WY 82721-2342	25
Dear Ms. Shepard	29

Are you interested in serving on a planning committee for a women's — 43
historical museum in Wyoming? The state's nickname (Equality State) — 56
stems from the fact that Wyoming women were the first women in the — 70
U.S. to achieve voting rights (1869). — 78

Since then, many women have played an important part in shaping — 90
the history of Wyoming. Are you aware that the first woman governor — 104
in the U.S. came from Wyoming? Nellie Tayloe Ross became governor — 118
of Wyoming in 1925. — 122

Let's build a museum to recognize these women--a place for people to — 136
reflect on events of the past and contemplate the future. I will call you — 151
next week to see if you are willing to serve on the committee. — 164

Sincerely \| William P. Shea \| xx — 170

Activity 6

References List

Use the information at the right to create a references list on a separate page. Proofread and correct all spelling, keying, and format errors.

Save as: **CA1 ACTIVITY6**

REFERENCES

A&E, *America's Castles*, "The Breakers." http://www.aetv.com/tv/shows/castles/breakers.html (26 January 2000).

Architecture, "Vanderbilt Marble House." http://www.architecture.about.com/library/blmarblehouse.htm (17 November 2003).

Encyclopedia Americana Vol. 27, "Cornelius Vanderbilt." Danbury, CT: Grolier Incorporated, 2001.

Smith, Helen Ainslie. *One Hundred Famous Americans*. Reprint of 1886 ed. Freeport, NY: Books for Libraries Press, 1972.

"Visitor's Guide to the Biltmore Estate." http://www.willowwinds.com/biltmore-estate-guide.htm (4 December 2007).

Activity 7

Assessment: Keying Skills

1. Key a 1' timing on each ¶ of Activity 4, p. 133; determine *gwam*.

2. Key two 3' timings on ¶s 1–2 combined (Activity 4, p. 133); determine *gwam* and number of errors.

Activity 8

Create the table at the right using the Dark List – Accent 3 table style. Center the table on the page.

Main heading: row height 0.7"; align center; 14-pt. font for 1st line.

Column headings: row height 0.4" align center; 12 pt. font.

Data rows: row height 0.3"; align column 1 bottom left, align column 2 bottom center.

Column widths: Adjust column widths to arrange material attractively on the page.

Save as: **CA1 ACTIVITY8**

VAN NOY ART GALLERY	
June—August Exhibits	
Exhibit	**Opening/Closing Dates**
Emerging Artists	June 1–June 10
19th-Century European Paintings	June 11–June 20
Colonial American Art	June 21–June 30
Old Masters' Paintings	July 1–July 15
American Oil Paintings	July 16–July 31
19th-Century French Prints	August 1–August 15
American Impressionists	August 16–August 30

OBJECTIVES

- To review personal-business letter formatting.
- To improve language skills.
- To increase proficiency in keying opening and closing lines of letters.

51B Formatting

Personal-Business Letters

Letter 1

Review the model personal-business letter on p. 66. Key in block format the letter shown at the right.

Save as: 51B LETTER1

672 Saratoga Place | Boston, MA 02120-3857 | July 15, 20--

Ms. Annette Banks | 91 Kenwood Street | Brookline, MA 02446-2412 | Dear Ms. Banks |

At our meeting this summer, we decided to dedicate one unit of instruction to John F. Kennedy. As you will recall, I was assigned the responsibility for proposing a curriculum for this particular unit of instruction.

The possibilities of what to include in this unit were unlimited. It was very difficult squeezing everything into a one-week unit (see enclosure). However, I enjoyed the challenge of trying to do so. JFK is one of my favorite Presidents; many of my childhood memories are centered around the few short years that he was President.

What do you think of taking our classes on a tour of his birthplace? The home he was born in at 83 Beals Street is now a National Historic Site. Wouldn't this be a great way to conclude our unit and impress upon our students that the 35th President of the United States lived in a modest home only a few blocks away from our school?

If this is of interest to you, I will start making arrangements for both of our classes. I'm already getting excited about returning to school in the fall.

Sincerely | Blake Finley | xx | Enclosure

Letter 2

Format and key in block format the letter shown at the right.

Save as: 51B LETTER2

325 Manhattan Avenue | New York, NY 10025-3827 | May 7, 20--

Ms. Suzanne E. Salmon | 1116 Tiffany Street | Bronx, NY 10459-2276 | Dear Ms. Salmon

I would be more than happy to meet with you to discuss my experiences during my assignment in the Persian Gulf region. It was one of the most, if not the most, exciting assignments I've worked on. The night the attack on Baghdad began will be with me for the rest of my life.

I will share with you the events in Kuwait that precipitated the war. I believe we should also discuss how these events led up to the next conflict, *Iraqi Freedom*.

Please call me at 212-183-8211 so we can arrange a time and location to meet. I'm looking forward to meeting you.

Sincerely | Mitchell Clevenger | Reporter | xx | bc Enrique Jaden

Activity 9

Create the table shown at the right using Colorful Grid – Accent 1. Center the table and adjust column widths to arrange material attractively on page.

Include the following source note: A&E, *America's Castles*, http://www.aetv .com/tv/shows/castles/ index2.html (26 January 2000).

Save as: CA1 ACTIVITY9

AMERICA'S CASTLES

Eastern Region

Castle	Location
The Breakers	Newport, Rhode Island
Chesterwood	Stockbridge, Massachusetts
Drumthwacket	Princeton, New Jersey
George Eastman House	Rochester, New York
Hildene	Manchester, Vermont
Longwood	Kennett Square, Pennsylvania
Lyndhurst Mansion	Tarrytown, New York
Marble House	Newport, Rhode Island
Sunnyside	Tarrytown, New York

Activity 10

Create the table shown at the right using Colorful List – Accent 6. Use the table formatting features that you learned to attractively arrange the information at the right as a table.

Save as: CA1 ACTIVITY10

THEATER VOCABULARY WORDS

April 7–25

Week of April 7	Week of April 14	Week of April 21
Blackout	Callbacks	Choreography
Conflict	Critique	Cues
Dialogue	Ensemble	Feedback
Floor plan	Illusion	Imagination
Improvisation	Intermission	Literary merit
Melodrama	Narrator	Playwright
Run-throughs	Screenplay	Soliloquy
Theme	Tragedy	Visualization

Activity 11

Electronic Presentations

Create the slides shown at the right. Choose appropriate clip art if the art shown at the right isn't available with your software.

Slide 1: Title slide
Slides 2 & 5: Section Headers slides
Slides 3: Comparison
Slides 4, 6, 7: Title and Content slides

Note: Text on some slides has been enlarged for readability.

Save as: CA1 ACTIVITY11

Slide 1

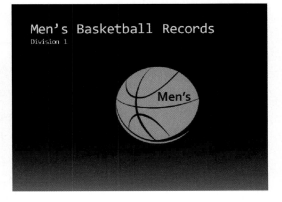

Slide 2

• To increase proficiency in formatting and keying memos.

50B   Formatting

Memos

Memo 1

Format and key a memo to **John Ewing** from **Duncan Sedgwick** using the current date. Include your reference initials and a blind copy notation to **Sally Enders**.

Save as: **50B MEMO1**

SUBJECT: FIELD TRIP PROPOSAL | In our American History class, my students are studying the American Revolution. To bring this unit to life, I would like to take the class on a field trip to the Valley Forge Historical Society Museum.

According to their website, the museum

. . . offers visitors to Valley Forge the opportunity to understand the value of the sacrifice made by the 12,000 men who camped here during the winter of 1777-78. The spirit of Valley Forge is chronicled through galleries and displays that present the letters, weapons, and personal effects of the great and everyday Continental soldier.

I believe this would be an excellent educational experience for our students. When would you be available to meet with me to discuss a field trip of this nature?

Memo 2

Format the text at the right as a memo to **Kara Hundley, Chair**. The memo is from **Richard Ashmore**. Use the **current date** and a subject line of **RECOMMENDATION FOR CORPORATE GIVING FUNDS**.

Save as: **50B MEMO2**

Remember the Alamo!!! As part of our annual corporate giving program, I am recommending that we make a contribution to the Alamo, managed by the Daughters of the Republic of Texas. They depend entirely on donations and proceeds from the gift shop for covering operating costs.

I believe it is important for us to honor those who played integral roles in the history of our state. Our children need to be reminded of the lives of James Bowie, David Crockett, and William Barret Travis, who made the ultimate sacrifice for freedom. And who can forget the role Sam Houston played as the commander in chief of the Texan army in the revolution against Mexico? Memories of Texan legends are preserved at the Alamo.

Please list the Alamo as a potential recipient in our corporate giving program next year. Of course, we will discuss it when we meet. | xx

Memo 3

Compose a memo using the information shown at the right.

Save as: **50B MEMO3**

50C

Drill: Memos

Key two 2' timings on Memo 2. Try to key at least four additional words on the second 2' timing.

Jason Lopez, the FBLA president, would like you to send a memo to four of your teachers asking them to announce the first FBLA meeting of the year in their classes. The purpose of the meeting is to recruit new members; Mr. Chen will be the guest speaker, talking about the importance of co-curricular activities. The meeting will be held on September 8 at 3:30 in Ms. Jackson's room (308). Compose and format an appropriate memo; send a copy of the memo to Jason Lopez.

Slide 3

Slide 4

Slide 5

Slide 6

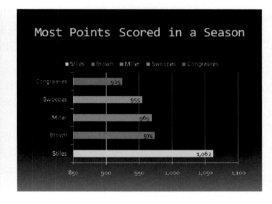

Slide 7

Activity 12

Timed Writings

1. Key a 1' timing on each ¶; determine *gwam*.
2. Key two 3' timings on ¶s 1–2 combined; determine *gwam*; count errors.

A all letters used (MicroPace)

	gwam	1'	3'

The Arlington House is a place filled with the very interesting history of our country. The exquisite house built for the grandson of Martha Washington, George Custis, in time became the home of General Lee. The house was built in an amazing location which today looks out over the capital city of our nation.

The home and land are also linked to other famous people of United States history. Soon after the Civil War started, the home became the headquarters of the Union army with much of the land to ultimately be used for what is today known as Arlington National Cemetery. President Kennedy and President Taft are just a few of the notables buried on the former estate of General Lee.

gwam	1'											
	1	2	3	4	5	6	7	8	9	10	11	12
3'		1			2			3			4	

1' column values: 11, 23, 33, 44, 55, 63, 11, 23, 34, 45, 57, 69, 77

3' column values: 4, 8, 11, 15, 18, 21, 25, 29, 32, 36, 40, 44, 47

OBJECTIVES

- To increase proficiency at formatting memos.
- To format memo distribution lists.

49A–54A

Conditioning Practice

Key each line twice.

alphabet 1 Gavin Zahn will buy the exquisite green jacket from the old shop.

figures 2 Check No. 183 was used to pay Invoices 397 and 406 on October 25.

speed 3 Glen may pay the haughty neighbor if the turn signals work right.

gwam 1' | 1 | 2 | 3 | 4 | 5 | 6 | 7 | 8 | 9 | 10 | 11 | 12 | 13 |

49B Formatting

Memos

Memo 1

After reviewing the formatting guides on p. 150, key the model memo on p. 151. Use Light List – Accent 1. Do not bold the entries in Column 1.

Save as: 49B MEMO1

Memo 2

Format and key the text at the right as a memo. Include a blind copy notation to **Kevin Hefner**.

Save as: 49B MEMO2

TO: Marsha Hanson, Director | FROM: Jack Vermillion | DATE: Current Date | SUBJECT: ANTHONY AND STANTON DISCUSSION

Even though the Virginia Women's Museum is primarily for recognizing those women who contributed greatly to Virginia's history, I think it appropriate to recognize some early leaders of the women's movement on a national level.

Susan B. Anthony and Elizabeth Cady Stanton are two women who led the struggle for women's suffrage at the national level. They organized the National Woman Suffrage Association. Shouldn't they be recognized for their gallant efforts in our museum as well?

Please include a discussion of this issue on the next agenda. | xx

Memo 3

Format and key the text at the right as a memorandum. Send copies of the memo to **Timothy Gerrard** and **Maria Valdez**.

Save as: 49B MEMO3

TO: Andrew Nelson, Manager; Amy McDonald, Assistant Manager; Judith Smythe, Assistant Manager | FROM: Malcolm McKinley, Travel Agent | DATE: May 3, 20-- | SUBJECT: CIVIL WAR BUS TOUR

Yes, I think there would be an interest in a bus tour of some of the battle campaigns of the Civil War. My recommendation would be to start with a six-day tour that includes some of the most famous battlefields.

Of course, the one that comes to mind right away is Gettysburg, where over 158,000 Union (George G. Meade) and Confederate (Robert E. Lee) soldiers fought courageously for their causes. This battle (July 1-3, 1863) resulted in an estimated 51,000 lives being lost. Being able to visit the place where President Lincoln delivered the Gettysburg Address would also be of real interest to those considering the trip. I've looked at several websites, and evidently something of interest is always going on in or near Gettysburg.

The other battlefields that I recommend including on the tour are Manassas (Virginia) and Antietam (Maryland). Both of these battlefields were key encounters of the Civil War.

Within the next week, I will provide you with more details on a tour such as the one I've briefly presented. | xx

Communicating
YOUR PERSPECTIVE | 2

A growing number of "fair trade" organizations provide artists, artisans, and farmers, often from developing countries, with a means of marketing their goods globally at a fair price. One such organization, PEOPLink, works with a network of Trading Partners (more than 1,400 organizations in 44 countries, representing over 200,000 artisans).* PEOPLink gives its Trading Partners digital cameras to photograph products and markets those products in its online catalog. The organization also provides online information about the work and lives of the artisans, teaches them to build and maintain their own Web catalogs, gives them online training, and helps them develop their products. The table below shows a few of the partners.

FAIR TRADE ARTS AND CRAFTS

Country	Product
Cameroon	Wood Carving
Guatemala	Ceramics
Nepal	Artwork
Panama	Molas
Uzbekistan	Chess Sets
Uganda	Baskets

*Source: PEOPLink. "Linking People Around the Globe via E-commerce." (15 May 2008) http://www.PEOPLink.org/EN/history.html.

Global Awareness

1. Key and format the table at the left. Use the table formatting features that you have learned to arrange the information attractively on the page.

2. Form a group with some other students. Develop a plan for a school fair in which you could showcase the work of artists from your school and community. Include details such as the date of the fair, where it would be held, how you would invite participants, how many you could invite, and where and how you would advertise the event.

Music has a rich cultural history. From ancient times, different cultures have developed their own styles of music and have invented different instruments with which to express them.

In music, the influence of one culture on another can be clearly seen and can produce exciting results. Take the American composer Aaron Copland, for example. Some of Copland's best-known compositions were based on American folk music, such as the ballets *Billy the Kid* (1938), *Rodeo* (1942), and *Appalachian Spring* (1944). His *El salon Mexico* was inspired by Mexican folk music.

Radio, television, the Internet, and high-quality sound and video recording have made music from many different cultures accessible to listeners worldwide. They have also helped to make music even more multicultural. For example, South Indian *cine*, or motion-picture music, uses both Indian and Western musical instruments and mixes classical Indian music with Western rock and jazz.*

*Source: David Butler, B.SC., M.A., Ph.D. "Music." Microsoft® Encarta® Online Encyclopedia 2008 http://encarta.msn.com (16 July 2008).

Cultural Diversity

1. Pair up with a student who likes a musician that you also like. Talk about this musician. Address the following questions, taking notes on the answers.

   • Does this musician's work show the influence of other musicians or other kinds of music? If so, in what way?
   • Do you think people in another country might form perceptions of this musician's country based on his or her music? If so, what might they be?
   • Think of the music you like to listen to and the music your parents like. How important is culture to being able to appreciate a particular kind of music?

2. Develop your notes and key them into a one-page unbound report.

2" TM

Memo
Distribution List

TO: American History I
                American History II ↓1

FROM: Ms. Schultz ↓1

DATE: February 1, 20-- ↓1

SUBJECT: FINAL PROJECT ↓1

Body   The table below lists the topics that you can choose from for your final project in American History. After you select a topic, sign up for it on Desire2Learn. Remember that only two students can select the same topic. The sooner you sign up, the more likely you are to get your first choice. ↓1

Default or 1"
Left Margin

American History Topics for Final Project		
American Revolutionary War	Cuban Missile Crisis	Reconstruction
California Gold Rush	Great Depression	September 11, 2001
Civil Rights Act of 1964	Industrialization	Vietnam War
Civil War	Korean War	Wall Street Crash of 1929
Cold War	Louisiana Purchase	War of 1812
Colonial America	Persian Gulf War	Watergate
Constitutional Convention	Prohibition	World War I
Continental Army	Reaganomics	World War II

Default or 1"
Right Margin

↓1

The guidelines for the final project are attached. Look them over before class on Monday, and I'll answer any questions you have at that time. Remember that each of you will be assigned to a faculty member of the English department to work with on the written part of this project. ↓1

Reference
Initials   xx ↓1

Attachment
Notation   Attachment ↓1

Copy Notation   c Ms. Conway
                   Mr. Brockton
                   Mr. Dickson
                   Ms. McGee

Shown in 11-point Calibri with 2" top margin and 1" side margins, this memo appears smaller than actual size. Table heading is keyed in 13-point.

Memo with Special Features

CYCLE 2

No matter what career you choose or what jobs you have along the way, a computer—and a computer keyboard—almost certainly will be at the center of your work. You will use new technology to build on existing keying skills.

In Cycle 2 you will refine keying techniques, increase communication skills, and learn advanced word processing features. You will work on your electronic presentation skills. You will process e-mail with attachments, reports with footnotes, and tables with borders and shading, to name a few. And that's not all.

You will go to work in the home office of a growing organization with branches in five cities. Your work for the President/CEO often takes you to the company's Web page.

Let's get started!

Social Studies

Format Guides

In Unit 8, you learned to format memos and personal-business letters. In this unit, you will learn to format business letters and memos with special features.

Since business letters have the return address printed as part of the letterhead, the return address does not need to be keyed.

Special Features for Memos and Letters

In addition to the basic parts presented in Unit 8, memos and letters may include the special features described below and illustrated on pp. 151 and 156.

Reference initials. If the memo or letter is keyed by someone other than its originator, the initials of the keyboard operator should be placed in lowercase letters at the left margin one line below the body (memos) or the originator's name and title (letters).

Attachment/Enclosure notation. If another document is attached to a memo or letter, the word *Attachment* is keyed at the left margin one line below the reference initials. If a document is included but not attached, the word *Enclosure* is used instead. If reference initials are not used, the notation is keyed one line below the body (memos) or the writer's name and title (letters).

Copy notation. A copy notation indicates that a copy of a memo or letter is being sent to someone other than the addressee. Use *c* followed by a space and then the name(s) of the person(s) to receive a copy. Place a copy notation one line below the last line of the enclosure notation or the reference initials if there is no enclosure. If there is more than one name, list names vertically.

c   Hector Ramirez
    Ursula O'Donohue

Blind copy notation. When a copy of a memo or letter is to be sent to someone without disclosing to the person receiving the memo or letter, a blind copy (*bc*) notation is used. When used, *bc* and the name of the person receiving the blind copy are keyed at the left margin one line below the last memo or letter part on all copies of the memo *except* the original.

bc Arlyn Hunter
    Miguel Rodriguez

Memo distribution list. When a memo is sent to several individuals, a distribution list is used. Format the memo distribution list as shown below:

To: Tim Burroughs
     Charla Dunwoody
     Alexandra Williams
     Ramon Garcia

Attention line for letters. An attention line should only be used when the writer does not know the name of the person who should receive the letter. For example, if a writer wants a letter to go to the director of special collections of a library but doesn't know the name of that person, *Attention Special Collections Director* or *Attention Director of Special Collections* could be used. When an attention line is used in a letter addressed to a company, key it as the first line of the letter and envelope address. Within the letter, the correct salutation is *Ladies and Gentlemen*.

Subject line for letters. The subject line specifies the topic discussed in the letter. Key the subject line in ALL CAPS, a SS below the salutation.

Tables. Tables may be inserted in memos and letters. Single-space before and after the table. To leave extra space following the table, click the Line spacing drop-down list arrow, and click Add Space Before Paragraph. This will make the spacing before and after the table equal. If space allows, indent the table at least .5" from the right and left margins.

UNIT 13
Lessons 46-48

Build Keyboarding Skill

Lesson 46 — KEYING TECHNIQUE

OBJECTIVES
- To improve keying techniques.
- To improve keying speed and control.

46A-48A

Conditioning Practice
Key each line twice.

alphabet	1	Extensive painting of the gazebo was quickly completed by Jerome.
figures	2	At least 456 of the 3,987 jobs were cut before November 18, 2005.
speed	3	Keith and I may go to the island to dismantle the bicycle shanty.

gwam 1' | 1 | 2 | 3 | 4 | 5 | 6 | 7 | 8 | 9 | 10 | 11 | 12 | 13 |

46B — Skill Building

Technique: Letter Keys
Key each line twice.

Technique Cue
Limit keystroking action to the fingers; keep hands and arms motionless.

Emphasize continuity and rhythm with curved, upright fingers.

A	1	Katrina baked Marsha a loaf of bread to take to the Alameda fair.
B	2	Barbara and Bob Babbitt both saw the two blackbirds in the lobby.
C	3	Carl, the eccentric character with a classic crew cut, may catch.
D	4	David and Eddie dodged the duck as it waddled down the dark road.
E	5	Ellen needed Steven to help her complete the spreadsheet on time.
F	6	Before I left, Faye found forty to fifty feet of flowered fabric.
G	7	George and Greg thought the good-looking neighbor was gregarious.
H	8	John, Hank, and Sarah helped her haul the huge bush to the trash.

gwam 1' | 1 | 2 | 3 | 4 | 5 | 6 | 7 | 8 | 9 | 10 | 11 | 12 | 13 |

46C — Skill Building

Technique: Number Keys/Tab
Key each line twice (key number, tap TAB, key next number).

Concentrate on figure location; quick tab spacing; eyes on copy.

95	107	403	496	572	824	590	576	871
82	458	314	307	891	103	721	980	645
73	669	225	218	600	206	843	109	312

Activity 8

Navigate a Document

1. Read the copy at the right. Learn to move the insertion point using HOME, END, PgUp/PgDn, and CTRL + arrow keys.

2. Key sentence 1; edit as instructed in sentences 2, 3, and 4, using only the insertion point to navigate.

Save as: OF5 ACTIVITY8

The **HOME**, **END**, **PgUp**, and **PgDn** keys can be used to *navigate* (move the insertion point quickly from one location to another) in a document.

The **CTRL** key in combination with the arrow keys can be used to move the insertion point to various locations.

1. Key the following sentence.

   The basketball game is on Friday.

2. Make the following changes, using the insertion point move keys.

   The basketball game is on Friday, **next** **February 20.**

3. Make these additional changes, using the insertion point move keys.

   The next basketball game is on Friday, February 20, **varsity** **at 7 p.m.**

4. Make these changes.

   The next varsity basketball game is on ~~Friday,~~ **Saturday** *February 20, at 7 p.m.* **against Sundance.**

Activity 9

Inserting the Date

1. Read the copy at the right; learn to use the features described.

2. Key the information at the right using the Insert Date and AutoComplete features as indicated. If AutoComplete is not available with your software, use the Insert Date feature.

Save as: OF5 ACTIVITY9

Use the **Insert Date** feature to enter the date into a document automatically. Some software has an Update Automatically option along with Insert Date. When the update option is used, the date is inserted as a date field. Each time the document is opened or printed, the current date replaces the previous date. The date on your computer must be current to insert the correct date in a document.

Some software provides an **Automatic Completion (AutoComplete)** feature, which also inserts the date automatically. When you start keying the month, AutoComplete recognizes the word and shows it in a tip box above the insertion point. By tapping the **ENTER** key, you enter the remainder of the month automatically, without keying it. When you tap the Space Bar, the tip box shows the complete date. Tapping the **ENTER** key enters the complete date.

Part I

<Insert Date>

Mr. Gavin Garfield
5104 Hyde Park Blvd., S
Chicago, IL 60615-3291

<Insert hard page break>

Part II

<Insert Date Field, Update Automatically>

Ms. Tabitha Cicero
3678 Regal Street
Charleston, SC 29405-1348

<Insert hard page break>

Part III

1. Today is <AutoComplete>.
2. Your balance as of <Insert Date Field, Update Automatically> is $42.83.
3. I received your check today, <Insert Date>.
4. You will need to make sure that today's date, <Insert Date Field, Update Automatically>, is included on the form.

Speed Forcing Drill

Key each line once at top speed; then try to complete each sentence on the 15", 12", or 10" call as directed by your instructor. Force speed to higher levels as you move from sentence to sentence.

Emphasis: high-frequency balanced-hand words

	gwam	15"	12"	10"
Hal paid the men for the work they did on the rig.		40	50	60
Orlando and I did the work for the eight busy men.		40	50	60
Helen and Rodney may do the handiwork for the neighbor.		44	55	66
When I visit the neighbor, Jan may go down to the dock.		44	55	66
Alan and I laid six of the eight signs by the antique chair.		48	60	72
Pamela and Vivian may sign the proxy if they audit the firm.		48	60	72
Chris may go with the widow to visit the city and see the chapel.		52	65	78
The maid may go with them when they go to the city for the gowns.		52	65	78

Skill Check

1. Key a 1' timing on ¶ 1; determine *gwam*.
2. Add 2–4 *gwam* to the rate attained in step 1; determine quarter-minute checkpoints from the chart below.
3. Key two 1' guided timings on ¶ 1 to increase speed.
4. Practice ¶ 2 in the same way.
5. Key two 3' timings on ¶s 1 and 2 combined; determine *gwam* and the number of errors.

Quarter-Minute Checkpoints

gwam	1/4'	1/2'	3/4'	Time
16	4	8	12	16
20	5	10	15	20
24	6	12	18	24
28	7	14	21	28
32	8	16	24	32
36	9	18	27	36
40	10	20	30	40

A all letters used (MicroPace)

	gwam	1'	3'
Which of the states has the least number of people?		10	3
Few people realize that this state ranks first in coal,		21	7
fifth in natural gas, and seventh in oil production. Quite		33	11
a significant number of deer, antelope, and buffalo dwell		44	15
within the boundaries of this exquisite state. A major		55	18
portion of Yellowstone National Park is located in the		66	22
state. If you still don't know which state is being		77	26
described, it is Wyoming.		82	27
Wyoming is located in the western portion of the		92	31
United States. The state is bordered by six different		103	34
states. Plains, mountain ranges, and national parks make		114	38
up a vast portion of the landscape of the state. Several		126	42
million people come to the state each year to view the		137	46
beautiful landscape of this unique state. Visitors and		148	49
the extraction of natural resources make up a major portion		159	53
of the economy of the state.		165	55

gwam	1'	1	2	3	4	5	6	7	8	9	10	11	12
	3'		1			2			3			4	

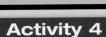

Activity 4

Review Features
Envelope

Use the Envelopes feature to format a small envelope (No. 6 ¾) for Envelope 1 and a large envelope (No. 10) for Envelope 2.

Save as: OF5 ACTIVITY4-1

Save as: OF5 ACTIVITY4-2

Return address:

Envelope 1
Felix S. Vidro
720 Dorado Beach NE
Albuquerque, NM 87111-3827

Envelope 2
Jesus Rios
310 Joe Louis Avenue
Raleigh, NC 27610-3386

Delivery address:

Ms. Erin Cooper
840 Torinita Avenue
Trenton, NJ 08610-3728

Ms. Kendra Eastwick
748 Gertrude Lane
Lafayette, IN 47905-3882

Activity 5

Review Features
Tabs

1. Set a left tab at .5", a right tab at 3", and a decimal tab at 5".
2. Starting at 2" from the top of the page, key the text (DS) at the right.

Save as: OF5 ACTIVITY5

Left tab at .5" ↓	Right tab at 3" ↓	Decimal tab at 5" ↓
One-eighth	1/8	.125
One-sixth	1/6	.1667
One-fourth	1/4	.25
One-third	1/3	.3333
One-half	1/2	.5
Two-thirds	2/3	.6667
Three-fourths	3/4	.75
One	1/1	1.0

Activity 6

Copy Text to Another File

1. Read the copy at the right.
2. Open *Microsoft Word*.
3. Open *DF OF5 ACTIVITY 6-1*; copy sentences 6–10.
4. Open *DF OF5 ACTIVITY 6-2*; place the copied text a DS below sentence 5.

Save as: OF5 ACTIVITY6

Use the **Copy** and **Paste** features to copy text from one file to another.

Use the **Cut** and **Paste** features to move text from one file to another.

Steps to Copy, Cut, and Paste:

1. Select the text.
2. Copy (or cut) the selected text.
3. Open the document in which you want to place the copied (or cut) text.
4. Place the insertion point where you want to place the text.
5. Paste the text at the insertion point.

Activity 7

Reinforce Copying Text to Another File

Open the files:
DF OF5 ACTIVITY7-1
DF OF5 ACTIVITY7-2
DF OF5 ACTIVITY7-3
Create a copy of the Gettysburg Address as directed at the right.

Save as: OF5 ACTIVITY7

The initial words of each of the three ¶s of the Gettysburg Address are shown at the right. The names of the files where these ¶s can be found are shown in parentheses.

Copy the ¶s from *OF5 ACTIVITY7-2* and *OF5 ACTIVITY7-3* and place them in the correct order in *OF5 ACTIVITY7-1*. Leave a DS between ¶s.

Paragraph 1: Four score and seven years ago, our fathers brought forth on this continent . . . (*OF5 ACTIVITY7-1*)

Paragraph 2: Now we are engaged in a great civil war, testing . . . (*OF5 ACTIVITY7-2*)

Paragraph 3: But in a large sense we cannot dedicate, we cannot consecrate, we cannot hallow this ground. The brave . . . (*OF5 ACTIVITY7-3*)

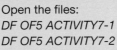

Lesson 47 KEYING TECHNIQUE

OBJECTIVES
• To improve keying techniques.
• To improve keying speed and control.

47B Skill Building

Technique: Letter Keys

Key each line twice.

Technique Cue

Keep fingers curved and upright.

Emphasize continuity and rhythm with curved, upright fingers.

I 1 Michigan, Illinois, Indiana, and Missouri are all in the Midwest.

J 2 Jeff juggled jobs to join Jane for juice with the judge and jury.

K 3 Katie knocked the knickknacks off the kiosk with her knobby knee.

L 4 Please allow me to be a little late with all legal illustrations.

M 5 Mary is immensely immature; her mannerisms make me extremely mad.

N 6 Nancy knew she would win the nomination at their next convention.

O 7 Roberto opposed opening the store on Monday mornings before noon.

P 8 Pam wrapped the peppermints in purple paper for the photographer.

Q 9 Qwin quietly queried Quincy on the quantity and quality of quail.

gwam 1' | 1 | 2 | 3 | 4 | 5 | 6 | 7 | 8 | 9 | 10 | 11 | 12 | 13 |

47C Skill Building

Technique: Number Keys/TAB

1. Set tabs at 2" and 4".
2. Key the copy at the right.

Technique Cue

Eyes on copy.

Concentrate on figure location; quick tab spacing; eyes on copy.

703 Sandburg Trl.	65 Yates Ave.	656 Winter Dr.
5214 Chopin St.	423 Clement St.	187 Ocean Ave.
3769 Orchard Rd.	641 Boone Ct.	410 Choctaw St.
158 Hartford St.	901 Cassia Dr.	792 Fairview Dr.

47D

Speed Building

1. Key a 1' timing on ¶ 1; key four more 1' timings on ¶ 1, trying to go faster each time.
2. Repeat the procedure for ¶ 2.

 all letters used MicroPace   gwam 1'

Government is the structure by which public laws are   11

made for a group of people. It can take many forms. For   22

example, in one type of structure, the populace has the right   34

to elect citizens to govern for them and make the laws and   46

policies. This way of making the laws is called a represen-   58

tative government.   62

Democracy or republic form of government are two names   12

that are quite often used to refer to this type of governance   24

by the people. This type of a structure is in direct contrast   37

to a dictatorship, in which all the decisions are made by just   49

one person.   52

gwam 1' | 1 | 2 | 3 | 4 | 5 | 6 | 7 | 8 | 9 | 10 | 11 | 12 |

Office Features 5

For each activity, read and learn the feature described, then follow instructions at the left.

Activity 1

Review Features
Key sentences 1–5; underline, *italicize,* and **bold** text as you key. Use the Hanging Indent feature to align the second line of text under the first line.

Save as: OF5 ACTIVITY1

1. **Benjamin Britten's** *Four Sea Interludes* include ***Dawn, Sunday Morning, Moonlight,*** and ***Storm***.

2. **Brad Pitt, Cate Blanchett, Kimberly Scott,** and **Jason Flemyng** star in ***The Curious Case of Benjamin Button.***

3. The titles of **books** and **movies** should be underlined or *italicized*.

4. The Bourne Ultimatum is an **adventure/action** movie; Fred Clause is a **comedy**; and The Assassination of Jesse James is a **western**.

5. *Success* was written by Henry Wadsworth **Longfellow;** Samuel **Longfellow** wrote *Go Forth to Life.*

Activity 2

Review Features
1. Open DF *OF5 ACTIVITY2.*
2. Underline, *italicize,* and **bold** text as shown at the right.

Save as: OF5 ACTIVITY2

6. During the first week of February, *The Testament* by **John Grisham** was No. 1 on the Best Sellers list.

7. Time and Newsweek featured articles on **Princess Diana** a decade after her tragic death.

8. Cut, Copy, and Paste were presented in **OF1**; margins were presented in **OF2**.

9. Do you know the difference between **their** and **there**?

10. *The Village Blacksmith* (**Longfellow**) and *The Road Not Taken* (**Frost**) were discussed in class on Friday.

Activity 3

Review Features
1. Open *DF OF5 ACTIVITY3.*
2. Use the Format Painter feature to copy formatting from line 1 and apply it to lines 2–6.

Save as: OF5 ACTIVITY3

1. The state capital of Alabama is Montgomery.

2. The state capital of Arizona is Phoenix.

3. The state capital of Georgia is Atlanta.

4. The state capital of Indiana is Indianapolis.

5. The state capital of New Jersey is Trenton.

6. The state capital of Ohio is Columbus.

Skill Building

Speed Forcing Drill

Key each line once at top speed; then try to complete each sentence on the 15", 12", or 10" call as directed by your instructor. Force speed to higher levels as you move from sentence to sentence.

Emphasis: high-frequency balanced-hand words

	gwam	15"	12"	10"

Glen and I may key the forms for the city auditor.   40 | 50 | 60

He may make a sign to hang by the door of the bus.   40 | 50 | 60

They may make a profit if they do all of the busy work.   44 | 55 | 66

Six of the men may bid for good land on the big island.   44 | 55 | 66

If he pays for the bus to the social, the girls may also go.   48 | 60 | 72

The neighbor paid the maid for the work she did on the dock.   48 | 60 | 72

It is their civic duty to handle their problems with proficiency.   52 | 65 | 78

Helen is to pay the firm for all the work they do on the autobus.   52 | 65 | 78

Lesson 48   KEYING TECHNIQUE

OBJECTIVES

- To improve keying techniques.
- To improve keying speed and control.

Skill Building

Technique: Letter Keys

Key each line twice.

Technique Cue

Limit keystroking action to the fingers; keep hands and arms motionless.

Emphasize continuity and rhythm with curved, upright fingers.

R 1 Raindrops bore down upon three robbers during the February storm.

S 2 The Mets, Astros, Reds, Twins, Jays, and Cubs sold season passes.

T 3 Trent bought the teal teakettle on the stove in downtown Seattle.

U 4 Ursula usually rushes to the music museum on Tuesday, not Sunday.

V 5 Vivacious Eve viewed seven vivid violets in the vases in the van.

W 6 We swore we would work with the two wonderful kids for two weeks.

X 7 Rex Baxter explained the extra excise tax to excited expatriates.

Y 8 Yes, Ky is very busy trying to justify buying the yellow bicycle.

Z 9 Dazed, Zelda zigzagged to a plaza by the zoo to see a lazy zebra.

gwam 1' | 1 | 2 | 3 | 4 | 5 | 6 | 7 | 8 | 9 | 10 | 11 | 12 | 13 |

Skill Building

Technique: Number Keys/TAB

1. Set tabs at 2" and 4".
2. Key the copy at the right.

Concentrate on finger location; quick tab spacing; eyes on copy.

331 Summit St.	589 Gabriel Ave.	364 Topaz Ave.
2490 Tucker Ave.	981 Toweridge Rd.	72 Viking Rd.
587 Telemark Ct.	207 Maplewood Trl.	481 Osceola Ave.
6021 Mission Hills	365 Westover St.	2963 Hunt St.
467 Sycamore Dr.	440 Radcliff Blvd.	50 Saratoga Ln.
809 Danbury Ave.	13 Plum Way	83 Ravine Dr.
9987 Park Pl.	224 Norton Way	745 Sinclair Ct.

2. Key Proofread & Correct, using correct verbs.
   a. Check answers.
   b. Using the rule number at the left of each line, study the rule relating to each error you made.
   c. Rekey each incorrect line, using correct verbs.

Save as: CS5 ACTIVITY1

ACTIVITY 2

Reading

1. Open *DF CS5 ACTIVITY2*
2. Read the document; close the file.
3. Key answers to the questions using complete sentences.

Save as: CS5 ACTIVITY2

ACTIVITY 3

Composing

1. Study the quotations.
2. Compose a ¶ to show your understanding of honesty and truth.
3. Compose a 2nd ¶ to describe an incident in which honesty and truth *should* prevail but don't.
4. Proofread and correct.

Save as: CS5 ACTIVITY3

ACTIVITY 4

Math: Finding What Percent One Number Is of Another

Proofread & Correct

Rules		
1	1	Sandra and Rich (is, are) running for band secretary.
1	2	They (has, have) to score high on the SAT to enter that college.
2	3	You (doesn't, don't) think keyboarding is important.
2	4	Why (doesn't, don't) she take the test for advanced placement?
3	5	Neither of the candidates (meet, meets) the performance criteria.
3	6	One of your art students (is, are) likely to win the prize.
5	7	The number of people against the proposal (is, are) quite small.
4	8	The manager, as well as his assistant, (is, are) to attend.
6	9	Neither the teacher nor her students (is, are) here.
3	10	All the meat (is, are) spoiled, but some items (is, are) okay.

1. What kinds of positions are being filled?
2. What is the minimum number of hours each employee must work each week?
3. Is weekend work available?
4. What kind of service is being offered to those who have to care for elderly people?
5. Is the pay based solely on performance?
6. When are the openings available?
7. Does everyone work during the day?
8. How can you submit a resume?

Honesty's the best policy.
—Cervantes

Piety requires us to honor truth above our friends.
—Aristotle

To be honest . . . here is a task for all that a man has of fortitude.
—Robert Louis Stevenson

The dignity of truth is lost with protesting.
—Ben Jonson

1. Open *DF CS5 ACTIVITY4* and print the file.
2. Solve the problems as directed in the file.
3. Submit your answers.

CAREER Clusters

ACTIVITY 5

You must complete Career Activities 1–3 before this activity.

1. Retrieve the printed Career Cluster Plan of Study for the career cluster that is your second choice.
2. Review the plan and write a paragraph or two about why you would or would not consider a career in this cluster. Print your file, save it as Career5, and keep it open.
3. Exchange papers with a classmate. Have the classmate offer suggestions for improving the content and correcting any errors he or she finds in your paragraph(s). Make the changes that you agree with and print a copy to turn in to your instructor. Save it as Career5 and close the file.
4. Return your folder to the storage area. When your instructor returns your paper, file it in your Career folder.

Speed Forcing Drill

Key each line once at top speed; then try to complete each sentence on the 15", 12", or 10" call as directed by your instructor. Force speed to higher levels as you move from sentence to sentence.

Emphasis: high-frequency balanced-hand words

	gwam	15"	12"	10"
Janel may go to the dock to visit the eight girls.		40	50	60
She is to go with them to the city to see the dog.		40	50	60
The sorority girls paid for the auto to go to the city.		44	55	66
She is to go to the city with us to sign the six forms.		44	55	66
Dick may go to the big island to fix the auto for the widow.		48	60	72
Hank and the big dog slept by the antique chair on the dock.		48	60	72
Rick is to make a turn to the right at the big sign for downtown.		52	65	78
Vivian may go with us to the city to do the work for the auditor.		52	65	78

Skill Check

1. Key a 1' timing on ¶ 1; determine *gwam*.
2. Add 2–4 *gwam* to the rate attained in step 1; determine quarter-minute checkpoints from the chart below.
3. Key two 1' guided timings on ¶ 1 to increase speed.
4. Practice ¶ 2 in the same way.
5. Key two 3' timings on ¶s 1 and 2 combined; determine *gwam* and the number of errors.

Quarter-Minute Checkpoints

gwam	1/4'	1/2'	3/4'	Time
16	4	8	12	16
20	5	10	15	20
24	6	12	18	24
28	7	14	21	28
32	8	16	24	32
36	9	18	27	36
40	10	20	30	40

A all letters used (MicroPace) gwam 3'

	3'	
Extraordinary would be an appropriate word to use to de-	4	71
scribe Michelangelo. It would be a good word to express how	8	75
an individual may feel about the statue of David. It would	12	79
also be an excellent choice of words for describing the exqui-	16	84
site works of art on the ceiling of the Sistine Chapel. It	20	88
would be just as fine a word to use to describe the dome of	24	92
St. Peter's Basilica. Each of these outstanding works of art	28	96
was completed by Michelangelo, quite an extraordinary person.	32	100
The paintings, sculptures, and architecture of this man	36	104
are recognized throughout the world. Michelangelo was born in	40	108
Caprese, Italy, but spent much of his early life in the city	44	112
of Florence. Here he spent a great deal of time in the work-	48	116
shops of artists. His father did not approve of his doing so,	52	120
because artists were considered to be manual laborers. His	56	124
father considered this to be beneath the dignity of his family	61	128
members. This did not stop the young artist, who would even-	65	132
tually become one of the greatest of all times.	68	135

Communication & Math
SKILLS 5

SUBJECT/VERB AGREEMENT

Subject/Verb Agreement

1. Study each of the six rules.
   a. Key the *Learn* line(s) beneath each rule, noting how the rule is applied.
   b. Key the *Apply* line(s), choosing correct verbs.

Subect/Verb Agreement

Rule 1: Use a singular verb with a singular subject (noun or pronoun); use a plural verb with a plural subject and with a compound subject (two nouns or pronouns joined by *and*).

Learn	1	The speaker was delayed at the airport for over thirty minutes.
Learn	2	The musicians are all here, and they are getting restless.
Learn	3	You and your assistant are to join us for lunch.
Apply	4	The member of the chorus (is, are) to introduce the speaker.
Apply	5	Dr. Cho (was, were) to give the lecture, but he (is, are) ill.
Apply	6	Mrs. Samoa and her son (is, are) to be at the craft show.

Rule 2: Use the plural verb *do not* or *don't* with pronoun subjects *I, we, you,* and *they* as well as with plural nouns; use the singular verb *does not* or *doesn't* with pronouns *he, she,* and *it* as well as with singular nouns.

Learn	7	I do not find this report believable; you don't either.
Learn	8	If she doesn't accept our offer, we don't have to raise it.
Apply	9	They (doesn't, don't) discount, so I (doesn't, don't) shop there.
Apply	10	Jo and he (doesn't, don't) ski; they (doesn't, don't) plan to go.

Rule 3: Use singular verbs with indefinite pronouns (*each, every, any, either, neither, one,* etc.) and with *all* and *some* used as subjects if their modifiers are singular (but use plural verbs with *all* and *some* if their modifiers are plural).

Learn	11	Each of these girls has an important role in the class play.
Learn	12	Some of the new paint is already cracking and peeling.
Learn	13	All of the dancers are to be paid for the special performance.
Apply	14	Neither of them (is, are) well enough to sing today.
Apply	15	Some of the juice (is, are) sweet; some (is, are) quite tart.
Apply	16	Every girl and boy (is, are) sure to benefit from this lecture.

Rule 4: Use a singular verb with a singular subject that is separated from the verb by the phrase *as well as* or *in addition to*; use a plural verb with a plural subject so separated.

Learn	17	The letter, in addition to the report, has to be revised.
Learn	18	The shirts, as well as the dress, have to be pressed again.
Apply	19	The vocalist, as well as the pianist, (was, were) applauded.
Apply	20	Two managers, in addition to the president, (is, are) to attend.

Rule 5: Use a singular verb if *number* is used as the subject and is preceded by *the*; use a plural verb if *number* is the subject and is preceded by *a*.

Learn	21	A number of them have already voted, but the number is small.
Apply	22	The number of jobs (is, are) low; a number of us (has, have) applied.

Rule 6: Use a singular verb with singular subjects linked by *or* or *nor*, but if one subject is singular and the other is plural, the verb agrees with the nearer subject.

Learn	23	Neither Ms. Moss nor Mr. Katz was invited to speak.
Learn	24	Either the manager or his assistants are to participate.
Apply	25	If neither he nor they (go, goes), either you or she (has, have) to.

Resources

© ARNE TRAUTMANN 2008/USED UNDER LICENSE FROM SHUTTERSTOCK.COM

directly in front of the chair. The front edge should be even with the edge of the table or desk.

Place the monitor for easy viewing. Some experts maintain that the top of the screen should be at or slightly below eye level. Others recommend placing the monitor even lower. Set it a comfortable distance from your eyes—at least an arm's length away.

Position the monitor to avoid glare (an antiglare filter can help). Close blinds or pull shades as needed. Adjust the brightness and contrast controls, if necessary, for readability. Keep the screen clean with a soft, lint-free cloth and (unless your instructor tells you otherwise) a nonalcohol, nonabrasive cleaning solution or glass cleaner.

If you cannot adjust your equipment and the desk or table is too high, try adjusting your chair. If that does not work, you can sit on a cushion, a coat, or even a stack of books.

Use a straight-backed chair that will not yield when you lean back. The chair should support your lower back (try putting a rolled-up towel or sweater behind you if it does not). The back of your knees should not be pressed against the chair. Use a seat that allows you to keep your feet flat on the floor, or use a footrest. Even a box or a backpack will do.

Position the mouse next to and at the same height as the keyboard and as close to the body as possible. Research has not shown conclusively that one type of pointing device (mouse, trackball, touch pad, stylus, joystick, etc.) is better than another. Whatever you use, make sure your arms, hands, and fingers are relaxed. If you change to a new device, evaluate it carefully first and work up gradually to using it all the time.

Arrange your work material so you can see it easily and maintain good posture. Some experts recommend positioning whatever you look at most often (the monitor or paper material) directly in front of you so you do not have to turn your head to the side while keying.

EXERCISE AND TAKE BREAKS

Exercise your neck, shoulders, arms, wrists, and fingers before beginning to key each day and often during the workday. Finger exercises appear on the next page. Neck, shoulder, wrist, and other exercises appear at the Cornell University ergonomics Web site listed below.

Take a short break at least once an hour. Rest your eyes from time to time as you work by focusing on an object at least 20 feet away. Blink frequently.

USE GOOD POSTURE AND PROPER TECHNIQUES

Sit erect and as far back in the seat as possible. Your forearms should be parallel to the slant of the keyboard, your wrists and forearms low, but not touching or resting on any surface. Your arms should be near the side of your body in a relaxed position. Your shoulders should not be raised, but should be in a natural posture.

Keep your fingers curved and upright over the home keys. Strike each key lightly using the finger*tip*. Grasp the mouse loosely. Make a conscious effort to relax your hands and shoulders while keying.

For more information on mouse and keyboard use and CTS/RSI, visit the following Internet sites:

- http://kidshealth.org/kid/ (search for *ergonomics*)
- http://www.tifaq.org
- http://www.berkeley.edu (locate the Ergonomics Program and look for Computer Use Tips)
- http://www.office-ergo.com
- http://www.cornell.edu (search for *ergonomics*)

Ergonomic Keyboards

Ergonomic keyboards (see illustration at left) are designed to improve hand posture and make keying more comfortable. Generally they have a split design with left and right banks of keys and the ability to tilt or rotate the keyboard for comfort. More research is needed to determine just how effective ergonomic keyboards are in preventing RSI injuries and carpal tunnel syndrome.

Know Your Computer

The numbered parts are found on most computers. The location of some parts will vary.

1. **CPU (Central Processing Unit):** Internal operating unit or "brain" of computer.
2. **CD-ROM drive:** Reads data from and writes data to a CD.

3. **Monitor:** Displays text and graphics on a screen.
4. **Mouse:** Used to input commands.
5. **Keyboard:** An arrangement of letter, figure, symbol, control, function, and editing keys and a numeric keypad.

© FRANKSITEMAN.COM 2007

KEYBOARD ARRANGEMENT

© FRANKSITEMAN.COM 2007

1. **Alphanumeric keys:** Letters, numbers, and symbols.
2. **Numeric keypad:** Keys at the right side of the keyboard used to enter numeric copy and perform calculations.
3. **Function (F) keys:** Used to execute commands, sometimes with other keys. Commands vary with software.
4. **Arrow keys:** Move insertion point up, down, left, or right.

5. ESC **(Escape):** Closes a software menu or dialog box.
6. TAB: Moves the insertion point to a preset position.
7. CAPS LOCK: Used to make all capital letters.
8. SHIFT: Makes capital letters and symbols shown at tops of number keys.
9. CTRL **(Control):** With other key(s), executes commands. Commands may vary with software.

10. ALT **(Alternate):** With other key(s), executes commands. Commands may vary with software.
11. **Space Bar:** Inserts a space in text.
12. ENTER **(RETURN):** Moves insertion point to margin and down to next line. Also used to execute commands.
13. DELETE: Removes text to the right of insertion point.

14. NUM LOCK: Activates/deactivates numeric keypad.
15. INSERT: Activates insert or typeover.
16. BACKSPACE: Deletes text to the left of insertion point.

Repetitive Stress Injury

Repetitive stress injury (RSI) is a result of repeated movement of a particular part of the body. It is also known as repetitive motion injury, musculoskeletal disorder, cumulative trauma disorder, and by a host of other names. A familiar example of RSI is "tennis elbow." RSI is the number-one occupational illness, costing employers more than $80 billion a year in health-care fees and lost wages.

Of concern to keyboard and mouse users is the form of RSI called **carpal tunnel syndrome** (CTS). CTS is an inflammatory disease that develops gradually and affects the wrists, hands, and forearms. Blood vessels, tendons, and nerves pass into the hand through the carpal tunnel (see illustration below). If any of these structures enlarge, or the walls of the tunnel narrow, the median nerve is pinched and CTS symptoms may result.

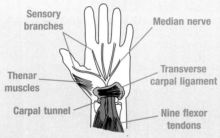

Palm view of left hand

SYMPTOMS OF RSI/CTS

CTS symptoms include numbness in the hand; tingling or burning in the hand, wrist, or elbow; severe pain in the forearm, elbow, or shoulder; and difficulty in gripping objects. Symptoms usually appear during sleeping hours, probably because many people sleep with their wrists flexed.

If not properly treated, the pressure on the median nerve, which controls the thumb, forefinger, middle finger, and half the ring finger, causes severe pain. The pain can radiate into the forearm, elbow, or shoulder. There are many kinds of treatment, ranging from simply resting to surgery. Left untreated, CTS can result in permanent damage or paralysis.

The good news is that 99 percent of people with carpal tunnel syndrome recover completely. Computer users can avoid reinjuring themselves by taking the precautions discussed later in this article.

CAUSES OF RSI/CTS

RSI/CTS often develops in workers whose physical routine is unvaried. Common occupational factors include (1) using awkward posture, (2) using poor techniques, (3) performing tasks with wrists bent (see below), (4) using improper equipment, (5) working at a rapid pace, (6) not taking rest breaks, and (7) not doing exercises that promote graceful motion and good techniques.

RSI/CTS is not limited to workers or adults. Keying school assignments, playing computer or video games, and surfing the Internet are increasing the incidence of RSI/CTS in younger people.

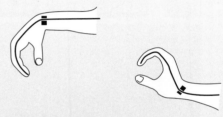

Improper wrist positions for keystroking

CTS is frequently a health concern for people who use a computer keyboard or mouse. The risk of developing CTS is less for those who use proper furniture or equipment, keyboarding techniques, posture, and/or muscle-stretching exercises than for those who do not.

REDUCING THE RISK OF RSI/CTS

By taking the following precautions, keyboard and mouse users can reduce the risk of developing RSI/CTS and can keep it from recurring. Experts stress that good computer habits like these are very important in avoiding RSI/CTS. They can also help you avoid back, neck, and shoulder pain, and eyestrain.

ARRANGE THE WORK AREA

Arrange your equipment in a way that is natural and comfortable for you. Position the keyboard at elbow height and

Windows® Tutorial

Microsoft® Windows® is an **operating system**, a program that manages all the other programs on a computer. Like other operating systems, *Windows®* provides a **graphical user interface** (**GUI,** pronounced "gooey") of **icons** (picture symbols) and **menus** (lists of commands).

Currently, the newest version of *Windows®* is called *Windows® Vista*. The version before *Vista* was called *Windows® XP*. This tutorial will show you how to use basic *Windows®* features. A few features may look, work, or be named slightly differently on your computer, depending on your operating system version and setup.

THE DESKTOP

After you turn on your computer and it has powered up, it will display the **desktop**, your main working area. The first illustration below shows a *Windows® Vista* desktop.[1] The second illustration shows the *Windows® XP* desktop. Your desktop will have many of the same features; but because the desktop is easy to customize, some items will be different.

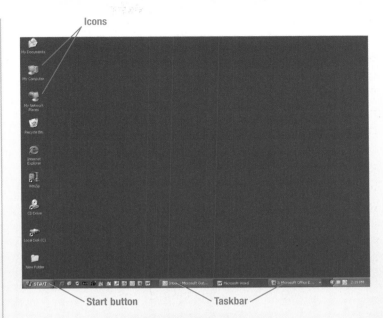

Windows® XP desktop

On the desktop, you will see icons and a **taskbar** (a tool for opening programs and navigating on your computer). Icons provide an easy way to access programs and documents that you use frequently. Double-click an icon to open the program, document, or **folder** (storage place for files and other folders) that it represents. (If the single-click option is selected on your computer, you will find that you can click an icon once instead of double-clicking. For more information about this option, open the Help Index—click *Help and Support* on the Start menu—and key **single-click**.)

On the right side of the *Vista* desktop, the Sidebar contains small programs called gadgets. *Vista* ships with several interesting gadgets including a clock, a calculator, and news headlines. You can add or remove gadgets from the Sidebar, and additional gadgets are available online.

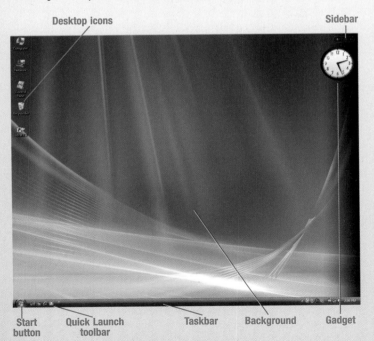

Windows® Vista desktop

---

[1]*Microsoft®* and *Windows®* are registered trademarks of Microsoft Corporation in the United States and/or other countries.

Electronic Resume (Resume 1)

Print Resume (Resume 2)

Application for Employment — An Equal Opportunity Employer
Regency Insurance Company

PERSONAL INFORMATION

NAME (LAST FIRST):	SOCIAL SECURITY NO.	CURRENT DATE	PHONE NUMBER
Ruckert, Douglas H.	368-56-2890	5/11/06	(713) 555-0121

ADDRESS (NUMBER, STREET, CITY, STATE, ZIP CODE)	U.S. CITIZEN	DATE YOU CAN START
8503 Kirby Dr., Houston, TX 77054-8220	☒ YES ☐ NO	6/10/06

ARE YOU EMPLOYED NOW?	IF YES, MAY WE INQUIRE OF YOUR PRESENT EMPLOYER?	IF YES, GIVE NAME AND NUMBER OF PERSON TO CALL
☒ YES ☐ NO	☒ YES ☐ NO	James Veloshi, Manager (713) 555-0181

POSITION DESIRED	SALARY DESIRED	STATE HOW YOU LEARNED OF POSITION
Customer Service	Open	From Ms. Anne D. Salgado Eisenhower Business Technology Instructor

HAVE YOU EVER BEEN CONVICTED OF A FELONY?
☐ YES ☒ NO   IF YES, EXPLAIN.

EDUCATION

	NAME AND LOCATION OF SCHOOL	YEARS ATTENDED	DID YOU GRADUATE?	SUBJECTS STUDIED
COLLEGE				
HIGH SCHOOL	Eisenhower Technical High School Houston, TX	2002 to 2006	Will graduate 06/06	Business Technology
GRADE SCHOOL				
OTHER				

SUBJECTS OF SPECIAL STUDY/RESEARCH WORK OR SPECIAL TRAINING/SKILLS DIRECTLY RELATED TO POSITION DESIRED

Windows and Office Suite, including Word, Excel, Access, PowerPoint, and FrontPage

Office Procedures course with telephone training and interpersonal skills role playing

FORMER EMPLOYERS (LIST LAST POSITION FIRST)

FROM - TO (MTH & YEAR)	NAME AND ADDRESS	SALARY	POSITION	REASON FOR LEAVING
9/05 to present	Hinton's Family Restaurant, 1264 S. Wayside Avenue, Houston, TX 77023-8841	$6.85/hr.	Server	Want full-time position in my field
6/04 to 9/05	Tuma's Landscape and Garden Center 10155 East Freeway, Houston, TX 77029-4419	$5.75/hr.	Sales	Employed at Hinton's

REFERENCES (LIST THREE PERSONS NOT RELATED TO YOU, WHOM YOU HAVE KNOWN AT LEAST ONE YEAR)

NAME	BUSINESS ADDRESS	PHONE NUMBER	TITLE	YEARS KNOWN
Ms. Anne D. Salgado	Eisenhower Technical High School, 100 W. Cavalcade, Houston, TX 77009-2651	(713) 555-0134	Business Technology Instructor	Four
Mr. James R. Veloshi	Hinton's Family Restaurant, 1264 S. Wayside Avenue, Houston, TX 77023-8841	(713) 555-0181	Manager	One
Mrs. Helen T. Landis	Tuma's Landscape and Garden Center, 10155 East Freeway, Houston, TX 77029-4419	(713) 555-0149	Owner	Three

I UNDERSTAND THAT I SHALL NOT BECOME AN EMPLOYEE UNTIL I HAVE SIGNED AN EMPLOYMENT AGREEMENT WITH THE FINAL APPROVAL OF THE EMPLOYER AND THAT SUCH EMPLOYMENT WILL BE SUBJECT TO VERIFICATION OF PREVIOUS EMPLOYMENT DATA PROVIDED IN THIS APPLICATION, ANY RELATED DOCUMENTS, OR DATA SHEET. I KNOW THAT A REPORT MAY BE MADE THAT WILL INCLUDE INFORMATION CONCERNING ANY FACTOR THE EMPLOYER MIGHT FIND RELEVANT TO THE POSITION FOR WHICH I AM APPLYING, AND THAT I CAN MAKE A WRITTEN REQUEST FOR ADDITIONAL INFORMATION AS TO THE NATURE AND SCOPE OF THE REPORT IF ONE IS MADE.

Douglas H. Ruckert
SIGNATURE OF APPLICANT

Employment Application Form

8503 Kirby Drive
Houston, TX 77054-8220

May 10, 2009

Ms. Jenna St. John
Personnel Director
Regency Insurance Company
219 West Greene Road
Houston, TX 77067-4219

Dear Ms. St. John:

Ms. Anne D. Salgado, my business technology instructor, informed me of the customer service position with your company that will be available June 15. She speaks very highly of your organization. After learning more about the position, I am confident that I am qualified and would like to be considered for the position.

Currently I am completing my senior year at Eisenhower Technical High School. All of my elective courses have been computer and business-related courses. I have completed the advanced computer application class where we integrated word processing, spreadsheet, database, presentation, and Web page documents by using the latest suite software. I have also taken an office technology course that included practice in using the telephone and applying interpersonal skills.

My work experience and school activities have given me the opportunity to work with people to achieve group goals. Participating in FBLA has given me an appreciation of the business world.

The opportunity to interview with you for this position will be greatly appreciated. You can call me at (713) 555-0121 or e-mail me at dougr@suresend.com to arrange an interview.

Sincerely,

Douglas H. Ruckert

Enclosure

Employment Application Letter

COMMON DESKTOP ICONS

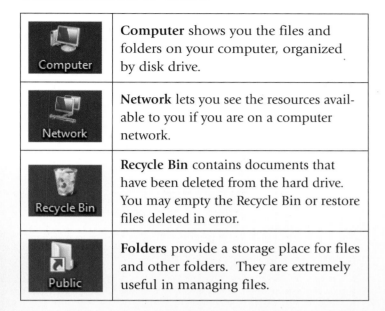 Computer	**Computer** shows you the files and folders on your computer, organized by disk drive.
Network	**Network** lets you see the resources available to you if you are on a computer network.
Recycle Bin	**Recycle Bin** contains documents that have been deleted from the hard drive. You may empty the Recycle Bin or restore files deleted in error.
Public	**Folders** provide a storage place for files and other folders. They are extremely useful in managing files.

The taskbar usually appears at the bottom of the screen. The standard *Windows*® taskbar consists of the Start button, a button for each program or document that you have open, and an icon for your computer's internal clock. Your taskbar may have additional icons.

The **Start button** opens the **Start menu**, shown on p. R6. Like a restaurant menu, a software menu offers you choices—commands you can choose. You can accomplish almost any task in *Windows*® from the Start menu.

The left pane of the Start menu shows the pinned program list and the Search results box. Pinned programs are programs that you use regularly, so *Vista* creates a shortcut to them. You can pin or unpin an icon by right-clicking it and then choosing *Pin to Start Menu* or *Remove from this list*. The right side of the Start menu contains shortcuts to many predefined folders. Quick access to features such as Search, Control Panel, and Help are available here. You can install updates, lock the computer, restart it, shut it down, or switch users from here as well.

> Note: The *Windows*® operating system requires a mouse or other pointing device. For help with using a mouse, see the Computer Concepts section at the front of this text.

START MENU

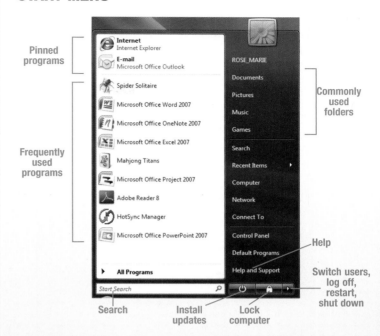

BASIC FEATURES OF WINDOWS

Microsoft® *Windows*® displays folders, applications, and individual documents in **windows**. The basic features of all windows are the same.

The **title bar** lists the name of the window.

From the **Ribbon**, you can access all the commands available in the software. Ribbon names are similar in application programs that run under the *Microsoft*® *Windows*® operating system (as are icons and other features).

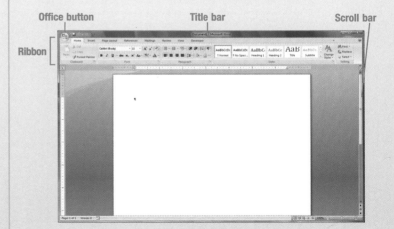

WOODWARD HIGH SCHOOL BIOLOGY CLUB

AGENDA

March 2, 20--

2:45 p.m. in Room 214

Type of Meeting: Regular meeting

Meeting Facilitator: Marcie Holmquist, President

Invitees: All members and faculty sponsor

1) Call to order

2) Roll call

3) Approval of minutes from last meeting

4) Unfinished business

    a) Finalize team assignments for candy sale that begins May 1

    b) Plan approved community service project to care for one mile of State Route 163

    c) Discuss recommendation that the Club help support an international student

5) New business

    a) Appoint nominating committee

    b) Discuss plans for regional leadership conference on April 12

    c) Discuss annual give-back gift to Woodward High

6) Adjournment

Agenda

TRAVEL ITINERARY FOR LISA PEROTTA
222 Pine View Drive
Coraopolis, PA 15108
(412) 555-1320
perotta@fastnet.com
Pittsburgh, PA to Santa Ana, CA—April 18-22, 20--

Date	Time	Activity	Comments
Tuesday April 18	3:30 p.m. (ET)	Depart **Pittsburgh International Airport** (PIT) for Santa Ana, CA Airport (SNA) on **USEast Flight 146**. *Arrival time is 5:01 p.m.(PT).*	The flight is non-stop on an Airbus A319, and you are assigned seat 22E.
	5:30 p.m. (PT)	Reservation with **Star Car Rental** (714-555-0190). Return by 12 noon (PT) on April 22.	Confirmation No.: 33-345. Telephone: 714-555-1030.
	6:00 p.m. (PT)	Reservations at the Hannah Hotel, 421 Race Avenue, Santa Ana for April 18 to April 22 for a single, non-smoking room at $145 plus tax. Telephone: 714-555-0200.	Confirmation No.: 632A-04/18. Check-in after 6 p.m. is guaranteed. Check out by 11 a.m.
Saturday April 22	1:25 p.m. (PT)	Depart **Santa Ana Airport** (SNA) for Pittsburgh International Airport (PIT) on **USEast Flight 148**. *Arrival time is 8:52 p.m. (ET).*	The flight is non-stop on an Airbus A319, and you are assigned seat 16A.

Travel Agency Contact Information—Agent is Mary Grecco; 444 Grant Street, Pittsburgh, PA 15219; Telephone: 412-555-0087; Fax: 412-555-0088; E-Mail: greccom@netway.com

Itinerary

WOODWARD HIGH SCHOOL BIOLOGY CLUB

MEETING MINUTES

March 2, 20--

1. Call to order: President Marcie Holmquist called the Biology Club meeting to order at 2:45 p.m. on March 2, 20-- in Room 214.

2. Attendance: Jerry Finley, Secretary, recorded the attendance. All officers, 23 members, and the faculty sponsor were present.

3. Approval of minutes: The minutes were approved as read by Jerry Finley.

4. This unfinished business was acted upon:

    a. There will be five teams of four members each for the candy sale that begins on May 1. Team captains are Bruce Holstein, Anita Jones, Roberto Nuez, Ty Billops, and Gracie Walton. Each captain will select three members for his/her team.

    b. Bill Eaton will organize a team of volunteers for the Route 163 project. He will try to get at least 15 members to clean up the litter on May 15. The Chamber of Commerce will provide adult supervision, safety vests and gloves, road signs, and collection bags. The volunteers will begin at 9:15 a.m. and work until about 11:30 a.m. They are to meet at the Carriage Inn parking lot at 8:45 a.m.

    c. The officers recommended that the Club not provide financial support for an international student this coming year since all members who attend the Fall Regional Leadership Conference will need financial assistance for travel, food, and lodging. The officers' recommendation was approved.

5. This new business was discussed and acted upon:

    a. President Holmquist appointed the Nominating Committee (Sissy Erwin, Roberta Shaw, and Jim Vance), and they are to present a slate of officers at the April meeting.

    b. The membership approved officers to attend the Spring Regional Leadership Conference at Great Valley Resort and Conference Center on April 12. Their expenses for travel and meals will be reimbursed.

6. The next meeting is April 3 at 2:45 p.m. in Room 103. The meeting was adjourned at 3:35 p.m. by Marcie Holmquist.

Minutes submitted by Jerry Finley, Secretary

Meeting Minutes

News Release

For Release: Immediate
Contact: Heidi Zemack

CLEVELAND, OH, May 25, 20--. Science teachers from school districts in six counties are eligible for this year's Teacher Excellence awards funded by The Society for Environmental Engineers.

Nominations can be submitted through Friday, July 31, by students, parents, residents, and other educators. Nomination forms are available from the participating school districts or on the Society's website at http://www.tsee.webhost.com.

An anonymous committee reviews the nominations and selects ten finalists. From that group, seven "teachers of distinction" and three award winners are selected. The top award winner receives $5,000, the second receives $2,500, and the third receives $1,500. Each teacher of distinction receives $500. The teachers of distinction and the award winners will be announced on September 5 at a dinner at the Cleveland Inn.

School districts participating in the program include those in these counties: Cuyahoga, Lorain, Medina, Summit, Lake, and Geauga.

###

News Release

For more information on Windows programs, see the section on Computer Concepts at the front of this text.

If the window contains more material than you can see at once, **scroll bars** may appear at the right and/or bottom. Clicking a scroll bar arrow moves the document in small increments. Clicking the empty area of a scroll bar moves the document in larger increments. Dragging the bar portion of a scroll bar moves the document exactly as much and as fast as you want.

At the right end of the title or menu bar are the Minimize, Maximize, and Close buttons. Clicking the **Minimize button** reduces a window to a button on the taskbar. This is useful when you want to **multitask** (perform more than one task at a time) and do not want to exit a program. To restore the window, click the button on the taskbar.

Clicking the **Maximize button** enlarges a window to take up almost the entire screen. Many people like to maximize application documents to have more room to work.

Minimize   Maximize   Close   Restore

After you have maximized a window, the **Restore button** will replace the Maximize button. Clicking this button restores the window to its original size and location.

Clicking the **Close button** closes a window.

To move a window, drag it by the title bar. To resize a window, move the mouse pointer to a side or corner of the window. The pointer will become a double-headed arrow (↔). Drag until the window is the size you want.

When more than one window is displayed at a time, clicking a window makes it the **active window**—the one you can work in. The other window(s) will have a gray title bar to indicate that it is **inactive**.

DIALOG BOXES

A **dialog box** displays when software needs more information to carry out a task. The illustrations at the right show how to choose common dialog box options. Clicking OK executes the selected option; clicking Cancel closes the dialog box.

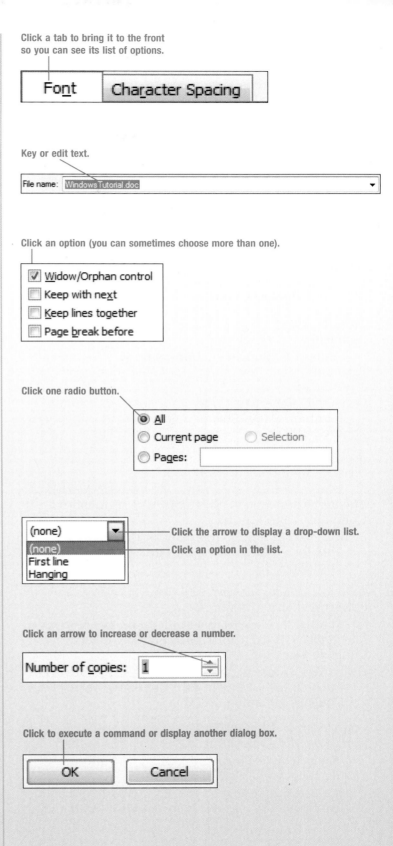

Click a tab to bring it to the front so you can see its list of options.

Key or edit text.

Click an option (you can sometimes choose more than one).

Click one radio button.

Click the arrow to display a drop-down list.
Click an option in the list.

Click an arrow to increase or decrease a number.

Click to execute a command or display another dialog box.

REPORT DOCUMENTATION

Good report writing includes proof that the reported statements are sound. The process is called **documenting.**

Most school reports are documented in the body and in a list. A reference in the body shows the source of a quotation or paraphrase. A list shows all references alphabetically.

In the report body, references may be noted (1) in parentheses in the copy (textual citations or parenthetical documentation); (2) by a superscript in the copy, listed on a separate page (endnotes); or (3) by a superscript in the copy, listed at the bottom of the text page (footnotes). A list may contain only the sources noted in the body (REFERENCES or Works Cited) or include related materials (BIBLIOGRAPHY).

Two popular documenting styles are shown: *Century 21* and MLA (Modern Language Association).

Century 21
Examples are listed in this order: (1) textual citation, (2) endnote/footnote, and (3) References/Bibliography page.

Book, One Author
(Schaeffer, 1997, 1)

[1]Robert K. Schaeffer, *Understanding Globalization,* (Lanham, MD: Rowman & Littlefield Publishers, Inc., 1997), p. 1.

Schaeffer, Robert K. *Understanding Globalization* (Lanham, MD: Rowman & Littlefield Publishers, Inc., 1997).

Book, Two or Three Authors
(Prince and Jackson, 1997, 35)

[2]Nancy Prince and Jeanie Jackson, *Exploring Theater* (Minneapolis/St. Paul: West Publishing Company, 1997), p. 35.

Prince, Nancy, and Jeanie Jackson. *Exploring Theater.* Minneapolis/St. Paul: West Publishing Company, 1997.

Book, Four or More Authors
(Gwartney, et al., 2009, 9)

[3]James D. Gwartney, et al., *Economics: Private and Public Choice* (Cincinnati: South-Western, Cengage Learning, 2009), p. 9.

Gwartney, James D., et al. *Economics: Private and Public Choice.* Cincinnati: South-Western, Cengage Learning, 2009.

Encyclopedia or Reference Book
(*Encyclopedia Americana*, 2008, Vol. 25, p. 637)

[4]*Encyclopedia Americana*, Vol. 25 (Danbury, CT: Grolier Incorporated, 2008), p. 637.

Encyclopedia Americana, Vol. 25. "Statue of Liberty." Danbury, CT: Grolier Incorporated, 2008.

Journal or Magazine Article
(Harris, 1993, 755)

[5]Richard G. Harris, "Globalization, Trade, and Income," *Canadian Journal of Economics*, November 1993, p. 755.

Harris, Richard G. "Globalization, Trade, and Income." *Canadian Journal of Economics*, November 1993, 755–776.

Web Site
(Railton, 1999)

[6]Stephen Railton, "Your Mark Twain," http://www.etext.lib.virginia.edu/railton/sc_as_mt/yourmt13.html (September 24, 1999).

Railton, Stephen. "Your Mark Twain." http://www.etext.lib.virginia.edu/railton/sc_as_mt/yourmt13.html (24 September 1999).

Modern Language Association
Examples include reference (1) in parenthetical documentation and (2) on Works Cited page.

Book, One Author
(Schaeffer 1)

Schaeffer, Robert K. *Understanding Globalization.* Lanham, MD: Rowman & Littlefield, 1997.

Book, Two or Three Authors
(Prince and Jackson 35)

Prince, Nancy, and Jeanie Jackson. *Exploring Theater.* Minneapolis/St. Paul: West Publishing, 1997.

Book, Four or More Authors or Editors
(Gwartney et al. 9)

Gwartney, James D., et al. *Economics: Private and Public Choice.* Cincinnati: South-Western, Cengage Learning, 2009.

Encyclopedia or Reference Book
(*Encyclopedia Americana* 637)

Encyclopedia Americana. "Statue of Liberty." Danbury, CT: Grolier, 2008.

Journal or Magazine Article
(Harris 755)

Harris, Richard G. "Globalization, Trade, and Income," *Canadian Journal of Economics.* Nov. 1993: 755–776.

Web Site
(Railton)

Railton, Stephen. *Your Mark Twain Page.* (24 Sept. 1999) http://www.etext.lib.virginia.edu/railton/sc_as_mt/yourmt13.html.

File Management in Windows®

Establishing a logical and easy-to-use file management system will help you organize files efficiently and find them quickly and easily. You can manage files on the desktop or in your file management program, *Windows Explorer*. This feature may be somewhat different on your computer, depending on your *Windows®* version and setup.

NAMING FILES AND FOLDERS

Good file organization begins with giving your files and folders names that are logical, relevant, and easy to understand. For example, you might create a folder for your English assignments called *English*. In this folder, you might have a journal that you add to each day (called *Journal*); monthly compositions (e.g., *Comp10-09*, *Comp3-10*); and occasional essays (such as *EssaySports* or *EssayEthics*). A system like this would make finding files simple.

UNDERSTANDING THE FILE SYSTEM

You can use *Windows Explorer* to see how files and folders are organized on your computer. *Windows Explorer* shows files and folders in a **hierarchical** or **tree** view. At the top is Desktop. Desktop contains all the items that appear on the desktop of your computer. The first item in Desktop, My Computer, contains the files and folders on your computer, organized by drives.

Drill 1: Navigate the File System

1. Click the *Start* button, point to *All Programs* (then to *Accessories*, if you have the *Windows® XP* operating system), and click *Windows Explorer*.
2. Click a plus sign beside a drive or folder to display below it a list of any folders that it contains. Click the minus sign to close the folder.
3. Click a folder (icon or name) in the left pane. All its contents (files and/or folders) will be displayed in the right pane.
4. Double-click a folder with a plus sign (double-click the icon or name, not the plus sign). Any folders inside the folder will be listed below, and all the contents of the folder (files and/or folders) will be displayed in the right pane.
5. Practice Steps 2–4 with other folders.

You do not have to be in *Windows Explorer* to locate a file or folder. You can use the My Computer icon on the desktop, the Search option on the Start menu, or the Address box (if available) in a drive or folder window.

CREATING FOLDERS

You will want to create folders to store files. You can do so using *Windows Explorer* or the desktop. In addition to putting files in your folders, you can create folders within folders if you need to.

- In *Windows Explorer*, click the drive or folder that will contain the new folder, click the *File* menu, point to *New*, and click *Folder*.
- On the desktop, double-click the drive or folder that will contain the new folder (if the drive or folder is not on the desktop, you can access it by double-clicking *My Computer*). In the window that opens, click the *File* menu, point to *New*, and click *Folder*. To create a folder on the desktop itself, right-click in a blank area of the desktop, point to *New*, and click *Folder*.

LEADERSHIP SEMINAR PROGRESS REPORT

Kimberly Jurgaitis

The Kemp Group

August 15, 20--

Title Page

1" TM

Henderson 1 — Header

DS I.D. Information:

James Henderson

Professor Lewis

HC101 Composition

15 February 20-- ↓ 2

Career Planning ↓ 2

Indent ¶ 0.5" and DS ¶s → Career planning is an important, ongoing process. It is important because the career you choose will affect your quality of life.

One important step in career planning is to define your career goals.

Indent long quotes 1" from LM and DS:

> Whatever your present plans for employment or further education, you should consider your long-term career goals. You might wonder why someone who is considering a first job should be thinking beyond that job. Thinking ahead may help you choose a first job that is closely related to long-term interests. . . . With a career goal in mind, you can evaluate beginning job offers in relation to that goal. (Oliverio, Pasewark, and White 528)

1" LM and RM — 1" LM and RM

Another useful step in career planning is to develop a personal profile of your skills, interests, and values.

An analysis of your skills is likely to reveal that you have many different kinds: (1) functional skills that determine how well you manage time, communicate, and motivate people; (2) adaptive skills that determine your efficiency, flexibility, reliability, and enthusiasm; and (3) technical skills such as keyboarding, computer, and language skills that are required for many jobs.

Values are "principles that guide a person's life" (Fulton-Calkins and Stulz 543), and you should identify them early so that you can pursue a career that will improve your chances to acquire them. Values include the importance you place on family, security, wealth, prestige, creativity, power, and independence.

At least 1" BM

MLA Report, page 1

1" TM

Henderson 2 — Header

Interests are best described as activities you like and enthusiastically pursue. By listing and analyzing your interests, you should be able to identify a desirable work environment. For example, your list is likely to reveal if you like to work with things or people, work alone or with others, lead or follow others, or be indoors or outdoors.

MLA Report, page 2

1" TM

Henderson 3 — Header

Works Cited

DS

Fulton-Calkins, Patsy and Karin M. Stulz. *Procedures & Theory for Administrative Professionals*. 5th ed. Cincinnati: South-Western, 2004.

Hanging indent with 0.5" indentation →

Oliverio, Mary Ellen, William R. Pasewark, and Bonnie R. White. *The Office: Procedures and Technology*. 4th ed. Cincinnati: South-Western, 2003.

Works Cited Page for MLA Report

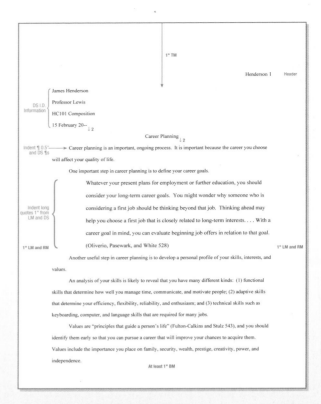

Drill 2: Create Folders

1. In the left pane of *Windows Explorer*, click *Desktop* (you may need to scroll up a little to find it).
2. Click the *File* menu, point to *New*, and click *Folder*. A new folder called *New Folder* will appear in both panes of the window. In the right pane, the name will be highlighted.
3. Key a name for the folder (**Century21**) and tap ENTER.
4. Minimize *Windows Explorer* (click the minus sign at the upper right of the window). Right-click in a blank area of the desktop, point to *New*, and click *Folder*.
5. Key a name for the folder (**Compositions**) and tap ENTER.

RENAMING FILES AND FOLDERS

You can rename a file or folder in one of these ways:

- In *Windows Explorer* or in a window opened by double-clicking a drive or folder, click the file or folder, choose *Rename* from the File menu, key the new name, and tap ENTER.
- Right-click the file or folder, choose *Rename*, key the new name, and tap ENTER.

In the filename *Lesson1.wpd*, the *wpd* **extension** indicates that the file is a *Corel® WordPerfect®* document. When you rename a file, be sure to include the extension that is recognized by your software program, or you may not be able to open the file.

Drill 3: Rename Folders

1. Right-click the *Century21* folder on the desktop, choose *Rename*, key **Keyboarding**, and tap ENTER.
2. Bring up *Windows Explorer*. If necessary, click the *Compositions* folder. Choose *Rename* from the File menu, key **English**, and tap ENTER.

MOVING AND COPYING FILES AND FOLDERS

You can move or copy files or folders in *Windows Explorer* or on the desktop.

- To move a file or folder, drag it to its new location.
- To copy a file or folder, hold down the CTRL key while dragging. The pointer icon will change to include a plus sign to indicate that you are copying.

Drag your file or folder on top of the destination drive or folder. You will know you are doing it correctly if the destination drive or folder is darkened, just as when you click it. If you are moving or copying to the open window for a drive or folder (as you will in Drill 5), drag the item anywhere inside the window.

When you are moving or copying files or folders, **selecting** (clicking) several items at once can save time.

- To select consecutive items, click the first item, hold down the SHIFT key, and click the last item.
- To select items in different places, hold down the CTRL key while you click each item.

Drill 4: Copy Files

1. In the left pane of *Windows Explorer*, locate and click the drive or folder from which you retrieve data files for this text. The files will be displayed in the right pane.
2. If necessary, scroll in the left pane until you can see the *English* folder.
3. Hold down CTRL and drag one of your data files to the *English* folder.
4. Select a block of data files to copy by selecting the first file and pressing SHIFT as you select the last file. Hold down CTRL and drag the files to the *English* folder.
5. Select several separate data files to copy from your student disk by pressing CTRL as you select each file. Hold down CTRL and drag these files to the *English* folder.
6. Close *Windows Explorer* (click the X at the upper right of the window).

Oops! We put keyboarding files in the *English* folder. Now we'll use the desktop to move the files to the *Keyboarding* folder.

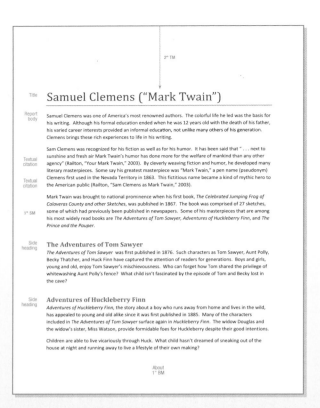

Samuel Clemens ("Mark Twain")

Samuel Clemens was one of America's most renowned authors. The colorful life he led was the basis for his writing. Although his formal education ended when he was 12 years old with the death of his father, his varied career interests provided an informal education, not unlike many others of his generation. Clemens brings these rich experiences to life in his writing.

Sam Clemens was recognized for his fiction as well as for his humor. It has been said that " . . . next to sunshine and fresh air Mark Twain's humor has done more for the welfare of mankind than any other agency" (Railton, "Your Mark Twain," 2003). By cleverly weaving fiction and humor, he developed many literary masterpieces. Some say his greatest masterpiece was "Mark Twain," a pen name (pseudonym) Clemens first used in the Nevada Territory in 1863. This fictitious name became a kind of mythic hero to the American public (Railton, "Sam Clemens as Mark Twain," 2003).

Mark Twain was brought to national prominence when his first book, *The Celebrated Jumping Frog of Calaveras County and other Sketches*, was published in 1867. The book was comprised of 27 sketches, some of which had previously been published in newspapers. Some of his masterpieces that are among his most widely read books are *The Adventures of Tom Sawyer*, *Adventures of Huckleberry Finn*, and *The Prince and the Pauper*.

The Adventures of Tom Sawyer
The Adventures of Tom Sawyer was first published in 1876. Such characters as Tom Sawyer, Aunt Polly, Becky Thatcher, and Huck Finn have captured the attention of readers for generations. Boys and girls, young and old, enjoy Tom Sawyer's mischievousness. Who can forget how Tom shared the privilege of whitewashing Aunt Polly's fence? What child isn't fascinated by the episode of Tom and Becky lost in the cave?

Adventures of Huckleberry Finn
Adventures of Huckleberry Finn, the story about a boy who runs away from home and lives in the wild, has appealed to young and old alike since it was first published in 1885. Many of the characters included in *The Adventures of Tom Sawyer* surface again in *Huckleberry Finn*. The widow Douglas and the widow's sister, Miss Watson, provide formidable foes for Huckleberry despite their good intentions.

Children are able to live vicariously through Huck. What child hasn't dreamed of sneaking out of the house at night and running away to live a lifestyle of their own making?

Unbound Report with Textual Citations, page 1

Perhaps the greatest testimony to this book was given by Ernest Hemingway when he said, "All modern American literature comes from one book by Mark Twain called Huckleberry Finn . . . . There was nothing before. There had been nothing as good since" (Waisman, "About Mark Twain," 2003).

Unbound Report with Textual Citations, page 2

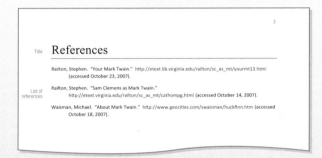

References

Railton, Stephen. "Your Mark Twain." http://etext.lib.virginia.edu/railton/sc_as_mt/yourmt13.html (accessed October 23, 2007).

Railton, Stephen. "Sam Clemens as Mark Twain." http://etext.virginia.edu/railton/sc_as_mt/cathompg.html (accessed October 14, 2007).

Waisman, Michael. "About Mark Twain." http://www.geocities.com/swaisman/huckfinn.htm (accessed October 18, 2007).

References Page

Globalization

We live in a time of worldwide change. What happens in one part of the world impacts people on the other side of the world. People around the world are influenced by common developments.[1]

The term "globalization" is used to describe this phenomenon. According to Harris, the term is being used in a variety of contexts.[2] However, in the broadest context globalization can be defined as:

> . . . a process of interaction and integration among the people, companies, and governments of different nations, a process driven by international trade and investment and aided by information technology. This process has effects on the environment, on culture, on political systems, on economic development and prosperity, and on human physical well-being in societies around the world.[3]

The business world uses this term in a narrower context to refer to the production, distribution, and marketing of goods and services at an international level. Everyone is impacted by the continued increase of globalization in a variety of ways. The types of food we eat, the kinds of clothes we wear, the variety of technologies we utilize, the modes of transportation available to us, and the types of jobs we pursue are directly linked to globalization. Globalization is changing the world we live in.

Causes of Globalization
Harris indicates that there are three main factors contributing to globalization. These factors include:

[1] Robert K. Schaeffer, *Understanding Globalization* (Lanham, MD: Rowman & Littlefield Publishers, Inc., 1977), p. 1.

[2] Richard G. Harris, "Globalization, Trade, and Income," *Canadian Journal of Economics*, November 1993, p. 755.

[3] "Globalization 101.org," http://www.globalization101.org/What_is_Globalization.html (accessed November 1, 2007).

Bound Report with Long Quotation and Footnotes

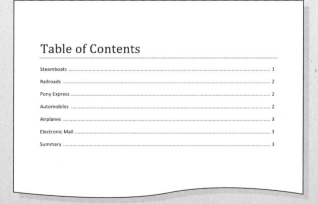

Table of Contents

Table of Contents

Drill 5: Move Files

1. Double-click the *English* folder on the desktop to open the *English* window. Move the window, if necessary (drag it by its title bar), so you can see the *Keyboarding* folder on the desktop.
2. Drag the first file from the *English* window to the *Keyboarding* folder.
3. Double-click the *Keyboarding* folder on the desktop to open the *Keyboarding* window. You need to be able to see all of the *English* window and at least part of the *Keyboarding* window. If you cannot, move the window(s) until you can see them.
4. If the *English* window has a gray title bar, select it to make it the **active window** (the window in which you can work).
5. Select a group of files in the *English* window and move them anywhere inside the *Keyboarding* window. Continue until all the files have been moved. Do not worry if the files are not neatly arranged. You will organize them in the next drill.
6. Close the *English* window.

ARRANGING FILES AND GETTING DATA

You can arrange the icons in a window by name, type, size, or date modified. You can also get details about files such as the file size and the date the file was last modified. In Drill 6, you will organize the file folders in the *Keyboarding* window, then look at details of these files.

Drill 6: Arrange Files and Get Data

1. In the *Keyboarding* window, click the *View* menu, point to *Arrange Icons by*, and select *Name*.
2. With no files selected, note (between the window and the taskbar) how many files the *Keyboarding* window contains and the total file size.
3. Select one file. What does the window tell you about it? What does it tell you about a group of selected files?
4. Select *Details* from the View menu. If necessary, scroll to see the information this view provides.
5. Click the *View* menu, point to *Arrange Icons by*, and choose *Modified*. When might this view be useful?

DELETING FILES AND FOLDERS

You can select and delete several files and folders at once, just as you selected several items to move or copy. If you delete a folder, you automatically delete any files and folders inside it. Here are two ways to delete a file or folder:

- In *Windows Explorer* or in a drive or folder window, select the file or folder and choose *Delete* from the File menu. Answer *Yes* to the question about sending the item to the Recycle Bin.
- Right-click the file or folder and choose *Delete*. Answer *Yes* to the question about sending the item to the Recycle Bin.

Drill 7: Delete Files

1. In the *Keyboarding* window, right-click a file, choose *Delete*, and answer *Yes* to send the file to the Recycle Bin.
2. Select several files in the *Keyboarding* window, choose *Delete* from the File menu, and answer *Yes* to send the files to the Recycle Bin.

RESTORING DELETED FILES AND FOLDERS

Assume that there was one file you didn't mean to delete from the *Keyboarding* window. When you delete a file or folder, the item goes to the Recycle Bin. You can restore files and folders from the Recycle Bin.

Drill 8: Restore a Deleted File

1. Minimize the *Keyboarding* window. Double-click the *Recycle Bin* icon on the desktop to open the Recycle Bin window.
2. Select one of the files you just deleted and click *Restore this item* (you may need to scroll down in the left pane to see the option). Or select *Restore* from the File menu, depending on your *Windows*® operating system version.
3. Close the Recycle Bin window. Click the *Keyboarding* button on the taskbar to bring up the *Keyboarding* window. It should contain the file you just restored.
4. Close the *Keyboarding* window and delete the *Keyboarding* and *English* folders from your desktop.

ENVELOPE GUIDES

Return Address

Use block style, SS, and Initial Caps or ALL CAPS. If not using the Envelopes feature, begin as near to the top and left edge of the envelope as possible—TM and LM about 0.25".

Receiver's Delivery Address

Use block style, SS, and Initial Caps. If desired, use ALL CAPS instead of initial caps and omit the punctuation. Place city name, two-letter state abbreviation, and ZIP Code +4 on last address line. One space precedes the ZIP Code.

If not using the Envelopes feature, tab over 2.5" for the small envelope and 4" for the large envelope. Insert hard returns to place the first line about 2" from the top.

Mailing Notations

Key mailing and addressee notations in ALL CAPS.

Key mailing notations, such as SPECIAL DELIVERY and REGISTERED, below the stamp and at least three lines above the envelope address.

Key addressee notations, such as HOLD FOR ARRIVAL or PERSONAL, a DS below the return address and about three spaces from the left edge of the envelope.

If an attention line is used, key it as the first line of the envelope address.

Standard Abbreviations

Use USPS standard abbreviations for states (see list below) and street suffix names, such as AVE and BLVD. Never abbreviate the name of a city or country.

International Addresses

Omit postal (ZIP) codes from the last line of addresses outside the U.S. Show only the name of the country on the last line. Examples:

```
Mr. Hiram Sanders
2121 Clearwater St.
Ottawa, Onkia  OB1
CANADA

Ms. Inge D. Fischer
Hartmannstrasse 7
4209 Bonn 5
FEDERAL REPUBLIC OF GERMANY
```

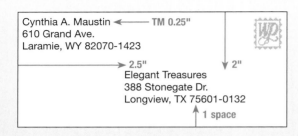

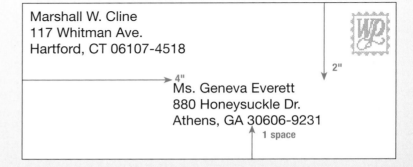

Folding Procedures

Small Envelopes (Nos. 6¾, 6¼)

1. With page face up, fold bottom up to 0.5" from top.
2. Fold right third to left.
3. Fold left third to 0.5" from last crease.
4. Insert last creased edge first.

Large Envelopes (Nos. 10, 9, 7¾)

1. With page face up, fold slightly less than one-third of sheet up toward top.
2. Fold down top of sheet to within 0.5" of bottom fold.
3. Insert last creased edge first.

Window Envelopes (Letter)

1. With page face down, top toward you, fold upper third down.
2. Fold lower third up so address is showing.
3. Insert sheet into envelope with last crease at bottom.
4. Check that address shows through window.

State and Territory Abbreviations

Alabama	AL	Illinois	IL	Nebraska	NE	South Carolina	SC
Alaska	AK	Indiana	IN	Nevada	NV	South Dakota	SD
Arizona	AZ	Iowa	IA	New Hampshire	NH	Tennessee	TN
Arkansas	AR	Kansas	KS	New Jersey	NJ	Texas	TX
California	CA	Kentucky	KY	New Mexico	NM	Utah	UT
Colorado	CO	Louisiana	LA	New York	NY	Vermont	VT
Connecticut	CT	Maine	ME	North Carolina	NC	Virgin Islands	VI
Delaware	DE	Maryland	MD	North Dakota	ND	Virginia	VA
District of Columbia	DC	Massachusetts	MA	Ohio	OH	Washington	WA
Florida	FL	Michigan	MI	Oklahoma	OK	West Virginia	WV
Georgia	GA	Minnesota	MN	Oregon	OR	Wisconsin	WI
Guam	GU	Mississippi	MS	Pennsylvania	PA	Wyoming	WY
Hawaii	HI	Missouri	MO	Puerto Rico	PR		
Idaho	ID	Montana	MT	Rhode Island	RI		

Language and Writing References

CAPITALIZATION GUIDES

Capitalize

1. The first word of every sentence and complete quotation. Do not capitalize (a) fragments of quotations or (b) a quotation resumed within a sentence.

   Crazy Horse said, "I will return to you in stone."
   Gandhi's teaching inspired "nonviolent revolutions."
   "It is . . . fitting and proper," Lincoln said, "that we . . . do this."

2. The first word after a colon if that word begins a complete sentence.

   Remember: Keep the action in your fingers.
   These sizes were in stock: small, medium, and extra large.

3. First, last, and all other words in titles except articles, conjunctions, or prepositions of four or fewer letters.

   The Beak of the Finch
   Raleigh News and Observer
   "The Phantom of the Opera"

4. An official title when it precedes a name or when used elsewhere if it is a title of distinction.

   In what year did Juan Carlos become King of Spain?
   Masami Chou, our class president, met Senator Thurmond.

5. Personal titles and names of people and places.

   Did you see Mrs. Watts and Gloria while in Miami?

6. All proper nouns and their derivatives.

   Mexico   Mexican border   Uganda   Ugandan economy

7. Days of the week, months of the year, holidays, periods of history, and historic events.

   | Friday | July | Labor Day |
   | Middle Ages | Vietnam War | Woodstock |

8. Geographic regions, localities, and names.

   the East Coast   Upper Peninsula Michigan
   Ohio River   the Deep South

9. Street, avenue, company, etc., when used with a proper noun.

   Fifth Avenue   Wall Street   Monsanto Company

10. Names of organizations, clubs, and buildings.

    National Hockey League   Four-H Club
    Biltmore House   Omni Hotel

11. A noun preceding a figure except for common nouns, such as line, page, and sentence.

    Review Rules 1 to 18 in Chapter 5, page 149.

12. Seasons of the year only when they are personified.

    the soft kiss of Spring   the icy fingers of Winter

NUMBER EXPRESSION GUIDES

Use words for

1. Numbers from one to ten except when used with numbers above ten, which are keyed as figures. Common business practice is to use figures for all numbers except those that begin a sentence.

   Did you visit all eight Web sites, or only four?
   Buy 15 textbooks and 8 workbooks.

2. A number beginning a sentence.

   Twelve of the new shrubs have died; 48 are doing well.

3. The shorter of two numbers used together.

   fifty 33-cent stamps   150 twenty-cent stamps

4. Isolated fractions or indefinite numbers in a sentence.

   Nearly seventy members voted, which is almost one-fourth.

5. Names of small-numbered streets and avenues (ten and under).

   The theater is at the corner of Third Avenue and 54th Street.

Use figures for

1. Dates and times except in very formal writing.

   The flight will arrive at 9:48 a.m. on March 14.
   The ceremony took place the fifth of June at eleven o'clock.

2. A series of fractions and/or mixed numbers.

   Key 1/4, 1/2, 5/6, and 7 3/4.

3. Numbers following nouns.

   Case 1849 is reviewed in Volume 5, page 9.

4. Measures, weights, and dimensions.

   6 feet 9 inches   7 pounds 4 ounces
   8.5 inches by 11 inches

5. Definite numbers used with percent (%), but use words for indefinite percentages.

   The late fee is 15 percent of the overdue payment.
   The brothers put in nearly fifty percent of the start-up capital.

6. House numbers except house number *One*.

   My home is at 8 Weber Drive; my office is at One Weber Plaza.

7. Amounts of money except when spelled for emphasis (as in legal documents). Even amounts are keyed without the decimal. Large amounts (a million or more) are keyed as shown.

   $17.75   75 cents $775
   seven hundred dollars ($700)
   $7,500 $7 million $7.2 million $7 billion

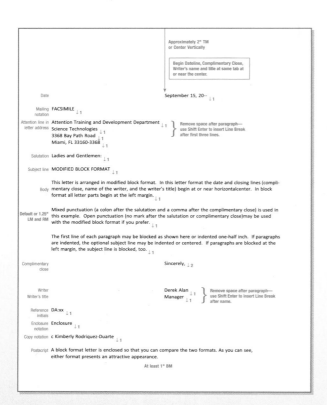
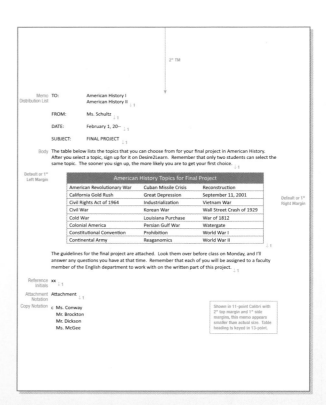

Letter in Modified Block Format with Postscript

Memo with Special Features

Current date

Ms. Valerie E. Lopez
207 Brainard Road
Hartford, CT 06114-2207

Dear Ms. Lopez:

SHADOWING AT BRIGHTON LIFE INSURANCE CO.

I'm pleased that you have chosen Brighton Life Insurance Co. as the place where you want to complete your shadow experience. I believe that you will learn a great deal about being an actuary by spending two days at Brighton with me.

To help you prepare for your visit, I have listed some of the things you should know about actuaries:

- Gather and analyze statistics to determine probabilities of death, sickness, injury, disability, unemployment, retirement, and property loss.

- Specialize in either life and health insurance or property and casualty insurance; or specialize in pension plans or employee benefits.

- Hold a bachelor's degree in mathematics or a business area, such as actuarial science, finance, or accounting.

- Possess excellent communication and interpersonal skills.

Also, I have enclosed actuarial career information published by the Society of Actuaries (life and health insurance), Casualty Actuarial Society (property and casualty insurance), and American Society of Pension Actuaries (pensions). These three associations offer actuaries professional certification through a series of examinations. We can discuss the societies and the importance of obtaining the professional designations they offer.

Letter in Modified Block Format with Paragraph Indentations and List

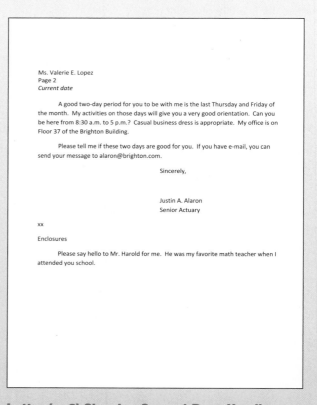

Letter (p. 2) Showing Second-Page Heading

PUNCTUATION GUIDES

Use an apostrophe

1. As a symbol for *feet* in charts, forms, and tables or as a symbol for *minutes*. (The quotation mark may be used as a symbol for *seconds* and *inches*.)

   12' x 16'   3' 54"   8' 6" x 10' 8"

2. As a symbol to indicate the omission of letters or figures (as in contractions).

   can't   do's and don'ts   Class of '02

3. To form the plural of most figures, letters, and words used as words rather than for their meaning: Add the apostrophe and *s*. In market quotations and decades, form the plural of figures by the addition of *s* only.

   7's   ten's   ABC's   Century 4s   1960s

4. To show possession: Add the apostrophe and *s* to (a) a singular noun and (b) a plural noun that does not end in *s*.

   a woman's watch   men's shoes   girl's bicycle

   Add the apostrophe and *s* to a proper name of one syllable that ends in *s*.

   Bess's Cafeteria   James's hat   Jones's bill

   Add the apostrophe only after (a) plural nouns ending in *s* and (b) a proper name of more than one syllable that ends in *s* or *z*.

   girls' camp   Adams' home   Martinez' report

   Add the apostrophe (and *s*) after the last noun in a series to indicate joint or common possession by two or more persons; however, add the possessive to each of the nouns to show separate possession by two or more persons.

   Lewis and Clark's expedition
   the secretary's and the treasurer's reports

Use a colon

1. To introduce a listing.

   These poets are my favorites: Shelley, Keats, and Frost.

2. To introduce a question or a long direct quotation.

   The question is this: Did you study for the test?

3. Between hours and minutes expressed in figures.

   10:15 a.m.   4:30 p.m.   12:00 midnight

Use a comma (or commas)

1. After (a) introductory phrases or clauses and (b) words in a series.

   When you finish keying the report, please give it to Mr. Kent.
   We will play the Mets, Expos, and Cubs in our next home stand.

2. To set off short direct quotations.

   Mrs. Ramirez replied, "No, the report is not finished."

3. Before and after (a) appositives—words that come together and refer to the same person, thing, or idea—and (b) words of direct address.

   Colette, the assistant manager, will chair the next meeting.
   Please call me, Erika, if I can be of further assistance.

4. To set off nonrestrictive clauses (not necessary to meaning of sentence), but not restrictive clauses (necessary to meaning).

   Your report, which deals with that issue, raised many questions.
   The man who organized the conference is my teacher.

5. To separate the day from the year in dates and the city from the state in addresses.

   July 4, 2005   St. Joseph, Missouri   Moose Point, AK

6. To separate two or more parallel adjectives (adjectives that modify the noun separately and that could be separated by the word *and* instead of the comma).

   The big, loud bully was ejected after he pushed the coach.
   The big, powerful car zoomed past the cheering crowd.
   Cynthia played a black lacquered grand piano at her concert.
   A small red fox squeezed through the fence to avoid the hounds.

7. To separate (a) unrelated groups of figures that occur together and (b) whole numbers into groups of three digits each. (Omit commas from years and page, policy, room, serial, and telephone numbers.)

   By the year 2005, 1,200 more local students will be enrolled.
   The supplies listed on Invoice #274068 are for Room 1953.

Use a dash

Create a dash by keying two hyphens or one em-dash.

1. For emphasis.

   The skater—in a clown costume—dazzled with fancy footwork.

2. To indicate a change of thought.

   We may tour the Orient—but I'm getting ahead of my story.

3. To emphasize the name of an author when it follows a direct quotation.

   "All the world's a stage. . . ."—Shakespeare

4. To set off expressions that break off or interrupt speech.

   "Jay, don't get too close to the—." I spoke too late.
   "Today—er—uh," the anxious presenter began.

Format References

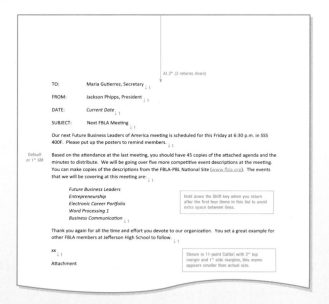

At 2" (3 returns down)

TO: Maria Gutierrez, Secretary ↓1

FROM: Jackson Phipps, President ↓1

DATE: *Current Date* ↓1

SUBJECT: Next FBLA Meeting ↓1

Our next Future Business Leaders of America meeting is scheduled for this Friday at 6:30 p.m. in SSS 400F. Please put up the posters to remind members. ↓1

Default or 1" SM

Based on the attendance at the last meeting, you should have 45 copies of the attached agenda and the minutes to distribute. We will be going over five more competitive event descriptions at the meeting. You can make copies of the descriptions from the FBLA-PBL National Site (www.fbla.org). The events that we will be covering at this meeting are: ↓1

Future Business Leaders
Entrepreneurship
Electronic Career Portfolio
Word Processing 1
Business Communication ↓1

> Hold down the Shift key when you return after the first four items in this list to avoid extra space between lines.

Thank you again for all the time and effort you devote to our organization. You set a great example for other FBLA members at Jefferson High School to follow. ↓1

xx ↓1

Attachment

> Shown in 11-point Calibri with 2" top margin and 1" side margins, this memo appears smaller than actual size.

Interoffice Memo

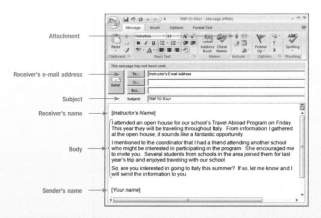

Attachment

Receiver's e-mail address

Subject

Receiver's name

Body

Sender's name

E-mail Message

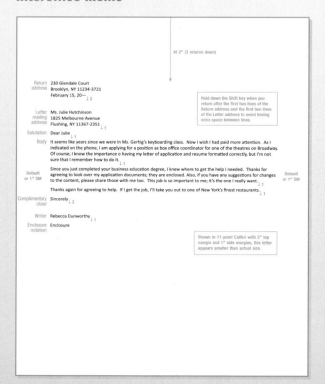

At 2" (3 returns down)

Return address 230 Glendale Court
Brooklyn, NY 11234-3721
February 15, 20— ↓2

> Hold down the Shift key when you return after the first two lines of the Return address and the first two lines of the Letter address to avoid having extra space between lines.

Letter mailing address Ms. Julie Hutchinson
1825 Melbourne Avenue
Flushing, NY 11367-2351 ↓1

Salutation Dear Julie ↓1

Body It seems like years since we were in Ms. Gerhig's keyboarding class. Now I wish I had paid more attention. As I indicated on the phone, I am applying for a position as box office coordinator for one of the theatres on Broadway. Of course, I know the importance o having my letter of application and resume formatted correctly, but I'm not sure that I remember how to do it. ↓1

Default or 1" SM

Since you just completed your business education degree, I knew where to get the help I needed. Thanks for agreeing to look over my application documents; they are enclosed. Also, if you have any suggestions for changes to the content, please share those with me too. This job is so important to me; it's the one I really want. ↓1

Default or 1" SM

Thanks again for agreeing to help. If I get the job, I'll take you out to one of New York's finest restaurants. ↓1

Complimentary close Sincerely ↓2

Writer Rebecca Dunworthy ↓1

Enclosure notation Enclosure

> Shown in 11-point Calibri with 2" top margin and 1" side margins, this letter appears smaller than actual size.

Personal-Business Letter in Block Format with Open Punctuation

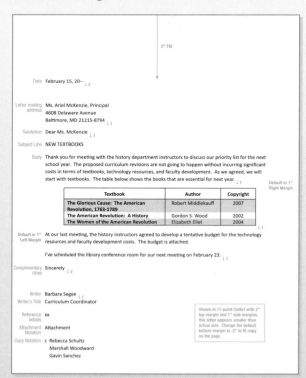

2" TM

Date February 15, 20-- ↓2

Letter mailing address Ms. Ariel McKenzie, Principal
4608 Delaware Avenue
Baltimore, MD 21215-8794 ↓1

Salutation Dear Ms. McKenzie ↓1

Subject Line NEW TEXTBOOKS ↓1

Body Thank you for meeting with the history department instructors to discuss our priority list for the next school year. The proposed curriculum revisions are not going to happen without incurring significant costs in terms of textbooks, technology resources, and faculty development. As we agreed, we will start with textbooks. The table below shows the books that are essential for next year. ↓1

Default or 1" Right Margin

Textbook	Author	Copyright
The Glorious Cause: The American Revolution, 1763-1789	Robert Middlekauff	2007
The American Revolution: A History	Gordon S. Wood	2002
The Women of the American Revolution	Elizabeth Ellet	2004

↓1

Default or 1" Left Margin

At our last meeting, the history instructors agreed to develop a tentative budget for the technology resources and faculty development costs. The budget is attached. ↓1

I've scheduled the library conference room for our next meeting on February 23. ↓1

Complimentary close Sincerely ↓2

Writer Barbara Segee ↓1

Writer's Title Curriculum Coordinator ↓1

Reference Initials xx ↓1

Attachment Notation Attachment ↓1

Copy Notation c Rebecca Schultz
Marshall Woodward
Gavin Sanchez

> Shown in 11-point Calibri with 2" top margin and 1" side margins, this letter appears smaller than actual size. Change the default bottom margin to .5" to fit copy on the page.

Business Letter in Block Format with Special Features

PUNCTUATION GUIDES (continued)

Use an exclamation point

1. After emphatic interjections.
   Wow!   Hey there!   What a day!

2. After sentences that are clearly exclamatory.
   "I won't go!" she said with determination.
   How good it was to see you in New Orleans last week!

Use a hyphen

1. To join parts of compound words expressing the numbers twenty-one through ninety-nine.
   Thirty-five delegates attended the national convention.

2. To join compound adjectives preceding a noun they modify as a unit.
   End-of-term grades will be posted on the classroom door.

3. After each word or figure in a series of words or figures that modify the same noun (suspended hyphenation).
   Meeting planners made first-, second-, and third-class reservations.

4. To spell out a word.
   The sign read, "For your c-o-n-v-i-e-n-c-e." Of course, the correct word is c-o-n-v-e-n-i-e-n-c-e.

5. To form certain compound nouns.
   WGAL-TV   spin-off   teacher-counselor   AFL-CIO

Use italic

To indicate titles of books, plays, movies, magazines, and newspapers. (Titles may be keyed in ALL CAPS or underlined.)
A review of *Runaway Jury* appeared in *The New York Times*.

Use parentheses

1. To enclose parenthetical or explanatory matter and added information.
   Amendments to the bylaws (Exhibit A) are enclosed.

2. To enclose identifying letters or figures in a series.
   Check these factors: (1) period of time, (2) rate of pay, and (3) nature of duties.

3. To enclose figures that follow spelled-out amounts to give added clarity or emphasis.
   The total award is fifteen hundred dollars ($1,500).

Use a question mark

At the end of a sentence that is a direct question. But use a period after requests in the form of a question (whenever the expected answer is action, not words).
What has been the impact of the Information Superhighway?
Will you complete the enclosed form and return it to me.

Use quotation marks

1. To enclose direct quotations.
   Professor Dye asked, "Are you spending the summer in Europe?"
   Was it Emerson who said, "To have a friend is to be one"?

2. To enclose titles of articles, poems, songs, television programs, and unpublished works, such as theses and dissertations.
   "Talk of the Town" in the *New Yorker*   "Fog" by Sandburg
   "Survivor" in prime time   "Memory" from *Cats*

3. To enclose special words or phrases or coined words (words not in dictionary usage).
   The words "phony" and "braggart" describe him, according to coworkers.
   The presenter annoyed the audience with phrases like "uh" and "you know."

Use a semicolon

1. To separate two or more independent clauses in a compound sentence when the conjunction is omitted.
   Being critical is easy; being constructive is not so easy.

2. To separate independent clauses when they are joined by a conjunctive adverb, such as *consequently* or *therefore*.
   I work mornings; therefore, I prefer an afternoon interview.

3. To separate a series of phrases or clauses (especially if they contain commas) that are introduced by a colon.
   Al spoke in these cities: Denver, CO; Erie, PA; and Troy, NY.

4. To precede an abbreviation or word that introduces an explanatory statement.
   She organized her work; for example, naming folders and files to indicate degrees or urgency.

Use an underline

To call attention to words or phrases (or use quotation marks or italic).
Take the presenter's advice: <u>Stand</u> up, <u>speak</u> up, and then <u>sit</u> down.
Students often confuse <u>its</u> and <u>it's</u>.

Proofreaders' Marks

Proofreaders' marks are used to mark corrections in keyed or printed text that contains problems and/or errors. As a keyboard user, you should be able to read these marks accurately when revising or editing a rough draft. You also should be able to write these symbols to correct the rough drafts that you and others key. The most-used proofreaders' marks are shown below.

Mark	Meaning
‖	Align copy; also, make these items parallel
¶	Begin a new paragraph
Cap ≡	Capitalize
⌒	Close up
ℓ	Delete
<#	Delete space
No ¶	Do not begin a new paragraph
∧	Insert
⋏	Insert comma
⊙	Insert period
∜	Insert quotation marks
#>	Insert space
∨	Insert apostrophe
stet	Let it stand; ignore correction
lc	Lowercase
⌊⌋	Move down; lower
⊏	Move left
⊐	Move right
⌐	Move up; raise
sp	Spell out
∼ tr	Transpose
___	Underline or italic

E-MAIL FORMAT AND SOFTWARE FEATURES

E-mail format varies slightly, depending on the software used to create and send it.

E-mail Heading
Most e-mail software includes these features:

Attachment: line for attaching files to an e-mail message

Bcc: line for sending copy of a message to someone without the receiver knowing

Cc: line for sending copy of a message to additional receivers

Date: month, day, and year message is sent; often includes precise time of transmittal; usually is inserted automatically

From: name and/or e-mail address of sender; usually is inserted automatically

Subject: line for very brief description of message content

To: line for name and/or e-mail address of receiver

E-mail Body
The message box on the e-mail screen may contain these elements or only the message paragraphs (SS with DS between paragraphs).
- Informal salutation and/or receiver's name (a DS above the message)
- Informal closing (e.g., "Regards," "Thanks") and/or the sender's name (a DS below the message). Additional identification (e.g., telephone number) may be included.

Special E-mail Features
Several e-mail features make communicating through e-mail fast and efficient.

Address list/book: collection of names and e-mail addresses of correspondents from which an address can be entered on the To: line by selecting it, instead of keying it.

Distribution list: series of names and/or e-mail addresses, separated by commas, on the To: line.

Forward: feature that allows an e-mail user to send a copy of a received e-mail message to others.

Recipient list (Group): feature that allows an e-mail user to send mail to a group of recipients by selecting the name of the group (e.g., All Teachers).

Reply: feature used to respond to an incoming message.

Reply all: feature used to respond to all copy recipients as well as the sender of an incoming message.

Signature: feature for storing and inserting the closing lines of messages (e.g., informal closing, sender's name, telephone number, address, fax number).

BASIC GRAMMAR GUIDES

Use a singular verb

1. With a singular subject.

   Dr. Cho was to give the lecture, but he is ill.

2. With indefinite pronouns (*each, every, any, either, neither, one*, etc.)

   Each of these girls has an important role in the class play.

   Neither of them is well enough to start the game.

3. With singular subjects linked by *or* or *nor*; but if one subject is singular and the other is plural, the verb agrees with the nearer subject.

   Neither Ms. Moss nor Mr. Katz was invited to speak.

   Either the manager or his assistants are to participate.

4. With a collective noun (*class, committee, family, team*, etc.) if the collective noun acts as a unit.

   The committee has completed its study and filed a report.

   The jury has returned to the courtroom to give its verdict.

5. With the pronouns *all* and *some* (as well as fractions and percentages) when used as subjects if their modifiers are singular. Use a plural verb if their modifiers are plural.

   Some of the new paint is already cracking and peeling.

   All of the workers are to be paid for the special holiday.

   Historically, about 40 percent has voted.

6. When *number* is used as the subject and is preceded by *the*; use a plural verb if *number* is the subject and is preceded by *a*.

   The number of voters has increased again this year.

   A number of workers are on vacation this week.

Use a plural verb

1. With a plural subject.

   The players were all here, and they were getting restless.

2. With a compound subject joined by *and*.

   Mrs. Samoa and her son are to be on a local talk show.

Negative forms of verbs

1. Use the plural verb *do not* or *don't* with pronoun subjects *I, we, you*, and *they* as well as with plural nouns.

   I do not find this report believable; you don't either.

2. Use the singular verb *does not* or *doesn't* with pronouns *he, she*, and *it* as well as with singular nouns.

   Though she doesn't accept the board's offer, the board doesn't have to offer more.

Pronoun agreement with antecedents

1. A personal pronoun (*I, we, you, he, she, it, their*, etc.) agrees in person (first, second, or third) with the noun or other pronoun it represents.

   We can win the game if we all give each play our best effort.

   You may play softball after you finish your homework.

   Andrea said that she will drive her car to the shopping mall.

2. A personal pronoun agrees in gender (feminine, masculine, or neuter) with the noun or other pronoun it represents.

   Each winner will get a corsage as she receives her award.

   Mr. Kimoto will give his talk after the announcements.

   The small boat lost its way in the dense fog.

3. A personal pronoun agrees in number (singular or plural) with the noun or other pronoun it represents.

   Celine drove her new car to Del Rio, Texas, last week.

   The club officers made careful plans for their next meeting.

4. A personal pronoun that represents a collective noun (*team, committee, family*, etc.) may be singular or plural, depending on the meaning of the collective noun.

   Our women's soccer team played its fifth game today.

   The vice squad took their positions in the square.

Commonly confused pronouns

it's (contraction): it is; it has
its (pronoun): possessive form of *it*

It's good to get your e-mail; it's been a long time.

The puppy wagged its tail in welcome.

their (pronoun): possessive form of *they*
there (adverb/pronoun): at or in that place; sometimes used to introduce a sentence
they're (contraction): they are

The hikers all wore their parkas.

Will they be there during our presentation?

They're likely to be late because of rush-hour traffic.

who's (contraction): who is; who has
whose (pronoun): possessive form of *who*

Who's seen the movie? Who's going now?

I chose the one whose skills are best.

NOTE: See p. R13 for other confusing word groups.

CONFUSING WORDS

accept (vb) to receive; to approve; to take
except (prep/vb) with the exclusion of; leave out

affect (vb) to produce a change in or have an effect on
effect (n) result; something produced by an agent or a cause

buy (n/vb) to purchase; to acquire; a bargain
by (prep/adv) close to; via; according to; close at hand

choose (vb) to select; to decide
chose (vb) past tense of "choose"

cite (vb) use as support; commend; summon
sight (n/vb) ability to see; something seen; a device to improve aim
site (n) location

complement (n) something that fills, completes, or makes perfect
compliment (n/vb) a formal expression of respect or admiration; to pay respect or admiration

do (vb) to bring about; to carry out
due (adj) owed or owing as a debt; having reached the date for payment

farther (adv) greater distance
further (adv) additional; in greater depth; to greater extent

for (prep/conj) indicates purpose on behalf of; because of
four (n) two plus two in number

hear (vb) to gain knowledge of by the ear
here (adv) in or at this place; at or on this point; in this case

hole (n) opening in or through something
whole (adj/n) having all its proper parts; a complete amount

hour (n) the 24th part of a day; a particular time
our (adj) possessive form of "we"; of or relating to us

knew (vb) past tense of "know"; understood; recognized truth or nature of
new (adj) novel; fresh; existing for a short time

know (vb) to be aware of the truth or nature of; to have an understanding of
no (adv/adj/n) not in any respect or degree; not so; indicates denial or refusal

lessen (vb) to cause to decrease; to make less
lesson (n) something to be learned; period of instruction; a class period

lie (n/vb) an untrue or inaccurate statement; to tell an untrue story; to rest or recline
lye (n) a strong alkaline substance or solution

one (adj/pron) a single unit or thing
won (vb) past tense of win; gained a victory as in a game or contest; got by effort or work

passed (vb) past tense of "pass"; already occurred; moved by; gave an item to someone
past (adv/adj/prep/n) gone or elapsed; time gone by

personal (adj) of, relating to, or affecting a person; done in person
personnel (n) a staff or persons making up a workforce in an organization

plain (adj/n) with little decoration; a large flat area of land
plane (n) an airplane or hydroplane

pole (n) a long, slender, rounded piece of wood or other material
poll (n) a survey of people to analyze public opinion

principal (n/adj) a chief or leader; capital (money) amount placed at interest; of or relating to the most important thing or matter or persons
principle (n) a central rule, law, or doctrine

right (adj) factual; true; correct
rite (n) customary form of ceremony; ritual
write (v) to form letters or symbols; to compose and set down in words, numbers, or symbols

some (n/adv) unknown or unspecified unit or thing; to a degree or extent
sum (n/vb) total; to find a total; to summarize

stationary (adj) fixed in a position, course, or mode; unchanging in condition
stationery (n) paper and envelopes used for processing personal and business documents

than (conj/prep) used in comparisons to show differences between items
then (n/adv) that time; at that time; next

to (prep/adj) indicates action, relation, distance, direction
too (adv) besides; also; to excessive degree
two (n/adj) one plus one

vary (vb) change; make different; diverge
very (adv/adj) real; mere; truly; to high degree

waist (n) narrowed part of the body between chest and hips; middle of something
waste (n/vb/adj) useless things; rubbish; spend or use carelessly; nonproductive

weak (adj) lacking strength, skill, or proficiency
week (n) a series of seven days; Monday through Sunday

wear (vb/n) to bear or have on the person; diminish by use; clothing

where (adv/conj/n) at, in, or to what degree; what place, source, or cause

your (adj) of or relating to you as possessor
you're (contraction) you are